Streets of Memory

Streets of Memory

Landscape, Tolerance, and National Identity in Istanbul

AMY MILLS

The University of Georgia Press   *Athens and London*

© 2010 by the University of Georgia Press
Athens, Georgia 30602
www.ugapress.org

Set in 11/14 Adobe Garamond Pro by BookComp, Inc.

Printed digitally in the United States of America

Library of Congress Cataloging-in-Publication Data

Mills, Amy, 1972–
    Streets of memory : landscape, tolerance, and national identity
in Istanbul / Amy Mills.
        p. cm.
    Includes bibliographical references and index.
    ISBN-13: 978-0-8203-3573-5 (hardcover : alk. paper)
    ISBN-10: 0-8203-3573-8 (hardcover : alk. paper)
    ISBN-13: 978-0-8203-3574-2 (pbk. : alk. paper)
    ISBN-10: 0-8203-3574-6 (pbk. : alk. paper)
    1. Kuzguncuk (Istanbul, Turkey)—Social life and customs.
    2. Kuzguncuk (Istanbul, Turkey)—Ethnic relations.
    3. City and town life—Turkey—Istanbul.
    4. Nostalgia—Turkey—Istanbul.
    5. Cosmopolitanism—Turkey—Istanbul.
    6. Landscape—Social aspects—Turkey—Istanbul.
    7. Toleration—Turkey—Istanbul. 8. Nationalism—Turkey—Istanbul.
    9. Istanbul (Turkey)—Social life and customs.
    10. Istanbul (Turkey)—Ethnic relations. I. Title.
    DR738.5.K89M55 2010
    956.3—dc22   2009047885

British Library Cataloging-in-Publication Data available

This book is dedicated with gratitude and respect to all Kuzguncuklu people, without whom that place, and this book, would not be.

CONTENTS

ACKNOWLEDGMENTS

So many people have helped me with this project that this book feels like a gift from the community of friends and scholars forged through my work over the last several years. Thanks to Derek Krissoff at the University of Georgia Press for enthusiastically taking on my manuscript and to the other excellent people at the press for skillfully shepherding it through the process of becoming a book. Thanks also to the anonymous press readers whose extremely helpful comments contributed so importantly to the final manuscript. I thank especially Ian Manners, whose insightful questions and incredible support contributed in uncountable ways to shaping this project.

Faculty at the Center for Middle Eastern Studies at the University of Texas at Austin gave me the skills to do research in Turkey and the foundational knowledge I needed to develop the larger contributions of this research, something that happened years after I completed my PhD. I thank Abe Marcus. The seed for this book was my dissertation, and each committee member contributed an essential element that still inspires me: thanks to Steven Hoelscher for the landscape, to Robin Doughty for place, to Barbara Parmenter for the city, and to Carel Bertram for Turkish memory. The graduate students with whom I studied in the Department of Geography are my first real group of colleagues, and I thank them. Thanks also to the institutions that funded my research and writing: in a very real way this book would not have been were it not for their material support. Thank you to Fulbright-Hays, the Institute of Turkish Studies, the University of Texas Population Research Center, the Mellon Foundation, the Title VI FLAS Fellowship program, and the University of Texas at Austin Graduate School.

Many people and institutions provided insight, contacts, resources, and information. I thank Tony Greenwood and the staff at the American Research Institute in Turkey for important support and library access. Thanks to the French Institute of Anatolian Studies in Istanbul for library access and stimulating connections with other local researchers. The network of people I interviewed, and the written materials I used to contextualize my ethnographic work, depended on other people who took an interest in my research. Thanks to Rıfat Bali, David Behar and Tolga Islam, the Center for Asia Minor Studies in Athens, Caroline Finkel, Tan Morgül, Leyla Neyzi, Christine Philliou, Murat Ruben, Aydan Sayın, Simurg Kitabevi, Amy Spangler, and Kızılca Yürür, among others. Sharing stories about Kuzguncuk is something I cannot thank people for directly because of my commitment to preserving their anonymity: their help and friendship, however, is something I'll never forget. Thank you. Friends in Istanbul sustained me during challenging times, and I thank especially Linda Robinson and Nancy Öztürk.

While most of the ethnographic research in Kuzguncuk was completed for my dissertation, the years immediately afterward involved important follow-up research in Istanbul and new research in Tel Aviv. I also needed collaborative spaces and relationships to enlarge the focus of the project and deepen its contribution. Many people and institutions helped me during this period: for help in Tel Aviv, I thank David Angel, Yaalom Bovete, and the Türkiyeliler Birliği. For opportunities to refine my ideas in collaborative contexts, I thank Kamran Asdar Ali, Martina Rieker, and participants in the Shehr Workshop on Gender and Urban Space at the American University in Cairo. Thanks also to Georges Khalil, Stefan Weber, Modjtaba Sadria, and the other sponsors and participants in the International Summer Academy in Istanbul on Plurality and Cosmopolitanism in the Ottoman Empire and Beyond. Editors and reviewers for the following journals provided thoughtful readings of earlier versions of some of the research that contributed to the book: thanks to colleagues at *Cultural Geographies*; *Gender, Place, and Culture*; the *International Journal of Middle East Studies*; and the *Geographical Review*. Thanks to Maria Lane for making the initial versions of the maps and for her extremely insightful suggestions on early drafts of some of the chapters. Thanks also to Christine Philliou for sharing her incredible knowledge of the historical and social interconnectedness of people and places in Istanbul and beyond. And thank you to Carl Dahlman, Owen Dwyer, and Patricia Ehrkamp.

Thanks to the University of Kentucky for the Women in Under-Represented Areas Postdoctoral Fellowship. That support paid for research in Istanbul, stacks of amazing books, and time to read and write. Much more importantly, however, the Department of Geography at the University of Kentucky provided the richest, kindest, and most brilliant group of colleagues, who helped me mature my ideas and demonstrated that departmental academic life can be both intellectually fulfilling and personally rewarding. I thank Anna Secor for her mentorship and friendship, especially. Thanks also to Rich Schein, Karl Raitz, and Sue Roberts for particular contributions to my postdoctoral experience.

I am lucky to have begun my career as a faculty member at the University of South Carolina. Gordon Smith has provided incredible personal and professional support. I thank him and the Walker Institute of International Studies for enriching International Studies, supplying financial support to develop Turkish Studies at USC, and funding research in Istanbul and Tel Aviv. Thanks to Ken Perkins and my Islamic Cultures Studies colleagues. Thanks also to Kara Brown, Ed Carr, Yvonne Ivory, Ann Kingsolver, Tom Lekan, Caroline Nagel, and Doyle Stevick, among others, for being my intellectual community at home. Thanks to Kevin Remington for the final maps.

I am fortunate to have an extremely fine group of colleagues at the Department of Geography. I thank Will Graf especially for his outstanding mentorship and support. I thank my fellow faculty members who supported my decision to publish a book as an untenured faculty member, something I consider crucial for my intellectual contribution to cultural geography and to area studies, but not something that is possible in every geography department.

I also thank the department for help in the months before and after my brain surgery in May 2008. I had a very rare tumor, and I thank Dr. Derald Brackmann and his incredible team at the House Ear Clinic in Los Angeles for removing it, for caring for me so expertly, and for ensuring many more years of research in interesting places. The House Ear Institute supports Dr. Brackmann's research, including improving surgical techniques for removing acoustic neuromas, and is supported by donations. Thanks to Dr. Daniele Rigamonti and Dr. Ari Shokek at Johns Hopkins for sending me to Dr. Brackmann. Thanks to my many friends and neighbors for support in Columbia, including Tara and Mike, Natalie, Mike, Billy, Eli, Kimberly, Sarah, Joanne, Cat and Paul, Ed and Lisa, and Banu. Thank you to Amy Benson and Scott Squire, Zeynep and Ben Kleiman, Ruth Bowers, and especially Lucy Griffith. The work for this book has demanded most of my time and attention over the last several years, and I thank my sister, Carrie Lamoureux, and especially my mother, Joanne Mills, for their infinite love, patience, and help. Writing the final manuscript and securing a publishing contract were more difficult than having brain surgery, and I can't imagine how I could have succeeded in either situation without Leon Jackson. I thank him for helping me achieve my dreams, for his unwavering love and loyalty, and for always having me on belay. Our home with Mango, Oscar, and Sam nourishes my mind and my heart.

Part of Chapter 5 appeared in different form as "Gender and *Mahalle* (Neighbourhood) Space in Istanbul," *Gender, Place, and Culture* 14, no. 3 (2007): 335–54, copyright, Routledge. Some of the other research for this book appeared in different form in the following previously published peer-reviewed journal articles:

> "Boundaries of the Nation in the Space of the Urban: Memory and Landscape in Istanbul," *Cultural Geographies* 13, no. 3 (2006): 367–94, copyright, Sage.
> "Narratives in City Landscapes: Cultural Identity in Istanbul," in "Geographical Dimensions of the New Middle East," special issue, *Geographical Review* 95, no. 3 (2005): 441–62, copyright, American Geographical Society.
> "The Place of Locality for Identity in the Nation: Minority Narratives of Cosmopolitan Istanbul," *International Journal of Middle East Studies* 40, no. 3 (2008): 383–401, copyright, Cambridge University Press.

I thank the publishers of these journals for permission to use this material in the preparation of this book.

Note: All maps are meant to orient the reader by providing relative locations of places in Istanbul and in Kuzguncuk. However, the locations and spatial information are approximate and are not the result of formal surveys. The maps should not be used as authoritative reference sources.

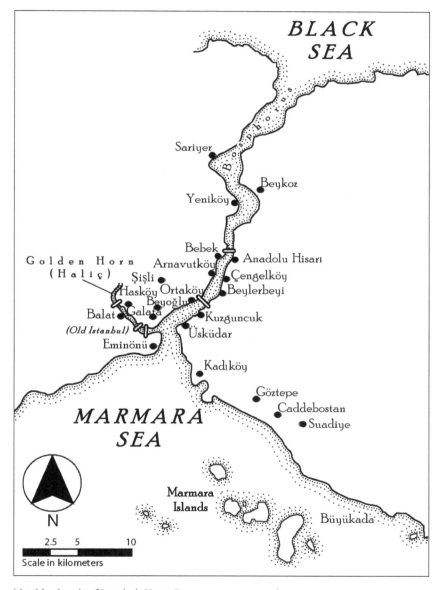

Neighborhoods of Istanbul. Kevin Remington, cartographer

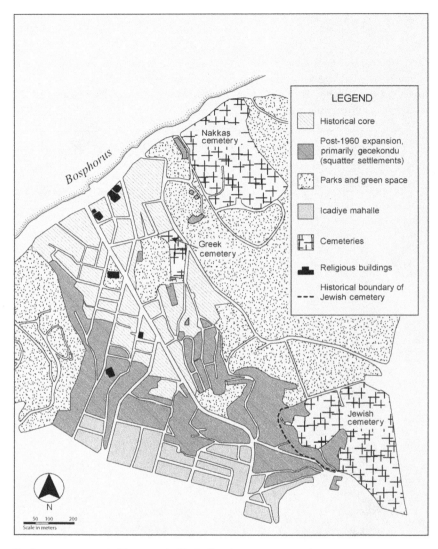

LEGEND

	Historical core
	Post-1960 expansion, primarily gecekondu (squatter settlements)
	Parks and green space
	Icadiye mahalle
	Cemeteries
	Religious buildings
---	Historical boundary of Jewish cemetery

Nakkaş cemetery

Bosphorus

Greek cemetery

Jewish cemetery

N

50 100 200
Scale in meters

Settlement patterns in Kuzguncuk. Kevin Remington, cartographer.

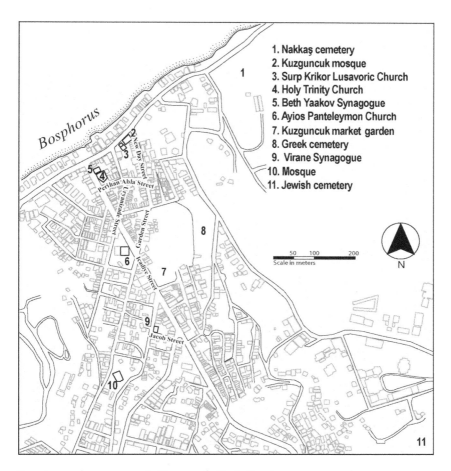

1. Nakkaş cemetery
2. Kuzguncuk mosque
3. Surp Krikor Lusavoric Church
4. Holy Trinity Church
5. Beth Yaakov Synagogue
6. Ayios Panteleymon Church
7. Kuzguncuk market garden
8. Greek cemetery
9. Virane Synagogue
10. Mosque
11. Jewish cemetery

50 100   200
Scale in meters

N

Locations and street names in Kuzguncuk. Kevin Remington, cartographer.

Streets of Memory

Introduction
Identity and Urban Memory in Landscape

One of the first Turkish words I learned was "Nerelisiniz?" Turks ask, "Where are you from?" almost before they ask anything else about any new person they meet for the first time: to figure out *who* someone is, people ask about *where*.[1] The first reason to ask "Nerelisiniz?" is to discover where a person's family originates or where a person grew up. The answer expresses a personal place identity with a special suffix (-lu/-li/-lı) after the place name. The suffix is also used in Turkish to describe national identity, as American becomes "Amerikalı," and Brazilian becomes "Brezilyalı." The case of Turkey, however, is unusual because the national identifier is not the place-based "Türkiyeli" but, rather, the word "Türk," which indicates both Turkish ethnicity and Turkish national identity, marking the commonly held understanding of national belonging in Turkey in ethnic-religious rather than place-based terms.

Nationalism, ethnicity, identity, and place intersect in particular ways in Turkey. The deeper reason Turks ask "Nerelisiniz?" is to locate a new person, however roughly, on an imagined national map—not with a literal absolute location somewhere in Turkey or in a neighborhood of Istanbul but, rather, with an imagined geography that situates a person in some way within the nation in terms of culture, socioeconomic status, political, or even ethnic identity. The word "Ankaralı," for example, means "from Ankara" or, more precisely, to be "of Ankara"—to be part of it, representative of it, to know its places intimately, to have lived one's life there, and to be a part of an ineffable something, an imagined community, with other Ankaralı people.

Istanbul is a city of more than fourteen million people, and most of them are from somewhere else. Learning that a new acquaintance is Ankaralı, from the capital city, endows that person with a different imagined geography than someone from Diyarbakır in the Kurdish Southeast or from Kayseri, a conservative city in the center of Anatolia, or from Trabzon in the Black Sea region. Massive rural-urban migration contributes to the significance of linking people with their places of origin, although identifying people by their region and neighborhood (*mahalle*) has historical roots as an Ottoman legal and cultural practice. Istanbul's population explosion has also caused a cultural debate, or identity crisis, concerning the word "Istanbullu" itself, as people argue about the true identity of the city and of its inhabitants. Notions of the proper Istanbullu Turkish accent or reactions to behaviors deemed to be too rural or uncultured for the city inhere in a cultural memory of the manners, languages, and ways of life of the Christian and Jewish minorities who once dominated the city's culture but who are today almost completely diminished in number.[2] Debates over what it means to be Turkish work through competing notions of what it means to be Istanbullu. It is through the everyday life of the city that people negotiate among themselves to accommodate Kurdish accents, conservative Islamic dress, or memories of a local Greek or Armenian past in the ethnically Turkish, secular, and Muslim nation of Turkey.

As I became familiar with Istanbul, I began to detail my own mental map of the city, developing my own understanding of the sociocultural identities coded in mahalle place names: I knew Suadiye as an upper-class neighborhood near an expensive shopping district on the Asian side. I thought of Cihangir, located near the cultural center, as a gentrified neighborhood with an interesting leftist political history. I was less familiar with Fatih, a poorer neighborhood on the historical peninsula with an Islamist cultural-political identity. Although Kuzguncuk is a very small Bosphorus neighborhood, I soon came to realize that it has an extremely powerful image on the imagined city map as a place with a typical, old-fashioned mahalle landscape, an intimate social character, and a multiethnic history. Being Kuzguncuklu (of, or from, Kuzguncuk) is something in which all Kuzguncuklu people take great pride. What it means to be Kuzguncuklu, and the ways in which people construct their identities in relationship to this place, however, are complex and contested issues that reflect the tensions at the core of notions of national belonging in Turkey, both in terms of an attachment to place and to an imagined community.

The Kuzguncuk Mahalle

I made my first trip to Kuzguncuk to attend a neighborhood festival organized by the Kuzguncuk Neighborhood Association (Kuzguncuklular Derneği) in the summer of 2000. The association was trying to raise media awareness and gather signatures to prevent the local market garden from being destroyed for a development project. A friend and I boarded a crowded blue minibus in Üsküdar to travel the short ride along the Bosphorus. We traveled up a hill, where our view was obscured briefly by walls. On the left the walls hid private waterfront mansions, and on the right they surrounded the Fetih Paşa Korusu, a tea garden and municipal park surrounding a restored nineteenth-century mansion. The road curved down to the right, the walls widened, and we came to the first stoplight, the Kuzguncuk stop. When I stepped off the minibus, my view turned from the sea inward to the glittering mirrors of the pastry shop in front of me on the corner. Icadiye Street looked small and protected; the arcade of trees shaded the main street, and it felt cooler and quieter than the bustling coast road. I admired the fruit on display at the *manav* (greengrocery) and peeked into the *kebap* (grilled meat) restaurant and into the coffeehouse as we passed, walking slowly to both satisfy my curiosity and avoid colliding with the people strolling, sitting, and standing on the sidewalk to talk. I could see that people knew each other well here, and as people looked at me, some of them smiling as I walked past, I felt more foreign than I did in the crowded parts of the European side of the city. We turned left on Garden Street and came to a table with people distributing information about earthquake-preparedness activities. The group from Arnavutköy had a petition against the proposed third bridge project. People gathered a little farther down the street to watch a clownlike performance by men dressed as old-fashioned firefighters, with a water tank and pump. Behind me, the market garden's back wall was painted in bright yellow, pink, and green, declaring in earnest children's handwriting that "the garden should remain green!" As I stood in the happy crowd listening to a singer, I noticed a beautiful dark wooden Ottoman house leaning against its neighbor. Its overhanging balcony sagged, one corner hanging more heavily toward the ground, and a little oval red metal marker with a white number displayed the house address.

Soon afterward the Kuzguncuk Neighborhood Association became my entry into the social space of the mahalle. The group met one evening every week in one of the little shop fronts on the main street across from the market garden. The metal trim of the building was a cheery purple, and fliers taped to the window advertised guitar lessons. Members talked about earthquake preparedness, a problem a neighbor had with a nearby empty lot, and the activity to save the garden from the proposed development project. A diversity of people—women and men, young people and retired folks—participated in the group discussions. They made me feel very welcome, inviting me to drink tea after the meetings. We sat outside on the sidewalk and looked at the garden. Someone reminisced about picking fruits in the garden as a child, and another described listening to the nightingale that sang from the garden. They were proud of their neighborhood's special history, explaining that the garden was once owned by a Greek man called Ilya. They had dreams of making the garden into a preserved green space, perhaps an environmental educational center for their children. They planned to live in Kuzguncuk for a long time. I could see they knew every single person who walked by as we talked, for they repeatedly exchanged greetings, asking after families and friends.

As I became acquainted with the association and their struggle to save the garden from the development project, I began to see how this particular issue intersected with many others in the neighborhood. Different perspectives on the neighborhood's past, its current situation, and its future illuminated the ways in which ethnicity, religion, class, gender, place of origin, or length of residence in the neighborhood all factored in staking claims to Kuzguncuk as a place or to Kuzguncuklu as an identity. Early on, I met with a man in the garden of the Greek Orthodox Church, after I learned the garden had once been a "Greek" property. I assumed that he would be enthusiastic about the activities to preserve the garden. I felt naive when I learned that he not only was cynical about the association's ability to prevent the development project but wanted nothing to do with the association's efforts. I met Cengiz Bektaş, a famous architect (although, as I learned, not the only famous person in this neighborhood of well-known artists and writers) who told me about activities he did with the aim of invigorating Kuzguncuk's mahalle culture and developing community involvement in the neighborhood. Later, some association members told me that they felt that they, not he, were responsible for the successful organizing that developed into the market garden campaign. Other residents told me that they felt that Bektaş and the intellectuals who followed him to restore houses on Uryanizade Street were socially exclusive. Later on in my research I began neighboring with people I met through my walks in the mahalle or through people I had come to know in my everyday life as a resident, and I learned that some people were critical of the association as well, which surprised me because I knew that members were enthusiastic to expand their numbers and include anyone who wanted to participate. What were the cultural politics behind these different perspectives?

Kuzguncuk became, to me, like a multifaceted puzzle, and as I turned it around and around, holding it like a prism to my questions, the different social spaces I experienced and the narratives I heard each refracted a unique light on the same mahalle to reveal a different place entirely. I saw multiple Kuzguncuks, each of them connected and dependent on the other, yet when I looked at any one of them too closely or felt too deeply embedded in its story, the others were obscured. The experience of doing research on Kuzguncuk meant living there, developing friendships, sharing food, and becoming a neighbor. My fieldwork was an embodied experience during which I often felt torn between impassioned and often competing loyalties of the people I knew. This book brings these diverse voices into conversation with each other. I hope that by addressing a multiplicity of perspectives, my work will provide ground for a mutual acknowledgment of difference.

I adopted the convention of naming book chapters after streets in Kuzguncuk for a few reasons. First, I do this to bring the neighborhood landscape into the foreground. Kuzguncuk's narrow streets are what makes it famous, as its old houses, shops, and religious buildings have made it probably the most frequently used setting for television series in Turkey (at least five television series were being filmed there in 2007). Second, the other well-known aspect of Kuzguncuk, frequently discussed in news media, and also an important source of pride for its residents, is its neighborliness. Kuzguncuk's neighborliness is a close sociality that depends on its streets as semiprivate social spaces for the daily interactions that link people as neighbors. An often recited "complaint" is that it takes a resident more than a half hour to walk down the main street, Icadiye Street, to get to the bus stop or the ferry station because of the time it takes to greet everyone she knows along the way. Third, naming chapters after streets was a way to structure the book around contesting narratives that converge in a particular place, to examine "the street as locus of collective memory."[3] In the book, and in reality, contrasting memories and experiences of neighborhood life meet in the street. My focus on streets expresses my goal to move away from a study of formal monuments or intentionally commemorative landscapes to focus on the cultural work of lived, everyday landscapes, the "accumulation of memories from below, through the physical and associative traces left by interweaving patterns of everyday life."[4] Kuzguncuk's streets open paths to understanding how Istanbul's larger urban process is conditioned by cultural, economic, and political forces.[5] By paying attention to the role of the urban, vernacular landscape in mediating the tensions of national belonging, I examine the cultural politics of national identity in Turkey from the perspective of regular people's lives and experiences. As Joelle Bahloul writes, regarding Muslim and Jewish memories of an Algerian household, "The house is like a family, and in its history the family appears as solid as a built structure. As we go through the house, memories not only describe physical space but also tell a social history."[6] As we go through the mahalle streets of Kuzguncuk, bringing diverse narratives of the past together, we can read some of the individual narratives against the grain of the dominant collective memory of historical multiethnic tolerance and belonging so often told about the neighborhood.[7] I do not aim to deny that the cosmopolitan space of cultural memory existed in fact; rather, I examine the reasons why the stories continue to be told.

Memories of cosmopolitan Kuzguncuk reveal the complex attachments and contradictions that lie at the heart of both violent and peaceful events concerning minority history and national identity in Istanbul in recent years. The political and cultural significance of remembering and forgetting the city's Christian and Jewish past cannot be overstated. Efforts to recognize historical and current minority human rights violations continue in the context of the European Union integration process.[8] Turkey's minority past has become grounds for symbolic violence, as nationalist lawyers attempt to persecute authors writing about the city's multicultural history for "insulting Turkishness" under Penal Code 301.[9] This symbolic violence periodically becomes tragically real in bombings of religious buildings and in symbolic assassinations. Just as importantly, gestures to recognize minority cultures, histories, and political perspectives express a hope for a tolerant, multicultural Turkey. After Armenian newspaper editor Hrant Dink was murdered in January 2007, by a young man linked to an extremist, secularist, Turkish ethnonationalist group, thousands of Turks gathered in public spaces to chant, "We are all Hrant! We are all Armenian!" in a passionate gesture of support for his family and rejection of ultranationalist violence. As Turkish professor and columnist Haluk Şahin writes, "'Who are we?' continues to be one of our most burning topics, even eighty years after the founding of the republic."[10]

The Nation in the City

Since the foundation of the Turkish Republic in 1923, Istanbul has had unique importance as a site through and against which the Turkish state asserts and represents national identity. Istanbul's historically rich cosmopolitan urbanism was similar to other cities of the Middle East, where Greeks, Jews, Armenians, and other non-Muslim residents had significant roles in the Ottoman administration, urban economy, and the modernization processes of the empire. Until the middle of the twentieth century, Istanbul's culture and daily life was characterized by a multiplicity of languages and cultural practices that required a mutual recognition of difference as well as a cultural system of sharing urban space.[11] This culture, which people in Kuzguncuk remember as a "mosaic," was destroyed by Turkish nationalism as minorities increasingly faced prejudice and discrimination both at the level of the state and in the social practices of everyday life, which began to change with rural-urban migration. Turkey's founder, Mustafa Kemal Atatürk, defined the nation with a primary emphasis on secularism but also as ethnically Turkish and culturally Muslim. (Islam was considered an integral and inseparable root of Turkish culture, which resulted in the ideological exclusion of non-Muslim minorities. Secularism meant that Islamic religiosity and religious practices, however, were to be separated from public life and strictly defined and controlled by the state.)[12] At this moment, the state created its own ethnic category—the Turk—to define the nation, which then became the ideal space of belonging.[13] By defining the minority as those not ethnically Turkish and not Muslim, the state circumscribed an imaginary national boundary to legitimize its power.[14] The exclusion of the many religious, ethnic, linguistic, and other social minorities in Turkey from this ideal created an identity crisis that continues to undermine a cohesive national identity in Turkey today. Studies of the identity politics resulting from the tensions between the exclusionary national identity promoted by the state and the multiple ways in which people self-identify constitute a major research trend in Turkish Studies. Many of these studies focus on cities, including those that address the expression of modernist and nationalist ideologies in the built environment and others that examine identity as produced through experiences of daily urban life.[15]

The ways in which Turkish nationalism worked through urban image and design can be compared with other cities in the region, although Turkey did not emerge from a colonial context. In colonial cities, European power was represented in architectural form and in urban planning, a system that also reproduced, through social and spatial segregation, a sense of ethnic and religious difference between European expatriates and local residents, and among local Christians, Jews, and Muslims.[16] As a result, postcolonial national identity was also forged, represented, and produced through the urban spaces of colonial rule and oppression. In Istanbul, although the city never became the site of direct colonial rule, by the end of the nineteenth century, Christian and Jewish ethnic minorities had come to symbolize European economic and political dominance, which was weakening the Ottoman Empire. After the founding of the republic, those minorities were seen both as betrayers of the Turkish nation-state and as uncomfortable reminders of the Ottoman imperial past, and although Christian and Jewish minorities were granted formal legal equality in Turkey, in practice they have experienced discrimination and thousands have been forced, or have chosen, to leave Turkey.

The processes of forgetting and remembering minority urban histories in Turkey resemble those in other formerly cosmopolitan cities of the Ottoman Empire where religious identities are politicized.[17] In Damascus, for example, nostalgic restoration of the old city is laden with debate concerning the identity of the city, as struggles over who is a Damascene are figured through Sunni, Christian, Jewish, and Alawi claims to places in the nation through their histories in the city.[18] In Beirut, where, in the quarter of Zuqaq al-Blat, Christian families were displaced and replaced by rural migrants moving to the city, collective amnesia of this process is so serious, that, unlike in Istanbul, public debate on the ethnic and national transformations of the city are impossible.[19] As a result, state-sponsored amnesia produces ongoing enmity among confessional groups, and competing memories of the past struggle for representation in the city. A nostalgic popular memory has developed, which "gloss[es] over the latent conflict with the myth of harmonious conviviality."[20] Cosmopolitan memory serves a political function through urban culture in cities of the former Ottoman Empire. The current nostalgia for cosmopolitanism not only occurs in a globalized context where notions of what cosmopolitanism is are informed by contemporary international discourse concerning tolerance, democracy, transnationalism, or westernization, but is produced in a local context where cosmopolitanism is believed to have real meaning as a lived, historical reality that was fundamentally altered by the effects of state-driven nationalism on urban landscapes and daily life.[21]

When the Turkish Republic was founded in 1923, its capital was located in Ankara, to ground the identity of the new nation in the heartland of Anatolia and leave the symbolic Ottoman city behind. Istanbul, the former imperial city, became the cultural remnant of the Ottoman past. The dominant presence of Christian and Jewish minorities in the city undermined the geographic imaginary of the nation as ethnically Turkish and Muslim. Istanbul's cosmopolitan neighborhoods were affected by linguistic and economic Turkification policies intended to remake the social character of the city. Most significant for the fate of Istanbul's cosmopolitan urban fabric were policies and events that targeted minority ownership of property, particularly in minority-dominated neighborhoods, some of which, like Beyoğlu, were where the city's cultural and economic pulse was located. In Istanbul, at the turn of the twentieth century, non-Muslim minorities and foreigners constituted 56 percent of the population of the city; they were even more significantly represented as property owners, tradespeople, and workers in skilled occupations.[22] By the end of the twentieth century, after massive minority emigration and the rural-urban migration of Kurds and Turks to Istanbul, Christians and Jews constituted less than 1 percent of the population of a city of more than ten million people. Remnants of their communities remain, however, and have left traces in Istanbul's culture and in its landscapes.

By focusing on the layers of history—material and imagined—in the urban landscape, I illustrate how the process of nation-imagining occurs through a transformation of the city. In this way, my work builds on research that has centered on formal national architecture and urban planning, or on symbolic buildings and monuments, to examine the nationalization of vernacular social and residential spaces and the experiences of ordinary residents in this process. In the first chapter, I introduce the neighborhood, the mahalle, as an element of Ottoman urban form that was linked to Ottoman administrative policies regarding non-Muslims. The cosmopolitan cultures of mixed mahalles was torn apart by Turkification policies such as the Citizen, Speak Turkish campaign; the 1942–43 Wealth Tax, which was disproportionately levied on Christian and Jewish minorities; the 6–7 September 1955 riots, which destroyed minority properties; and the 1964 deportation of Greek citizens. These events have only very recently begun to be acknowledged in Istanbul and are nearly totally denied to have happened in Kuzguncuk because of its special tolerant culture.

In spite of the Turkish state's efforts to render minorities invisible from the national narrative and to erase their traces from contemporary public spaces, a national memory crisis erupted toward the end of the twentieth century as traces of minority pasts became currency in a national debate surrounding cultural memory and minority human rights.[23] A secular memory of cosmopolitan neighborhood life among minorities began to emerge in the 1990s. This countermemory challenged the state-authored historical narrative of Turkey as ethnically Turkish and Muslim by emphasizing the city's ethnic minority history. (A similar, but Islamist, cultural memory of the Ottoman past also emerged at this time to support a growing Islamist cultural and political movement.)[24] It was produced not only in print media, television, and film but also in the restoration of formerly multiethnic neighborhoods of Istanbul.

Nation, Memory, and Landscape

Nation

There exists a very broad literature on the idea of the nation; the relationships between religious, ethnic, and national identities; the relationship between the nation and the state; and the historical and mythical roots of nations.[25] Scholarship on nationalism has challenged the notion that national identity is something primordial and examines it, rather, as produced through a process.[26] Rogers Brubaker frames it in this way: "Instead of focusing on nations as real groups, we should focus on nationhood and nationness, on 'nation' as practical category, institutionalized form, and contingent event. 'Nation' is a category of practice, not (in the first instance) a category of analysis."[27] One of the most influential works in this area is *Imagined Communities* by Benedict Anderson, who introduces the notion of the nation as an imagined community to explain how thousands of people can share an imagined sense of belonging that transcends their inhabited locality.[28] He reveals the role of the state in producing and disseminating the identity of the nation through mass print media, the standardization of state language and education, the census, the national map, and the museum. Research inspired by Anderson's theory thus examines how state agencies construct a coherent identity for the nation to legitimize state power.[29] Studies on the role of the state as the primary agent in the processes through which the nation comes to be imagined provide an important framework for research on Turkish nationalism, in part because of the very significant role of the state in creating the nation.[30] For example, research has illustrated the ways in which state historians define the Turkish nation with a historical narrative that grounds Turkey's foundations in the migration of Turkish tribes from Central Asia who carried a distinctive ethnic, linguistic, and cultural Turkish and Muslim identity.[31] This narrative is represented in Turkish national museums and in the architectural style of Atatürk's mausoleum, was taught in the History of the Turkish Revolution course at Turkish universities between 1923 and 1942, and was employed to oppress political dissent in the 1970s.[32]

Since the impact of *Imagined Communities*, other theoretical approaches have widened the scope of analysis to include a broader range of methods, groups, and sites of study. These studies rely on ethnography or oral history to understand contemporary lived experiences, or employ discourse analyses of individual narratives, cultural media, and material forms such as landscapes or monuments. Underlying much of this research is a critical focus on plurality and inequality and on the failures of the nation, as an imagined community, to cohere in reality. Two broad and interrelated contributions of this research inform the thinking behind this book.

The first contribution questions the totalizing nature of the national narrative to draw attention to the complexity inherent in the nation. National identity is not seen as unitary but, rather, as something fluid that embodies multiple and contested meanings. The focus of this research is to understand the discursive processes, and experiential moments and spaces, through which individuals and social groups produce and challenge notions of national identity. Homi Bhabha's work on national narrative is foundational, as he argues for an examination of the cultural signs and symbols through which the national narrative gathers meaning. This approach, grounded in cultural studies and literary criticism, reveals the inconsistencies embedded in national narratives. Bhabha also exposes what he calls the margins of the nation, that is, the moments and spaces through which the national narrative is interpreted and contested.[33] An important dimension of this and similar approaches is the focus on nationalism as something that is not static or predetermined but continually re-created and thus vulnerable to change and to a multiplicity of interpretations and practices.

An example of a similar approach, but in a historical study, grounds the work of Zachary Lockman. He argues that national identity should be examined as "not a thing but a set of relations and forces that in each particular case unfolds and takes shape within a specific historical conjuncture, social context, and discursive arena. It is moreover always the object of struggles among various sociopolitical forces over its meaning and over what is to be 'done' with it."[34] Lockman eschews formal or elite national narratives and examines, rather, particular historical episodes. For example, in studying the actions of Palestinian Arab workers who accepted support from Zionists in the mandate period, he demonstrates the sometimes unexpected and seemingly contradictory ways in which national identity gathers meaning in particular spaces and moments. The complex religious, rural, urban, and other dimensions of Palestinian national identities present a very clear challenge to any overarching or exclusive understanding of the nation.[35] As recent scholarship demonstrates (and to which this book contributes), the same is true for Turkey.[36]

The second contribution of recent nationalism studies raises questions regarding the assumed top-down direction of the process that places the state in the position of primary authorship of the nation.[37] Other research challenges the notion that the nation, as an ideal, originated in Europe.[38] Critical ethnographies focus on the indivisibly political, social, and cultural processes through which the nation comes to have meaning. Ana Maria Alonso, for example, analyzes the nation as a "structure of feeling."[39] Michael Herzfeld offers a way of thinking about the nation in terms of cultural intimacy, or humor, embarrassment, and pride—elements of social life that produce a sense of shared identity, which can facilitate a negotiation with state power.[40] Other studies focus on the languages and interactions that constitute "everyday ethnicity" among Romanians and Hungarians in Romania or on the gendered social practices of daily household life through which villagers articulated Muslim and Christian identity in pre-war Bosnia.[41]

Research on national identity in Turkey has similarly examined the roles of cultural practices and political symbols in everyday life in reproducing, and also challenging, the notion of Turkish national identity as secular, modern, ethnically Turkish, and culturally Muslim.[42] Geographers have contributed with a focus on the spatial practices that contest hegemonic notions of Turkish identity in public space.[43] Recent research on citizenship has destabilized the traditional scholarly emphasis on the top-down role of the state in the processes of identity construction.[44] My work is similarly concerned with the ways in which Turkish national identity gathers meaning in urban life, among ordinary people. What are the sociospatial processes through which diverse people imagine, articulate, and sustain ethnic-religious identities in a context where ethnic-religious identity becomes a marker of belonging or exclusion for the state? What is the role of the city—of the material urban fabric and of urban culture—in these processes?

The strength of the geographic approach I take to theorizing nationalism is that, through a conceptual emphasis on place, landscape, and social space, it goes beyond assuming that the state takes a primary role in the processes of nation imagining and also breaks down a dichotomous view that places the state and people in opposition in this process. While critical scholarship on Turkey has drawn attention to the historical and contemporary experiences of particular minority groups, my focus on place makes it possible to center an analysis on where, and in what ways, a diversity of people come together and negotiate belonging. Approaching national identity through place and landscape also shifts the question away from an emphasis on ethnic-religious identity itself, an approach that may set up an implicit and erroneous assumption that ethnicity and religious identity are bounded and discrete categories.[45] However powerful the state may be in producing nationalist ideology, the ways in which people negotiate with it are inconsistent and unpredictable; individual identities are multiple and fragmented, and cohere, sometimes only briefly, in specific places. Furthermore, boundaries of belonging and exclusion may overlap, and individuals may accommodate multiple identities in relation to the nation. Examining the role of culture, and of the city, in the processes of imagining and challenging national identity is extremely important in contexts where religion and ethnicity have been employed as markers of political belonging and exclusion. This question is significant because of the ways in which both Turkish nationalist ideologies and global popular and political discourse frame Christian, Jewish, and Muslim identities as essential, static, or ultimately opposed.

Memory

One of the most important elements in the processes through which people come to imagine themselves as sharing a particular identity, including national or cultural identity, is the reproduction of a shared memory of the past. This works in several ways, including the selective appropriation of particular events in history by an elite or a state body, and their representation in invented traditions or commemorations that then come to shape a national memory.[46] Although shared national memory is known as collective memory, this memory is not truly collective, in that tensions exist between individual and collective memories, particularly when those authored by dominant social groups or the state disguise social inequality.[47] The construction of (and reference to) memory is thus deeply imbricated in national identity politics.

One important assumption behind my study is the understanding that memory (like the nation) is not static or predetermined and cannot be objectively assessed. Rather, memory is a process that occurs in the present day, and although it refers to a past, that past is remembered in particular and selective ways.[48] And so, while memory appears to be a coherent, natural unfolding of past events into a narrative, perception and experience are always partial and incomplete.[49] Memory of the past is thus always fragmented. By bringing this understanding of the nature of memory to thinking about the processes of imagining the nation, this book contributes to that body of research that challenges an understanding of national memory as unitary. I examine multiple individual memories alongside representations of memory in popular culture to understand how individuals negotiate national belonging in partial, multiple, or even contradictory ways. National and minority identity politics in Turkey often search for and depend on historical evidence to bolster claims about what did or did not happen in the past. The aim of my project, in contrast, is to identify and explain important themes, moments, and debates regarding contemporary memory. I am interested in cultural memory as a medium through which people reconcile tension associated with difficult moments in the past, moments that "impinge, sometimes fatally, on the present."[50] What distinguishes this study is my attention to the ways in which these processes of memory both rely on and also come to shape landscapes and places in the city.

One of the ways in which society copes with the nation's failure to live up to its implicit promises of harmony and inclusivity is through nostalgia, an interpretation of history that compensates for a contemporary malaise, a lack of community and identity that is the result of rapid, alienating change.[51] For example, in Istanbul, nostalgia for the mahalle as a familiar space of shared belonging arose in a context of extremely rapid social and environmental change, resulting from overurbanization, massive rural migration, and an increasingly visible polarization of wealth. Nostalgia for mahalle life, where everyone knew everyone else and religion never separated neighbors, may appear to be escapist, romantic, or even regressive. However, scholars of memory argue that nostalgia "is only a structure of relation to the past, not false or inauthentic in essence."[52] "Structural nostalgia," for example, is a cultural practice of negotiating with contemporary tensions through memories of social balance, reciprocity, moral parity, and the observance of self-enforcing rules.[53]

Nostalgia thus serves a cultural function where past traumatic events resurface persistently in a contemporary cultural context.[54] The dominant silencing, and forgetting, of Istanbul's multicultural, Ottoman past and of the state's role in nationalizing the city has produced a society divorced from its own history.[55] The cultural politics of memory—the power dynamics conditioning who does the remembering and what is remembered—work through contestations over the histories and identities of places.[56] Memory requires a "display," an articulation in object or representation, to give it meaning.[57] Where nostalgia for a particular past becomes embodied, it transforms places.[58] Memory thus becomes embedded in the cultural landscapes of the city, whether they are formally commemorative or vernacular and understood to be historical.[59] As an essential element in the processes through which powerful discourses are materialized and contested, the landscape is central to the imagining of the nation.[60]

Landscape

The cultural landscape is a concept foundational to geography and has been defined in various ways throughout the history of the discipline.[61] Early studies defined landscape as the cultural imprint of human activity on the environment or as society's "unwitting autobiography," approaches that, in general, understand the layers of the physical landscape as traces of cultural history.[62] The notion that the landscape is a combined, layered residue of the past, or a composite material reality that is merely there, is also an important part of the way the landscape is popularly understood. A careful observer of an urban landscape on the old peninsula of Istanbul, for example, might see the traces of the city's history in the Byzantine city walls, an Armenian church, a recently renovated Ottoman house, a modern apartment building, and an informal squatter house sandwiched in between these other elements. This book contributes to critical cultural geographic scholarship aimed at looking critically at landscapes that appear, on their surfaces, to be innocent traces of the past, because it is these understandings of landscapes that facilitate the mysterious work they do to sustain particular ways of seeing the world. What do these composite landscapes come to mean in contemporary Istanbul culture? Do people look at them as investment opportunities, signs of urban renewal, results of overcrowding amid ancient infrastructure, or historical evidence of the city's multiculturalism? What shapes these views? This book examines the role of everyday ordinary landscapes in Istanbul in reproducing taken-for-granted understandings about the way things are.

One way of investigating the ideologies embedded in landscapes is to read them like a text and to study the meanings embedded in symbols in the landscape, whether they are architectural elements or monuments.[63] This critical perspective views landscapes as "transformations of ideologies into a concrete form" and makes it possible to link the material landscapes with the processes that reproduce social relations.[64] Research in this field interrogates how landscapes produce cultural meaning by making ideology (or, in this case, a particular narrative of Turkish history) appear natural and reveals the power of landscapes to make historical social inequalities seem normal, and thus uncontestable.[65] This interpretation makes the cultural landscape a useful conceptual framework with which to examine questions of nationalism, identity, and minority history in Turkey.

Contemporary landscape studies examine the processes shaping landscapes to understand their role in representing and reinforcing ideologies that perpetuate unequal social relations. Landscapes are viewed as a medium through which various social groups exert power in the cultural-political sphere. Thinking of the "landscape as material discourse" highlights the power relations embedded in the transformation of material landscapes by examining the ways in which they reflect a multiplicity of intentions of various actors who stake competing claims to place, and to identity, through efforts to shape the material landscape.[66]

Far more than just illustrating historical traces or intended representations of historical narratives, landscapes have a peculiar kind of power inherent in the fact that they are visual, material forms. Their materiality makes them appear neutral, as mere traces of history. Yet, when we look at them, we perceive a composite whole with a cohering logic. Landscapes are also thus a way of seeing that extends farther than simply their materiality.[67] As observers, we normally take the narratives embedded in landscapes for granted, even though they may employ a synthetically created sense of authenticity to make the historical narratives they tell seem even more real.[68] Because the origins of landscapes are rarely questioned, they become naturalized: when we look at landscapes, *we see what they represent* and we don't interrogate this representation or the cultural work it performs to perpetuate social norms. The landscapes' visual materiality makes the representation we see appear to be objective, and in this way, the politically laden and socially conditioned processes that actually produced the landscapes become obscured.[69]

Narratives of memory embedded in landscapes, then, also come to have a seemingly uncontestable authority and thus work to obstruct alternative narratives of history. Nicola King writes similarly of the process of memory, that because the very nature of memory is conventionally understood to have a quality of truth, one memory can acquire authority and can obscure competing memories.[70] In this way, I view the informal urban, cultural landscape—and by this I mean not monuments, formal architecture, or urban planning but the seemingly spontaneous, resident-generated landscape—as the cultural materiality of the process of interpreting and negotiating national identity politics through cultural memory. Neither memory nor landscapes are fixed, although they may appear to be static. Rather, they are always in process. There is a logic that coheres the actions of individuals who participate in the processes of cultural memory that resonates through the larger cultural and political sphere.[71] This logic conditions the ways in which people relate to, or negotiate their positions within, a larger system, a process that creates the complex and heterogeneous social spaces through which memory and forgetting take place. In this sense, landscapes do not merely represent, commemorate, or challenge memory but are *the means through which* Istanbullus *perform* urban memory.

The city is thus the site and medium through which memory and forgetting, and nation-imagining, takes place.[72] The Ottoman past is always present in the urban landscape of Istanbul and contains remnants, reminders of what has not successfully been forgotten. Its materiality is always undergoing interpretation and is full of meaning continually produced through the narration of the city as a place.

Cultural Memories of Cosmopolitanism in Istanbul

In Istanbul, memories of the city's Greeks, Jews, and Armenians have variously been the subject of nostalgia, regret, debate, and heated political controversy. Places in the landscape, symbols, or *lieux de memoire*, of Istanbul's

Christians and Jews became the subject of new attention at the end of the twentieth century.[73] Tensions existed between the state's memory enforced through the national historical narrative and what is known or suspected to have happened to minorities. Minorities had come to occupy an uneasy balance that relied on a distinction between public and private spheres of life.[74] As Leyla Neyzi describes it, "the rejection of the past resulted in a potential conflict between family identity and national identity on the part of [minority] individuals."[75] By the 1990s, minority rights activism, most vocally on the behalf of Kurdish refugees from the southeast, had put minorities on the public agenda. An increasing interest in topics related to minority history emerged.[76] By the early to mid-1990s, several books began to be published in Turkish on what were once taboo topics, demonstrating not only decreasing censorship but also increasing social and cultural openness toward these issues in Istanbul.[77] Works that expose the targeting of minorities in the 1942–43 Wealth Tax and the 6–7 September 1955 riots; relate the consequences of the forced deportation of Greek citizens from Istanbul in 1964; and cover social, cultural, and political Jewish history in Turkey and in Istanbul are direct interventions by historians to rewrite the national narrative.[78] Other works focus on the histories of specific minority places in the city or on minority human rights issues in general.[79] Turkish academic journals, such as *Toplum ve Bilim* (Society and Knowledge), and semiacademic popular magazines about Istanbul, like *Istanbul Dergisi* (Istanbul Magazine; published between 1992 and 2008), devote space to minority history. An important and increasingly large focus of this critical scholarship (and the body of literature to which this book most directly contributes) has been on the study of memory itself as a way to understand the political, cultural, and social processes through which national memory is constructed through processes that condition what is remembered and what is forgotten.[80]

The cultural-political movement to remember the minority past also constitutes a small but important genre of Turkish literature, including memoirs and fiction set in historically minority-dominated areas of the country and also of Istanbul.[81] For example, Buket Uzuner's book *Kumral Ada, Mavi Tuna* (published in English translation as *Mediterranean Waltz*) was a best seller in Kuzguncuk. The novel explores the consequences of mandatory military service, as well as the state-Kurdish conflict in the southeast for how it reshaped local identities and friendships between

Muslims, Greeks, and Jews. Minority history in Istanbul reached the national popular consciousness when a novel about a Jewish family and their experiences during World War II was made into a film and this counter-narrative of history became a topic of widespread discussion in the media and among the general public. This film, *Salkım Hanımın Taneleri* (Salkım Hanım's Necklace) was based on a book of the same title.[82] It is a fictional account of one Jewish family's experience with the antiminority 1942–43 Wealth Tax and addresses the widespread devastation of minority communities and their forced labor in work camps. Although it later faced periodic censorship, the film was widely popular, won several awards in Turkey, and was considered to represent Turkey at the Oscars.

One of the avenues through which remembering and forgetting takes place is through the building and restoration of landscapes in the city that recall Istanbul's cosmopolitan past. Old neighborhoods where Greeks, Jews, Armenians, and other minorities lived are undergoing gentrification. Some of these areas, such as the neighborhoods of Tepebaşı, Galata, and Çukurcuma (near the European district of Beyoğlu) or Balat and Fener (former Jewish and Greek neighborhoods on the Golden Horn), were, through the 1970s, commonly thought of by Istanbul's elite as run-down and not desirable. These areas at that time were the spaces of the poor, including Roma and Kurdish migrants, and later of refugees from countries in Central Africa and Southwest Asia. They lived (many continue to do so today) in Greek or Armenian or Jewish apartment buildings because these buildings were abandoned or rented at extremely low prices by owners living far from Istanbul. In the 1980s many of these areas began to be renovated, some of them explicitly for the purpose of tourism.[83]

These areas became popular for investment, in part, because of the ways in which their minority histories intersected with what, by the early 1990s, had emerged as a larger cultural movement to remember the city's historical cosmopolitanism. In many cases, people who move to or visit the new historical areas are not interested in any critical revisioning of history but rather articulate an elite and European lifestyle through locations that represent a Western identity.[84] Some, however, articulate visions of a multicultural national identity through the urban cultural landscape and the cultural memory of cosmopolitanism it signifies. Restoration of these and other parts of the city known for minority history locate a nostalgia for the lost Istanbullu, for the Greeks, Jews, and Armenians who took the character of the city with them when they departed.

I encountered these places first as a foreigner walking through Beyoğlu. Beyoğlu is located on the northern European side of the city, which developed in the late nineteenth and early twentieth centuries as Istanbul expanded outward from its historical peninsula. Here, ports were developed for trade with European countries, and European businesses and consulates located in the city; the turn-of-the-century apartment buildings and shops seen there today were home, almost exclusively, to local Jews and Christians and foreign expatriates. Beyoğlu was the cosmopolitan, European heart of the city, until it began to decline when non-Muslim minorities emigrated in large numbers after the 1955 riots. This decline worsened during the 1970s and early 1980s, after more minority emigration and increased political tensions in the city, until the area became a focus of urban investment in the early 1990s. Today it is the location of a major shopping and entertainment district and an area of tourism, as well as of Istanbul's countercultures and political activism. The past is made deliberately present in Beyoğlu's landscape as the area has become a beloved subject of restoration and representation. One consumes this "historical" landscape by purchasing postcards and books about its history or through eating and drinking in restored historical buildings. The popular Ara Café, for example, is owned by a famous photographer called Ara Güler. Filled with old artifacts of the city (antique telephones, stained glass), the café also offers free postcard reproductions of Güler's photographs of 1950s Beyoğlu.[85] Sometimes nostalgia for the minority-owned businesses that used to characterize Beyoğlu's landscape is written in new shop or restaurant signs in languages other than Turkish, such as Greek, an irony given the fact that in 1930s Beyoğlu, speaking non-Turkish languages in public spaces was discouraged and local words that came to be thought of as "foreign" were erased from street signs.

In addition to resurrecting the histories of minority neighborhoods, remembering Istanbul's past also works through a cultural memory of old-fashioned mahalle life, a space and image represented in nostalgic memoirs, by reissuing old works of fiction set in traditional mahalles and by producing commercials and a long string of mahalle television shows, which began with one filmed in Kuzguncuk in the late 1980s. No longer referring to the segregated ethnic neighborhood of the Ottoman city, today the word *mahalle* refers to the neighborhood, the space of everyday urban life in the contemporary city. As a Turkish cultural concept, the idea of the mahalle also carries associations of belonging and familiarity, and of social and spatial intimacy; it is the space where everyone knows everyone else. The mahalle of cultural memory refers to a time when Istanbul's neighborhood landscapes were composed of old, small apartment buildings, single-standing Ottoman houses, and a mix of family-owned shops. The Ottoman house, an integral part of the imagined typical mahalle landscape, is a traditional space that embodies Turkish cultural memory and identity.[86] The mahalle is a space that signifies a more tolerant, inclusive way of life where people lived on a local scale and neighbors were like members of an extended family. As I began to notice the nostalgia for old Istanbul and ask people about the history of the city and mahalle life, someone told me that if I want to see a real mahalle, I should go to Kuzguncuk.

Landscape and Memory in Kuzguncuk

The idea that Kuzguncuk retained much of its historical mahalle landscape and culture, or had not been *bozuldu* (ruined) like new parts of Istanbul, popped up repeatedly in conversations and in texts about the neighborhood during my fieldwork. It became a theme that connected the threads of my research and prompted me throughout to examine what it was that was so special about Kuzguncuk, and why Kuzguncuk, in particular, was described by so many as a typical mahalle. Kuzguncuk was frequently pictured in local newspapers, on television, and in photograph essays in magazines, in part because of the activity of its neighborhood organization, but also, I believe, because the portrayal of Kuzguncuk's friendly mahalle culture and its multiethnic historical landscape struck a nerve in larger Istanbul culture; it was the cosmopolitan cultural memory made real.

In the early months after my arrival in Kuzguncuk it was difficult for me to make sense of the relationship between how Kuzguncuk was represented—its beautiful, romantic landscape and its image as a real mahalle—and the actual regular daily life in the mahalle itself, which was at once complex and confusing but also seemingly fairly ordinary. As I studied the historical and contemporary processes that resulted in Kuzguncuk's material landscape, I tracked its representations in cultural media and in conversations to understand the symbols embedded in its form, in the Ottoman wooden houses, the mixed small-scale shops on the main street, and the propinquity of churches, mosques, and synagogues. I tried to notice what the landscape represented and why it was important, and also asked questions about what was *not* represented: the social, political, and cultural realities obscured by the landscape itself. As the trails I followed continually returned to issues of contemporary social difference and to Greek, Jewish, and Armenian history, I began to see how the themes of multicultural harmony and belonging in the cultural memory of the mahalle related to the historical and contemporary life of the mahalle on the ground. It is this process that is the true subject of my study and the window through which I explore national identity. I began to understand that Kuzguncuk's landscape, as a material form, served as evidence of a particular memory of the past, both for residents living in the neighborhood and in the larger cultural sphere. This representation obscured other, rarely told narratives of place and the very processes through which the landscape was built.

The minibus to Kuzguncuk from Üsküdar stops at a pastry shop that faces the Bosphorus, diagonally across from the Çınaraltı Café, which is next to the locally famous fish restaurant Ismet Baba on the seaside. In the summer, people sit on the benches in the small square next to the café. There might be a group of young men smoking cigarettes, telling stories, and watching girls; or a smiling couple; or a small child tumbling after a pigeon; or an elderly man feeding scraps to a lucky cat. All the windows will be open at the Çınaraltı, and on a weekend morning the place is full and a cluster of little tables and chairs spills out into the park, filled with people reading newspapers, eating breakfast, and drinking tea or fresh juice. The sea breezes cool the bright sunlight glinting off the swiftly moving water, and the nearby bridge soars overhead across the sea, landing behind the waterfront and the lovely ornate Ortaköy Mosque across the Bosphorus. In the winter, the café is a warm and smoky respite from hurrying on the narrow sidewalk along the noisy road, dodging potholes and tree roots and cars parked on the sidewalk while trying to avoid muddy splashes from passing buses. The little square is where Kuzguncuklu people come to see each other and feel part of the neighborhood. Elderly people remember promenading down the main street to the seaside park on summer nights, being seen as young couples and socializing with neighbors.

The old marble fountain there used to have the sweetest drinking water in Kuzguncuk.

This area nearby the ferry station was once Kuzguncuk's heart, when entering the neighborhood meant arriving by boat and Kuzguncuk faced the sea. The coastal road was developed later, carved through the water-front buildings or built on top of fill that extended the coastal edge farther into the sea. In 1836 Armenian workers who were building a palace in the neighboring mahalle of Beylerbeyi built a small church in Kuzguncuk. Today the church sits right on the coastal road, less than a block away from the café. To look at the church means to look straight up at the building itself; it's very difficult to take a photograph of the front of the building in its entirety from street level because, like most churches in Is-tanbul, it sits behind a tall metal gate and its facade is obscured from view. Next to it, immediately on the other side of its wall, is a small mosque. This mosque was built more than a hundred years after the church, in 1952. That was the first moment in the neighborhood's long history when there were enough Muslim Kuzguncuklus to necessitate a local, regular, community gathering space.[87] By the mid-1990s, local media had begun representing the church and mosque as symbols of multiethnic harmony in Kuzguncuk. By the time the Kuzguncuk mosque was built next to the Armenian church, however, Kuzguncuk's Armenian community had all but completely disappeared.

The narrative of Kuzguncuk's past multicultural harmony is rarely criti-cally interrogated, although it should raise several questions: why does the legend that the church gave the land to the mosque continue to be told? Why does the current congregation of the church come not from Kuz-guncuk but from other neighborhoods? Why did Kuzguncuk in the 1990s become so popular in the media, and why did so many (Turkish Muslim) people move there to buy historical houses? Why is the neighborhood now the most popular setting for nostalgic television shows? I open this discus-sion in chapter 2, where I examine the nostalgic mahalle landscape and the processes that create it, and link it to contemporary social and cul-tural tensions in the neighborhood that resonate back to larger issues of national belonging. I continue to explore this theme in chapter 3, where I introduce contesting place narratives of the Kuzguncuk market garden to examine the mechanics of how one particular former minority property became the subject of various efforts to appropriate it or preserve it. I also bring in the voice of one of the descendants of the family that used to own the property to reveal one of the perspectives obscured by the dominant cultural memory narrative. I continue by focusing on the nature of memories, both told and untold, in chapter 4, where I introduce collective and individual memories (told by Muslims, Greeks, and Jews) of daily life and intercommunity harmony on the main street of Kuzguncuk. Icadiye Street is the setting for nostalgic memories of people of different religions sharing religious celebrations, funerals, foods, and exchanges of daily life. Narratives of past neighborhood life are characterized by silence, tension, and contradiction, however, because they generally ignore or deny the violence of the anti-Greek riots that shook this street in 1955.

Rather than providing objective evidence of a specific history in Kuzguncuk, place narratives reveal the dimensions of the larger cultural political arena in Turkey, which conditions what is remembered and concealed, as "memory is active and it is situated in the present."[88] How interethnic relationships, and events that targeted Christian and Jewish minorities, are remembered and forgotten involve specific cultural politics that reproduce notions of belonging or exclusion in the nation, a process that occurs at the local scale. Belonging as a Turk is partly negotiated through what one should or should not say about the state's role in minority oppression and emigration. Belonging as a Kuzguncuklu involves being careful about what is or is not remembered about how these events took place in Kuzguncuk and the roles and experiences of individual neighbors. Belonging, in Turkey, as a non-Muslim minority involves denying to others any knowledge or experience of these and similar events, while simultaneously living in families and communities that can never forget they happened. Because memories "do not allow the distinction between private and public," they are produced at the intersection between individuality and community: "cultural memory is collective, yet, by definition, subjective."[89] One of the reasons, perhaps, why intercommunity life is remembered with such nostalgia and fondness is that memories of life before traumatic events are conditioned by the knowledge of what came afterward: memories of the period before the 1955 riots, for example, involve remembering a more innocent time for the narrator.[90] Emphases and silences in the narratives reveal how the nostalgic collective memory reproduces the idea of the mahalle as the space of collective belonging and home, and obscures nationalism and the unequal claims to place it supports with stories of extraordinary multiethnic tolerance.[91]

Methods

Memories of Kuzguncuk tell of moments, spaces, and feelings of belonging or exclusion, thus expressing, as place narratives, identities as Kuzguncuklu, Jewish, Karadenizli (from the Black Sea region), and so on. What emerges is that the landscape's process—of representing and obscuring—is not twofold; rather, how various people read Kuzguncuk's landscape is sometimes consistent with the dominant memory and sometimes, even for the same person, dissonant. Furthermore, the processes that are obscured are extremely complex, reflecting both Kuzguncuk's intricate social geography and the many ways in which people construct their identities in relation to the neighborhood as a place. This varied complexity reveals not only that national identity is always constituted in relation to place but that the nation itself is local and complicated.

To understand the contemporary dynamics that condition remembering and forgetting, I became involved in neighborhood life in Kuzguncuk. I interviewed people and acted as a neighbor to understand the relationship between how Kuzguncuk is represented and how its historical landscape is being created, by studying what people say about why they moved there and what they think is special about the neighborhood's social character and environment. I viewed the mahalle as a social space, governed by propriety (notions of what should or should not be said and done) and produced through daily sociospatial interactions that reflect conceptual boundaries defining who is a neighbor, boundaries that also circumscribe the terms of belonging in the imagined space of the nation.[92] As I lived in Kuzguncuk, the paradoxes I observed in what was emphasized or concealed in place narratives and in daily sociospatial relations revealed a number of tensions, particularly surrounding issues of contemporary and historical social difference.

I interviewed many predominantly secular Muslim Turks.[93] They included descendants of early Black Sea migrants and recent migrants from this same region, people who came from parts of central Anatolia, and well-educated artists or professionals who moved from other cities or other parts of Istanbul to live in Kuzguncuk. I spoke with remaining non-Muslim minorities who still live in Kuzguncuk and other Greeks, Jews, and Armenians who live in other parts of Istanbul, many of whom return on weekends for religious services. During a trip to Tel Aviv, I conversed with Kuzguncuklu people who emigrated to Israel. While living in Kuzguncuk, I participated regularly with three groups of diverse neighbors (one group of predominantly Black Sea migrant long-time residents; one mixed-marriage minority family and their neighbors; and the neighborhood association, including people from the professional elite). These groups were located in different parts of Kuzguncuk, and I visited the same places and people regularly, once or twice per week. My visits lasted anywhere between two hours to as long as twelve hours and included visits with the same people each time, as well as with new people I met only once or twice throughout the research period.

Over the years in Istanbul, I had hundreds of conversations with architects; urban planners; historians; urban issues activists; people affiliated with the larger Jewish, Greek, and Armenian communities of Istanbul; academics; and others involved or interested in Istanbul's social history and minority cultures. Two significant groups, however, that I did not interact with substantially were Kurdish migrants and activists working on Kurdish issues, and political Islamists or nonpolitically active but overtly religiously conservative people.[94] My methodologies reflect the chance encounters I experienced in Kuzguncuk as I began my research; my own identity as a foreign woman and the spaces and people that were open to me; and what emerged, in my opinion, as significant issues for the neighborhood's current cultural geography and its cultural memory.

Importantly, many of my interviewees, and almost all of the people I neighbored with regularly, were women. This was not an intentional aspect of my research design but reflects, rather, the ways in which my own identity conditioned my research.[95] Being a woman made possible particular types of interactions (such as being invited by other women for tea) and impossible other types of interactions (hanging around men's coffeehouses, for example). One impact of my positionality is that my method revealed the important ways in which women's neighboring practices help sustain a sense of community belonging and propriety in the mahalle. In chapter 5, I draw on an important contribution of feminist geography, which has been to foreground the ways in which gender is spatially contextual. The concept of paradoxical space—the possibility of inhabiting several spaces at once (public and private space, or center and margin)—is a way of thinking spatially about how an individual may inhabit multiple and mixed-identity categories.[96] By visiting with women inside their homes, I developed trust, ensured confidentiality, and participated in the relationships with the women I met on their own terms. This strategy helped us develop friendships and destabilized my authority as an "objective" researcher, and also produced a great deal of information regarding the ways in which ethnic-religious identity, class, and gender overlap in local places, in ways informed by national imaginaries. The focus on gender was one of the strategies (like the emphasis on religious-ethnic identity in chapter 6) for understanding the cultural politics of national belonging and exclusion as they are negotiated in everyday life. Moments of defining or perceiving belonging and exclusion are articulated and experienced in different moments, in different spaces, and sometimes simultaneously; one can be both a Turk and a minority, or a neighbor and an outsider, for example. I examine the gendered social relationships that produce the mahalle as the space of belonging to understand it as a semiprivate space likened both to the extended family and to the nation.

One of the people I came to know well in Kuzguncuk is a Jewish woman whose family has been in Kuzguncuk for several generations. Although she has little extra money, she lives comfortably and is very generous with her hospitality. She visits every day with her neighbors, and with one Muslim woman in particular, with whom she shares daily companionship and who helps her with errands such as buying bread or paying bills at the post office. One day, as we sat together inside her house, she began to tell me her story of what happened to Jews in Kuzguncuk during the time of the 1942–43 Wealth Tax. Her neighbor knocked on the door, and before she answered it, my friend put her finger to her lips, silencing her narrative, whispering that I could never trust a Turk. She had revealed her Jewish identity—her Jewish memory of Kuzguncuk—to me but concealed aspects of it from her neighbor, a woman she knows far better than she does me and with whom she shares daily life.

In another example, I interviewed a Greek woman who used to live in Kuzguncuk. She showed me pictures of the neighborhood and lamented how it had changed since the arrival of the Muslim migrants from the

Black Sea region. They live in the houses that used to belong to Greeks, she said, and they ruined Kuzguncuk's special culture. Identifying herself as a witness to the loss of the city's cosmopolitanism articulated her identity as truly of Kuzguncuk and also as Rum (Istanbul's native Greek Orthodox, Greek-speaking community). However, months later, she came to Kuzguncuk to visit a friend, and as we sat with neighbors, Muslims from the Black Sea region, they reminisced together about people and stories they remembered about Kuzguncuk. By sharing memories aloud in that space they articulated their shared identities as fellow Kuzguncuklus.

In a third example, a middle-aged Turkish woman described to me, as we shared a meal, the multicultural history that makes Kuzguncuk a special place. Her family arrived in Kuzguncuk when she was a child, and she remembers having minority neighbors in the past. She also told me that she would never eat Jewish food. I wondered how the person across the table, another guest at lunch, a woman who is secular and Muslim but married to a Christian, felt. From a distance, or from a focus on state ideology or on ultranationalist events, it appears that state-authored nationalism in Turkey is rigid and unchallenged; it is only through a focus on the geography of the city as it is lived, remembered, and imagined that the shifting and complex ways in which ordinary residents sustain, reinterpret, and unmake nationalist boundaries become visible.

In the last chapter of the book, I examine how Kuzguncuklu Jews imagine their own individual, cultural, religious, and community identities and histories through their relationship to Kuzguncuk.[97] This strategy illustrates the ways in which ethnic-religious identity is imagined geographically, through place narratives and in spatial practices that retain links to Kuzguncuk from other parts of the city and of the world. I also relate Kuzguncuklu narratives told in Israel that provide information about midcentury Turkification policies. These interviews demonstrate that the state's policies worked through material, local places to affect real people and families and thus transform the social spaces and landscapes of the city. These narratives are extremely important because they are never told in Istanbul and thus illuminate the pervasive silence surrounding these events. A second and equally important but seemingly contradictory theme emerges here as well: the theme of continued attachment to Kuzguncuk as a place and of memories of neighbors who shared an identity bound to place and were never divided by religion.

While some academics claim that the nation has declined in relevance amid an emerging deterritorialization and transnationalization of identity in globalization, this study reveals that in Turkey the nation continues to be a relevant and structuring concept for identity, even while the notion of who is a Turk continues to be debated.[98] However, while this process takes place within what is indeed an increasingly interconnected global context, identities continue to be produced through the relationship to local places because that is where national imaginaries are endowed with (and undone of) their power, through the social-spatial relationships of everyday life. What emerges is that identities as Turk or Armenian, Jew or Greek, do not always work oppositionally, as binary nations and Others, but are rather produced in inconsistent and unpredictable ways. Sometimes, a common belonging to a local place transcends national imaginary categories, as people intermarry, share memories of the past, and imagine a collective identity as neighbors, as Kuzguncuklu. Kuzguncuklus use the word *kozmopolit*, together with words such as "mosaic," "little Paris," and "dream," to describe the past, where "everyone was like siblings" and they "knew no difference between religions" and "there was a very special neighborliness."[99] This cultural memory of cosmopolitanism signifies both the idealistic as well as the normative aspects of that ideal.

Cosmopolitanism, Nationalism, and Local Geographies

Cosmopolitanism, as a concept, has its roots in Immanuel Kant's political project for a universal law of humanity involving an ethic of responsibility toward others.[100] It came to mean a sense of world citizenship, in opposition to the rigidly defined, violently upheld, and exclusionary sense of belonging that was nationalism.[101] This book responds to the relationship between cosmopolitanism and nationalism in a few ways.

The first way is to view nationalism and cosmopolitanism as distinct; this aspect of the project speaks to the politics of cosmopolitanism as an ideal. On one level, cosmopolitanism has been critiqued for the ways in which it travels with imperialism to enforce a worldview that upholds Western political and economic dominance in a world characterized by globalizing capitalism. One dimension of the memory of cosmopolitanism written and reinforced by Turkish economic and cultural elites conforms closely to this view. These elites reproduce landscapes that represent a cosmopolitan ideal but actually work to reinscribe class differences. So-called cosmopolitan spaces represent European identity and are economically and culturally exclusive, as they leave out many others, be they religious, rural, Kurdish, or otherwise not secular, upper class, and Turkish. This version of cosmopolitanism that produces seemingly historical landscapes, such as in Kuzguncuk, conforms to larger processes transforming other spaces in the region, including in Cairo, Alexandria, Damascus, and Fez.[102] In these cases, elites resurrect particular imaginations of heritage to reinforce cultural, political, and economic dominance, through processes that depend on the increasing polarization of the global economy and ground global economic and political disparity in exclusive, local urban environments around the world. In Istanbul, this kind of cosmopolitanism is definitely positioned in relation to nationalism, in that it sustains traditional upper-class Kemalist notions of Turkish identity as secular, modern, and located in the West.

Something more complex is going on as well, however. Some of the same upper-class elites, together with many more who are antielitist or leftist, or who occupy oppositional countercultural political spaces, are resurrecting memories of cosmopolitanism as a strategy to put forward a progressive agenda for Turkish politics. These efforts are also grounded in unearthing and representing Istanbul's diverse histories, but they are very explicitly political. This cosmopolitanism is activist, vernacular, bottom-up, and explicitly positioned against nationalism. It is also produced through international geographic processes in which agendas promoted by the European Union, for example, touch ground in Istanbul, where they become inspiration and justification for arguing for minority human rights, civil liberties, the freedom of expression, and an openness to examine difficult moments of Turkey's national past for the purpose of creating a more peaceful and inclusive society. This movement would include those Turks who in 2008 initiated and signed a petition to apologize for the Armenian Genocide (a movement that remains very visible but relatively small: more than thirty thousand people had signed the petition by July 2009).[103] Diane Singerman and Paul Amar "[use] the term cosmopolitan . . . to draw attention to the world-scale cultural claims and nostalgia of elite projects, but also to shift debates toward questions of agency (of elites as well as subalterns), and to processes of vernacular world-making among Cairenes that may not constitute resistance at all, but which do reconstitute worlds that cross or challenge class, urban, and national borders."[104]

The third point regarding the relationship between nationalism and cosmopolitanism views nationalism as a historical development that redrew ethnic and religious boundaries in ways that transformed the cultural and economic cosmopolitanism of cities in former empires, as in the case of Istanbul.[105] Evridiki Sifneos, for example, argues that commercial diasporas in Odessa and Alexandria that were linked with the internationalization of trade in the early industrial period were cosmopolitan because they possessed economic and cultural traits that gave them a common worldview and a set of publicly oriented practices inspired by Europe. Nationalism and the emergence of new nation-states not only restructured the roles of old imperial port cities and altered the trade routes that facilitated internationally oriented diasporic communities but also recast ethnic and religious identities in those cities, thus destroying their cosmopolitan nature.[106] In Sarajevo, for example, by 1994 the "cosmopolitan character of the city and all that it stood for were finally destroyed."[107] Memories of cosmopolitanism in Kuzguncuk refer to what was an actually existing, particular, local environment, for Istanbul possessed a historical cosmopolitan culture. This study thus differs from mainstream contemporary research that sees cosmopolitanism as a product of contemporary globalization and transnationalism and that raises questions about the relationships between territoriality, citizenship, and identity in new urban contexts.[108]

The contribution of this research on memories of a historical cosmopolitanism is that cosmopolitanism and nationalism emerge as not oppositional but rather interrelated ideals as they were lived out in urban neighborhood space.[109] As imaginaries that inspired local practices, cosmopolitanism and nationalism worked together for many decades through Istanbul's transformation from an imperial to a nationally Turkish city. Ideas one may recognize as nationalist or cosmopolitan flowed through spatial situations to inform individual thoughts and actions in sometimes unpredictable ways, as people formed social relations based on what one, from the current Turkish national context, might wrongly assume would have been naturally opposed identities. For example, take the case of this Kuzguncuklu man's stories of the 1930s and 1940s (he appears in chapter 6): he was a Jew, a member of a religiously circumscribed community; as a Zionist, he participated in a political movement that operated within an oppressive ethnic Turkish nationalist context and that was devoted to creating a Jewish nation-state. He was also a Kuzguncuklu and felt a deep sense of attachment to others in his neighborhood, where others' identities as Muslim or Christian were mere aspects of their fellow identities as Kuzguncuklu, not terms for exclusion. The sense of cosmopolitanism that emerges from the study of memories of past social life in Kuzguncuk is an example of "actually existing cosmopolitanism," that is, a cosmopolitanism that is lived and experienced in particular and multiple ways and that is contingent on specific geographic context.[110]

Memories of Kuzguncuk of the several decades after the foundation of modern Turkey reveal, indeed, a transformation of Istanbul from what may be termed cosmopolitan to a national city. Exploring the ways in which the past continues to be present in contemporary Turkey and how people negotiate cosmopolitan identities in everyday life opens ways of thinking about the processes through which nationalism and cosmopolitanism are embedded within one another and how actual places and specific geographies contribute and are transformed by these processes.[111] In this sense, this project brings a specific geographic knowledge of "the banality of mundane everyday local experiences" to understanding cosmopolitanism.[112]

Cosmopolitan people of Ottoman Empire cities, including Alexandria, Beirut, and Istanbul at the turn of the twentieth century, were expatriate Europeans and local Christian, Jewish, and Muslim elites. The lives and relationships of these cosmopolitans, and the urban landscapes they created, were conditioned by their relationships with imperial Europe. They thus reflected the local connection to the increasingly core-dominated world economy and political system. Nostalgic memories of cosmopolitanism tend to occlude colonial and imperial contexts and the social exclusionary practices of cosmopolitans, as is at play in some of the dimensions of how secular Turkish elites employ it to create exclusionary spaces in Istanbul.[113] However, memories of cosmopolitanism also refer to and appeal to ideals of peaceful coexistence; reflect notions of common, place-based belonging that go beyond ethnic or religious categories; and are employed to support a radical leftist politics within a contemporary nationalist context. Examining these different roles can illuminate some of the subtleties of the larger-scale processes of nationalism, globalization, and imperialism, exposing the ways in which they gain meaning and traction on the ground.

Streets of Memory thus takes an approach of "embracing ambivalence."[114] In this sense it responds to the work of Sheldon Pollock, Homi Bhabha, Carol Breckenridge, and Dipesh Chakrabarty, who argue that cosmopolitanism is not a fixed idea but rather a still undefined project and who suggest that "specifying cosmopolitanism positively and definitely is an uncosmopolitan thing to do."[115] In this way, understanding memories of cosmopolitanism in Kuzguncuk involves taking the following ambivalent stances: approaching them as a vision of relationships that is ethically opposed to rigid nationalism and that is remembered in a contemporary nationalist context; examining the interrelation between processes and imaginations that literally, and necessarily, *take place* in a specific locality, and the ways in which these processes are conditioned by power dynamics and flows of ideas occurring at many geographic scales; and critiquing the ways in which nostalgic memories of cosmopolitanism are employed to reify existing imperialist, national, ethnic, class-based, or gendered spaces of exclusion, while considering that memories of cosmopolitanism, articulated or employed in other spaces, may potentially offer possibilities for transgressing exclusionary imaginaries and practices.[116] Cultural memories of cosmopolitanism at the turn of the millennium in Istanbul, then, are produced together with the ongoing, sometimes violent, debates regarding the nature of Turkish national identity and the place of the past in contemporary urban life, processes that continue to transform the landscapes of the city.

I The Turkish Nation in the Urban Landscape
Cultural Geographies of a Nationalizing City

At the beginning of his book about Kuzguncuk's history and culture, resident and writer Nedret Ebcim explains why he decided to write about his mahalle: "Kuzguncuk, as a place where cultures blended with each other, were transferred to each other, where different religions and races lived as siblings in the same place for several centuries, must be explained. In a world where friendships, exchanges of help, and neighborliness are decreasing, where people feel increasingly alone even when in a crowd, Kuzguncuk resists losing these values. Openly showing its differentiation. Kuzguncuk is a neighborhood with identity."[1] Kuzguncuk, for Ebcim, is a place that retains a memory of the cosmopolitan past, even as this past has slipped away in the rest of Istanbul.

Cultural memories of cosmopolitanism are grounded in Istanbul's cultural geography. The landscapes and places of the city are the product of daily cultural, economic, and political exchange among Muslims, Christians, and Jews; and Ottomans and Europeans. This chapter provides a brief sketch of the transformation of Istanbul from a cosmopolitan urban center of empire into a Turkish city and situates Kuzguncuk within this milieu. Its specific aims are twofold: first, it grounds cosmopolitan cultural memory in a specific historical, urban context and provides readers unfamiliar with Turkey with enough information to understand my later analyses of contemporary cultural memory through landscape and place. I emphasize nationalist policies such as the Citizen, Speak Turkish campaign, the 1942–43 Wealth Tax, the 6–7 September 1955 riots, and the 1964 deportation of Greek citizens because these events are not mentioned in mainstream history books in Turkey.[2] My interviews, which suggest that these events had dire consequences in Kuzguncuk, provide important perspectives that are generally obscured by nostalgic representations of Kuzguncuk's past.

A second purpose of this chapter is to demonstrate how the Turkish state produces its imaginary of the Turkish nation through a transformation of inhabited urban space.[3] I examine the mahalle as the space through which cosmopolitan urban life was produced and experienced by urban residents as they migrated through mahalles and created economic and residential social spaces. The mahalle is also important as a spatial reflection of Ottoman administrative policies regarding non-Muslim, or *millet*, communities.[4] As millets became minorities, and their social practices and spaces became the focus of Turkification, mahalles too were fundamentally transformed to become, much later, the focus of contemporary urban nostalgia. After a brief discussion of mahalles and Ottoman administration, I describe the cosmopolitan social geography of Istanbul and (to the extent it is possible to do so while relying primarily on secondary and semipopular sources) of Kuzguncuk. I then discuss Turkification and its impact on the city. While the historical framework in this chapter focuses on the roles of state administration and on inter- and intracity migration patterns to understand the mahalle as a cosmopolitan social space, the rest of this book examines how residents inhabit this nationalizing city and make sense of the state's national imaginary after the impact of Turkification.

The Mahalle, Space of Cosmopolitanism

The Turkish word for neighborhood is mahalle, which, in its basic meaning, is the residential space of the city. Mahalle also refers to a space of social memory in Turkish popular culture defined by familiarity, belonging, and tolerance in a local, urban place.[5] The social memory relies, in part, on the long and varied social history of the mahalle as the space of urban daily life, not only in Istanbul but in other cities of the former Ottoman Empire (the word is derived from the Arabic *mahalla*). Historically, the mahalle reflected the administrative structure of the Ottoman millet system in the city.[6] Millets were religiously defined groups (although the term also came to mean "nation"), and people lived under the authority and within the community of the millets within which they were born. The millet system was rooted in a long history of administrative and religious differentiation between Muslim and non-Muslim subjects of the empire. The three non-Muslim millets had a semiautonomous status within the empire because they were governed by the leaders of their own religious communities: the Greek Orthodox millet was governed by the Greek Patriarchate; the Jewish millet by the Hahambaşı, or Chief Rabbinate; and the Armenian Gregorian millet by the Armenian Patriarchate. The local religious leader of each millet would govern and represent his religious community in a particular neighborhood. And so the mahalle, as a social space, located the ethnic and religious identity of a particular community.

Millets were not homogenous communities, however, which makes thinking about the geography of the city's cosmopolitanism quite complex. Istanbul residents possessed fluency in a variety of languages and were conversant with a plurality of cultures. Roel Meijer describes historical cosmopolitanism in the cities of the former Ottoman Empire in this way: "During the Ottoman period, the Middle East was an open undefined territory in which groups of different religious and ethnic backgrounds intermingled and exchanged ideas and lifestyles. Cosmopolitanist cities—Alexandria, Istanbul and Beirut—formed freehavens for cultural exchange. *No definite and rigid boundaries had been drawn* and the state did not yet exert its power of standardization or impose its norms on its citizens."[7] Thinking about this historical cosmopolitanism in terms of the intermingling of groups, however, belies the fact that groups were not bounded, and an individual may have been part of, or felt affinity with, many social groups. Millets were not necessarily ethnically or linguistically homogenous, as people within the same millet came from different places and spoke different languages. Jews who migrated from Spain, for example, spoke Ladino (Judeo-Spanish), while Jews from Europe spoke

Yiddish and Jews from Arabic-speaking areas spoke Arabic. Ethnic and religious identity sometimes also crossed group boundaries, as in the case of Greek Orthodox communities that spoke Turkish, or Greek Jews who spoke Ladino.[8]

Mahalles were not always ethnically and religiously monochromatic or static, either, as the long history of one particular mahalle might witness changes in millet communities living there over time.[9] Changes in the ethnic and religious populations of mahalles were a result of migration in between Istanbul mahalles and from outside the city. Migration flows were shaped by connections through millet communities, as, for example, Jews migrated to Kuzguncuk from other neighborhoods because they knew there were other Jews there or because of marriages facilitated through Jewish connections outside the neighborhood. Migration was also facilitated by shared connections with places of origin outside the city, through important social and economic links that were organized regionally and that transcended millets.[10] Both Greeks and Armenians from Sinesos, a village outside Kayseri, for example, migrated to Kuzguncuk.[11]

To complicate the sociospatial picture of mahalles even further, the boundaries of mahalles themselves were unmapped, flexible, and subject to interpretation.[12] The city's cosmopolitan geography was thus much more than a mere patchwork of different ethnic mahalles that together formed a multicultural urban fabric. Rather, Istanbul's culture was characterized by a blurring of ethnic-religious boundaries and the sharing of words and customs across millet communities. Urban cosmopolitanism meant that elite members of millet communities formed relationships and mixed frequently outside their religious communities, sometimes within the multiethnic Ottoman bourgeoisie and also in secular, mixed spaces that transcended class lines. Modern identities in cosmopolitan Istanbul were produced through interactions with others in new kinds of public spaces such as the coffeehouse, municipal associations, and Masonic lodges, "where the ideal was the ability to juggle local and cosmopolitan identities successfully."[13] Jacob Barnai describes the social life of Sephardi Jews in the Ottoman Empire in a similar way:

> Although the social and religious life of each religious community
> was self-contained, there was still some degree of contact and mutual
> influence between the various groups. Jewish, Christian, and Muslim

men constantly met at the workplace and in the markets; they spent hours together, working and drinking coffee in coffeehouses. The women, however, almost always remained at home, and the few who ran stalls in the market had little contact with the surrounding society. The men developed personal and cultural ties thanks to mixed guilds, businesses requiring close cooperation, and the interaction between buyers and sellers. Many Jews spoke Turkish, Greek, or Arabic, and words from these languages began to infiltrate Judeo-Spanish, the Sephardi's first language. The surrounding culture also influenced popular music and dance. Thus, despite their closed religious and family life, there was an openness to the day-to-day contact between the various communities.[14]

The mahalle was the space through which complex ethnic-religious, linguistic, and urban identities were blended and articulated. The mahalle was also important as a constitutive element of identity in that cosmo-politan context, as personal identity depended not only on membership in the millet community but also on locality.[15] Legal documents, for ex-ample, identified individuals by mahalle in Istanbul before the creation of surnames.[16] Local cultural practices bound residents together through ties of mutual responsibility, in the collection of taxes and in the enforcement of social norms.[17] Practices of neighboring (*komşuluk*) and expressions of knowing (*tanımak*) created networks of support between neighbors and in resident-owned shops and businesses and defined the mahalle, making it the space of familiarity and belonging. The mahalle was thus fundamental to how residents located themselves in a cosmopolitan urban social and cultural milieu, and the social spatiality of the mahalle was defined by cultural practice rather than a bounded physical geography or rigid place in the urban administrative system.[18] Place identity also contributed to the historical social development of the mahalle.

Social Geography

Historical settlements in Istanbul were clustered on the old peninsula and in Kadıköy and Üsküdar, while outlying provincial settlements, such as Kuzguncuk, existed on the Asian side and on the Bosphorus. Kuzguncuk, a small fishing and artisan village built along a creek that flowed along the bottom of a valley into the sea, did not become a mahalle of the larger city of Istanbul until the turn of the twentieth century. However, proximity to the imperial city influenced the development of its social geography. Located just north of Üsküdar, it was connected to that transportation node by a coastal road. Kuzguncuk's market garden products and other materials produced by its tradespeople, craftspeople, and artisans were sent to this port for transport to Istanbul. Migration to Kuzguncuk from Anatolia and other parts of Istanbul was also influenced by policies and practices located in the urban core. Life in Kuzguncuk was thus interconnected with administrative and economic processes occurring in old Istanbul from an early period.

The cultural geography of the mahalle is richly layered with traces left by the movement throughout its long history of Greeks, Jews, Armenians, and Muslims, to and from the mahalle and to other areas of Istanbul and places outside the city.[19] Kuzguncuk's name traces back to several possible origins, possibly from an old Byzantine name, Chrysokeramos, reflecting the description of a church with gilded tiles built by Justinian II (669–711).[20] It may also trace back to the Slavic or Albanian Kotsinitsa.[21] The name also possibly reflects a tie to the legend of Kuzgun Baba, who is buried there and who is said to have been a dervish who lived there during the time Sultan Mehmet conquered Istanbul in the fifteenth century.[22] In its early history, Kuzguncuk was possibly a Byzantine settlement connected to a monastery called the Hermolaos Monastery.[23] In 1492, when Jews were expelled from Spain, many emigrated to the Ottoman Empire and to Kuzguncuk.[24] Graves in the Jewish cemetery there date back to its early Sephardic migrants of the sixteenth century. Literature on Bosphorus history refers to this cemetery as the holiest and most preferred burial place for Jews of old Istanbul, and legend states that it was the last stopover on European Jewish pilgrimages to Jerusalem.[25] It is presumed that the oldest graves in the cemetery belonged to Kuzguncuk's own Jewish community.

According to P. Ğ. Inciciyan's travel narratives (1758–1833), Kuzguncuk was a mixed settlement of Greeks, Jews, and Armenians:

> The Greeks had a church known as Haghia Pantaleimon and an *ayazma* [holy spring], as well as the seat of the Metropolitan of Halketon (Kadıköy). Most of the houses belonging to wealthy Jews

were situated on the shore, but there were also Jews and Armenians living further inland. There was a Jewish cemetery on the slopes behind. As the Jews reckoned Kuzguncuk as being adjacent to the territory of Jerusalem they regarded it with particular favour and preferred to bury their dead in the cemetery there. The cemetery therefore covers a very large area. Kuzguncuk was also the seat of the deputy Chief Rabbi, the leader of the whole Jewish community.[26]

Inciciyan also states that its population was so small that "a large part of Kuzguncuk is a cemetery, and those buried there number more than the live inhabitants."[27] It population grew significantly in the nineteenth century, however.

Kuzguncuk's Virane Synagogue is located in the upper part of the neighborhood on the edges of Kuzguncuk's historical settlement core. One source dates the construction of this synagogue to 1664.[28] This synagogue served the farming mahalle of Jews who lived in this area, known later by popular convention as the upper neighborhood, or *yukarı* mahalle. Its population grew through the 1800s, as indicated by a request submitted in 1870 to expand the synagogue by one floor to accommodate the growing population.[29] Kuzguncuk's Jews also attended the larger Beth Yaakov Synagogue located on the main street close to the coastal road.[30]

Fires were a significant element in the nineteenth-century development of Istanbul, as they caused the destruction of massive areas of wooden building stock and the migration of large numbers of people from destroyed areas. In 1865 a fire swept Kuzguncuk and burned five hundred shops along the main street. When the market area was restored, the Şirket Hayriye company built a boat station in Kuzguncuk for new steamboat service to Istanbul.[31] Steamboats connected Istanbul to Anatolia, calling in at provincial cities such as Trabzon along the Black Sea coast, a development that increased seasonal and permanent migration to the city. People who rode these vessels to Istanbul originated not only from the Black Sea region but also from areas in the southeast of Turkey. Many settled in the Bosphorus villages like Kuzguncuk, as they weren't all able to find work in the city.[32]

Migration from Anatolian provinces to Istanbul in the nineteenth century occurred for several reasons. First, voluntary economic migration increased in the mid-1800s. The pull factors were opportunities created by the central bureaucracy and the boosts of foreign investment in Istanbul.[33] Push factors included economic pressures on peasants in the east as a result of new tax collections and threats to subsistence farming, as well as political pressures, violence, and population displacements from the aftermath of the Ottoman-Russian war of 1877–78 and later pogroms against Armenians.[34] Another factor was the Ottoman policy of *sürgün*, the forced exile of some groups (including Christians and Jews) from provinces to Istanbul, a policy that aimed to boost population and improve the economy in the capital and also to keep certain populations, including Armenians, under the closer watch of the state.[35] Between the 1840s and 1880s Istanbul's population increased from four hundred thousand to eight hundred thousand.[36] Among them were Christian craftspeople, artisans, and construction workers from the east, some of whom were recruited to work on construction sites of large imperial projects such as mosques.[37] In 1885, in the district of Üsküdar (nearby and probably including Kuzguncuk), Muslims were in the majority, but Armenians were a very significant minority, numbering approximately half as many. The Greek, and then Jewish, population in that district overall was much smaller, although in Kuzguncuk, Muslims were by far the minority.[38] So, along with Kuzguncuk's Jewish population, the neighborhood's Greek and Armenian populations also grew significantly during the nineteenth century.

Migrants to Istanbul from Anatolian provinces frequently built new religious buildings, re-creating with new congregations the localities they left behind. Migrants in Kuzguncuk, too, built new congregations affiliated by common origins, languages, and confessional ties. It was not unusual for a single mahalle to contain more than one congregation of the same millet but of different origin.[39] The increase in religious buildings in Kuzguncuk during the nineteenth century reflects this type of migration pattern.

Ohannes Amira Serverian completed Kuzguncuk's Armenian church, St. Gregory the Illuminator (Surp Krikor Lusavoriç), in 1835. The church was rebuilt in 1861 and repaired in 1967.[40] The architect hailed from the Anatolian city of Kayseri, and the church was built for a group of Armenian migrants who in turn were building the Beylerbeyi Palace. According to local legend, the church in Bağlarbaşı was so far away from Beylerbeyi that the head worker was late to work every morning because of his daily visit to church. The pasha gave the architect money and his permission to build a church closer to the palace, so it was built in Kuzguncuk. This community grew, and in 1868 they requested an addition of a priest's room to their church.[41]

The two Greek Orthodox churches in Kuzguncuk were built by people from Kayseri, as well. The smaller church, Holy Trinity Church, was located on the main street close to the coastal road and was built in 1821 with financial support from a sailor and a fisherman originally from Sinesos, a village near Kayseri. This church was rebuilt from its foundations in 1871 and restored in 1951.[42] Ayios Panteleymon, the second Greek Orthodox church, farther up the main street and much larger in scale, was built in 1836 on the foundation of a much older Byzantine-era church called Ayios Yeoryios Church.[43] This building was restored in 1911 by workers from Sinesos and Konya.[44]

As the steamboat integrated Kuzguncuk into Istanbul's urban fabric, Istanbul's urban elite built residences there. The hills above Kuzguncuk and the shores of the Bosphorus provided views for the summer estates and *yalis* (waterfront mansions) of pashas and wealthy Ottomans. Kuzguncuk's earliest Muslim population is from this elite community.[45] The Uryanizade family, descendants of Cemil Molla Pasha, constructed a small *mescit* for this Muslim minority on the seaside.

By the turn of the twentieth century, as a result of migration patterns conditioned by Ottoman administrative policies, economic and administrative developments in Istanbul, membership in millet communities, and shared ties to places of origin, Kuzguncuk, like other mahalles of the city, had become a multiethnic space remembered today as cosmopolitan. In Kuzguncuk in 1914, there were 1,600 Armenians, 400 Jews, 70 Muslims, 250 Greeks, and 4 foreigners.[46] The relatively large Armenian population identified in this assessment declined shortly afterward as Armenians in Kuzguncuk began to leave, many of them to resettle in the hills above the neighborhood in nearby Bağlarbaşı. They were also perhaps affected even before the 1914 census, by the expulsion in 1896 of Armenian workers from Istanbul, as Kuzguncuk was home to many carpenters, builders, and artisans.[47] One source that lists all Armenian associations in Istanbul in 1922 and that identifies many located in nearby Scutari (Üsküdar) does not mention any Armenian associations located in Kuzguncuk at that time.[48]

The early twentieth-century character of Kuzguncuk became cosmopolitan as stronger ties to the city impacted its local culture. The Alliance Israelite Universelle, a French-Jewish association, founded French-language boys' and girls' schools in Kuzguncuk. There was also an Armenian school on Yenigün Street and a Greek school on Behlul Street. A Jewish charity, La Unyon, provided aid to Kuzguncuk's poor. Greeks, Jews, and Armenians worked locally as tradespeople and craftspeople and also operated businesses along the main street, including pastry, pudding, and sweet shops; pharmacies and doctors' offices; family-run corner stores; and a shoe store. Others commuted to the old city for work via steam ferry.

The period between the turn of the century and the 1940s is one for which not a great deal of written information survives to describe life in Kuzguncuk. Significantly, this is also the period during which Turkification and urbanization began to transform the neighborhood.[49] A book written in 1931 describes non-Muslim businesses in the neighborhood, including restaurants owned by Todoraki and Kiriyako, a butchery owned by Madam Raşel, and a *köfte* (meatball restaurant) owned by Madam Marika.[50] It is believed that the first day care was located in Kuzguncuk because of the prevalence of women who worked outside the home.[51] By the 1940s migrants from villages near the Black Sea cities of Inebolu and Rize began to arrive in Kuzguncuk in significant numbers, building perhaps on an earlier migration pattern established by the connections between Kuzguncuk and Black Sea ports via the steamboat ferry system. They constructed a mosque next to the Armenian church in 1952.[52] They built new houses and grew food in gardens by their homes and began to work for the minority-owned shops on Kuzguncuk's main street. Women also worked, sewing, printing scarves in the factory, or cleaning homes. Others maintained their sea-related trades, fishing and working on ferry boats; for example, one of the most prominent of the Black Sea migrant families, the Kaptanoğlu family (whose name means "son of the captain"), came from Rizeli and Çayeli and had long worked in seafaring.[53]

Kuzguncuk residents who remember this period describe a culture in which it was not uncommon for every resident to speak a little Ladino, Greek, Armenian, or French. Kuzguncuk's older residents also remember the special qualities of different religious holidays and sharing them with their neighbors. A mix of social classes shared the spaces of the main street, but Kuzguncuk, in comparison to newer minority-dominated neighborhoods that developed on the European side, such as Galata or Pera, was not a predominantly wealthy neighborhood, and many of its Greeks, Jews, and Armenians were poor. Sayings about Kuzguncuk reflect its identity as a warm and folksy place: "In Beylerbeyi, the mahalle is polite; in Kuz-guncuk, if they're polite, they're famous."[54] A story about a steam ferry captain and why he was always late coming back from the Bosphorus line compares Kuzguncuk with the nearby elite neighborhood of Beylerbeyi: "What can I do, sir, what with all the politeness in Beylerbeyi and all the pushy crowds in Kuzguncuk? I can't take off on time."[55]

Today's Kuzguncuk remains in close proximity to and connected ad-ministratively to the municipality of Üsküdar, which is now an important economic and transportation hub. The historical core of Kuzguncuk is concentrated along its main street, which was once divided by a creek that flowed down the valley into the Bosphorus and that was covered by many small bridges in front of the many *meyhanes* (Greek restaurants that served alcohol and where couples would socialize together in mixed com-pany) that once lined each side of the street. Later, probably in the 1960s, the creek was channeled into a pipe and paved over. Today there are no meyhanes in Kuzguncuk, although there are several predominantly male spaces, such as coffeehouses, where men sit around and talk. There are also small grocery stores; bakeries; a butcher shop; a bank; a few restaurants and cafés; dentist and doctor offices; stores that sell toys, stationery, or appliances; and other businesses run by artists, architects, engineers, and computer technicians.

Because of its valley location and the relative lack of contiguous bound-aries with neighboring developed residential areas, Kuzguncuk has an en-closed geography that has helped preserve its historical fabric. The upper part of Kuzguncuk, where the creek originated on the hill, is where the historical Jewish cemetery forms a border on the north side and the ma-halle of Icadiye meets the edge of Kuzguncuk on the other. Kuzguncuk is also bordered to the north, on the seaside, by the (Muslim) Nakkaş cemetery and a military area that was formed in 1973 to protect the first Bosphorus bridge. To the south is the Fetih Paşa Korusu, a small park with walking paths. Kuzguncuk has a large population of new migrants, how-ever, who built squatter settlements on these areas in the neighborhood's periphery, including along the main street up along the hillside away from the core; on the old Jewish cemetery; next to the Fetih Paşa Korusu, where they also built a mosque in 1985; and around the Nakkaş cemetery. These settlements are visually quite distinctive, as they are prevented from being improved beyond the original structures that were built quickly during the migration process. As a result, many are small in size with short cement walls and gardens and may contain irregular building materials, such as corrugated iron or borrowed tiles, and lack natural gas or other basic infrastructure common in the richly developed landscape in the historical core of the neighborhood. Some of the people who live in the squatter settlements own animals, which provide goods sold to other residents in the neighborhood. For example, I met a man who lives in a squatter settlement on the northern edge of Kuzguncuk who owns a cow. He told me that he once regularly sold milk just a couple of blocks away to people living near the main street of Kuzguncuk.

Today, Jewish and Christian families resident in Kuzguncuk number merely a handful. Most of them are married to Muslims—one member of the synagogue's leadership told me that he believes that there are twelve Jewish families in Kuzguncuk, including single elderly residents, and that all are intermarried. Census information in Istanbul at the mahalle level is collected by the *muhtar*, the neighborhood administrator, and is formally closed to researchers. However, a local neighborhood historian, Nedret Ebcim, was able to obtain census information. He states that in 1933 Kuzguncuk's population was 90 percent non-Muslim. (Another source cites the 1933 census and lists, out of 4,000 people, the majority as Jews, followed by Greeks, Turks, and Armenians.)[56] Ebcim writes that in 2004, out of a total population of 5,940, only 64 were Christian and 30 were Jewish, although far lower numbers for those groups are given in a different source for a 1992 census.[57] The churches and synagogues are maintained largely by people who live in other neighborhoods and return to Kuzguncuk to attend weekend services and maintain the buildings. The Kuzguncuk synagogue's congregation, for example, lives mostly in Gayrettepe, Şişli, Caddebostan, and Bostancı. The Armenian church has a very small congregation that comes from other areas in Istanbul, as there are almost no remaining Kuzguncuklu Armenians. Turkification and urbanization transformed minority mahalles of Istanbul in dramatic and visible ways.

Minorities in the Transition from Empire to Nation-State

The spatial and cultural fluidity of the mahalle was an important geographic dimension of the processes sustaining the larger cosmopolitan culture of Istanbul. Yet, to refer back to Roel Meijer's words, if "no definite and rigid boundaries had been drawn" in the time of empire, the early years of the Turkish Republic and the nationalist era between the 1940s and 1960s witnessed the drawing of firm boundaries of ethnic identities such as Turk and the non-Muslim minority. Former millet communities became minorities (*azınlık*) marking a social distinction that would eventually undermine the historically cosmopolitan character of the mahalle and of daily life in Istanbul.

From its foundation in 1923, the Turkish state worked to align its territorial boundaries as they were drawn on the map with the imagined boundaries of the Turkish nation as Muslim and Turkish. This Turkification, which eroded the religious and ethnic plurality of Turkey and which had such dire consequences for its ethnic and religious minorities, should be seen as the continuation of a process of demographic transformation that began before the turn of the twentieth century and that took place in the context of the territorial and political dissolution of the empire.[58]

During the nineteenth century, internal nationalist movements were fragmenting the Ottoman Empire at its edges, and European powers were penetrating it economically with capitulations that privileged European states and companies. European states were planning to divide Ottoman territories among themselves with the demise of the empire. The Paris Peace Conference proposed to cede Balkan and Arab provinces of the empire to European powers and to place areas occupied by Turkish populations in Anatolia under foreign or minority control. Izmir was captured by Greek armies in 1922. European governments also formed political relations with millet communities that gave local Christians and Jews in the empire ties of privilege.[59] And so, in spite of the fact that many Christians and Jews were loyal to the empire and held important positions as administrative and economic elites, they occupied a precarious position because non-Muslim millets were perceived by Turks to pose an internal threat to the territorial integrity of the empire.

Throughout the processes of economic and political interaction between European states and the empire, Ottoman leaders responded with attempts to both modernize the empire and define a national identity to prevent its total dissolution. The Tanzimat reforms of the nineteenth century were modernizing legal reforms intended to make all Ottoman subjects equal under the law by giving each group state protection and autonomy regardless of religion or language. However, in practice, the millet system reinforced notions of separate group identities.[60] Social difference and prejudices remained, as the system came to institutionalize inequality along religious lines.[61] Another consequence was that it "ended up cementing a bond between ethnicity and religion, thereby reinforcing the very centrifugal ethnonationalist forces it was meant to suppress."[62] As a result, linguistic, ethnic, and religious identity had become linked, and later Turkish state policies regarding language, for example, were employed as a strategy of ethnic and religious Turkification.

As the empire attempted to modernize, its leaders struggled to define national identity, a process that also politicized religious and ethnic identity. The ethnic and cultural-religious terms with which Turkish nationalism later came to be defined thus had roots in the nineteenth century.[63] Sultan Abdülhamid (r. 1876–1909) attempted to define an Ottoman identity in Islamic terms, in an attempt to suppress ethnic nationalisms. The focus on Islam unintentionally fostered the growth of Turkism as an ideology, however, as Turks were disappointed by this policy that placed them, as a group, on the same tier as other Muslims, including Albanians and Kurds.[64] The process of secularization was also contested by the non-Muslim millets, as it shifted the identification of those communities from religious to national terms, and they protested in large crowds in urban centers.[65]

The struggle to define a national identity did not take place merely in the realm of ideas but also on the ground, as the state employed demographic strategies to create a nation-state in conformity with a Turkish, Muslim nationality. In the early decades of the twentieth century, the massacre of Armenians in 1915 and the 1923 population exchange with Greece succeeded in nationalizing Turkish territory by removing most of Turkey's non-Muslim minority populations.[66] At the same time, during the 1920s programs for population resettlement facilitated the immigration of Muslims from the Balkans and from Cyprus, Hatay, Iraq, Iran, and the Soviet Union to Turkey, and Kurds and Armenians were forcibly relocated from eastern to western provinces.[67] The aims and the results of demographic engineering were to tip the population balance in favor of Muslims.[68]

In 1923 the Lausanne Treaty recognized the Turkish state and meant the end of foreign interference in Turkish affairs.[69] This agreement also formalized the boundaries of the new republic, legislated the exchange of populations between Greece and Turkey, defined the legal equality of (non-Muslim) minorities in Turkey, and regulated their citizenship in the new nation-state. In complex ways, this agreement reinforced a sense of ethnic identity for the state by forcing ethnic-religious migration, although it also attempted to legislate the equality of those remaining minorities in Turkey. The issue of religious minorities that thus became embedded in Turkish national identity is grounded, in part, in the ways in which European powers mediated the creation of the new state out of the ruins of a formerly multiethnic empire and with an understanding of a nation-state in religiously and ethnically homogenous terms.

The compulsory population exchange of 1.5 million people involved the forced migration (with no option for return) of Muslims from Greece, and of Greek Orthodox people from Turkey, although many more non-Muslim minorities were displaced or perished during this period. While Turkey's population was 20 percent non-Muslim before 1923, non-Muslims constituted only 2.5 percent of the total population after that date.[70] Istanbul's Greek Orthodox population of approximately one hundred thousand was exempt from the exchange, though state-enforced Turkish nationalism targeted their community later, in the early decades of the republic.[71] The population exchange also provided a foundational legitimacy for Turkish nationalist ideas, as it enforced a notion of national ethnic and religious homogeneity and an intolerance of remaining minorities.[72] An additional consequence was the overall destruction of the cosmopolitan social, economic, and political structures that had developed over centuries in the area, including the loss of a significant portion of the people involved in finance, industry, and commerce.[73] Another important outcome was the loss of a shared relationship to place that could have formed a practical and ethical basis for tolerance and understanding for future relations; since the exchange, Greek and Turkish narratives of this event have historically been constructed through narratives of victimhood and demonization that rely on polarizing notions of national "others," a situation that has had serious repercussions for local minorities in both Turkey and Greece.[74]

In addition to the population exchange, the Lausanne Treaty protected remaining minorities in terms of their rights to education, religious practices, cultural foundations, and language.[75] How minorities were defined, however, reflected the earlier categorization of social groups through the millet system, in that minorities were defined as religious minorities. Ethnic or linguistic Muslim minorities outside Sunni Islam (Alevis, Druze, Kurds) were not given minority status and thus were not explicitly protected.[76] In this way the problem of ethnic and religious minorities in the state of Turkey was an inheritance of the Ottoman imperial past.

Mustafa Kemal Atatürk, the founder of Turkey, has become the symbol of the Turkish nation, and the nationalism he embodied synthesized some of the elements of Turkey's Ottoman heritage with the European-style modernization viewed as necessary for Turkey to survive among European nations. Atatürk supported a reformist agenda and proposed replacing Turkey's traditional civilization with a modern European one.[77] Secularism, Muslim cultural identity, and Turkish ethnicity combined in the idea of the "Turk," that is, the ideal member of the nation who was Muslim and ethnically Turkish. The category of minority effectively worked to produce a boundary, making the ethnically Turkish and Muslim imagined community the space of national belonging.[78] The ideological exclusion of non-Muslim minorities was enforced, in practice, by the state's repression of any activities that would promote or protect non-Turkish or non-Muslim languages and cultures.[79]

Istanbul, the former capital of the empire, remained a cultural remnant of the imperial Ottoman past in modern Turkey and came to have special symbolic, economic, and demographic significance as a place with a relatively visible population of non-Muslim minorities. Although some early policies enacted in Istanbul targeted the economy and culture of minorities, it wasn't until midcentury that antiminority policies were employed to Turkify the city.

Turkifying Istanbul

In Istanbul, at the turn of the twentieth century, minorities and foreigners constituted 56 percent of the population of the city.[80] Between 1885 and 1914 the demography of the city changed in the general direction of an increasingly Muslim population, a slight increase in the Greek Orthodox population, a sharp decline in the Armenian Gregorian population, and a more or less stable Jewish population.[81] The trend toward an increasingly Muslim population of the city would continue through the century, as would its non-Muslim geography. After the turn of the century, Christians and Jews would leave old minority neighborhoods that were losing minorities to re-group in new neighborhoods, seeking to retain or improve social status and to live with other Jews or Christians. Non-Muslim minorities occupied important roles in the city's economy toward the end of the nineteenth and beginning of the twentieth century: in 1885 Muslims constituted 38.32 per-cent of those engaged in trade, industry, and commerce.[82] As the presence of non-Muslims in urban cultural life and in the economy became an issue, nationalist policies targeted minorities by attempting to remove not only the signs and symbols of their influence in urban culture but also buildings and places in the city. Although the loss of Turkey's Greeks and Armenians had enormous consequences for the Turkish economy, it also meant that the policies of Turkification faced little opposition.[83]

Turkification policies against minorities in the 1920s and 1930s reflected a Kemalist differentiation between Turkish citizens and "true Turks." Some of the policies included denaturalizing, or removing the citizenship, of non-Muslim minorities who lived abroad, a situation that had dire con-sequences for Jews in Europe.[84] Minorities were also taken from the army and put into special labor battalions.[85] The Turkish language was seen as the key to inclusive Turkish citizenship during that period, and so some minorities, such as Moiz Kohen (Tekinalp), promoted speaking Turkish because they favored assimilation as a path to ensured future equality. Ko-hen was himself a Jew, and his active promotion of the Turkish language reflects the efforts of Jewish community leadership to present itself as loyal to the Turkish state, as many Jews were active in the Young Turk and, later, Kemalist movements.[86] Indeed, Jews have been perceived as more loyal than Greeks and Armenians, resulting in the consequence that Jews, Greeks, and Armenians have experienced different legal and political rela-tionships to the Turkish state throughout the twentieth century. The fact that Jews have worked to prove state loyalty and were not seen as betray-ers of Turkey is an important dimension of their relatively greater degree of assimilation compared with Greeks and Armenians.[87] (This situation meant that Jews were far more open to being interviewed for my research while, in contrast, I experienced some hostile encounters with Greeks who, in general, were not open to participating in my research.) Jews are also historically more linguistically and ethnically heterogeneous and more pre-dominantly urban than Greeks and Armenians.[88] However, as minorities, non-Muslims have shared a similar history of social and cultural exclusion from the state's national imaginary. As Riva Kastoryano argues, "All minorities find themselves in the same situation, even if the distinctions between communities persist, sometimes rife with friction, a fact which further enforces the identity of each group."[89]

Turkish language as a criterion for citizenship and nationality was aggressively promoted, for example, in the Citizen, Speak Turkish campaign, which discouraged minorities from speaking non-Turkish languages in public spaces.[90] The policy was promoted several times in the Turkish press, beginning in 1928 and running through the 1950s.[91] It impacted social relationships in urban space, as Turks pressured non-Turkish speakers to speak Turkish, and non-Muslim minorities reacted by tearing up propaganda posters or by reacting physically to verbal pressure.[92] While I did not hear stories about how or whether this policy was enforced in Kuzguncuk, Greeks, Armenians, and Jews in Kuzguncuk would have known about the social dimensions of this policy as many worked or attended high school on the European side of the city.

Another, more material focus of Turkification during that period was the effort to transform the city's socioeconomic structure by decreasing the power of non-Muslim minorities and transferring economic ownership and activity to Muslim Turks, through what Ayhan Aktar describes as "a set of policies aimed at establishing the unconditional supremacy of Turkish ethnic identity in nearly all aspects of social and economic life." The policies mandated that accounting be done in the Turkish language, prohibited minority employment in particular jobs, and legislated that Muslim Turks be employed in at least three-quarters of all the positions in foreign companies.[93] Non-Muslim employees of foreign companies were fired, in spite of the fact that all of the employees with foreign language and commercial experience in Istanbul during the 1920s were non-Muslims.[94] In 1922 the National Turkish Trade Association was founded to determine which businesses were Turkish. The association discovered that 97 percent of the import-export trade in Istanbul and all shops, stores, restaurants, and entertainment centers in Beyoğlu were owned by minorities.[95] In 1923 non-Muslims were expelled from trading jobs and insurance companies. In 1924 minorities were barred from service jobs, including working in bars, restaurants, and coffeehouses, as well as from trades such as boat captain, fisherman, and streetcar driver, jobs previously dominated by non-Muslims. In 1934 a law identified further minority-dominated professions to be prohibited to foreigners (in the same year of the state-led boycotts and pogroms against Jews in Thrace).[96] More than nine thousand Rum people were left out of work, causing most of them to migrate to Greece. Greek, Bulgarian, and Spanish non-Jewish citizens and Italian Jewish citizens also began to depart, and their property was taken by the Turkish state. And so, in spite of the protection they were guaranteed by the Lausanne Treaty, discrimination against minorities continued in practice in the early years of the Turkish state.

Economic discrimination continued along nationalist lines between 1942 and 1943, when the Wealth Tax "reflected the deep-seated perception in Kemalist circles that Muslim equals Turk, and non-Muslim equals non-Turk."[97] The stated rationale for the tax was that it was meant to meet wartime expenses at a time of national crisis. Some of the Muslim Turks I met in Istanbul who knew about the tax believed that if minorities were disproportionately affected by the tax, this was because they owned a disproportionate share of the wealth in the economy. This understanding of the tax basically reinforces nationalist claims that minorities unfairly constituted an upper class and that perhaps they may even have posed a threat to the nation at a vulnerable period. However, minorities were taxed to a level outrageously disproportionate to the amount of property they actually owned, and the wealthiest Turks were never taxed in the same way.[98] The true aims of the tax were thus political and cultural.[99]

In 1942 a committee was formed to determine the rates of taxation, using a subjective assessment of last names to determine which Istanbul residents were part of particular minority groups. A member of this committee, Faik Ökte, later wrote an account of his own participation in those activities and described how people were taxed arbitrarily according to their religious identities.[100] Of all properties sold to pay the tax, 97 percent were owned by non-Muslims.[101] Payment was required in fifteen days, and nonpayers were sent to work camps. Six thousand to eight thousand minorities (most of them Jews and none of them Muslim) who couldn't pay the tax were sent to work camps in Aşkale, near Erzurum in northeast Turkey.[102] People over fifty-five, even men as old as seventy-five and eighty years old, were sent to work camps, and sick people were taken from hospitals and sent as well. The majority of Jews in Istanbul during the 1940s were not wealthy but belonged to the lower and middle classes. Many sold their possessions at far less than their value to pay the tax.[103] The municipality set up centers for the sale of personal items to pay the tax, and some property was confiscated by the government if the owners couldn't pay; in this way property was transferred to the state.[104] The tax resulted in state confiscation of much minority property in Istanbul, effectively Turkifying not only the city's economy but also its landscape. The tax was probably the most significant causal factor in the emigration of thirty thousand Jews to Israel in 1948. In spite of Turkey's formal neutrality during World War II, the tax was also a contributing factor to the perception among Jews that anti-Semitism was increasing in the city during the 1940s. I discuss the tax in much more detail in chapter 6, where I relate memories of the tax as it was experienced in Kuzguncuk, including by families with only moderate or little income.

The situation for local Istanbul minorities became even more difficult as the Cyprus issue began to increasingly impact Greek-Turkish relations, and in 1955 local Greeks became the target of a major riot, which also impacted Armenians and Jews.[105] In 1954 Greece took the issue of Cyprus to the United Nations. On 6–7 September 1955, a riot against Greek-owned properties swept the city. Although the incident was provoked by reports that Atatürk's birthplace in Salonica had been bombed, it was later discovered to have been a state-led riot.[106] The massive destruction of minority (particularly Greek) property and the violence created such an atmosphere of fear that after 1955 thousands of Greeks left Istanbul. This episode had a significant impact on Kuzguncuk and I examine memories of this event in detail in chapter 4.

In 1964 Istanbul's Rum community was again made a local target in an international conflict when the İnönü government punished Istanbul's local Greeks for the Bloody Christmas massacres of ethnic Turkish Cypriots in 1963. The prime minister revoked the residency permission of Greek citizens in Istanbul by canceling the 1930 Ankara Convention treaty with Greece, even though their rights to residency in the city had been guaranteed by the Lausanne Treaty. These people, many of them elderly, were born in Istanbul, and many had never even been to Greece. While 9,000 Istanbullus of Greek citizenship were legally deported, many more of the larger Greek Orthodox community departed in the wake of this deportation.[107] The total emigration was 40,000.[108] According to Baskin Oran, 13,000 Greek citizens living and working in Istanbul were deported, including not only Greeks who came from Greece to work in Turkey under the provisions of the 1930 convention but also local Rum who had Greek citizenship.[109] The entire Greek Orthodox population in Istanbul decreased from 120,000 to 3,000 after the decision.[110] The emigrants were permitted to take twenty kilos of possessions and the equivalent of twenty-two U.S. dollars with them, leaving behind property, much of which was confiscated by the Turkish state.[111] The Turkish treasury benefited with property valued between 200 million and 500 million U.S. dollars.[112] Other property owned by Turkish citizens married to Greeks was left in an ambiguous legal status. The fear generated by the forced deportation caused many more to leave, and today mere traces of Istanbul's historical Greek community remain. "By 1967, almost the entire Istanbul Hellene community had been expelled and their assets in Turkey frozen."[113]

In 1974 Turkey occupied and declared the Turkish Republic of Cyprus in northern Cyprus. Cyprus continued to be a bone of contention that placed minority citizens in Istanbul at risk.[114] As late as 1988 Foreign Minister Hasan Esat Işık stated, "There is no direct connection between the Cyprus problem and the Greek minority and the patriarchate," but he added, "if Athens refused to deal with Ankara over Cyprus this would have its effects on the Greek minority in Turkey."[115]

One of the most important dimensions of economic and cultural Turkification is the impact on urban landscapes. Property ownership in Turkey can be very difficult to determine.[116] Disputes regarding minority property ownership in Istanbul is even more difficult to document. When Christians and Jews left Istanbul, or were deported, their property was often unable or forbidden to be sold and so was abandoned and then confiscated by the state.[117] Some properties were sold in a hurry at very low prices. Property was bequeathed to friends or left to the names of saints so it would remain within the religious community, an act that paradoxically rendered it vulnerable later because of the Turkish state's declaration that any donations to foundations would become the property of the state and of the inability of minority foundations to buy or sell property.

One of the most disputed areas of this history concerns the status and consequences of the property that Greeks and Rums left behind in 1964. Legal situations concerning these properties are very complex, making it impossible to generalize as to their fate and status. Old property deeds in Istanbul are complicated by inheritance laws that split property among family members in shares. An individual property may be owned by dozens of absentee inheritors who may be deceased or live abroad. Sometimes dozens of people are involved and they reside in cities all over the world in diaspora. To inherit or sell property, however, all family members and their inheritors on the deed must agree on the sale and be present. This legal situation makes the sale or restoration of these properties exceptionally difficult or impossible and thus places them in a semiabandoned "limbo" status. Furthermore, lawsuits to reclaim property can be difficult because of the lack of clear birth and death records or the absence of surnames on old Ottoman property records.

The legal problems regarding the sale or transfer of historical properties are further intensified for Istanbul's non-Muslim minorities, particularly for its historical Rum community. One specific result of the 1964 deportation was a decree that resulted in the confiscation, by the state, of properties left by those who were forcibly deported. For example, any property abandoned for more than ten years was legally taken by the state Treasury. According to Hülya Demir and Rıdvan Akar *40 percent* of the properties abandoned in 1964 were lost to the Turkish state this way.[118] Furthermore, Greek citizens were forbidden "from being parties to any legal transactions resulting in the transfer of titles of real property in Turkey—in short, blatant confiscation without compensation."[119] Greeks were forbidden from selling, transferring, or inheriting property. Furthermore, Turkish courts appointed Turkish trustees for abandoned Greek properties, and those trustees were given the right to lease the property under whatever terms they desired. After ten years, these properties under trusteeship devolved to the state. The 1964 deportation was thus a vehicle for the appropriation of minority-owned properties by the Turkish state. And while the 1964 decree was lifted in 1988, the Turkish state continued, through the 1980s and in ensuing decades, to appropriate minority properties through similar legal rulings regarding the denial of Greek citizens to possess or inherit property and the refusal to remove Turkish trustees from Greek properties.[120] An additional current problem faced by the remaining Rum community in Istanbul is that any donations made to non-Muslim minority foundations have been declared, by the Turkish administration, to be the property of the Turkish state.[121]

For these reasons, large neighborhoods of the city formerly dominated by minorities, and that were evacuated during the late 1950s and through the 1960s, became filled with empty and decaying buildings. Some were

occupied by incoming rural migrants who achieved ownership after a period of uncontested occupation. Some properties that remained unclaimed
after a period of time were eventually permitted to be sold. Others were
sold through unclear legal processes. In Kuzguncuk, all of the shops on the
main street and many of the houses were transferred in various (and some
believe through legally ambiguous) ways to Muslim Turks, some of whom
had arrived in Kuzguncuk as rural migrants and worked as employees for
minority-owned businesses and others who arrived to purchase houses or
property on which to build. Areas where former minority properties remained in a legal limbo status for many years have begun, over the last
fifteen years, to become places for smart investment in Istanbul.[122]

The result of Turkification policies has been that, by the late twentieth
century, the cosmopolitan quality of cultural spaces in Istanbul had largely
disappeared with the emigration of most of Istanbul's historical minorities. In this way, the hegemonic processes that define and create the nation
as ethnically Turkish and Muslim were inscribed on the city landscape,
altering the spaces and practices of daily life. Today Turkey (and Istanbul)
is approximately 99.9 percent Muslim.[123] Ayhan Aktar argues that this is
a result of the 1942 tax, the 1955 riots, and the 1964 deportation: "From
a cultural perspective, the result of these important developments is that
the non-Muslim minorities, the Ottoman world's treasure to the Republic, were erased from the scene by a few decisions of the state."[124] Other
factors are also important, including the incentive for remaining minorities to emigrate from Turkey for economic opportunity, an atmosphere of
political stability, and low population growth.[125] This tumultuous period
between the 1940s and the 1960s, in which minority properties in the city
were sold or confiscated, also witnessed the first very large wave of rural-
urban migration. According to Turkish state census data, between 1945 and
1975 Istanbul's population increased four times, from one to four million.
In spite of these tumultuous population shifts that fractured urban communities, it is this very period that is nostalgically narrated in the dominant collective memory as one of tolerance, siblinghood, and belonging
in the mahalle. After the decades of antiminority policies, the "frequently
encountered" tropes of "tolerance" and "living together in peace" in memories of cosmopolitan Istanbul betray a certain irony.[126]

As overurbanization and the increasing polarization of wealth create
new and alienating landscapes, Istanbul residents lament that the city lost

its character.[127] Social life in the city, and in Kuzguncuk, has witnessed other sociocultural changes, such as the loss of its open-air cinema and the increase in private televisions. Mahalle landscapes changed as chain stores pushed out small family-owned businesses. As the social practices that characterized traditional mahalle life erode, the mahalle as a Turkish, urban, cultural space moved into the realm of social memory as the embodiment of familiarity in place. Kuzguncuk's historical landscape became famous as its old buildings were restored or their facades re-created, and it was used as the setting for numerous television shows, films, and commercials that romanticize the mahalle. Historical mahalles in Istanbul become symbols that embody cultural memory, while the social fragmentation and disjunctures in their landscapes manifest the tensions underlying recent cultural change in the city.

2 Uryanizade Street
Landscape of Collective Memory

The Theater of Mahalle Life

On my last day in Kuzguncuk in 2003 I walked down Icadiye Street and stopped to watch the crowd of people at the bakery. Loaves of bread were lined up in the window, and the carved wooden placard hanging outside read "Ekmek Teknesi" (Bread Boat) (see figure 1). Local family-owned businesses such as bread ovens are trademark features of the traditional mahalle, and this shop blended seamlessly into Kuzguncuk's neighborhood landscape. The crowd around Ekmek Teknesi was watching two men in a heated discussion in front of the shop. It was a typical scene that normally wouldn't attract an audience. However, these people were well-known actors whose faces appeared regularly on the new and popular mahalle television series called *Ekmek Teknesi*. The mahalle place that set the scene was none other than the local kebap restaurant, its front redecorated to look like a traditional bakery. In 2003 *Ekmek Teknesi* was so popular that the actors and film crews created a spectacle, and although film crews were a common sight in Kuzguncuk, crowds of onlookers appeared every time cameras and lights were set up along the main street. By 2007 the situation had changed, and television film sets became so pervasive in Kuzguncuk—five different programs were being filmed per week—that the neighborhood association filed an official complaint against the disruption they caused. The spokesperson for the neighborhood association traced the frustration back to the disturbance caused by the film crew of *Ekmek Teknesi*.[1]

According to Kanal 1, the channel that broadcast the program, *Ekmek Teknesi* "narrated the cheerful stories lived in a typical Turkish mahalle," and the main character, the baker Nusrettin, "resembled the character Nasrettin Hoca of the traditional folk legends of Turkey."[2] An important element of the program was its setting in Kuzguncuk. The series brought to life, in "one of Istanbul's old mahalles" a "beautiful fairy tale, one that is untrue but that is desired to be true."[3] Kuzguncuk's landscape was the theater, in *Ekmek Teknesi*, for a nostalgic portrayal of mahalle life, and the program soared in popularity because it brilliantly matched the cultural memory of the mahalle developed in previous television series, advertisements, and print media.

Kuzguncuk's landscape has served the crucial role of providing *the* stage for nostalgic memory making in Istanbul. The street that intersects the main road to form the corner where *Ekmek Teknesi* was filmed is called Perihan Abla. The street is named for the first, and most famous, mahalle television series in Turkey. *Perihan Abla* (Sister Perihan) was filmed in Kuzguncuk in the late 1980s and starred Perran Kutman in the role of Perihan. Its success inspired an entire genre of mahalle television series that were to follow over the next twenty years, several of which were filmed in Kuzguncuk and others that were filmed in other old Istanbul neighborhoods, including the Bosphorus neighborhood of Çengelköy and the neighborhood of Samatya on the historical peninsula on the European side of the city. Setting popular films in historical districts has been a practice since the 1960s in Istanbul, where areas restored for tourism, such as Soğukçeşme Street in the Sultanahmet district of the historical peninsula, convey a "romantic old flavor" appropriate for movies.[4]

In Kuzguncuk, Perihan Abla Street is not the street where the character Perihan lived in the television series. Rather, Uryanizade Street, the most

Figure 1. Set for the television program *Ekmek Teknesi* (Bread Boat) on Icadiye Street in Kuzguncuk. Author's photo.

carefully restored street in Kuzguncuk, named for a wealthy Muslim family, was the primary setting for the program.[5] This historical street of restored Ottoman wooden houses, along with the small local shops of Kuzguncuk's main street, Icadiye Street, constituted the theater for the intimate mahalle life portrayed in *Perihan Abla*. On the Turkish Web site called anilarim. net (mymemories.net) viewers of *Perihan Abla* write that "we grew up with *Perihan Abla*. From that program we learned about friendship. Turkey really has a need for these kinds of television series" and "A few years ago *Ekmek Teknesi* was filmed in the same place [as *Perihan Abla*]. Kuzguncuk is one of Istanbul's undestroyed precious, rare places."[6] Kuzguncuk's landscape and the television program *Perihan Abla* became popular together because of a growing collective nostalgia for the traditional mahalle as a place of belonging and familiarity. Kuzguncuk's material landscape made the memory appear to be real and was popular precisely because the seeming reality of the memory so successfully obscured the tensions and disharmony of actual everyday life in Istanbul. Kuzguncuk's mahalle landscape had become a simulacrum through its frequent portrayals on television and the attendant transformations on the ground to accommodate those representations.[7] As the cultural meanings and values were embedded in symbols in the landscape, acquiring material form, they also inherited a corresponding sense of authenticity, as what was visually observable came to constitute a seemingly objective, uncontestable reality.[8]

Kuzguncuk's mahalle landscape as portrayed in *Perihan Abla* provides an authentic feel of a traditional mahalle because the old wooden houses and their interior spaces connect to public places along the main street in a blending of public and private space that characterizes mahalle life.[9] The character Perihan lived in a traditional Ottoman-era wooden house, and the problems and scenarios of the mahalle that center around her unfold primarily on the neighborhood street in front of her house, as well as in the public spaces of the neighborhood.

The frequent representations of the friendly, close mahalle in television shows like *Perihan Abla* work together with other popular media—such as memoirs, short stories, advertising, and reproductions of old photographs displayed in coffee-table books or for sale in historical parts of the city—to reproduce a collective memory of Istanbul's past. Kuzguncuk's historical landscape began to be cited in books, journals, and newspapers and on television as evidence of the reality of the collective memory of mahalle life, particularly as it related to remembering a cosmopolitan, tolerant past in Istanbul. As the neighborhood of Kuzguncuk began to signify the mahalle of collective memory in the popular imagination, the neighborhood's landscape itself was increasingly transformed: by the time *Ekmek Teknesi* began to be filmed in 2002, the film set for the television show necessitated the creation of a setting more authentic, that is, more evocative of the collective memory, than Kuzguncuk's actual landscape. The kebap restaurant was rented for a high price and its facade was remade to look like a real bread bakery, although two working bread bakeries were already located on the same street.

The collective memory of the mahalle and the mahalle landscape in Kuzguncuk thus became dependent on each other. The cycle of cultural reproduction that creates and reproduces cultural landscapes is conditioned by the cultural politics that structure the "lived relations of places," in this

Figure 2. Restored houses on Uryanizade Street, the set for the television program *Perihan Abla*. Author's photo.

case, the social dynamics of everyday life in Kuzguncuk.[10] As Kuzguncuk's landscape became popularized through media representation, increasing numbers of people moved to the neighborhood seeking the associated values of mahalle life. They purchased and restored or rebuilt old houses, developing the historical atmosphere of the neighborhood. Paradoxically, however, the arrival of these newcomers altered the socioeconomic composition of the neighborhood in ways that intensified the fragmentation of stable and consistent neighborly relations in the mahalle (a process that began with earlier migrants and the departure of old minority families).

Although Kuzguncuk's landscape is known as historical, it is not a mere relic of the past but a landscape under continual and deliberate reproduction. This process is sustained by two interrelated nostalgic themes: the mahalle, as the urban space of belonging and familiarity, and the narrative of historical multiethnic harmony. These two narratives themselves respond to and reproduce a social memory of a past cosmopolitanism, of harmony and neighborliness grounded in the shared belonging to the mahalle as a place. The current divisions of class and origin in Kuzguncuk, as well as the circumstances under which Kuzguncuk's minorities departed, however, are obscured by the cultural memory.

In this chapter, I examine the symbolic dimensions of the mahalle landscape.[11] I introduce the notion of the mahalle as a space of collective memory and link the processes reproducing this space of collective memory to the cultural landscape in Kuzguncuk that represents it on the ground. I also discuss some of the social dynamics of gentrification in Kuzguncuk. This chapter focuses on the work of the landscape to make a representation appear to be real, and as such, it sets the stage for the discussion in the next chapter, which examines what exactly the landscape, with its representative power, conceals.

Mahalle of Collective Memory

In 2001 a book titled *Bir Maniniz Yoksa Annemler Size Gelecek: 70'li Yıllarda Hayatımız* was published in Istanbul and rapidly became a bestseller. The title is a colloquial phrase that roughly means, "if it's convenient my mom will visit." The subtitle reads, "our lives in the 1970s." The expression suggests a child sent over to a neighbor, on an errand for her mother to ask politely if the neighbor could receive visitors, indicating perhaps that her mother had news or something to ask. The title recalls, for the book's audience, the time and place of close neighborly relations of urban life in the past. Published in April of that year, by August it was in its twenty-fourth printing, and in 2003 it went on to win an international award for regional literature. The author, Ayfer Tunç, was born in 1964 in Adapazarı, a city not far from Istanbul. Her family moved to Istanbul, where she attended high school and would remain a resident.

Bir Maniniz Yoksa was published at a moment when the popularity for nostalgic cultural forms, including books and television series reproducing the collective memory mahalle, was reaching its height. In the introduction to her book, Tunç begins with her own memory of a favorite landscape she'd see from the train as she returned home from school, a mural in three dimensional relief of girls dressed in beach wear. She explains that although the pictures weren't very good, because the girls' heads were too large, she always liked them and assumed that anytime she wanted to she'd be able to see them. One day, however, the wall was destroyed to make way for the new coastal road, which today extends along the Asian coast of the Marmara Sea. The road expanded residential development and boosted the construction of large apartment buildings along what, at that time, were becoming new upper-class areas of Istanbul—the neighborhoods of Göztepe, Caddebostan, and Suadiye. She writes, "For the first time, when I felt the absence of those walls, I understood that the small things that colored our lives will, could, disappear."[12]

Tunç describes her book as a collection of the small, unimportant, common things of her childhood and of her generation. The titles of the brief chapters read like a list of her memories. A chapter titled "Stealing Quinces from Peaceful Trees" describes the kinds of flowers and herbs that grew in empty lots before they were filled with apartment buildings and cement, and recalls the pastime of children climbing walls to steal fruit from neighbors' gardens. In a chapter about childhood games, Tunç writes that while hopscotch is still played today, it's very difficult to find streets where there is no traffic, and the game is now restricted to school playgrounds. The chapter titled "Paste, Pickles, Noodles, Jam," after foods that were once always homemade, describes how in those times seasons were predictable and foods grew only in the appropriate season. Foods sold out of season were very expensive. Homemade food was prized above ready-made food, and anything served for a guest was to be made at home, to properly show respect for a visitor.[13] Tunç reflects that as a child, grown-ups began their sentences with the words "in our times." In this book Tunç writes from this same voice, as if speaking for a generation remembering its shared history. The book recalls the ways of life that were lost when modernization and urbanization altered urban spaces and society, and it speaks to a nostalgia for a better, slower pace of life.

Ayfer Tunç's book is one of many media that engaged in reproducing the social memory of mahalle life, including television shows, comic strips, and Web sites that brought historical Istanbul landscapes to life in the imagination. Other memoirs, essays, and fiction published in the mid-1990s and early 2000s, such as Sait Faik Abasıyanık's *Mahalle Kahvesi* (Mahalle Coffeehouse), a collection of short stories written and set during 1940s Istanbul and reissued in 2002, both satisfied and created a need for forms and images through which people could consume and remember mahalle life.

Advertising took advantage of this nostalgia by using the mahalle concept to create name-brand images that signify familiarity and community. In September 2002, the telecom firm Aria broadcast a television commercial with the logo "communication is an art" (*"iletişim sanattır"*). Viewers watch a handsome, young male artist painting a large scene of Beyoğlu, a formerly minority-dominated neighborhood in Istanbul, which is the subject of much contemporary nostalgic interest. The artist listens to an elderly man talking about the good old days. The theme of the commercial, and the man's conversation, is communication. We hear nostalgic music as the elderly man says, "in our times, there were nice conversations; there was wonderful neighborliness . . . where has it gone, where has it gone?"[14] The young man nods and smiles, understanding and respecting his older friend. The point of the commercial is that Aria, with their art of communication, can restore good relationships in today's city like in the old days.

Another commercial, this one for the international banking company HSBC, used the mahalle concept to market HSBC, ironically, as the local banking option. A young boy has a handheld camera and he's making a video to introduce us to his neighborhood. "This is our mahalle," he says. We see the streets of upper-class Nişantaşı (again an old minority neighborhood) and its old European-style apartment buildings. He introduces us to one of the elderly people who recognize him as a local neighborhood kid. He shows us the local corner store. Then he says, "This is our bank," and the ad focuses in on HSBC.

Mahalle landscapes began to be represented on television and in magazines, special weekend editions of newspapers, popular fiction, and memoirs because the landscapes signified or represented something very much desired but absent, remembered and longed for, in contemporary Istanbul culture.[15] In representations of Kuzguncuk and in narratives of the mahalle's history, nostalgia for familiar community life refers to the time before Istanbul's older urban fabric and open green spaces were replaced with apartment buildings to house new migrants. Alongside rapid urbanization, other sociocultural changes had begun to erode the traditional practices of mahalle social life. People of Kuzguncuk say that when more families began to own televisions, fewer people visited each other outside in the evenings, and the open cinema in Kuzguncuk closed down. Kuzguncuk once had many small family-owned corner groceries, but today most shopping is done in two larger supermarkets. Traditionally, neighboring practices created networks of support between neighbors and in resident-owned shops and businesses, defining the mahalle and making it the space of familiarity and belonging. Yet by the 1980s, these practices, and the collectivity of social life in the mahalle, had nearly faded away.

As the social practices that characterized traditional mahalle life eroded, the mahalle as a Turkish, urban, cultural space moved into the realm of social memory as the embodiment of familiarity in place. Other neighborhoods of Istanbul (including the Bosphorus neighborhoods of Çengelköy, Beylerbeyi, and Arnavutköy, and other parts of the city known for minority history, such as Fener, Samatya, and most especially Beyoğlu) also locate nostalgia for past community life, as well as for the lost Istanbullus, the Greeks, Jews, and Armenians who took much of the character of the city with them when they departed.[16] David Lowenthal writes that both nostalgia and heritage rely on interpretations of history to compensate for a present malaise for a lack of community and a need for identity in place.[17] Both the nostalgia for Istanbul's minorities and for the local-scale historical urban landscape inform social memory in Kuzguncuk, a memory that narrates the past in an attempt to cope with the present and articulate an imagination for the future.[18]

Perihan Abla and the Spaces of Mahalle Life

When Kuzguncuk was chosen as the setting for the *Perihan Abla* television show, its historical landscape became known not only for its physical beauty but also as the theater for the acting out of mahalle life in the popular imagination. In each episode, a problem touches several members of the community and mahalle residents come together to solve it, demonstrating the interconnectedness of mahalle relations. Characters refer to Kuzguncuk as "*bizim mahalle*" (our mahalle), and all mahalle members are treated as one of the community. Everyone knows everyone else's business and most of the show takes place in the mahalle spaces of the streets and shops, where news of fellow neighbors is the subject of discussion. An important part of this familiarity is the goodness of people in helping each other.

Fundamental to the structure of social life in the show is the landscape, in which streets and shops become an extension of the private space of the home or a transition between private and public spaces. Episodes often start and finish on the street. In one episode, Perihan and her friends get lost on a boat trip and eventually return back to the mahalle after a series of adventures, and the entire neighborhood meets them and embraces them at the boat dock. Scenes that take place inside the home continue as the character moves out onto the street, and her interactions with others continue through this space into the next space of the corner store.[19] The social space in the television show is thus continuous: the mahalle space in *Perihan Abla* includes, and moves through, both inside and outside spaces, which set the scene for intimate and personal, as well as public and collective interactions between characters.

The episode called "Hediye" (The Gift) demonstrates the role of street space in the complex interconnectedness of neighbor relationships. In the beginning of the episode, Perihan's dress is ruined by a rich business associate of her husband's who splashes mud on it when he drives away from the curb. He feels obliged to give her a new dress in compensation. However, a series of misunderstandings between his wife, his secretary, Perihan's neighbors, and her sister culminate in a street scene in which the rich businessman's wife accuses Perihan's neighbor, mistaking her for Perihan, of having an affair with her husband. During the fight we see scenes of men talking at the fruit stand, telling passersby "there's a fight, a fight!" The barber, along with other neighbors, looks out the window to see the fight. Eventually people come onto the street and break up the fight. The private matter becomes public because of the spreading of rumors and the constant observation resulting from living in small neighborhood space. The misunderstanding is resolved collectively as neighbors contribute their observations to piece together what happened. The story is acted out in the public space of the residential street with all the neighbors' participation.

In "Acemi Kumarbaz" (The Novice Gambler), Perihan's fiancé Şakir succumbs to a gambling habit. The whole mahalle gradually becomes aware of it because he starts to borrow money, first from his mother and then from the barber. Then he misses payments on his bill at the local appliance shop owned by another friend. He also looks for money in his friend's taxi. Mahalle residents start to share concerned comments about Şakir's strange behavior and they follow clues he leaves behind to discover his problem. The mahalle bands together in a plot to cure him by setting up their own card game, where they plan to cheat him out of everything, thus embarrassing him enough to want to quit, but in a safe way so they can give him back the money. Perihan is urged to leave him if he doesn't give it up, and she makes this threat in front of all the neighbors as he stands on the front stoop in his pajamas. Close neighbor relationships are demonstrated in the lending of money and in the communication of news and concern about Şakir, and the community acts as a collective in addressing what has transcended an individual problem to become a community project.

Perihan Abla is remembered today as the show that most successfully represents typical or old-fashioned mahalle life. The characters symbolize average Istanbul residents as well: they are middle class, Turkish, and Muslim. According to Hülya Tanrıöver, the broadcasting of *Perihan Abla* in 1986 was important, not only for starting an era of family-mahalle series but also for "transforming [the mahalle] by the masses into a beloved modern legend." The mahalle television show was such a popular concept that by 1997 the mahalle had become the context for almost all Turkish television serials. Tanrıöver argues that the mahalle space of the Turkish television serials is popular precisely because it so closely simulates a kind of reality common to how Turkish people imagine everyday life, because the mahalle is a determinant concept of the collective identity of Turks and yet is also imbued with a nostalgia and romanticism for the past.[20]

Tanrıöver also argues that the mahalle provides the most convenient type of place for the narrative structure of the serials because the characters can meet in a realistic and natural manner in public places. The landscape of the mahalle is ideal because it offers a possibility of transition from interior to exterior spaces without disturbing the audience. A character can "leave her apartment, greet a neighbor, and go to the grocery, without the sudden jump from bistro to house like in 'Western' serials." The mahalle presents a unity and renders possible a natural transition from one space to the other, and "with its resemblance to real life gives the audience a feeling of security."[21] On television, mahalle life is dependent on a landscape that is constituted by the places necessary for its performance. These places include the semiprivate residential streets of homes as well as the mahalle places of public interaction among neighbors, like the corner store (*bakkal*), the coffeehouse, and other common meeting places in the traditional neighborhood. These places form the landscape of the mahalle in collective memory.

Creating a Historical Landscape

It is no coincidence that by the time *Perihan Abla* was filmed, Kuzguncuk's landscape had already felt the impact of its first wave of historical restoration. In this way, "The exercise of imagination that conjures . . . representations . . . [is] intimately connected to the ongoing work of landscape production 'on the ground.'"[22] Cengiz Bektaş, an internationally known architect and 2002 winner of the Aga Khan Architectural Prize, is personally responsible for beginning historical renovation in Kuzguncuk and for bringing international attention to his project and to the neighborhood's historical characteristics.[23] He started in 1978 by purchasing and restoring an old house on Uryanizade Street. He takes credit for initiating a movement and has argued that the success of his project inspired others to patch up their own old houses.[24] While there is no doubt that some elderly, long-term Kuzguncuk residents were inspired by his work, the dramatic changes in Kuzguncuk's historical landscape were made by the artists and professionals who moved there after him to restore old houses. Bektaş began by bringing friends from his own circle of artists, architects, and engineers to the street. One artist explained to me that as a house went up for sale, Bektaş would bring in a friend, and the resident artist community would contribute help if the friend couldn't afford to buy the house right away. Today many of the residents of Uryanizade Street are thus connected by relations of friendship and acquaintance preceding their move to Kuzguncuk. This restoration movement gained media attention and was promoted by Bektaş himself, thus enhancing Kuzguncuk's visibility and popularity. It thus became a precursor to a larger wave of gentrification that boomed in the 1990s. This later stage of gentrification, however, did not largely involve the same early community of artists and professionals and also meant a direction away from the restoration of existing wooden structures, toward a focus on their total destruction and re-creation in cement with brightly painted wooden facades.[25]

For Cengiz Bektaş, neighborhood life and neighborhood space are dependent and intertwined. Bektaş used historical renovation in Kuzguncuk as a vehicle for specific aims and goals intended to create community and a sense of belonging in local neighborhood life. I was introduced to Bektaş soon after my arrival in Kuzguncuk. He explained the approach behind his project in Kuzguncuk. He worked first to try and engender a sense of care and responsibility among residents for their environment by asking everyone to help paint a wall on Uryanizade Street. Later he initiated community-oriented places in neighborhood spaces, hoping to nurture a sense of bonding among residents.[26] They included a small children's library and an open-air theater on Bereketli Street, where outside stairs formed a natural amphitheater. He also helped fellow neighbors with plans to refurbish their old houses. Bektaş claims that he made a broad effort to interact with local residents in projects of his own design, though the extent to which the projects were successful over a long term remains unclear. To my knowledge, none of them were ongoing during my residence in Kuzguncuk. Bektaş wrote himself into the history of the neighborhood, saying that he has been working for twelve years to help people learn to live together again. He believes he has been successful.[27] In a brief speech at Kadir Has University in May 2003 he said, "I am a Kuzguncuklu," defining his own identity as bound to Kuzguncuk.[28] He characterized his project in Kuzguncuk as a life passion, explaining that although he started in 1978 the idea occurred to him as early as 1965.

Throughout his writings and public lectures, Bektaş emphasizes the importance of tolerance at the center of his work. He aims to revive the tolerance of Kuzguncuk's multicultural past. "Holding a face against the destruction of community identity as members of a place of common origin, [residents of Kuzguncuk live in] an interesting settlement, given the social life of today's Istanbul, which has begun to resemble a migrant's relationship with the environment. For hundreds of years, people of four different beliefs lived among each other here (Muslims, Jews, Armenians, Greeks) . . . That is, until some things were broken with those who came from outside . . . in the riots of 6–7 September (1955) . . . But still today, even if their numbers . . . are changed, these people of four beliefs still live together in Kuzguncuk."[29]

Bektaş argues that this history has created a special culture of community in the neighborhood. He selected Kuzguncuk for his project of community building through historical restoration because of the neighborhood's history of multiethnic tolerance. "Come, I say, love the shared space you have; before everything, a person must know to love their geography. Our geography of course is made of people . . . Otherwise why would I have come to Kuzguncuk? It's a place where the whole mahalle is lived like an extended family."[30]

For Bektaş, the tolerance of Kuzguncuk's multiethnic past is embedded in its landscape. In his book *Hoşgörünün Öteki Adı: Kuzguncuk* (The Other Name for Tolerance: Kuzguncuk), he sketched the Bosphorus from a northern-facing Kuzguncuk hill. In the center of his view is Kuzguncuk's most often-cited image: the Armenian church next to the mosque. Bektaş challenges his audience: "Don't the Armenian church and the Muslim mosque, with their domes mingling among each other, demonstrate themselves the very idea of tolerance?"[31]

Kuzguncuk's landscape, in his text, becomes actual evidence of the ethnic inclusion of the living mahalle of collective memory. His descriptions of Kuzguncuk's landscape mixes past and present with the same tone of nostalgia adopted by the many magazine and newspaper articles about the neighborhood's tolerant history. Bektaş conveys a rich sense of the life of the main street, describing the elderly Armenian pudding maker, the synagogue and churches, and the shops and coffeehouses. He describes the funeral of the barber Muzaffer, attended by all the mahalle. A photo of solemn men gathered around the coffin in front of the barbershop helps us imagine the sense of community in the neighborhood, as well as the photograph of the inside of the shop, where the walls are covered with photographs of Kuzguncuk people.[32] Bektaş's narratives of Kuzguncuk emphasize that this place has not lost its sense of community like other places in Istanbul.

Kuzguncuk is exceptionalized not only in Bektaş's works but also in other media that merge representations of Kuzguncuk's historical landscape and its unusually integrated life. In one article, the neighborhood is described as "possibly the most beautiful" on the Bosphorus:

> The mansions protected until today, the historical boat station, and the people tightly bound by neighborly relationships make Kuzguncuk possibly the most beautiful neighborhood on the Bosphorus. The work there to protect the old structures is done with the aim of creating a new way of life. More than protecting the old structures is the true desire to protect the relationships, the love and understanding between

Figure 3. Armenian church and Kuzguncuk mosque side by side. Author's photo.

people. Kuzguncuk people are making decisions for themselves, trying to prevent Kuzguncuk from becoming foreign.[33]

In an article titled "Last Stop before Reaching the Holy Land: Kuzguncuk," the authors describe Kuzguncuk in this way:

> The things built in Kuzguncuk reflect a yearning for the past . . . More than preserving the old structures, the relationships, the love between the people, the real thing desired in protecting Kuzguncuk is that people should not become strangers, that Kuzguncuk people should decide by themselves for themselves, to represent themselves on their own terms in Istanbul . . . It became like a fairytale because Kuzguncuk is a fairytale.[34]

The links between Kuzguncuk's beautiful landscape and its special ma-halle culture are also emphasized in an article titled "The Last Heaven in Istanbul: Kuzguncuk," in which Kuzguncuk is referred to as a "Little Paris," and local artists are quoted as saying that Kuzguncuk's peaceful quality, its natural beauty, and its historical atmosphere is what drew them to the neighborhood. The article describes how even after Turks moved to Kuzguncuk, people of the four religious backgrounds—Muslim, Greek Orthodox, Armenian Orthodox, and Jewish—lived together in peace in Kuzguncuk.[35] In a different article, which also reiterates the theme of Kuz-guncuk as a Little Paris, the author writes,

> however small Kuzguncuk is, it is also that large . . . it has an enormous heart. Its neighbors are full of a simple but beautiful happiness. Waiting with open arms to hold you and never let you go. Don't think it's exaggerated, memories buried inside history; these are words that fall from the tongues of those who live here.[36]

The histories of its minority communities are detailed, as well as the ways they lived without religious or cultural divisions, all under one tent. The 6–7 September riots are said to have been more peaceful here than in other neighborhoods because neighbors helped each other.[37] "From those days until now, nothing has changed in Kuzguncuk. Remember *Perihan Abla*, how we loved it, how we never missed it? Why did that show influ-ence us so much? The inside of life, from it, from us, it showed our feel-ings, in every corner. Do you know where it was filmed? In Kuzguncuk." The things unforgotten about Kuzguncuk's past conclude the piece, which describes the smell of the sea and the celebrations on the street at Easter, the outside movies in the summer and trips to the baths, and the role neighbors took in lighting stoves for Jewish families who didn't light fire on the Sabbath. The piece also displays several full-color photographs of old restored wooden houses, the Armenian church next to the mosque, the bell tower of the Greek church, and scenes of Kuzguncuk's tree-lined streets.[38]

Representations of Kuzguncuk circulate in the same spaces in which mahalle television series are produced and gain popularity. One of the most famous mahalle television serials was *Ikinci Bahar* (Second Spring), produced by Uğur Yücel, a nationally famous comic actor and television series director, who was born in Kuzguncuk. He speaks and writes often about how his own identity is tied to the neighborhood where he was born, and at a talk in January 2002 in Kuzguncuk at a local organization he referred to himself as a *mahalle çocuğu*, or a "local kid" of Kuzguncuk.[39] He said, "I belong here; I'm not speaking here as a foreigner . . . The mahalle doesn't push away neighborhood children from the warmth of life. For me, Kuzguncuk was a cinema. It had a wonderful character . . . I left here nourished by my experience of the people here."[40]

His personal identity as a Kuzguncuklu underlies his vision behind the programs he produces for television, most recently in *Ikinci Bahar*. This program was filmed in the historical (and once predominantly Armenian) neighborhood of Samatya. The show centers on a Romeo-Juliet–type love story situated around two local shops on the main street. In my interview with him, Yücel claimed that Samatya resembles Kuzguncuk in terms of mahalle life. He looked at approximately fifteen neighborhoods for the filming of the show, and if he hadn't been able to work in Samatya, he probably would have gone to Kuzguncuk. Yücel said that the extended social family relationships of mahalle life don't exist as they used to, however, citing the Portuguese word *saudade*, which, he said, means "something you miss from the past that wasn't actually lived." "Like nostalgia for mahalle," I asked? He shrugged. He said even if old Istanbul life is gone, Kuzguncuk still has the *mahalle havası*, the mahalle atmosphere. Media reliance on Kuzguncuk as the best example of mahalle atmosphere has given it a primary place in the popular imagining of the city.

Gentrification Makes Mahalle Landscapes

The desire to vicariously participate in the collective memory of mahalle with various acts of consumption is nowhere more manifest than in the lifestyle centered around gentrification.[41] In this way, the collective memory changes Istanbul's urban landscapes by creating landscapes that evoke its atmosphere.[42] Sociologist Nil Uzun has identified a new urban cultural group of the 1990s that identifies with living in an old neighborhood. Her research on gentrification in Istanbul, in which she compares the neighborhoods of Cihangir and Kuzguncuk, illustrates the social differences embedded in the creation of historical, nostalgic landscapes in the city. She examined gentrification as a process driven by globalization, most especially the economic restructuring of the 1980s, when professionals and moneyed intellectuals moved into devalued historical neighborhoods, "attempting to distinguish themselves in space by imbuing their new place of residence with new status connotations."[43]

Uzun aligns herself with Christine Boyer by situating her study within the postmodern cultural shift of the 1970s and 1980s, when renewed interest in the past spurred historical preservation and the recycling of past architectural styles. She describes the aestheticization of urban life and the process by which the refurbishment of old houses became a lifestyle preference of a particular population. Uzun's surveys reveal that Kuzguncuk's gentrifiers form a cohort with consistent characteristics. They consist mostly of nuclear families, with lower numbers of children than their surrounding communities. The majority of household heads were born in urban environments, in contrast to the rural origins of their surrounding communities. A high percentage of the gentrifying group in Kuzguncuk has a university education, compared with residents of the nearby neighborhood of Icadiye, where the percentage of respondents with a high school education is equal to the percentage of respondents with a primary school education. Most households have both spouses employed in wage-earning labor outside the home, employed in prestigious and high-status occupations. Furthermore, nearly 70 percent of Uzun's respondents declared that their reason for choosing to live in Kuzguncuk was the scenic quality of its environment. Kuzguncuk's gentrifying population also watches more news programs and documentaries, reads more newspapers, and hires more outside help to do cleaning with much higher frequency than people in the surrounding area. Uzun concludes that Kuzguncuk's gentrifying population has lifestyle indicators that emphasize its "connection with the outside world and their engagement in more elite activities."[44] So, for the community of people moving to Kuzguncuk and restoring houses there, their choice of neighborhood is part of a lifestyle identity as a highly educated cultural elite.

Moving to Kuzguncuk for a lifestyle choice differs, of course, from the original aims of Cengiz Bektaş in restoring community by restoring neighborhood environments. Yet Kuzguncuk's gentrification landscape has come to symbolize an image. For one woman I interviewed, whom I will call Ebru, Kuzguncuk's neighborhood of set-apart houses was the defining factor for her move to the neighborhood in the mid-1990s. The desire for community was not as strong as the desire to live independently apart from the responsibilities and eyes of nearby neighbors. Ebru is an artist who works with film productions in Beyoğlu. She moved to Kuzguncuk in 1994, destroying and rebuilding in concrete a traditional wooden house she bought from a Greek Kuzguncuklu who now lives in Athens. She moved to Kuzguncuk to escape the crowds of the city. She confessed that she would have preferred to live in the more upscale neighborhood of Arnavutköy, but it was too expensive. She rejected the idea of living in a new gated community, although she acknowledged that these areas (called *sites*, borrowing a French term) are popular now because of their status. She argued that for artists like herself, gated communities are unattractive; she wanted an old house. She doesn't maintain relationships with her neighbors and said that while the elderly people who grew up in Kuzguncuk maintain these relationships, she works and goes out in the evening. She also said that these kinds of relationships would be invasive to her privacy. For Ebru, the quiet of Kuzguncuk made it desirable to live there, and her "old" house, a completely new house built of cement that boasts a historical facade, expresses her individual identity as an intellectual.[45]

As popularity of the initial restoration efforts drew more people to Kuzguncuk, Kuzguncuk's property values increased. The television show brought it to national observation and Kuzguncuk "became a model for the conservation of a valuable social and physical environment through modern democratic processes like participation, integration of local initiative, transparency, mediation, and cooperation." By 1999 the number of gentrified houses in Kuzguncuk had increased to about fifty.[46] As gentrification manifests the spatialization of class differentiation in Istanbul, Kuzguncuk has become a very popular real estate market.[47] Ali Akay speculates on the meaning of the mahalle for the city, reflecting that "mahalle is now a postmodern cultural concept, a sociocultural unit now based not on religious difference, as it was in the past, but on social-class difference."[48]

The Mahalle Is Fragmented

An article about Kuzguncuk that appeared in the *Turkish Daily News* in 2002, like the many other media representations of the mahalle in the early 2000s, romanticizes the close relationships in the neighborhood. The author writes that Kuzguncuk's historical fabric has been protected, that this place from the past actually represents an ideal future.

> As you walk the streets, there are your friends with whom you can exchange greetings . . . The sounds of the nightingale continually seep into the house via the window. To continually become lost in the peace of mind of being able to experience all these things, Can Yücel's lines spill from one's mouth: "I found a green branch in Kuzguncuk. To it I clung." Don't ask whether or not there is anyone who still experiences such happiness in Istanbul. Yes, there is. Those who live in Kuzguncuk. It is a place that contains the most beautiful things in the universal sense. Kuzguncuk housed all the religions and cultures within its structure . . . Here is a place in which lived people who could look with smiling faces on the world. Kuzguncuk is perhaps the last dinosaur in Istanbul whose historic fabric has been protected. It seems to lie there as the format for an ideal world, an ideal community for humanity.[49]

Yet while Kuzguncuk's landscape has come to represent an ideal of close and tolerant community life, the rips and tears of economic, social, and political difference within the neighborhood render impossible a truly cohesive mahalle collectivity. The gentrifying landscape of the mahalle is rent with the social tensions of its new geography.

In spite of the socioeconomic changes brought by restoration, in only one of hundreds of conversations did anyone ever openly criticize the representations of Kuzguncuk and its landscape as that of a true mahalle. A woman who worked on television film crews, who was familiar with the sets of various television programs and the recent mahalle series, opined that *Perihan Abla* was really the finest show of all the mahalle television serials, but that mahalles like Kuzguncuk are "fake" (she used this word in English). She said they are not real mahalles anymore, and the houses aren't real because they're torn down and rebuilt from the ground up. She also explained that the Jews, Armenians, and Christians aren't there anymore, and all the Bosphorus neighborhoods have been "lost" this way.

Cengiz Bektaş's efforts to improve community in Kuzguncuk and become part of the neighborhood have not met universal acceptance. One resident told me a story about what happened after "the Bektaş people" (as she refers to the people on Uryanizade Street) moved to Kuzguncuk.

This middle-aged neighbor was born in Kuzguncuk to parents of Black Sea regional origin and has always lived in modest economic circumstances. She said she hasn't talked to Bektaş since a conflict years ago over the issue of electricity brownouts caused by the computers and pottery kilns the "intellectuals" brought with them when they moved to Kuzguncuk. She gathered signatures from all the people in her mahalle (that is, everyone in her immediate surroundings) and petitioned the electric company to install a second electric generator for her part of the neighborhood that bordered Uryanizade Street. When they finally received permission and the electric company began installing the generator, she said the Bektaş people became agitated. They contacted people they knew in the planning ministry with claims that the generator would destroy the street's historical character and create environmental health problems. According to her story, my neighbor had been reading Bektaş's books, and so she went to him and asked, "After all this talk about komşuluk [neighborliness], why did you not come to us but instead go behind everyone who signed the petition to the people you knew in the government?" According to her, Bektaş denied being directly involved and didn't want to talk about it. She argued with some of the women who lived on that street and hasn't shared a greeting with any of them since. She is still angry.

Other women in the same group of neighbors as this resident referred to the people who live on Uryanizade Street as "the intellectuals." They were suspicious about their "meetings" and also complained about the rising rents.[50] One neighbor's corner store, a rented space, was threatened when the building went up for sale and the prospective buyer, an architect, planned to evict them to build his own office. As renters, the corner store family had few rights after the legal period of notification of change of ownership passed. In the end, a neighboring resident purchased the space for the corner store.

The unity of the neighbors on Uryanizade Street is sometimes perceived as exclusive, or unlike the old Kuzguncuklular. Members of the Kuzguncuk Neighborhood Association told me they conflicted with Cengiz Bektaş because he wanted to direct everything and wouldn't work with others' ideas. This resentment is likely related to the unintended socioeconomic and political effects of gentrification. The growth of the artist and architectural community has meant not only a rise in property values but the loss of older public spaces, such as local shops, and the opening of newer spaces that are exclusive and private, such as architecture studios. This gentrification, for all its claims to be preserving the landscape of the mahalle, brings with it a loss of communal mahalle spaces.

However, community in Kuzguncuk fails not only because of gentrification but simply because the same social and political divisions that fragment Istanbul society are also present in Kuzguncuk. I interviewed a member of the early artist community who has lived in Kuzguncuk for more than fifteen years and invested a lot of time in the neighborhood organization, trying to help the neighborhood. This person was angry about an article in a radical Islamist newspaper that claimed that intellectuals and artists (the article also accuses these people of alcoholism) had raised property values in Kuzguncuk, making it impossible for "good Turks" to be able to buy a house. Islamists are present in Kuzguncuk like they are throughout Istanbul, although their presence is denied in popular representations of the neighborhood.[51]

Mahalle Representations and the Living Mahalle

Kuzguncuk is taken so automatically in media representation to be the true theater for mahalle life that sometimes the actual neighborhood of Kuzguncuk and the ideas of mahalle embedded in collective memory become blurred. Media articles about the neighborhood reflect disappointment when the usual narrative of mahalle closeness is betrayed by a disappointing social reality. In a brief newspaper article in June 1999, for example, it was reported that the residents of the street on which *Perihan Abla* was filmed did not join the neighborhood-wide cleanup campaign. While "hundreds of Kuzguncuk residents joined hand in hand to clean their streets from end to end . . . those who live on the street that was the site of the *Perihan Abla* show were not seen all day." The Kuzguncuk residents said, "If Perran Kutman [the star of *Perihan Abla*] had seen this situation, she would have been very saddened."[52] Here the writer links the real social space of Kuzguncuk with the Kuzguncuk as it was portrayed in the television series, scolding the artists on Uryanizade Street for not joining in a cleanup campaign and for marking their social difference and separateness from other neighbors. In statements that Perran Kutman would be saddened as an individual to see the lack of neighborhood unity in Kuzguncuk, the television persona and real-life personality merge, reflecting the extent to which the real Kuzguncuk has become defined by its representation in the television series. A collage of photographs accompanies the article: a scene of a fictional group of neighbors from the television show is posited next to photographs of local residents sweeping streets. The real Kuzguncuk landscape and its representation meld together. Its real social tensions mar the image of neighborly cooperation so significant to its media representation.

This article is not the only example of disappointment over whether the real Kuzguncuk matches its romantic representation. An article in the book review section of the *Radikal* newspaper in March 2002 criticizes a new novel, Mehmet Ünver's *Kuzgun Bir Yaz*.[53] Ünver's Kuzguncuk describes a mischievous childhood, and the reviewer finds some of the descriptions to be too negative, as he quotes the book's back-cover summary: "The [book is colored] with descriptions of the novel's heroes fighting with children from other neighborhoods, or defecating in the backyards of unpleasant neighbors."[54] Other depictions in the book, however, have to do with describing the kinds of social change in the 1960s, including the author's reaction, as a child, to the behavior of his new rural migrant neighbors and their poverty and, to him, strange lifestyle. He wrote the book not only to specifically address the special aspects of life in Kuzguncuk as it had been in his childhood but to describe how these characteristics were lost, suddenly, with the huge influx of migrants. "Kuzguncuk changed a lot at that time, in front of the coffeehouses sat people I had never seen before."[55] It is these nonconformist descriptions of unpleasant social change that are smoothed over by the preferred nostalgic narrative.[56]

The Work of the Landscape

Kuzguncuk's contemporary landscape is one that recalls a particular historical memory and makes it seem incontestably real, even while the forms that signify this history are new and the landscape continues to be recreated in the image of collective memory. The persuasive nature of the landscape, its power, lies in the ways that its material form (whether synthetic, such as the kebap-restaurant-cum-bread-bakery of *Ekmek Teknesi*, or older, as in the case of the Armenian church) appears as objective evidence of the narrative represented by the landscape.

Uryanizade Street, the street with which Bektaş began his historical restoration movement, begins at the shoreline on the corner where the Armenian church sits. The church was built for the workers who were building the Beylerbeyi Palace. Some residents of Kuzguncuk suspect that the houses along Uryanizade Street belonged to these workers. If Uryanizade Street was the home of an Armenian artisan community, this is a past that has faded out of memory. These houses were made available for restoration in the 1980s in part because of the very cultural transformation of the neighborhood in which non-Muslims departed and their properties went up for sale. The nostalgic movement to "bring this history to light," such as in Cengiz Bektaş's works, does not actually work to bring out their history; the former residents of Uryanizade have slipped voicelessly into nostalgia. No one is in a better position to do research on the fate of the residents of Uryanizade Street (and even if they were not Armenian builders, they were most definitely a minority or foreign community) than the group of people who live there now. No one but current property owners, and their lawyers and real estate agents, can access the historical property deeds to examine the social histories of these buildings. An account of when and why the original owners left Kuzguncuk, or commemoration in the landscape of their history, would empower the historical voices of this community more than building restoration or nostalgic narratives.

Paradoxically, even as Cengiz Bektaş writes of the extended family of Kuzguncuk, the very movement he started has created a social divide in the neighborhood. Neighborhood relations are splitting further as the neighborhood comes to symbolize the collective memory mahalle of close relations and tolerance. The mahalle on the ground becomes more fragmented, divided, more like the conflicted postmodern city of Istanbul, as the mahalle in the imagination becomes more popular, more synthetic, more romantic, and perfect. However unintentionally, the narrative of peace and tolerance embedded in the landscape of collective memory mahalle works to support the nationalist historical narrative of Istanbul life in that it obscures the traumas and events that pushed out the minority communities. While the landscape acts like a real representation of history, it obscures the tensions of the past with a narrative of seamless community. The relationship between the landscape and its representation in Kuzguncuk structures social relations in terms of contesting claims to place. Why is it that the narrative of tolerance first promoted by Bektaş and then by others, which attempts to preserve and remember minority history and its idea of tolerance, rarely involves speaking directly to the nature of the change in Kuzguncuk's cultural geography? Because minority claims to place in the city, now, are denied.

Don Mitchell argues that the production of landscape "is a hugely mystified, ideological project that seeks to erase the very facts of its (quite social) production." The creation of a landscape that looks so real and historical signifies the nostalgic history embedded in the idea of collective memory. Yet "one of the purposes of landscape is to make a scene appear unworked, to make it appear fully natural. So a landscape is both a work and an erasure of work. It is therefore a social relation of labor, even as it is something that is labored over."[57] One of the purposes in creating the historical Kuzguncuk landscape by "restoring" (rebuilding) wooden houses is to make it appear as the natural theater of the collective memory of the mahalle. It is both a creation of the landscape and an erasure of the minority family history embedded in it. The connection between landscape creation and representation is significant when the historical landscape uses the "reality" of the images it signifies to obscure traumas of the past. Bringing the study of collective memory back to the production of space reveals a political economy in the creation of this collective memory: populations are displaced and new social groups with new identities articulate their claim to place with gentrification. The historical landscape of Kuzguncuk stands as evidence of the collective memory it signifies because of its material reality. The church and the mosque suggest that cosmopolitanism is alive and well in Kuzguncuk; what remains unspoken is the fact that the congregation of the nineteenth-century church is gone, replaced by the people who attend the twentieth-century mosque.

Maurice Halbwachs writes that a historical landscape serves an important function to soothe a disquiet society. A historical landscape, he states, has the capacity to suggest that, in spite of recent political violence, nothing has really changed for a city's residents:

> The districts within a city and the homes within a district have as fixed a location as any tree, rock, hill, or field. Hence the urban group has no impression of change so long as streets and buildings remain the same . . . The nation may be prone to the most violent upheavals. The citizen goes out, reads the news, and mingles with groups discussing

what has happened . . . Some inhabitants attack others, and political struggle ensues that reverberates throughout the country. But all these troubles take place in a familiar setting that appears totally unaffected. Might it not be the contrast between the impassive stones and such disturbances that convinces people that, after all, nothing has been lost, for walls and homes remain standing? Rather, the inhabitants pay disproportionate attention to what I have called the material aspect of the city. The great majority may well be more sensitive to a certain street being torn up, or a certain building or home being razed, than to the gravest national, political, or religious events. That is why upheavals may severely shake a society without altering the appearance of the city.[58]

This chapter examines how, in spite of its recent creation, the Kuzguncuk landscape appears as the historical and therefore natural theater of mahalle life, signified by the social memory, making the narrative appear to be true. The memory requires its symbols to give it authenticity, producing its landscape even while it erases history. What is the actual history behind the "historical" landscape? What are some of the minority perspectives that are obscured by the seeming truths of the nostalgic landscape? The next chapter examines the cultural politics of contesting historical memory in Kuzguncuk, with a focus on the Kuzguncuk market garden.

Garden Street
Narratives of Contested Place

At the start of my research, my relationship with the neighborhood was largely defined by the friendships I formed with core members of the Kuzguncuk Neighborhood Association. I only later realized the extent to which their perspectives on neighborhood issues were to shape my own understanding of Kuzguncuk's contemporary and historical cultural geography. People I met at weekly meetings and during other meetings where we shared tea or lunch explained why the garden was threatened by development and told me of their dreams of building an organic garden project and an environmental educational center, of restoring an environmental purpose to the space so it would remain green. "Our soul, our pride, our everything, our garden" was a slogan expressing their passion for the garden, printed on signs carried by children in the neighborhood of Kuzguncuk during protests in the year 2000. Members of the association asked me if I could help them apply for a grant for this project from the European Union. They were deeply involved in a range of urban issues and were excited by encouraging contacts they had made with organizations across the city, as well as with large international groups, such as the American Friends Service Committee and Habitat for Humanity. I was sympathetic to their cause because of their political identification as an environmentally active grassroots organization and their sincere belief that Kuzguncuk was a beautiful place and should be preserved, and because they showed me hospitality and respect from the beginning of my research.

The most active people in the neighborhood association were young adults born in Kuzguncuk to parents of Black Sea–origin migrant families who began arriving in the neighborhood in the late 1930s. They worked closely with the highly educated professionals and artists involved in the gentrification discussed in chapter 2. The organization drew even broader support from the neighborhood during signature campaigns. However, such a diverse social mix is uncommon in Istanbul. Not everyone supported or participated in association activities, including residents who were afraid of potential turbulent political activity; people who lived in peripheral, poorer settlements in the neighborhood; and the leadership of the local Greek and Armenian Orthodox churches and of the synagogue.[1] The association represents what are dominant visions of the past and future cultural geography of Kuzguncuk, in that these visions are most well known in and beyond Kuzguncuk and have been most influential in shaping its landscape. Association members expressed their attachment to Kuzguncuk with their activities to define its historical and future identity, and the garden was a powerful place for those involved in the movement to protect it.

I came to understand association members' actions as efforts to articulate their identities in terms of their relationship to Kuzguncuk as a place. My approach to thinking about place in this way is grounded in the cultural geographic literature that has theorized the coconstitutive nature of place and identity. Place, as a location endowed with cultural and social meaning—and narrative has a crucial role in this process—becomes significant as a cohering space for cultural politics that sustain or challenge power relations.[2] Cultural and political identities are articulated as debates over the character, nature, or visions of place.[3] In Kuzguncuk, and with particular respect to the market garden discussed in this chapter, narratives of this place's past and future are proxies through which residents stake competing claims to place in the neighborhood.

As this chapter demonstrates, the market garden is a contested place. The various visions of its pasts and futures reveal competing claims to place in the mahalle that inhere in the cultural politics of nationalism and identity as they relate to the right to property and the histories of non-Muslim residents in twentieth-century Istanbul. Debates over place thus employ the terms that inscribe belonging to or exclusion from the nation, as they protect or threaten the right to own and determine the future of property, the most geographic expression of belonging to the nation, the right to its territory. The Turkish state confiscated the garden in 1977 from a Greek family in an undisputable example of illegal dispossession of private property by the Turkish Ministry of Foundations. Dimitria Teyze ("Aunt Dimitria") is the last remaining member and inheritor in Istanbul of the Greek family who owned the garden.[4] For her, her family's link to the garden is proof of her identity as a real Kuzguncuklu. It also represents, however, her identity as an Istanbul Rum and a non-Muslim minority who was dispossessed through the larger political processes through which the state sustains an identity for Turkey as ethnically Turkish and Muslim and excludes local Greek Orthodox residents.

Throughout this chapter I read the *bostan* (market garden) as a complex and meaningful place of emotion and memory. Narratives of this place serve in different ways as identity markers for groups of people who share the same neighborhood space but stake differing and sometimes oppositional claims to being Kuzguncuklu. I begin with a description of the struggle of the neighborhood association to protect the historical market garden from development and examine the narratives used to endow the garden with particular cultural meanings. I then introduce Dimitria Teyze and her story to reveal the ways in which the nostalgic narrative of the garden, like the nostalgic narrative of Kuzguncuk introduced in chapter 2, obscures tensions over claims to place, particularly as they relate to minority rights to property and place-based identity. What emerges is that the residents involved with the association, the Ministry of Foundations, the man who tried to develop the property, and the family that used to own the garden do not revolve in separate social or political spheres but share the concern to control the future of a parcel of land and, in this way, confront each other through their relationships to this place.

Saving the Market Garden

Kuzguncuk's historical market garden lies in the heart of the neighborhood. This garden is remembered fondly by residents for its fresh fruits and vegetables and for its owner, Ilya, whose Greek name evokes a time when Greeks, Jews, and Armenians had a significant presence in Kuzguncuk. During the 1980s the garden was abandoned for a time, and residents picked figs and allowed their children to play. In practice, its status was in limbo, like many of the other Ministry of Foundations–owned properties previously belonging to minority families. It suffered the fate of similar spaces and was sometimes used for unregulated purposes, such as the seasonal slaughter of animals for the sacrifice feast or for dumping trash. In retrospect, however, it was valued by residents who treasured the open, quiet, green space in their neighborhood's center.

Opposition to the planned development of the garden began in 1992 when the Ministry of Foundations rented it with a ten-year lease to Mehmet Haberal, the director and owner of the Turkish Organ Transplant and Burn Treatment Foundation. Haberal immediately announced plans to build a private dialysis center on the property. One resident told me about a confrontation she had with him while she was walking in the garden and he was there assessing the space. She told him they wanted to keep the garden green; he told her they were mere women who couldn't stop him from building the hospital no matter how they tried. In mobilizing to prevent his plans, residents had to raise awareness of the problem of the potential illegal building in the neighborhood and in the city and to identify their options for action. They worked to persuade other residents that the stakes were high enough to be worth risking political action. They argued the hospital would create poisonous air pollution, physical waste, and traffic congestion and also crowd the neighborhood center. In a door-to-door campaign they collected more than a thousand signatures from local residents who demanded that the building project be stopped. The core group of activists (the initial activists were local and highly educated foreign-born professionals) defined specific roles to be managed by people who had useful or particular skills. One resident who lived close to the garden watched it daily and informed others immediately of any activity. A local writer connected to the press used all of her contacts to get articles about the issue published as widely as possible. Another resident wrote dozens of official letters to request action from local and national governmental bodies.

One of the most important avenues pursued by the neighborhood association involved research into the legal status of the garden. Residents worked together to compile a file about the history of the garden and its legal status. One person obtained a copy of the original property deed and researched its history and described in detail how it was acquired by the Ministry of Foundations. Local architects obtained a map of the Bosphorus plan that marks the garden as an agricultural area (*tarım alanı*) and thus protected by the Culture and Nature Preservation Committee as a historical green area unavailable for development. Another resident lawyer obtained a copy of the 2960 Bosphorus Law, stating that all green sites along the Bosphorus are protected from new building.[5] Residents also discovered that, according to building codes, the space was too small for development. Furthermore, the original rental contract between the ministry and Haberal stipulated that the garden was rented as a vacant lot to be used as a vacant lot, and the purpose of the lot to be used for building was not specified.[6]

By 2000 local residents had, through official requests as well as media exposure, sufficiently pressured Haberal regarding the dialysis center project that he changed his tactics, deciding instead to start planning a private school for the site.[7] The association consolidated their arguments against any development in a lawsuit filed against the Bosphorus Planning Bureau because the bureau changed the Bosphorus Master Plan to approve a school and granted a building permit, in spite of the multiple illegalities of such a decision. The Kuzguncuk Neighborhood Association sent a copy of the file they created to all the leaders of local political parties and to the local and national offices of administration responsible for the site. Because Haberal's lease started in 1992 and was good for ten years, the association prepared for the window of opportunity that would open when his lease would end in February 2002. In 2001 they founded a cooperative, which has a different legal status than an association, for the purpose of potentially renting the garden for an organic farming and community education project.

In 2000 the association held a neighborhood festival to raise awareness for their cause. They organized music and food and invited people from other neighborhood associations in Istanbul as well as friends and media from all over the city. Newspaper and magazine articles showed photographs of angry residents with protest signs ("Keep our garden green!" "The garden belongs to the people of Kuzguncuk!"). They experienced a huge, although tenuous, victory in 2002 when Haberal decided to give up his lease. The association organized a party that drew more than two hundred people to the garden for music, picnicking, and celebration.

The Kuzguncuk Neighborhood Association wanted to rent the garden, but the Ministry of Foundations raised the rent to 2 milyar TL, an exaggerated price of about 1,400 U.S. dollars per month. The association suspected it was set deliberately high and argued that because it was marked as an agricultural site on the Bosphorus Plan, the price must be accessible to someone who would use it for such a purpose. It was rented to a landscaping company. Their presence in the garden is the best possible compromise for the Kuzguncuk Neighborhood Association. The association is proud of its victory, but they must remain vigilant. Their lawsuit against the planning board for approving the building of a school has not yet reached a conclusion. Should the landscape company decide to leave the property, the association will have to find another green tenant. There is no official legal decision the association can rely on to preempt illegal development in the future. Ongoing success in keeping the garden green depends on the association members. Their victory is an excellent and unusual example of how a small neighborhood association can fight irregular building practices in Istanbul.

During their struggle, the Kuzguncuk Neighborhood Association became known as among the most politically active of Istanbul's neighborhood organizations, along with the Arnavutköy Neighborhood Initiative, which works to prevent the building of a third Bosphorus bridge that would destroy their neighborhood, and the Human Settlements Association, a group that aimed to form a network to share information among new civil society organizations concerned with urban issues.[8] After the August 1999 earthquake, local political activity centered on a sense of civil responsibility to preserve, protect, and inform city residents of their rights to a safe environment. Disaster preparedness became an important issue for the Kuzguncuk Neighborhood Association, and with support from the American Friends Service Committee, they started gathering emergency supplies and educating residents on mitigating the effects of disaster. When they formed a disaster plan, one of the arguments for not building on the

Figure 4. "The garden belongs to the people of Kuzguncuk!" Author's photo.

garden became the need to preserve an open space where the community could gather to distribute medical aid, information, and supplies in the event of a future earthquake. In a press release, the association linked this need back to the problem of the corrupt system: "Last year, we saw how few available places there are to gather in the event of an earthquake . . . Before even one year has passed since the recent huge earthquake disaster, another green space under protection along the Bosphorus came under scrutiny. First as a 'cheap open area' and then as a 'private school' this mentality was forced on us."[9] Kuzguncuk Neighborhood Association members felt that protecting Kuzguncuk was their collective responsibility and acted out of a sense of their own agency in determining, and holding accountability for, Istanbul's future.

The post-earthquake civil society movement in Istanbul, which began in August 1999, was a fragile but important moment of change in which local residents began to feel safe in their new convictions that they had the right to protect their environments. They were also angry at the corrupt construction and building practices that caused such extensive earthquake damage. The garden issue for the Kuzguncuk Neighborhood Association also concerned corruption, because throughout the ten years of his lease,

Haberal's actions marked him as powerfully connected politically and above normal legal and bureaucratic procedures.

Kuzguncuk residents have never been shy about speaking out regarding their suspicions of political connections behind the building project. When bulldozers entered the garden to test the soil for the foundation of the building, citizens gathered and protested, crying as they chanted a rhyme written by famous resident poet Can Yücel, "The cows have entered the garden."[10] The poem appeared in a newspaper essay in which Yücel accuses the government of being undemocratic and despotic, making direct associations between government leaders and illegal profiteering. In another essay regarding corruption and the struggle for the garden, Kuzguncuk resident and Boğaziçi University professor Uğur Tandoğan bitterly laments the fact that such a beautiful green space will likely be destroyed because Turkey's laws are not enforced. He says soon the garden will be gone, and "don't ask why, because in the words of Güngör Uras, 'brother, this is Turkey.'"[11] His tone of frustration represents the widespread and general hopelessness in Istanbul regarding the role of political and economic corruption in ruining the city by destroying the system that is supposed to prevent the future loss of historical or green spaces:

> Congratulations. We ate Istanbul and finished its greens. We made Istanbul a cement city. Those who go to civilized countries and cities know it. In those cities, the color that strikes the eye most is green. But in our country, green causes an allergy . . . In our country, it cannot be said that those in the municipality and other foundations charged with protecting these spaces are appropriately using the laws founded to protect our areas of cultural and historical value. If those concerned with this job of protecting had done their jobs in the past, Istanbul would not be in this situation today.[12]

Urbanization, Nostalgia, and the Garden

The frustration with corruption and unplanned urbanization underlying the Kuzguncuk movement was often expressed with nostalgic memories of the past and a vision for a better future. An article in *Nokta* magazine reported that Kuzguncuk residents "watched how cement masses surrounded Istanbul's green and treed places with sadness. Now they don't want the redbud trees in their garden covered with cement."[13] The garden became a symbol of what was lost for Istanbul and what will be lost for Kuzguncuk should the garden be developed. The garden became a store of Kuzguncuk's memories. "Now, inside this treasure chest, in our days, Ilya's garden, which is as valuable as gold with all its characteristics, will shortly be claimed with screams of panic that nothing will remain anywhere. Furthermore, our [places] we will claim, the places we are afraid of losing, our values, our culture, with the loss of our memories . . . Ilya's garden has become a symbol of all of this."[14]

Along with the longing for the greenness of Istanbul's past was a deep nostalgia for a time of closeness and familiarity in small neighborhoods, when everyone knew everyone else, the time when the neighborhood was a tolerant multiethnic space. The garden became a symbol for the good old days and the movement to protect it came from a desire to carry the neighborhood's past culture into the future. The discourse surrounding the struggle transformed the garden from a green space into a beloved place filled with memories. A local youth is quoted in a newspaper article on the garden issue:

> All of our childhoods were spent in this garden. It was a playground
> for all of us. It was until recently . . . until the hospital's influence,
> and a fence was put around it . . . The garden is Kuzguncuk's lungs.
> Kuzguncuk takes its breath from it. They should donate the garden to
> us . . . Kuzguncuk has a warm neighborhood quality to it. This quality
> is lost in Istanbul now. All of my friends here are friends of mine
> from childhood. We grew up on the same streets, studied at the same
> schools. The corner store grocer, the butcher, the vegetable seller, the
> driver, the painter, the mover, the doctor, the teacher . . . we are like
> a family here. Building a hospital will destroy this special quality in
> Kuzguncuk. How sad![15]

This boy identifies himself as Kuzguncuklu by describing himself as part of the extended family of the mahalle. The garden, as a place, carries the body of this family—the garden is its lungs; the garden gives it life. In framing the garden this way he inscribes his own identity as Kuzguncuklu and the garden as an inseparable part of the landscape to which he belongs.

Uğur Yücel, the famous comedy actor and television series director who was born in Kuzguncuk and who appeared in chapter 2, explains, "Kuzguncuk is one of the most important places along the Bosphorus. This area carries very huge meanings for me. If a hospital is built here, people can't walk around on the streets. In the old days they used to call this place 'Little Paris.' This place's trees and flowers, in short, all of its values, must be protected."[16] The Web site of the Kuzguncuk Neighborhood Association passionately laments the destruction of Istanbul's places and vows not to let this happen in their neighborhood:

> Those before us lost their generations, their open spaces, and didn't make a noise. Their pines, sycamores, redbuds were cut down, and they didn't make a noise. They were buried in cement masses without any aesthetic or architectural value, and they didn't make a noise. The beautiful buildings were burned and destroyed, and they didn't make a noise. The identity of their streets was lost, and they didn't raise their voices. But we, whatever the cost of our last stand, we have decided to protect our garden and never to submit.[17]

Their resistance throughout was vigilant and staked a passionate claim to the future of their place.

Markedly absent from the garden struggle, however, were the remaining non-Muslims of Kuzguncuk. While they are small in number, they are linked to the larger and active groups of Greek and Jewish Kuzguncuklu families who moved out of the neighborhood to other parts of Istanbul. These people return to the neighborhood on weekends to attend services in its church and synagogue. Minority communities are interested in Kuzguncuk's past: during my research, the Kuzguncuk synagogue together with the larger Istanbul Jewish community was collecting materials to celebrate Kuzguncuk's history with a festival in the neighborhood. However, as far as the garden is concerned, Kuzguncuk's remaining Jews and Greeks were not involved in the association's movement to protect it, nor did they otherwise become active regarding this issue. They also were not involved in creating or restoring other elements of the contemporary landscape of Kuzguncuk, aside from restoring and protecting its religious buildings, and they are not moving back to Kuzguncuk to buy and restore historical houses. While the churches and synagogue have organized congregations, they do not affiliate themselves with the Kuzguncuk Neighborhood Association, even though they share some similar aims, such as earthquake preparedness.[18] In what seems like a paradox, the movement to preserve Kuzguncuk's historical green space relies on nostalgia for the multiethnic, greener past, and yet those involved in the movement and who publicly remember this past are Kuzguncuk's newer, Muslim Turkish residents, not its minorities.

Dimitria Teyze's Claims to Place

The very day I heard the news that Haberal had given up his lease on the garden, a friend brought me to our arranged interview with Dimitria Teyze. As we rode the ferry across the Bosphorus I told my friend about my excitement for the neighborhood association. My friend's only reaction was to raise her eyebrows in a way that let me know she wasn't sharing my enthusiasm. Then she prepared me for our meeting and told me that although Dimitria Teyze no longer lives in Kuzguncuk, she is the last descendant living in Turkey of the family that used to own the Kuzguncuk garden.

I met Dimitria Teyze in her apartment on the European side and at the home of our mutual friend several times during the spring and summer of 2002. Meeting Dimitria Teyze made me realize how deeply I had overstepped my own critical boundary as a fieldworker during the first three months of my research regarding the community I studied; our conversations opened my eyes to the complexity of perspectives and histories involved in representations of Kuzguncuk, which became the focus of my questions over the next several months. The difference between Dimitria Teyze's relationship to the garden and that of the Kuzguncuk community that fought to protect it resonated throughout my entire project as it became clear that I had unconsciously begun to share in a cause that could potentially threaten my research perspective. I had forgotten how to be the researcher in favor of being a friend, association member, or neighbor, all roles I had come to play every day so well they felt like my own clothes. Encountering Dimitria Teyze was disturbing and exhilarating because she lives so deeply in the very past discussed and remembered by others—the past that I, too, had come to imagine.

Dimitria Teyze's house is full of her family's beloved but broken inheritance. A large mirrored cabinet displays cracked goblets of shimmery glass, and worn velvet chairs wait next to little tables draped with bits of rusty handworked lace. Her small rooms are stuffed to the ceiling with grand, old furniture that evokes the past civility of the large airy houses along the Bosphorus for which they were made. In her proper Istanbullu accent, Dimitria Teyze says, "*yavrum* (darling), eat," as she brings handmade pastries to the table. She serves us Turkish coffee together with almond liqueur after dinner and sits just long enough to smoke a cigarette and read my coffee fortune. She cooks her labor-intensive, old-fashioned foods in an old plug-in oven that was a modern convenience when most women were sending their pastries to the local neighborhood oven. Although Dimitria Teyze's family is generations-old Kuzguncuklu, they no longer live there. Her identity is bound up with her attachment to her family's historical property; as such, it is rooted in the past.

The dominant topic of conversation every time we met was the material, financial, and emotional loss experienced by her family as Istanbullu Rum of former great wealth who were tragically dispossessed. Dimitria Teyze's family once owned several small dairy farms and market gardens. They had a successful business shipping their products to the old city of Istanbul. Their wealth included mansions in several neighborhoods on the Asian side, including in Üsküdar, Salacak, Çengelköy, and Kuzguncuk. By the time we met, her family had lost nearly all of its property. Dimitria Teyze's claims that they were all taken illegally by the Turkish state may be true. At the very least, the property deed of the garden in Kuzguncuk provides evidence of one such illegal confiscation. Dimitria Teyze resents the neighborhood association's claim to the garden, which, she says, rightfully belongs to her family.

Dimitria Teyze had a brief relationship with the neighborhood association several years before I met her. One member of the association tried to help her with legal research to build a lawsuit to reclaim her property. In our interview, he explained that he initially hoped to assist her in reclaiming it from the Ministry of Foundations and, in this way, perhaps help the association prevent its illegal development. According to him, she wouldn't trust him, thinking he wanted to get the property away from her. Another association member told me separately that he wasn't aware of anyone from the garden family ever coming forward and that the neighborhood association hoped the family never would, because if the family reclaimed ownership they could interfere with the association's plans for the garden. Dimitria Teyze herself told me, however, that she wasn't on speaking terms with people at the association anymore because they had wronged her. When I first encountered the situation in fieldwork I naively assumed that she and the association might be able to accomplish something mutually beneficial if they shared efforts. It became obvious that their claims to the garden are incompatible.

While Dimitria Teyze told me about the market garden and her family's history there, she never showed me any documentation about it. My sources for the documents that constitute evidence of the garden's complex history as property came from the people affiliated with the association's campaign to prevent it from being developed.[19] Dimitria Teyze was open with me about her feelings about the property and her understanding of what happened to it. However, although she showed me very briefly that she had a similar deed to another property and took me to a house in another mahalle that her family had lost, she was reticent to share official documents regarding the garden with me as a researcher.[20] After she met with the lawyer in Kuzguncuk, her information became accessible to the association; copies of the file were sent to various official bodies as part of the association's lawsuit and a newspaper article about the property was published in *Radikal*.[21] In writing about the history of the property here, I rely on the documents that were compiled for the association's lawsuit and on my conversations with people who were involved with it, as well as on the newspaper article, which published in very specific detail the property's family history before it was taken by the Ministry of Foundations. The ways in which I myself came to this evidence illustrate the ways in which the family and the association encountered each other through this place, and the ways in which they moved away from that encounter because of their differing stakes in the eventual future outcome of the property.

This is what happened: The Kuzguncuk market garden once belonged to two Greek Orthodox families that were related by marriage. The property was parceled into nine shares, and eight of them passed at unknown times under unclear legal circumstances to the Ministry of Foundations.[22] Information in the documents from the association suggests that perhaps some of it was lost because of unpaid debt, perhaps in inheritance taxes. The last share of the garden passed to the Ministry of Foundations in 1977, and the plot became the property of the state. The last family gardener to own a share died in 1951. After his death, the share should have passed to his son, who continued to work the garden until his own death in 1984. But the property share was not transferred as it should have been, and in 1977 the Ministry of Foundations appropriated it, using a law that cites the abandonment of property.[23] The property was never abandoned, however, as the man and his son both worked on the garden until their deaths. The transfer of the property to the Ministry of Foundations was inappropriate and illegal for two reasons. First, the transfer was based on its having been abandoned, although the inheritor of the last property share never left the neighborhood. Second, according to a lawyer with experience in property law who helped me understand the language in the deed, this law's original purpose was to regulate the transfer of Armenian properties "abandoned" after the massacre of 1915 and was never intended to be used in transfers of Greek properties in Istanbul in the 1970s.[24] Furthermore, even if it had been abandoned, minority properties normally passed to the Treasury: this property mysteriously passed to the Foundations Ministry. And finally, the association's efforts to locate a legal ruling whereby the property formally passed to the Foundations Ministry revealed an absence of such a ruling; the ways in which it happened remain unclear. By the time the property was rented in 1992 its status and history were obscured by the complicated and corrupt transactions concerning the deed, rendering the potential success of a lawsuit to reclaim it unlikely. This specific case suggests that non-Muslim minority families lost properties in various stages and in various ways and at times other than the known instances of the 1942–43 Wealth Tax or the abandonment of property after the 1964 deportations. Their losses should be viewed as having taken place within this larger political context, as that is how minorities themselves view these circumstances.[25] Dimitria Teyze's own narrative suggests that this is how the place has become meaningful for her—as evidence of her status as a minority.

The very first day we met, Dimitria Teyze was excited by my interest in Kuzguncuk and told me she was going to prepare a report for me about her family and Kuzguncuk's history. Months later, she gave me a booklet, the kind of folded and stapled booklet used to take university exams, filled with handwritten information she collected by talking with elderly relatives, which she translated from Greek into Turkish for me. Her narrative starts with a description of what is known about the neighborhood's very distant past and explanations for how it earned its name. It continues with a history of its churches and well-known people and ends with her own family and the history of her grandmother. For Dimitria Teyze, Kuzguncuk's history is the history of herself and her family. Her identity is still powerfully bound to the neighborhood, but it is now tempered by her physical displacement from the neighborhood to which she rarely returns (although it is only a forty-minute bus and boat trip from her home). For Dimitria Teyze, Kuzguncuk is lost. The loss is made more painful because of the contrast between her personal continued financial failures and the increase of wealth in the neighborhood, brought by the people who have adopted her family's place as their own, investing in and beautifying it.

Dimitria Teyze writes what happened to the Greeks:

> ———'s daughter's gardens are lost. A Turkish family lives in her house now. They have a property deed to it in their hands, but it's not known how they obtained it . . . The house across from the Greek church is run as a restaurant now and owned by the mafia . . . Turkey's laws transferred Greek property to Turkish hands, and with their leaving and forced migration, Kuzguncuklu Rum properties were lost in various ways in 1944, 1955, and in the Cyprus events of 1964.

Her words about what happened to the Greek community in Kuzguncuk speak to the larger history of the city. Her place in this history is fundamental to her construction of her own identity.

In the mental map of Kuzguncuk I asked her to draw on the first day we met, she labeled the garden, "Yeşil Bostan ——— Ailesine Ait" (Green Garden Belonging to the ——— Family). She marked the main street of Kuzguncuk, Icadiye Caddesi, as Icadiye Deresi (Icadiye Creek) and showed the bridges that used to cross the stream when it flowed down and divided the main street—Icadiye Creek was paved over and the stream rerouted under the main street several decades ago. At either end of each bridge were meyhanes, eating establishments owned by Rum, where alcohol was served. They do not exist in Kuzguncuk today. She also marked, with domes and crosses, the locations of the Armenian and Greek Orthodox churches and put a star to perhaps represent the main synagogue, although it is not in what would be the correct relative location. At the top and center of the map, she inscribed her family name, identifying the garden as a central place in Kuzguncuk with an identity personal to her family. Her mental map of Kuzguncuk illustrates the characteristics of a place that exists in her memory, not the place that exists today.

Dimitria Teyze's identification with place is not only historical but also dependent on her *absence* from contemporary Kuzguncuk. She has almost no lived relationship with Kuzguncuk now. In marked contrast, the Black Sea migrants (some of whom are core members of the association) identify with Kuzguncuk through a living relationship to its present and by having *witnessed* its social transformation.

Competing Narratives of Place and Identity

In what may appear as a paradox, Black Sea Kuzguncuk residents, those Muslims whose families migrated to Kuzguncuk in the very late thirties and early forties, identify themselves as real Kuzguncuklu, with their memories of sharing the neighborhood with the non-Muslim minorities before they emigrated. As I discuss in the next chapter, they also claim that those who came after them are the outsiders, the ones who ruined the neighborhood's traditional tolerant and multiethnic culture, although the cultural geographic transformation of the mahalle indeed began with the arrival of the earliest rural migrants. The interactions between Dimitria Teyze and Black Sea Kuzguncuklu residents I observed were among the neighbors we both visited at the home of our mutual friend.

Kuzguncuk's Black Sea community remembers living among minorities, although the memories are located in the past and never linked to the present with stories of the minorities' departure. Unlike Dimitria Teyze, for whom the departure from the neighborhood is the primary theme in her narratives of Kuzguncuk, for contemporary Black Sea–origin residents the departure is over and never discussed in detail. Though memories of living with past neighbors are clear, the circumstances of their departure remain clouded in ambiguity. Neslihan Abla, a neighbor who was born in Kuzguncuk to a Black Sea family in the 1950s, says that the later rural migrants "took all the Greeks' houses." She remembers knowing Greek and Jewish adults as a child, and her mother talks freely about the neighborly relations she shared with minority neighbors. The leaving, though, is eclipsed and invisible in the narrative. The words of this middle-aged Muslim woman are typical of Muslim narratives of this history: "*Bir den biri gittiler,*" meaning "all of a sudden, they left." When I asked her to tell me more about what happened, she changed the subject. As another longtime resident told me in answer to the same question, "It's known but never discussed."

Dimitria Teyze's opinions that the people in the neighborhood association have no right to her garden, that they are all occupying homes that really belong to her people, legitimize her claim to place as a real Kuzguncuklu. However, this claim is challenged when she interacts with people of Kuzguncuk's Black Sea migrant community. One hot July evening I went to Zeynep's house to play a tile game called *okey*. Zeynep's middle-aged neighbors have Black Sea regional origins and were born in Kuzguncuk. They represent the community of people who witnessed Kuzguncuk's transformation and who have inherited its history as the old-timers. Neslihan Abla came downstairs to play with us when Dimitria Teyze arrived unexpectedly and agreed to be our fourth player. Dimitria Teyze and Neslihan Abla are strong personalities who share a mutual dislike of each other. The game involves taking and discarding a tile on each turn, slapping it down on the corner in a pass to the player on the right. Dimitria Teyze and Neslihan Abla sat next to each other, and as Dimitria Teyze passed tiles to Neslihan Abla, she spat on each one to wish her bad luck, a move made in jest but with bitterness that affected our game. Neslihan Abla tried to open a conversation with Dimitria Teyze and said, "I saw your house in Çengelköy, the furniture still inside. Are you going to be able to get it?" Dimitria Teyze explained they are working with a lawyer to rescind the illegal sale done through "a mafia deal." A few turns passed; tiles smacked on the table.

Neslihan Abla spoke up again, asking about the condition of the house and its history, concluding that "it was really wrong, what happened to the property of the non-Muslims." Dimitria Teyze said that it happened a lot, to all of them. The game moved on, some other conversation ended, and then Neslihan Abla said, "Well, they were all minorities [she used an old-fashioned word *ekaliyet*], and there aren't any left." Dimitria Teyze said, "Yes, there are." Zeynep and I exchanged glances over the tension in the game and the conversation.

Neslihan Abla said, "They're all in Maslak and in other places on the other side [of Istanbul]." Dimitria Teyze replied, "There are lots of them left." Neslihan Abla said, "Well, they all left Kuzguncuk; they're not *here* anymore; there aren't any *ekaliyet* left in Kuzguncuk is what I'm saying," and Dimitria Teyze retorted, "Well, if you'd seen the 6–7 September events [the infamous antiminority riots], you'd have left too!" Neslihan Abla said, "I know, they explained it to us." Silence fell with tense faces and Dimitria Teyze got to her feet and went out the door.

For Neslihan Abla, the minority life of the neighborhood is a thing of the past; it's gone. For Dimitria Teyze, it's still a living issue. There are, indeed, a handful of Greek families living in Kuzguncuk and many more who now live in other parts of Istanbul. Neslihan Abla identifies herself as Kuzguncuklu by acknowledging the past and sharing the witnessing of it by saying, "I know, they explained it to us," meaning her mother and her older neighbors. But Dimitria Teyze sees herself as the real Kuzguncuklu because her community actually experienced the events of 1955 and the deportation of 1964 and they continue to experience the effects of those events.

When Dimitria Teyze visited another time, she met Neslihan Abla again, this time with Neslihan Abla's mother, Emine Teyze, who saw that Dimitria Teyze was one of the old community. She started like her daughter did before, trying to empathize as a fellow Kuzguncuklu by saying, "When all those people left, so did the beauty of Kuzguncuk." They walked down memory lane together, although they hadn't met before, and Emine Teyze asked if Dimitria Teyze remembered Marko who sold vegetables. She talked about Ispiro's garden and Dimitria Teyze explained it was once her family's. They talked about an elderly neighbor whose father was Turkish but who had an Armenian mother, and about Rebeka and the other Jewish neighbors and their holidays, and how in general the olden days were so beautiful with wonderful neighbors and now nothing is left. Interestingly, though, Emine Teyze and Neslihan Abla kept supplying the names and memories and Dimitria Teyze kept saying, "That sounds familiar, but I don't really remember."

In this encounter, Emine Teyze was the real Kuzguncuklu. Dimitria Teyze left Kuzguncuk as a child and grew up in other parts of the city. With Emine Teyze she referred to herself as Çengelköylu and Beylerbeyli, from places where she had lived for periods of her life. Her identity as the real Kuzguncuklu she portrayed to me in her written narrative shifted in this context to being more specifically of a Kuzguncuklu family but of other neighborhoods. The conversation reflected a competition for authority of who really knows the past. Emine Teyze's naming all the old neighbors she really remembers and misses is an articulation of a lived identity as Kuzguncuklu, versus Dimitria Teyze's identity, which is related to family and the property of generations. I was struck, as I was on so many other occasions, by how the story remembering of the good old days revolves around the citing and describing of the non-Muslim people by name, as if their names carry the identity of Kuzguncuk as it was in the past, as if the names are the stuff of its history, even for the Black Sea community.

For the Black Sea community, Kuzguncuk is a home place, and their witnessing of the past and ability to remember its history places them in Kuzguncuk, making them Kuzguncuklu. Their stories of neighborhood history are part of their own personal histories. During a conversation with a friend called Reyhan, I asked her why was it that the Black Sea people came to Kuzguncuk and not another neighborhood, like Çengelköy for example. Her father poked his head out from another room to say that 90 percent of them came here because *we* came here. His own father came here because there was someone they knew who'd come to Kuzguncuk on holiday and liked it and bought a place. His father's friend saw the house for sale that his own father eventually bought. After that, they helped others come, and so they used to know everyone in the entire neighborhood. But he said, now, "we don't know the newcomers, and they don't know us." They distinguish themselves as the Kuzguncuk Black Sea community pioneers, different from later migrants, asserting their own primary claim to place in Kuzguncuk.

Forming Landscapes and Attachments to Place

The garden in Kuzguncuk is a rich place, a piece of the neighborhood landscape full of meaning for Kuzguncuklular. Its history makes it worth preserving in the eyes of the Kuzguncuk Neighborhood Association, who claim it for their future in the neighborhood. Its history also anchors the identity of Dimitria Teyze, who claims to be its rightful owner. As Doreen Massey argues,

> The past of a place is as open to a multiplicity of readings as is the present. Moreover, the claims and counter-claims about the present character of a place depend in almost all cases on particular, rival,

interpretations of its past . . . What are at issue are competing histories of the present, wielded as arguments over what should be the future.[26]

The contesting narratives of place, of contemporary and past Kuzguncuklu people, reveal tension concerning interpretations of its history and the future of the neighborhood. Places are created by layers of actions over time and by the telling of narratives that endow them with emotion, memory, and vision. The narratives and stories association members tell that endow the market garden with meaning as a valuable green space and a remnant of Kuzguncuk's multiethnic history are as valuable as Dimitria Teyze's mental map. Dimitria Teyze's story is silenced, however, while nostalgic media representations of the garden gain currency because they resonate with the nostalgia for Kuzguncuk's past that circulates in the larger cultural sphere. In chapter 2, I examine how the nostalgic image is constructed and given authority by the material cultural landscape. In this chapter, I explore how this narrative is contested by another, rarely told.

In his play dramatizing Kuzguncuk's changing social life, Güngör Dilmen gives silenced perspectives a voice on the stage. A Greek character, Saranda, confronts Cengiz Bektaş regarding his book *Hoşgörünün Öteki Adı: Kuzguncuk* (The Other Name for Tolerance: Kuzguncuk).

SARANDA: Is tolerance going to be shown to me as well?
BEKTAŞ: Of course, Saranda Bey!
SARANDA: Okay, but please tell me, what thing of mine are you going
    to tolerate? I go back and forth from my house and my workplace,
    and no one notices my presence. What of mine do they tolerate?
    What do they endure? The startling sounds of the bells ringing
    in the morning at eight, or at five in the evening? At a baptism, a
    wedding—what a joke! Even the bells that ring when someone dies
    have thinned out. Excuse me, but the tolerance should be coming
    from us.[27]

The work of Kuzguncuk's nostalgic mahalle landscape is to perpetuate a way of seeing that conforms to Turkish nationalism and imagines no place for non-Muslim minorities in contemporary space. Nostalgia relegates Greeks, Jews, and Armenians to history, if at all, and elides their current claims to place that remain unresolved. Locally, in Kuzguncuk, visions of the past and future of the market garden—the meanings it has come to embody as a place—jump scales as local claims to place are conditioned by, and speak to, decisions of state bodies and the ideologies they sustain. It is through the lived local place that nationalist ideology comes to have meaning for identity as well as for interethnic social relationships in everyday urban life. In the next chapter, I explore place narratives from a diversity of perspectives as they converge on the main street of Kuzguncuk, the place of remembered shared multiethnic celebrations and neighborly relations and the site of the anti-Greek riots of 6–7 September 1955.

4 Icadiye Street
Nostalgia for Home, before History

A profound sense of loss underlies place narratives of Kuzguncuk.
In former Kuzguncuk resident Zakire Büyükfırat's memoir, for example,
the author describes her disappointment that Kuzguncuk has lost the most
important qualities that, for her, made it a special place. The landscape
embodies both the place's past as well as the writer's feelings of loss surrounding the fact that this past is a place to which she cannot return:

> The magnolia tree in front of our house, in the church garden, was as
> old as the church itself. When the flowers of the tree bloomed, all of
> Kuzguncuk was perfumed with the fragrance of magnolia. Every time I
> go to Kuzguncuk I anticipate that smell. I don't know if my senses are
> dulled or if that tree is no longer speaking to nature, but I can't smell
> that tree in Kuzguncuk anymore.[1]

The magnolia tree, the remnant of Kuzguncuk's past that is as old as the church itself, has ceased to sweeten the neighborhood with its lovely fragrance. We can read, perhaps, in Büyükfırat's description of the tree, that the church garden, as a living place whose culture and character beautified the neighborhood, is no longer alive. Büyükfırat goes to Kuzguncuk, anticipating the smell of the tree, seeking the sweetness of what once was, but is disappointed. Her memory of and search for what the ancient magnolia represents is an act of nostalgia for Kuzguncuk as the place of home. In Svetlana Boym's words, nostalgia is "a mourning for the impossibility of mythical return, for the loss of an enchanted world with clear borders and values; it could be a secular expression of a spiritual longing, a nostalgia for an absolute, a home that is both physical and spiritual, the edenic unity of time and space before entry into history."[2] Kuzguncuklu memories of daily life among cosmopolitan neighbors are steeped in a nostalgia for the neighborly space of the mahalle as home, where belonging among Greek, Armenian, Jewish, and Turkish neighbors meant their "edenic unity" before the antiminority riots of 6–7 September 1955 brought their "entry into history."

In place narratives of Kuzguncuk, Icadiye Street *is* the space of that lost enchanted world.[3] The main street in Kuzguncuk was where every resident stood for funeral processions for neighbors of all faiths; the Greek, Armenian, and Jewish merchants and tradespeople located their businesses; Easter and other annual church celebrations took place; and neighbors promenaded together on summer evenings. Icadiye Street, the remembered space of neighborly kinship in which "there was no religious difference" and "we were all brothers" is the locus of both collective and individual memory.[4] As Kuzguncuklu resident Güngör Dilmen writes in his play dramatizing Kuzguncuk's past,

Mistakes were quickly repaired.
To apologize was like a cure.
Tough guys would never yell in front of the church, nor at
    Nightingale Creek.
Good manners were something one took very seriously
as rituals performed sincerely, never just for show.

Figure 5. Icadiye Street. Author's photo.

Let's walk together up Icadiye, to its end
in the evening.
From neighbor to neighbor, little trays, plates, bowls, coming and
    going, covered with care
as if the saying, "What's cooked at the neighbors' will come to us"
was written for Icadiye.
Sweets would go, stuffed grape leaves would go, and pudding would
    come back.

. . . .

The fragrance is gone, the neighbor is longed for.[5]

As I demonstrate in this chapter, place narratives of neighborhood life
along Icadiye Street represent, as Boym suggests, a place in memory that
does not actually exist. Those who remember the neighbors who departed
remember mahalle life through a lens colored by the knowledge of what
happened to break apart the bonds of neighbors, events that wrote the
mahalle into history. Remembering the cosmopolitan past occurs from
the perspective of the present, where the memory responds to loss, long-

ing, and disappointment. Büyükfırat continues to return to Kuzguncuk and to wonder why the magnolia tree doesn't exude its beautiful fragrance anymore.

During the night of the 6–7 September 1955, riots terrorized Icadiye Street with violence as rioters broke glass, pillaged shops, burned the church, and invaded the homes of Greeks, Jews, and Armenians. Although the events were state-led, the riots effected a dramatic change in the local mahalle, amplifying the social difference between Muslims and non-Muslims. The year 1955 is the point when interethnic social life in Kuzguncuk fundamentally changed, as Greeks and other minorities who had not yet emigrated finally left in significant numbers. And yet while this moment of loss underlies the telling and remembering of Kuzguncuk's past, Kuzguncuk's Christians and Jews have not been openly grieved. The circumstances of propriety and social relations in the mahalle protect a normative collective memory and preserve the power of a dominant nationalist ideology that conditions which memories are told and which remain hidden. Thus, although the 1955 riots are rarely described or remembered aloud, they constitute a powerful silence that underlies narratives of Kuzguncuk's past.[6] Feelings of shame and trauma, and of longing for unmourned but absent neighbors, are sublimated into the nostalgic collective memory.

Popular collective memory in Kuzguncuk denies that there was any social difference between people of different ethnicities in the past and disavows that the riots happened in Kuzguncuk, by claiming that the riots could never have happened in a neighborhood of such siblinghood between Muslims and non-Muslims. The hesitance of people to speak openly about what took place is grounded, in part, in the sorrow of remembering a distressing event. However, more traumatic than the event itself was the sense of betrayal that belonging in Kuzguncuk could be destroyed by nationalist riots or even by the complicity or inability of neighbors to prevent them from happening. Belonging in Kuzguncuk meant not only a respectful acknowledgement of difference but also a pleasure taken in sharing a multicultural place; the riots caused a shock, or a mental fracture, by destroying this cosmopolitanism. The event raised questions about what it meant to be Kuzguncuklu and how it would be possible to maintain propriety concerning the role of Kuzguncuklus and the role of the state, given knowledge of what had happened and the pain of the experience. The riots, as a trauma, "un[did] the self by breaking the ongoing narrative, severing the connections among remembered past, lived present, and anticipated future."[7]

The exclusionary aspects of ethnic-religious difference, which the collective memory normally obscures, become obvious through examining the tensions, silences, and inconsistencies that surround the instance of the riots. Denying that the riots took place at all, claiming that they occurred only on the European side of the city, or saying that they were done only by outsiders and that local Kuzguncuklu Turks were innocent protects not only the state-authored national narrative that denies any prejudice or violence against non-Muslim minorities but also the collective remembered history of Kuzguncuk as an always tolerant, cosmopolitan place. Memories of the riots are important, because "the myths and narratives that found and sustain modern national polities are situated at the intersection of competing collective memories of violence."[8] If we extend our analysis from this small local example to the larger issue of political and cultural silence surrounding antiminority violence in contemporary Istanbul, what this chapter suggests is that the silence and denial of these and related events serves to protect not the state, exactly, but perhaps the memory of the inclusive nation that could have or should have been. The silence of the collective memory reflects a nostalgia for a "unifying nation-state memory."[9] All Kuzguncuklus, not only ethnic minorities, were traumatized by this event. The cultural politics of memories of the riots of 1955 illuminate the contours of the cultural politics that structure the ongoing debate regarding the terms of belonging in the Turkish nation, a process that too is characterized by silences, inconsistencies, and trouble.

During my first summer of visiting Kuzguncuk in 2000, I began to suspect that narrative images of Kuzguncuk contained more than was immediately obvious. One afternoon in June, I sat with a new Turkish Kuzguncuklu friend in the Çınaraltı Café after he gave me an introductory tour around the neighborhood. During our walk, he emphasized that Kuzguncuk was known for its exceptionally close neighborly relationships. He told me (I was to hear this example countless times during my fieldwork) that it took him a half hour to walk to the boat station because of all of the greetings he shared with people on Icadiye Street. However, later in our conversation, he contradicted himself. He said relations in the past were much closer. He told me about the open-air cinema he loved as a child and the nights when, after everyone watched the movie together, they strolled down the main street to the seaside, eating melon seeds, flirting, and enjoying the summer evening. My friend said that today, however, no one goes out. The cinema is closed and everyone is inside watching television. People aren't interested in each other and the practice of neighborly relations, komşuluk, had mostly disappeared. This story struck me because the contradiction embedded in it was so natural and yet so inconsistent. The meaning of this little narrative, and of its contradictory nature, became clear over the course of hearing many memories of Kuzguncuk.

This chapter introduces and analyzes place narratives of Kuzguncuk that relate to the 6–7 September events as memories of the past that reinforce the collective memory and yet also reveal tensions concerning the multiethnic tolerance of the mahalle. I begin with a presentation and discussion of Turkish, Greek, and Jewish individual nostalgic memories of interethnic neighborly life in the past as told in place narratives. I explore the themes these memories share in common, including the beauty of Kuzguncuk's environment, the warmth of neighborly relationships, and social life and typical events and experiences on Icadiye Street. I also examine other recurring issues, such as the brief mention of, and narrative movement away from, the arrival of rural migrants, changes in mahalle culture, and the departure of minorities. I then move on to discuss in depth the ways in which memories of the riots of 1955 and the issues of interethnic difference and violence against minorities are embedded in memories as silences and contradictions. The chapter concludes with a discussion of individual and collective memory, which links the emphases, contradictions, and silences surrounding memories of interethnic neighborly life on Icadiye Street back to our larger discussion regarding collective memory and national belonging.

Memory

Often-repeated themes in place narratives of Kuzguncuk, such as the strolls along the main street on summer evenings, together create a collective memory of life in the good old days. When people of Kuzguncuk recall the mahalle's rosy past, they position themselves as members of the mahalle by repeating the collective story and thus identify themselves as Kuzguncuklu.[10] Collective memory narratives are like yarns that weave together to form a tapestry, looped over and over along the same warp so that from a distance the woven image appears clear and consistent. These threads reinforce each other as they reinforce the larger image: narratives conform to a particular perspective on history. Yet, a close examination of individual narratives that support the collective memory will reveal gaps in between the weaving, where threads escape and fray. Because individual narratives, from Muslims and non-Muslims alike, reflect responses to trauma, they contain tensions and fissures that betray the collective memory. Sometimes the narratives diverge from the collective memory with silence, or an ellipsis, and sometimes the narratives loop back unexpectedly to retrace parts of the story but to retell them with contradictions, in a paralepsis that reflects a dissociation from the trauma.[11] Other narratives, much more rarely told, contest the nostalgic memory directly by emphasizing ethnic tension and loss.

Knotty individual bumps that interrupt the larger tapestry of Kuzguncuklu memory concern the issues of belonging, familiarity, and interfaith harmony and are bound to the concepts of mahalle and komşuluk. The individual stories also assume a stance that positions the teller in relation to others: as an early migrant and not a later migrant or as a Muslim and not a non-Muslim, each division contesting the claim of other individuals to true belonging in the neighborhood. The nostalgia embedded in the collective memory of Kuzguncuk's past is a symptom of anxiety surrounding both past and contemporary fissures in what is imagined to be a commonly shared and tightly knit Kuzguncuklu identity. Because the collective memory of cosmopolitanism exists alongside knowledge of a violent history, all narratives betray, whether subtly or deliberately, the trauma surrounding the riots of 6–7 September 1955.

"The Olden Days Were So Beautiful"

Kuzguncuklu people most often begin narratives of what Kuzguncuk was like in the past with the words, "Kuzguncuk in the olden days was so beautiful; our neighborly relations were so wonderful." To examine the layers of meaning in this underlying and connecting theme, I chose the following narrative segments because they are typical representations of the overall nostalgic story and yet also contain elements of tension. Common elements of place narratives of Kuzguncuk are the beauty of the neighborhood, the presence and friendship with minorities by name, a gentler pace of life, the participation in social activities in outside street space as a group and among young men and women together, homemade food and vegetables from gardens, and the familiarity of everyone knowing everyone else. This collective memory is filled with longing for a time before urbanization and nationalism transformed the geography of everyday life and thus reveals what is missing in the contemporary cultural moment.[12] The communal mahalle identity is the element most longed for in Kuzguncuk today, and it is missed by Muslims, Greeks, and Jews—by everyone who remembers the past and by those who did not experience it but who move to Kuzguncuk, seeking its traces.

A Greek woman over sixty years old, for example, said that in the old days there were no Muslims. The first Muslim who came was the man who eventually became the muhtar (he migrated in 1938 from the Black Sea region and served as the muhtar for sixty years). She talked about the wonderful relationships with her neighbors and explained that there were Jews and Armenians, as well as other Greeks, who lived on their street. When it was time to ring the church bell, all the kids would go together to participate in doing it, not just Greeks. In the evening they sat outside with the neighbors and sang songs. Her family invited their Muslim friends for *iftar* (the evening meal to break the fast during Ramadan). Her parents told her not to chew gum outside during Ramadan because the others were fasting. By describing other Greeks and by mentioning the arrival of Muslims, she positions herself as non-Muslim, articulating a natural sense of ethnic-religious difference, even while she also emphasizes the civility and mutual respect between Muslims and non-Muslims. By locating cosmopolitanism in the past, she implies that such interfaith respect is no longer characteristic of Kuzguncuk culture.

Another Kuzguncuklu, a middle-aged Muslim man, also describes his memory of relationships between Muslims and non-Muslims:

> There used to be Turks, Greeks, Armenians, and Jews. On Sundays everyone would walk side by side on Icadiye Street. It was very pleasant. They were all one, all being Kuzguncuklu. There are a mosque and church next to each other in Kuzguncuk . . . There used to be an elderly Armenian watchman responsible for the security of

the whole neighborhood . . . My teacher was Greek; he had to go back to Greece but he didn't want to. We saw troubles . . . They [the non-Muslims] were quality people. There was a good Greek restaurant, and Greeks and Jews played in the theater. We had a football team and played football together. The team was mixed Jewish and Armenian, but because there were many more Greeks they made up their own team. Kuzguncuk changed a lot. No one is left. It was a mosaic, but not one beautiful thing remained.

While this narrative also emphasizes friendships and a shared oneness of belonging to Kuzguncuk, he also shares his sadness at the departure of the Greeks. While he acknowledges troubles, he doesn't detail them, focusing instead on the quality of what was lost, being close with others in the mahalle. His loss is bound together with silence regarding what exactly happened to destroy this culture.

Another Muslim man told me (I write here from notes I took while we spoke, for he declined to be recorded) that when his family arrived in the early 1940s, Muslims were a very small minority in Kuzguncuk and that they lived as brothers with the Jews and Armenians and Greeks who were already here. They went to weddings at synagogues; visited and helped each other with death rituals; went to the church, synagogue, or mosque for each other; and never had any problems. His neighbors were Greek and his mother visited the women in their homes. When the call to prayer rang out, the Greek family set up a prayer rug in an area of the house for their Muslim friends to pray. He told me that when the creek that used to flow down Icadiye Street was covered over, there remained a tunnel underneath it. As children they wore bathing suits. As teenage boys and girls together of all religions, they jumped in one end of the tunnel and came out the other end into the sea. No one's family said anything if the girl or boy was from a different religion. All the shopkeepers used to be Greek or Jewish or Armenian, like the fruit seller and the barber. People wore fine evening clothes to walk along the sea at night. He told me that Kuzguncuk was like a theater. Everyone knew each other. It was isolated, and everyone was tied together by love. Everyone loved to help each other. His friend in Greece who grew up in Kuzguncuk calls him every Bayram at the end of Ramadan, and he calls his friend every Christmas, and they wish each other happy holidays. He said that this generation of people was close and tolerant. They all used to sit in front of their houses at night and sing songs, visit, have fun, and collect fireflies. He said that this was what passed for entertainment in those times: each other.

Similar themes, of mixing in the main street, of remembering minorities no longer present, emerge in the narrative of this Greek woman who also describes a cosmopolitan life lived in the street spaces of the neighborhood:

> In the past Kuzguncuk was a mosaic. Turks, Greeks, Armenians, Jews, there were a mosque, churches, a synagogue—there's only one place like this in the world, no place else like this existed. The churches would empty out. The Armenians would walk out from their church. Everyone would walk together; it was famous, all together in a promenade . . . Kuzguncuk was a village. In those days it was all Greek. Dimitro the hairdresser was Greek. The vegetable seller, the corner stores. Toman had the restaurant; now it's a shoe store. The corner store across from the church was Evripides. The pharmacy was Koço. On Easter we carried candles from the church on the main street to our homes and made a cross above the door . . . Kuzguncuk was a small place . . . It was chance. It was all a mosaic.

Her description of Kuzguncuk as a mosaic makes it exceptional in her memory, when she says that no other such place in the world exists. She remembers the minority shops by name and the residents' social life. For her, this mosaic is gone.

The following narrative emphasizes the ways in which people of different religious backgrounds helped each other. This Muslim woman describes the people of her daily life who were not Muslim like herself:

> The unleavened bread for the Passover holiday was made by hand. A family friend would make a neat little packet of it for us. That Jewish family took care of me. At that time everyone was together; there was no difference except in a name. When someone from the [Christian] community died, Muslims would go to the church . . . I knew a Russian woman who came to Turkey during the time of the Bolsheviks. Her daughter Yorgi was my age. They had a garden and they'd collect beans, tomatoes, and peppers in a basket. They called me "daughter" because I looked like Yorgi, and they gave me vegetables, chocolate,

and food they made. Everything was good [with people] from the beginning, without asking for anything . . . The Jews and Greeks did the best embroidery. The women did it in their homes . . . [A Jewish neighbor] would ask me to come and talk to her so she wouldn't fall asleep while she was working, and I would finish the edges for her or read aloud a novel. We'd sit three or four nights in a row.

She refers to the kinds of neighboring bonds between women that, in her memory, were between Christians, Jews, and Muslims. This story's emphasis on good relations between Muslims and Jews, which typified past neighborliness, relies on a common understanding that such relations would be exceptional now. The special community relationships between Jews, and Greeks and Armenians, as shown in the following excerpt told by a Jewish man, was also an important part of public spaces on the main street. This story also expresses nostalgia for a slower pace of life, for a time when shopping and other errands were done with people one knew well rather than at large, chain supermarkets as they are today. He also comments on the relative importance of social relationships over financial transactions, reflecting a nostalgia for a different set of values.

When we went to school we all wore short hair, and who would we go to but Dimitro. Our father would say, "Hey, let's go see Dimitro." In Kuzguncuk there were two barbers, both Greek. The doctors were also non-Muslim. There was one called Minasyan, and Doctor Giorgo Vargarit. Karmona, he was Jewish, the other two were Armenian. They'd sit in the coffeehouse, playing games . . . This doctor Ohanes, he was someone who enjoyed life and would love to play in the coffeehouse, and when a patient came someone would run and tell him and he'd say, "Coming right away! Coming right away! There's a patient dying over there!" [laughing]. There were these kinds of people; there wasn't any rushing. People weren't always motivated to earn more money; the pace of life was slower, more patient, more comfortable. There was another corner store owned by a rabbi. He was a sweet man, to the last degree a nice person. When we went, he'd write our debts in a notebook or papers; then he'd lose them, then he'd forget, and put cheese and potatoes on someone else's list . . . Can you imagine such a storekeeper?

The warmth of neighborly relationships, as well as the beauty of the neighborhood's environment, however, contrasts with other narratives that emphasize very directly the departure of minority neighbors and the change that took place in the neighborhood when minorities departed and Turks arrived in greater numbers. Memories of the cosmopolitan past contain, within them, the awareness that within the social relationships that maintained a balance between ethnic-religious difference and place-based belonging were the seeds of fragmentation. Nationalism and urbanization would redraw ethnic-religious boundaries along national lines while displacing the people of the city and fracturing the ties of common belonging to the mahalle. Memories of cosmopolitanism, therefore, are memories of "events which took place in a kind of innocence," and express a profound sense of loss, pain, and regret that the teller couldn't do anything to prevent what would happen later.[13]

In those days the main street was a creek; it was a clean place . . .
We used to walk around along the seaside. There were Greeks and Jews, all friends together, everyone was close and loved to help each other . . . We had close Jewish friends, but they all sold their houses and went. When they were going to Palestine they were on a boat and someone exploded the boat and they all died. We were all very sad about it.[14] We loved those Jewish people. When they were sick we went to them. When you were sick, they would always come to you . . . In those days . . . everyone knew each other on the street; everyone visited; there was neighborliness. Today no one comes to the door. We celebrated Jewish holidays and ate unleavened bread with them. We also celebrated Easter with Greek friends and went to the church to light a candle. There were also Turks in the neighborhood but fewer. We didn't go to the synagogue. The Jews didn't go there much either; they didn't take people there. But everyone went to the church . . . It changed after all the people left. The houses remained but the beauty didn't remain. When I visit, I look out of the window; the houses look uncared for. The clean beauty of the past is gone; everything has totally changed; only the name has remained.

Yet although this Muslim woman emphasizes the goodness of past relations, her deliberate emphasis on this point suggests that ethnic-religious identity was, in reality, sometimes an issue of difference. She remembers going to the church but not the synagogue. The following informant, an elderly Muslim man, clearly feels regret concerning the departure of the old non-Muslim neighbors and the immigration of other Muslims, although he did not want to talk about any specific events or circumstances. Every time his narrative moved toward something unpleasant, he shifted back to a nostalgic memory.

> They went to Israel, Greece, America. We had such good neighbors. We went to the church for weddings. We'd go to the synagogue; they'd come to the mosque. My neighbor went to Greece, and they came back later to visit us. They were good people. Our renter was Greek; he had five or six children. Religion never separated us; we always got along well. If we needed something we'd go to them. Or our Jewish neighbors would come to us. We shared meat. Still they call us from Bostancı [this neighborhood is only twenty minutes away by car, yet the neighbors don't return for visits]. Most went to Israel, most Greeks to Greece. About 85 percent of them left . . . Civilization went with the minorities when they left. They took it with them; they took politeness. All has changed; this respect ended in a bad way. When the old people come here they don't know anyone anymore. Kuzguncuk is still beautiful; we help each other; we were all brothers, but then there became a difference; it was divided.

In this narrative, the speaker confuses present and past good relations in saying Kuzguncuk "was divided." He contrasts the politeness of the past with the rudeness of the present. The good neighbors of the past are unlike those who came later, even as the teller then says there continues to be good neighborliness. Even though he doesn't explain why people left, the pain he feels regarding the loss of his neighbors is embedded in his narrative.

The riots of 1955 mark the entry of Kuzguncuk into history, when cosmopolitanism was truly destroyed in a moment of trauma for everyone who witnessed them; the event is remembered as the moment when Turkish nationalism was propagated by outside, rural migrant Turks. As Cengiz Bektaş, the architect introduced in chapter 2, writes, "For centuries, people of different faiths (Muslims, Jews, Armenians, and Greeks) lived here together, proving that it is possible for them to live side by side in an atmosphere of tolerance and understanding. Until people from outside came to ravage and destroy . . . Until the inhabitants were terrified by the fanaticism of the 6–7 September riots . . . But, though there has been a radical change in respective numbers and proportions, there are still people of the four faiths in Kuzguncuk."[15] His words mark the riots as an exceptional event and not related to a larger social situation of Turkish and minority ethnic difference, either within the mahalle or in Istanbul in the context of Turkish nationalism. Narratives of the past in Kuzguncuk emphasize sameness and neighborliness between neighbors, while they are also imbued with expressions of loss and tension. The state-led local violence that shattered neighborhoods across Istanbul in 1955 made ethnic-religious difference visible and divisive as Greeks and other minorities in the city were targeted and their property violated. For minorities, the riots recalled earlier experiences of violence and fear as a result of Turkish nationalism. For Kuzguncuklus who experienced the riots, they mark a moment that heralded real social and demographic change in the mahalle.

The Events of 6–7 September 1955

The riots of 1955 started simultaneously in separate parts of the city after an evening newspaper announced that Kemal Atatürk's house in Salonica had been bombed. They occurred during a heightened period of tension between Greece and Turkey concerning Cyprus and made local Rum pawns in the international dispute. Importantly, they targeted symbolic elements of the material cultural landscape that signified the important place of local Rum in Istanbul's culture and economy, including churches, cemeteries, houses, and, most especially, commercial properties such as those along Istiklal Street in Beyoğlu. It is now known that the Turkish government planned the riots, in spite of initial claims that "communists" were responsible. The riots occurred in many parts of the city, and the sophistication in planning and organization and the fact that eyewitnesses report that police stood by and allowed the riots to occur reflect an administrative structure connected to the state.[16] The Turkish press was censored during the event, although the foreign press sent the following dramatic reports of the violence:

After news of the bomb outrage in Salonica had been received here a crowd, mostly young men, demonstrated before the Greek consulate and then marched through the main streets, shouting anti-Greek slogans . . . Thousands of people carrying Turkish flags and portraits of the late President Kemal Atatürk wrecked hundreds of Greek-owned stores and houses here to-night. Shouting Atatürk's name and "Cyprus is Turkish" they destroyed shops and their merchandise on Independence Street [Istiklal Caddesi] with stones and iron bars.[17]

Middle-aged persons recalled the destruction of Izmir, then called Smyrna and largely a Greek town, in 1922. Old people recalled earlier massacres of Christians.[18]

Greek churches, tombs and sacred ossuaries were rifled and wrecked, as well as the stores along the famed Avenue of Independence. A sea of olive oil flooded the streets before one large grocery store; spilled paints and dyes made the street a nightmarish rainbow before a paint store nearby. One aging priest was burned alive in his bed, another scalped. By next morning, Istanbul was quiet again, its rubble-strewn streets the property of prowling cats and patrolling soldiers, but a reporter from London . . . compared the debris to the worst in England during Hitler's blitz.[19]

More than 4,000 shops, mostly Greek or Armenian owned, were totally wrecked by the rioters the night of Sept. 6. Seven hundred homes were damaged . . . No non-Turkish witness to whom this correspondent talked during five days in Istanbul believes the riots were entirely spontaneous. The most widely accepted theory is that the Turkish Government quietly encouraged a demonstration in favor of Turkish claims on Cyprus and that it got completely out of hand. Observers of the early hours of the disturbance are unanimous in reporting that the police did nothing to interfere for some time.[20]

One of the most important observers of the riots was Demetrios Kaloumenos, a local Greek photographer who risked his life to take 1,500 photographs of the destruction around the city. Kaloumenos was standing, by chance, in Tophane at 5:00 p.m. on 6 September 1955. He noticed some soldiers removing their uniforms and changing into regular clothing, while others in nearby official-looking trucks were handing out crowbars and pickaxes. He rushed to his studio to get his camera because he thought there was going to be a demonstration and hurried to Taksim Square, where he "caught the tail end of the speeches to the gathered mob and then witnessed the onset of violence."[21]

In an exhaustive study of the events based, in part, around Kaloumenos's diaries and photographs, Speros Vryonis describes the extent of the destruction that marked the end of Istanbul's vibrant Rum community. For Vryonis, the cause of the riots was much more than the Turkish-Cyprus conflict but was rooted, rather, in the fact that during the early 1950s local Greeks had become very economically prosperous and very significant to the economic and social life of Istanbul, in spite of the antiminority economic regulations of the 1930s.[22] They thus came to be viewed as a threat to the state, which is why it was their properties that were targeted in the riots and why the Turkish state and its allies (including the United States) have worked so hard to suppress knowledge of the event. This silence has, very recently, been challenged, and in 2005 a book about the events written by Dilek Güven was published in Turkish by the Tarih Vakfı (History Foundation).[23] The foundation exposes silenced moments of Turkish history by publishing academic literature intended to reach a broader popular audience.

Vryonis gathered many eyewitness accounts of the events, many of them published in Greek. He describes the Greek populations of the city and writes that 90 percent of the Greeks on Istanbul's Asian shore lived in the southern coastal areas of Kadıköy, Üsküdar, Kuzguncuk, and Çengelköy. He cites a Greek source that gives the population of local Greeks for the years 1951–52 and states that Kuzguncuk had two hundred Greek families at that time.[24] These areas were thus important targets in the riots, and Vryonis transcribes many Greek-language sources openly describing what happened in those mahalles. According to the sources, the riots in Kuzguncuk began around midnight that night. Kuzguncuk suffered less damage than the nearby mahalle of Çengelköy, and the one transcribed account relating to Kuzguncuk in Vryonis's book states that this was because a local Turk, an assistant director of the civil police, refused to let demonstrators pass. The account also describes the destruction and vandalism of some shops, and Vryonis also notes that both Greek churches were damaged in the riots.[25] It appears that the riots did occur in Kuzguncuk, that they were propagated by Turks who arrived on a boat, and that Kuzguncuk was relatively less destroyed than other nearby neighborhoods, although the residents were terrified. The riots were devastating for Kuzguncuk, however, because many Greeks left Kuzguncuk afterward and because they wove Kuzguncuk, as a place, into the larger fabric of nationalism and economic and political tensions occurring across the city.

Remembering Conflict

The 6–7 September events were a state-organized act of violence that relied on already existing prejudices and resentment for its implementation. This reality of social prejudice, which led to violence, underlies all narratives of the 6–7 September events, which is precisely why stories of Kuzguncuk's past are conflicted on this topic. The interviews that touch on the 1955 riots are important because these events are popularly denied in Kuzguncuk, and they remain, largely, unspoken. This is clearly an event whose (un)remembering is significant because it undermines the values of equality and tolerance between Muslims and non-Muslims in the collective memory of the past. The moment of contradiction hinges on the neighborly relationships—that in a neighborly place like Kuzguncuk such a thing couldn't happen (yet it did), that there was no difference between religions (and yet there was). This static collective narrative refuses to acknowledge what is known by the tellers to have occurred and reflects the fact, perhaps, that the frequent telling of the event—that the riots did not take place in Kuzguncuk—actually distorts the memory itself by solidifying it into a fixed stereotype.[26] The italicized emphases in the following interview fragments emphasize what I see as significant points that are important for the analysis of memory.

This first narrative marks the 6–7 September events as the moment of change in Kuzguncuk. Two Greek women told me that during these events their Muslim friends protected the church and hid their Greek friends under their beds. But they say this

neighborliness has disappeared. *After the 6–7 September events, places died.* In the old days there was civilization. Between Jew, Armenian, and Greek, there was no rudeness. Then when they began to come (the rural migrants) it got ruined. There used to be two hundred thousand Greeks in Istanbul, but everyone has left. Jews went to Israel. The shops all used to be Greek, Jewish, Armenian. Kuzguncuk used to be a beautiful place. They were good people in our village.

This interview took place in a group. The two women and I were seated on folding chairs in a reception room in the building next to the Ayios Panteleymon Church. After we sat down, several men, other women, and the male representatives of the church pulled up chairs and gathered around us in a circle, in another group situation during which I felt that what was being said was heavily monitored for propriety. During our interview, everyone in the room started to talk about how and why Kuzguncuk changed, and the topic returned to the 6–7 September events. People disagreed over what exactly happened. One man said, "They broke in and took what was in the houses, and that's how they got rich." Then a woman said, "That didn't happen here; they broke some glass in the houses, in my own house for example, but they didn't take what was inside." Someone else mentioned that a mob came with "red and white" (the Turkish flag). It was agreed that after this event Greek people became afraid and began to leave Kuzguncuk in large numbers and that this event marks the moment of change in the neighborhood.

In another interview, this one with an elderly Muslim man, the speaker referred to the 1955 riots and spoke directly about the later occupation of non-Muslim property by Muslims:

Menderes came to power in 1944. Houses were destroyed. Bad things happened. Between 1950 and 1955 houses were destroyed. The 6–7 September riots were very bad. They, Muslims, came from the other side, from areas where houses were ruined like in Fındıklı, and moved to this part of the city *to occupy newly evacuated non-Muslim houses* here. In the 1955 events destruction happened against the Greek people in Kuzguncuk.

One of the most interesting interviews was with an elderly Muslim woman whose narrative was embedded with contradictions surrounding what exactly happened, in ways that illustrate some of the tensions surrounding memory of the events.

The 6–7 September events didn't happen in Kuzguncuk, but I heard about it. They stole . . . vandalism . . . it happened in [the districts of] Beyoğlu, Eminönü, and Sultanahmet. Our people [Muslims] put them [minorities] out on the street. Oh, the things that happened, the things that happened . . . Sounds of tanks were heard here. The noise carried from the other side of the city. On the other side there were *gazinos* [casinos, bars with music] and we heard the music from them across the water. On that night they destroyed the churches . . . I had three or four Christian friends and I protected them; they stayed in my house. Then after that the Greeks began to leave and go to America; my friends left. My close friends . . . during the bad times they stayed with me for fifteen days . . . After the 6–7 September riots, they began to look for reasons to make the Greeks and Armenians leave. The Greeks felt themselves part of Turkey; they said, "Greece doesn't want us." They cried, "We are Turks; where do we go? Will they kill us?" Some went to the islands. The Greeks sold their houses cheap. Jews went to Israel.

Much later the teller returns to the events, this time contradicting her statement that the events did not happen in Kuzguncuk by starting to describe them.

Turks, Jews, Armenians were not separate in those times. There was no anger at each other. It was when the doctor was killed in Cyprus that it got bad here [this is her explanation for why the 1955 riots started]. Then *those who came from Anatolia did it to us*. They took their goods; they hit the churches; there were Turkish houses next to the churches. It was the people who came from Anatolia who did it. They broke into the houses; they tied the tanks' wheels and tore fabrics in the houses . . . *We heard sounds* . . . They cut the rugs; they ruined things; they took the mattresses of the beds and cut them and threw the wool out of the windows. They broke the glass. *One of them sat in front of the jail*, wearing several layers of clothes, putting on shoes from a pile of shoes there. *What sins were committed here*. When they saw the Greeks they turned the other way.

Then the speaker tries to rationalize what happened by saying it was a war time:

We would have given our clothes, books to the poor; if a guest came we treated that person with great respect; we protected and respected everyone. We killed those who did bad things to us. We protected those who were good. In war it wasn't a normal time.

One of the ways to understand these contradictions is to see them as the confrontation between individual and collective memory, as "the imprint of a collision between a larger collective and myself . . . marks of catastrophic encounters."[27] By stating first that the riots did not happen in Kuzguncuk and then later describing the traumatic events as a witness, the teller reveals the ways in which she experiences conflict as an individual and as a Kuzguncuklu bound to maintain the propriety of silence surrounding the events. Although her narrative is filled with the "ambivalence, ambiguity, contradiction, and lack of cohesion that characterizes subjective experience," it can open understanding regarding the nature of national identity tensions.[28] To scale up from this situation to the issue of national-level tension and prevailing silence regarding antiminority violence in Turkey, this example reveals the pressure of being caught between maintaining loyalty to one's collective identity as a member of Turkish society and possessing personal knowledge of events or moments that challenge the popular historical narrative.

This tension is also at work in the following narratives, which retain an ambivalent position regarding national difference and interfaith belonging in Kuzguncuk. In the following excerpts, local goodwill between Muslims and non-Muslims in Kuzguncuk is emphasized, retaining the value of the collective memory:

> The 6–7 September events were against the Greeks and Armenians. Those who did it came from outside. The Turks hid their neighbors in their homes. Those who came were the attackers. *Those who protected the minorities were all Turks.* They broke into a shop and broke the refrigerator. They ripped up people's fabrics. The event was influential in these people's leaving Kuzguncuk.

And,

> During the 6–7 September riots everyone went into their houses and sat. They (the rioters) broke all the glass in the shops and in

the church. Our *civilized* Turkish friends were embarrassed, still are embarrassed at the event.

The following recollection of a Jewish interviewee is full of tension between his statements regarding good relations and the underlying issue of intracommunity friction. He said he heard from his parents that the 6–7 September events were

> very dramatic, very sad in Kuzguncuk, and Jews were also affected by these negative events. But in Kuzguncuk Greek houses were pillaged and vandalized with stones and it was done by people who came from Anatolia, although *some of the Turks here showed them the way,* saying, "This house is Greek; throw it over there; this house is Jewish; don't throw a stone here." These are sad things but they were *done by those who came later.* In Kuzguncuk, whether Muslim, Greek, Armenian, Jewish, there was a good relationship between them, there was a good feeling of siblinghood. This was a very sensitive time.

While he describes tension between Muslims and non-Muslims, saying the Turks (the Muslims) showed the rioters the way to minority homes and that it was done by recent migrants to Kuzguncuk, he pulls back from this idea to emphasize the good relationship between neighbors of different religions, preserving the collective memory.

Some older Turks' narratives betray an underlying social tension between religious groups, even if they contradict it later. However, open acknowledgement of differences between Muslims and non-Muslims occurred in my conversations not with Turks but with Greeks or Jews. In one conversation with a non-Muslim couple, I commented on the departure of so many non-Muslims from Kuzguncuk, and my friends said, "an entire world left" ("bir dünya gitti, bir dünya!") with them. They said that old Istanbul had completely gone with the people who left. I asked whether it was after the 6–7 September riots that people left, and the husband said, in an unusually direct statement, "This was a terrible event that happened all over the city. The riots were not just near Beyoğlu like people think. It was a mad, crazy violence that happened in Kuzguncuk, too." His wife told me that "terrible things happened to girls in their homes" and that she was twelve years old and remembers how scary it was. She said that after the riots, anyone with money left Kuzguncuk. A Muslim neighbor came to the door while we were talking and her husband told me to stop talking about it. In this case the memory of the events is definitely from a minority perspective, and they are telling me because I am American and Christian, not Turkish and Muslim.

Tensions and Difference

While there existed intercommunity civility in neighborhood life, religious difference was important. In spite of the usual assertion that religion never came between people, narratives make it clear that on an individual level religion was an important marker of identity. In his play about Kuzguncuk, Güngör Dilmen works out this tension in conversations between his characters:

> SARANDA [a Christian Kuzguncuklu]: They knew how to live beautifully, in a middle-class way.
> EKREM [a Muslim Kuzguncuklu]: So everything was all smiles and happiness?
> ALI [a Muslim Kuzguncuklu]: No dear, that would have been counter to human nature! There were also irritations and arguments.
> EKREM: When we'd call them "heathen" how quickly they'd be against us . . . hesitant to say anything . . .
> SARANDA: With the wisdom that comes from being a minority![29]

When people say, "in the past we were all like brothers" or "everyone celebrated everyone else's holidays," what goes unexplained is the complexity of interethnic relationships in which one may maintain neighborly relations but, as Greek and Jewish interviewees explained to me, one's closest friends and family friends were usually people of the same ethnic group. In my interviews with Kuzguncuklu Jews in Istanbul the issue of ethnic-religious differences emerged in statements such as "we were never very close to Muslims. Our close friends were always Jewish like us"; "Sometimes we heard things like 'scared Jew'"; and "sometimes Muslims called us 'heathen.'" Interethnic relationships were complex, and particularly after the riots, non-Muslim Kuzguncuklu people began to feel insecure. The mahalle characters in Dilmen's play react to the 6–7 September events the morning after: "The neighbor couldn't look at her neighbor's face. With the feeling of being excluded. The warm coals inside us cooled. The state didn't have our backs. What class of citizen are we?"[30]

In narratives of change in Kuzguncuk, when the teller states that people left one day and no one knows why, attention is deflected from what they do know: that ethnic-religious difference was significant for relationships of belonging, not just to the neighborhood but also to the nation. The fact that the Turkish state confiscated the property these people left behind, or local Kuzguncuklu Turks bought the property of minorities who left at extremely devalued prices, or that some Turks may have known what was going to happen to their neighbors but didn't warn them is denied, as is the fact that minority neighbors left because they were scared or forced to leave.[31] The ways in which cosmopolitan life before the 6–7 September events is remembered today is filtered through the knowledge of the national fragmentation that would follow the events, as minorities left and sold their properties to Turks. The character Saranda in Dilmen's play narrates this moment, saying, "Kuzguncuk's new era: 'Neighbor, how much is your house?' After we were swindled once, the name for our helplessness became Emigration."[32]

Memories of Change

The migration of non-Muslims out of Kuzguncuk (and out of Istanbul) that began in the late 1940s and continued through the 1960s occurred simultaneously with migration to Istanbul. The incomers were not only Muslim but rural. Religious difference was heightened as non-Muslim communities in Kuzguncuk became true demographic minorities at the same time that the state was initiating persecutory policies against these communities by divesting them of their property and rights to residency and safety. The nostalgic memories of the past contrast sharply with the narratives that bemoan how contemporary Kuzguncuk has been ruined by the new and unpleasant people and their ways of life, as "our suffering nightingale Kuzguncuk began to rush toward a rural boor [maganda] culture."[33] In the narratives, the newcomers become scapegoats for the problems of the ruined environment and the breakdown of good neighborhood relationships. The narratives thus reveal the urban bias against the cultural changes of rural migration that dominate contemporary discourse about Istanbul and its problems. In the words of an Armenian woman,

> The traders and jewelers used to be Jews. Then they became the
> Laz's . . . Everyone was such good neighbors.[34] Now there's nothing
> like that. Because cultured, enlightened people wouldn't do things like
> this. All the people on the street now, they're all Laz, conservative; their
> women are covered. They came to Kuzguncuk and now they're settling;
> they're coming from uncared-for places where there is no school or
> civilization.

A Greek woman tells it this way: "Then the villagers came. After the 1960s they came with lots of possessions and were brought here by their relatives and friends . . . In the old days the animals would never have been standing in the garden for the sacrifice; would Ilya do such a thing?" Our conversation was during preparation for the upcoming Muslim Feast of the Sacrifice holiday, and there were animals in the market garden waiting to be cut the next day.

Paradoxically, however, the very people whose presence is vilified in accounts by older migrants who condemn the immigration of rural people as destructive for Kuzguncuk's "civilized, urban culture" share the same collective memory of the past and an identity as Kuzguncuklu. When I met a couple who migrated from Sivas in 1972 to live in one of Kuzguncuk's squatter settlements and told them I was doing research on Kuzguncuk, they immediately launched into the same, predictable narrative:

> In the old days Kuzguncuk was so beautiful; there used to be lots of
> Jews and Christians but they are gone now. There used to be a summer
> theater we used to go to; it was wonderful. It was so green; there was
> no one, but now it's full of houses. The apartment buildings across
> from us weren't there; it was all green; it was so beautiful. Now people
> we don't know throw trash in front of our house after the garbage
> truck has already gone and it smells. They throw cigarettes in the
> grass next to our house. This is a fire hazard because the grass dries in
> the summer. People don't think; they're so impolite. Kuzguncuk has
> changed; it used to be so beautiful.

By adopting the collective memory, these migrants claim their own place in the neighborhood and identify themselves as Kuzguncuklu. The need to belong, to know and retell the narratives that build the collective memory, is powerful.

The Place of the Narrative in Collective Memory

Narratives of Kuzguncuk, with their tension concerning social difference in origin, class, and religion, center on issues of belonging. The nostalgic narratives always mention the life of the main street, the same street that became the site of violence during the 1955 riots. These riots forever fractured the sense of neighborliness and belonging by destroying the property and safety of non-Muslims. They made visible the difference that had always existed underneath the commonality of neighborhood life.

The silences regarding the riots in the collective memory indicate not that it is insignificant or forgotten but rather that the shame of it has made it deeply ingrained in memory.[35] The emphasis on friendship and siblinghood is a language with which to talk about what was lost, what was destroyed by this event and the changes that came later. While the shared nostalgic collective memory of the past fosters social cohesion among Kuzguncuklu residents now, the silent memories are also divisive for those who feel excluded from the collective.[36] Those who are willing to remember aloud the events in Kuzguncuk contradict the story that the events couldn't happen in Kuzguncuk because of the exceptional siblinghood and interfaith neighborliness. One confirms oneself as Kuzguncuklu with the nostalgic narrative and the sense of longing for the past. Narratives that describe the 6–7 September riots are unusual, and they transgress the norm. What remains emphasized is the neighborliness and the past is remembered as a civilized time. Not talking about painful events "plays an important social role in legitimizing a current society. In short, forgetting is one of the main processes found in collective memory."[37]

Remembering (or unremembering) the antiminority violence of the past serves in different ways to articulate Kuzguncuklu identity for the teller. For the older Muslim residents of Kuzguncuk who remember the early days of migration and the dominance of minority culture in the neighborhood, remembering minorities' presence, reciting their names, and describing their holidays, authenticates the identity of the teller as a true Kuzguncuklu by placing herself as a witness to the loss of these communities. For the few remaining Jews and Greeks, however, the loss of these people represents much more, a loss to claim to place and membership in a larger community and evidence that they are the "other" in a Turkish nation and a now Muslim neighborhood.[38]

In a poem titled "Odise," in a book of nostalgic poems about Kuzguncuk, Kuzguncuk-born writer Reza Suat Gökdel starts by describing the Greek caretaker of the old Greek cemetery. As he looks at the stones, the caretaker laments that no one comes anymore. He remembers his love of a girl called Despina and tells the story of change in Kuzguncuk:

> Greek, Jew,
> Turk, Armenian,
> we were all together as one.
> Before our nation,
> our society was Ottoman.
> We danced together at my wedding.
> We sang the same songs.
> . . . .
> With tolerance were observed
> the stormy love affairs.
> Evenings
> strolling on the streets and to the coffeehouses,
> women and men,
> in groups
> from the philosopher to the porter,
> close friendships,
> loving to help each other,
> neighbors.
> . . . . .
> Around 1960
> with those who were arriving
> and leaving
> it became confused.
> Kuzguncuk changed,
> became filled with other people.
> Some of them
> already knew how to live together.

But most of them
ruined
its beauty.

First the Jews
left quickly;
right behind them
escaped the Rum.
From different origins,
but who knew how to live together,
those honorable people,
in the new environment,
got lost.
They vanished.
Even the polite Turks,
they watched what happened,
with a wave
of silence.[39]

Memories of Kuzguncuk's past are what makes Kuzguncuklu people who they are. Those who tell the narrative count themselves as part of the Kuzguncuk mahalle. "Memory, which also includes forgetting, should not be taken literally. It is to be understood in its 'sacred context' as the variety of forms through which cultural communities imagine themselves."[40] The collective memory of mahalle life, however, has a cultural politics that produces it, that forms the context for its remembering. Who holds the collective memory of the mahalle, and who and what are the subject of nostalgia?

Placing the burden of nostalgic memory on the names of Istanbul's old minority populations by valuing them especially in the collective memory of Istanbul's tolerant multiculturalism betrays, in the end, a continued underlying sense of social difference between "us" and "them," Turk and non-Muslim. Istanbul's Greeks, Jews, and Armenians embody, in memory, what has passed.[41] They are present in contemporary memory precisely because they are no longer there. As writer Selim İleri notes, in a book of essays on Istanbul, "Koço was famous then, too, but he wasn't 'nostalgic.'"[42]

The nostalgic emphasis on minority people and places is a way of continuing to make them the "other." Minorities are memorialized in stories that reinforce the overall collective memory of cosmopolitan belonging but are otherwise invisible. Dipesh Chakrabarty makes a useful observation regarding Hindu and Muslim narratives of intercommunal relationships and violence in Bengali society during the Partition of 1947. He discovers, in those narratives, that placing exceptional value on some people, and denying even the possibility of ethnic hatred, actually works to continue and sustain prejudice.

> In treating the Bengali Muslim's ethnic hatred as something inherently inexplicable and, hence, profoundly shocking, the essays refuse to acknowledge their own prejudice. I say this to underline the intimate relation that necessarily exists between values and prejudices. When unattended by critique, and in moments of crisis, not only do our values play a role in producing a sense of home, a sense of community among ourselves and with others, but they can also stop us from hearing what the other might be saying to us at that moment. My argument, then, is not one that recommends the "homelessness" of the modern; being at home is not something that we choose at will. "Poetically, man dwells . . ."—true, but *within the poetry lies the poison of inescapable prejudice, all the more unrecognizable because it comes disguised as value.*[43]

If we bring Chakrabarty's conclusions to the mahalle in Istanbul, his words suggest that the nostalgia for the cosmopolitan mahalle disguises ongoing prejudice and enduring social difference between Turks and minorities. Because minorities are exceptionalized, their individual voices are silenced and the realities of interethnic difference are denied. The collective memory of mahalle life that narrates the past with the language of "we were all brothers" is important because it disguises the ways in which Turkish nationalism cut apart the spheres of difference in daily life.

Today, spheres of difference no longer overlap to constitute a cosmopolitan culture but cohabit the city in a fragmented way; the nostalgic collective memory, the exceptionalizing of minority cultures, disguises ongoing and unacknowledged friction and the potential of future violence.

The collective memory of life on Icadiye Street thus produces an imagined cultural space that refers not to the past but to what is happening now. It has become necessary to remember a tolerant multiculturalism to cope with the fracturing of the mahalle in contemporary life. And yet, "By now, traditions have been so thoroughly 'invented' or homogenized, and 'history' so absolutely marketed or commodified, misrepresented, or rendered invisible, that any oppositional potential rooted in collective memory has been eclipsed completely."[44] There is, today, no space for alternative narratives of Kuzguncuk.

This chapter examines in close detail the narratives that construct the nostalgic collective memory of cosmopolitan daily life and the ways in which they silence, or elide, issues of tension and difference, particularly as they surround the violence of the 6–7 September riots and the minority emigration and rural Turkish immigration that ensued. The next chapter situates these memories of the past within their current social context by examining how belonging and exclusion are created through daily neighboring practices among women and by interrogating the role of propriety that sets the price of belonging in the mahalle and that dictates what should and should not be done or told.

5

New Day Street
Neighboring and Belonging

What are the social and political dynamics of contemporary everyday life that condition the ways in which the past is remembered? In this chapter, I explore the cultural politics of the spatial practices that create the mahalle. I name this chapter for the street I lived on during my research because it is based on my participation in the ongoing neighborhood visits between women, although the visits I write about in this chapter took place in many different areas of the mahalle. Neighboring visits among women are important because they link homes and streets in the mahalle and create ties of belonging.[1] This chapter deepens the analyses in chapter 2, which link the emergence of the nostalgic cultural memory of the mahalle to the erosion of traditional mahalle life; in chapter 3, which explores contrasting claims to place in the mahalle; and in chapter 4, which examines tensions and silences in narratives of Kuzguncuk's past. In this chapter, I examine how neighboring practices reproduce yet another dimension of the complex inclusionary and exclusionary identity politics operating in the mahalle. Throughout, I view the mahalle as a proxy space through which national and urban conceptual terms of belonging and exclusion are made real through the social practices that define who is a neighbor in (and who is excluded from) the mahalle. Propriety functions on many levels in the mahalle, as it regulates social behavior, defines with whom people neighbor, prescribes what neighbors will talk about and how they talk about things, and determines how neighbors enforce a collective silence around particular issues. Understanding and maintaining propriety is the price of belonging in the mahalle. This belonging means community support and membership, especially significant at moments of personal or social crisis and in the context of increasingly fragmenting urban culture. It is this same propriety, however, that reproduces the collective memory of Kuzguncuk's past and silences transgressive stories or actions, including memories of state-led antiminority events and the roles of neighbors in acts of discrimination. Remembering and reproducing the nation thus takes place in the tiniest spaces of daily life: in the living room, around the kitchen table, on the front steps, and through windows overlooking the mahalle street.

Belonging in the Mahalle and in the Nation

The mahalle is the space of belonging and familiarity because it is, in part, a semiprivate space. For the Turkish mahalle (and specifically for Kuzguncuk), the public and private exist simultaneously in the same residential street. The residential space of the urban mahalle is a space that embodies tensions—created through disparate and contradictory expressions of social, financial, and physical mobility—between individuality and conformity with neighborhood norms. Roles and expectations for women are reproduced in shifting moments conditioned by mobility and confinement, support and isolation, and strength and weakness. By examining the ways in which (gendered) identity is implicated in complicated ways in mahalle space, we can understand the complex spatialities of national identity and belonging in urban life as well.

I have, in the previous three chapters, focused primarily on issues of class, origin, and religious and ethnic identity and have examined these distinctions through various representations of Kuzguncuk's past. In this chapter, I complicate these analyses by looking at the role of gender in belonging and exclusion, and move to a closer focus on daily life practices. As in previous chapters, the contribution of this chapter is structured around the assumption that the sociospatial actions, words, and narratives that articulate and rely on the terms of belonging are also those terms that illustrate the fractures within the nation. These fractures cause tensions in Istanbul because pressures to conform make it difficult for people to negotiate differences in class, origin, ethnicity, and religious identity. And yet what becomes particularly clear in this chapter is that the boundaries of belonging and exclusion in the mahalle are not rigidly defined but, rather, shift in different spaces or moments as different facets of identity are articulated or hidden; identity and space are produced together, but in unpredictable ways.

In the first part of the chapter, I compare neighboring practices of long-term Black Sea–origin resident women and recently arrived middle- and upper-middle-class women to argue that while the latter have more social and economic mobility and increased personal privacy, these characteristics do not compensate for the need for ties in the residential community. This part of the chapter uses ideas concerning gentrification, gender, and class to explore the impact of recent urban change in Istanbul on the spaces of local life. I then link these changes back to a need for the collective memory of the mahalle as a space of belonging and familiarity as a motivating factor behind people's decisions to buy and renovate old houses in Kuzguncuk. In this way, I expose a cultural dimension to the gentrification of the neighborhood that relates the transformation of the urban landscape to the larger issues of national belonging.

The second part of the chapter examines the dynamics of neighborhood life among intermarried, poor minority women and more recently immigrated, and sometimes conservative, Muslim women. By revealing some of the paradoxes of neighboring relationships, I challenge assumptions that national categories of belonging based on ethnicity or religious identity are always the most important factors for creating meaningful relationships in daily social life: gender and spatial proximity are sometimes more significant. I examine first the ways in which gender identity is conditioned by socioeconomic status and place of origin and then explore the ways in which these issues are complicated by ethnic-religious identity and place of residency in the mahalle, themes that introduce the next and final chapter of the book.

Gender and the Nation

Traditionally, the most important practice for creating and sustaining the familiar spaces of mahalle life is neighboring (komşuluk), which opens home spaces to neighbors. The cultural practice of neighboring is gendered, relying in part on traditional gender roles for women as wives and mothers, which place them at home during the day. Many factors have impacted mahalle life in the last several decades, including urbanization, the decline of small shops in the mahalle and the shift toward larger providers in central urban locations, and the replacement by television of other forms of entertainment and social life. Women's roles in the mahalle have also been changing in recent decades: women may work for pay, live alone, choose not to have children, or desire individual privacy, even while these same women may also desire intimate mahalle relationships, maintain close family ties, and feel desire and/or pressure to marry.[2]

Gentrification has brought people to Kuzguncuk who appreciate its historical landscape. Some of them also seek the qualities of warmth and closeness of community believed to exist in Kuzguncuk and that are symbolized by its traditional mahalle landscape. Some of the women who move to Kuzguncuk desire a sense of belonging there and yet do not form traditional gendered mahalle relationships. They are not socially integrated with the families of the Black Sea–origin community, who have been the most dominant group of people in Kuzguncuk since their arrival in the late 1930s. Many of those women do maintain some traditional mahalle practices that are gendered and that provide them a great deal of support even while they are also sometimes felt to be invasive of individual personal privacy.

Ethnicity and class also figure into gendered sociospatial practices that produce mahalle space. The newly arriving professional women, or women who are married to professionals, also are not integrated with the remaining minority women of Kuzguncuk, most of whom are intermarried, and mostly to Muslim men. Minority women are among the poorest of Kuzguncuk's residents and they form mahalle relationships of support with their neighbors in proximity, other Muslim women of a similar socio-economic status. Some of their Muslim neighbors have immigrated fairly recently from rural areas and some of them have lived in Kuzguncuk for decades and were among the earliest migrants from the Black Sea region. Minority women may share friendly relationships in everyday life even while they may conceal facets of their minority identities from these very same neighbors. The experiences and practices of these various groups of women illustrate the ways in which gendered identity intersects with other multiple facets of identity such as socioeconomic and family status, as well as origin, length of residence in the neighborhood, ethnicity, and religion. Sociospatial practices of neighboring vary and create bonds of belonging or boundaries of exclusion that may reify facets of difference in identity or produce unexpected spaces and moments of belonging.

Mahalle, Space of Tradition

The familiarity of mahalle life is created in several ways, including developing social relationships in public spaces by the frequent patronage of local shops and socializing on sidewalks or in the weekly market. Men and women both participate in this kind of neighborhood socializing, which is extended, for men, to the spaces of men-only coffee shops. Some social spaces of mahalle life have disappeared in the last twenty-five years, including the open-air movie theater, which used to attract all neighbors regularly in summer evenings to watch a movie and walk together to socialize along the waterfront. Some new social spaces have emerged, such as in the Kuzguncuk Neighborhood Association, which brings a diversity of residents together over concerns for neighborhood issues.

The mahalle as a social collectivity is likened to the extended family. A neighbor distinguishes one end of the street from the other by saying, "my mahalle" and "your mahalle"; the mahalle is thus a place defined by its proximity to home.[3] The mahalle space is produced by the actions of daily life that link neighbors together in bonds of sharing, support, and reciprocity. The residential street of the mahalle blends the spaces of the public arena of the main street and the inside of the house, linking neighbors and their homes.[4] I set aside the mixed-gender public spaces of the main street to examine the fluid quality of residential streets as extensions of home spaces, along with the social actions, or tactics, that create the public/private quality characteristic of the neighborhood.[5] Geographic research on gender similarly views the boundaries between the public and the private as fluid, "highlighting the ways in which power and experiences from one sphere infiltrate the other sphere."[6] I use these conceptual strategies regarding the interembeddedness of public and private spaces to examine how, through mahalle neighboring practices, the private space of the home extends into the public space of the city. This strategy helps us make the scalar jump between home spaces and national imaginaries: the social practices in homes that create belonging among neighbors are produced together, in the same discursive field, with state practices that author imagined boundaries of belonging in the nation.

Although my move to Kuzguncuk brought me into the physical neighborhood, it was not until I was made a neighbor that I entered the mahalle. Daily visits with Zeynep, the first person to make me a neighbor, taught me about the special roles of women in creating Turkish neighborhood space.[7] Zeynep introduced me to komşuluk (a sociospatial tactic), by initiating the habit of ongoing and reciprocal visiting. The responsibility of visiting frequently enough to demonstrate membership in the community and the ways of visiting with other women (talking, reading coffee fortunes, drinking tea, eating, helping prepare food, interacting with children, or keeping company while someone does chores) are important characteristics of mahalle life. Doors are always open to a visiting komşu (neighbor), and visitors come without calling first. Komşuluk is related to the cultural value of preferring being with people over being alone and usually depends on women staying at home during the day while their husbands are out.[8] By linking the insides of homes to streets, visiting makes the residential street of the neighborhood an extension of private family space.

The social relations and actions that make the mahalle a place also inscribe one's identity as bound in place, as a neighbor, one of the collectivity. The idea of knowing (tanımak) defines the mahalle: everyone knows each other or is known in the neighborhood. Because of the gendered dimensions of producing Turkish mahalle space, changes in women's activities at home, in paid employment, and in political activity (for example) in Turkey have combined with rapid urbanization to erode the cohesiveness that characterized traditional neighborhood life. Contesting ideals concerning women's social and family roles are but one dimension of the changing urban cultural context in Istanbul that produces so much nostalgia for the traditional mahalle, as Istanbul society negotiates the place of tradition in contemporary life.

In the next section, I take this conceptual framework of the mahalle as a space of belonging to gendered daily life practices in Kuzguncuk. I begin with a description and analysis based on my participant-observation of neighboring and explore practices such as reading coffee fortunes as means of creating the bonds of neighboring and knowing that create mahalle space.

Gender and Gentrification in Kuzguncuk

As I discussed in chapter 2, the paradox of the gentrification and historical renovation movement in Kuzguncuk is that the multiethnic tolerance for which Kuzguncuk's landscape and people are known is not exemplified by the current demographic makeup of this neighborhood. Kuzguncuk remains famously exceptional, however, for retaining its typical mahalle characteristics that continue to make it attractive to gentrifiers. Gentrification involves the introduction of new social actors, a predictable boost in property values, and the introduction of new elements in the cultural landscape. As I examine in this chapter, gentrification is also a gendered process. Women in Kuzguncuk's gentrifying community (in comparison to women in nearby nongentrified neighborhoods) are more likely to be employed outside the home, have a higher level of education, have been born in an urban area, and read newspapers, appreciate the arts, and watch documentaries and foreign films, all signs of "modern urban life."[9] My interviews and observation of women connected to the Kuzguncuk Neighborhood Association suggests that many women gentrifiers have additional reasons for moving to Kuzguncuk alongside the desire to live in a historical mahalle environment. Kuzguncuk, as a place, carries deep associations with feelings of belonging and familiarity, and desire for this social closeness draws newcomers to Kuzguncuk.[10] My ethnographic encounters with both long-term resident and newcoming women reveal, however, an embedded ambivalence toward mahalle life.

Neighboring: Connecting Homes and Selves

Zeynep was in her late twenties when we met. She is interested in U.S. and European cultures and ways of life. She enjoys studying English and reading Western literature in translation and loves U.S. eighties pop music. Zeynep defines herself as modern, and thus not religious, in a way consistent with the dominant sense of the Turkish modern.[11] Zeynep has two children and her highest priority is to provide them with a good education. She has not been able to find a stable job, in spite of her need and desire to earn money to supplement her husband's insufficient income. Zeynep has lived in Kuzguncuk for several years. Her generous and outgoing personality, combined with a socioeconomic situation similar to her neighbors', has helped her form strong neighborly connections with nearby women in spite of not being a lifelong resident. Neighbors visit Zeynep regularly and seek her advice, asking her to look at their coffee fortunes and sharing their problems. The women who visit her meet other people in her house and thus expand their networks of intimacy and support.

On my first visit, Zeynep made me some Turkish coffee and taught me how to invert my cup and let it cool so she could read my fortune (*fal*) in the grounds. I became a frequent visitor to her home, where I met many other neighbors as well as neighbors' family and friends from outside the neighborhood. Zeynep's acceptance of me as a neighbor and friend in her everyday life encouraged the women who visit her to accept me as a neighbor as well.[12] Reading coffee grounds is an activity almost exclusive to women, although women may "look at fal" for male family or friends. Reading coffee is not specific to particular classes or ethnic groups in Istanbul. I have seen independently wealthy women and well-educated professional women, as well as poor women living in basements and women who sell knickknacks on the sidewalk, look at fal in coffee grounds or ordinary playing cards. It is an activity common throughout the Arab world and the Mediterranean and is also an integral part of Istanbul culture.[13] My observations of neighborhood life among women suggest that women enjoy it, in part, because sharing burdens and receiving advice through coffee readings is an important vehicle for participating in a network of emotional support and personal contact.

In Kuzguncuk, reading fal does not necessarily indicate an expressed belief in the supernatural. It is common for women, while reading, to say,

"I don't know anything; I only say what I see in the coffee." Specific shapes are said to bear specific meanings, and so the burden of interpretation is alleviated if one claims merely to be reciting what is objectively obvious in the coffee. Some people who practice Islam with devotion do not participate, and I have witnessed some avid fal readers feign disinterest in front of someone who appears to be religious.[14]

The first time Zeynep looked at my fal, she drew me into her personal space—and entered mine—by addressing private subjects such as my family; stresses of life, including work and money; and my emotions. "Your work is very heavy right now. You're going through a period of difficulty and sometimes feel very stressed, but this period will soon end and your work will go very smoothly." By addressing what she saw in my coffee grounds, Zeynep placed herself in the realm of my friendship, offering words of comfort, forming a tie with me, and making me a neighbor. She looked at my coffee countless times over the next year, and on almost every visit I met other women. Zeynep taught me how to read fal and asked me to do it for people she wanted me to form friendships with, like her mother or her grandmother. In this way Zeynep made me part of her community.

Sometimes women came to Zeynep at difficult times because they "had a need"; looking at fal functions like therapy. It is a way to discuss difficult issues, like problems with finances, children, health, or husbands. The fal creates a space of intimacy in which women share information and emotions and receive support. Once an old friend came to visit Zeynep and immediately started crying, asking Zeynep to look at her coffee and give her advice. Though we'd never met, my being there made me a neighbor too, and she asked me for advice as well. The boundaries of knowing and not knowing someone intimately are overcome by neighboring with the practice of fal.[15]

Looking at coffee fal is part of women's ongoing reciprocal visits that link houses and families to create mahalle space. Visiting is a natural part of daily life, making the inside sitting or visiting space of the home always open to visitors and extending this interior space onto the street. Those who live nearby are known as neighbors and are welcome to visit, and much of the conversation during visits involves topics concerning the neighborhood and other neighbors. People experiencing illness or poverty receive help from neighbors in the mahalle. This kind of community support depends on effectively communicating problems; visits between women can make known the needs of others or involve offers of advice on practical matters like cooking or cleaning, shopping and finances, as well as dealing with a difficult family member or neighbor.[16] These visits create the "knowing" of everyone by everyone else, a primary defining quality of the Turkish mahalle.

The neighboring and knowing of the mahalle not only create spaces of familiarity and belonging but also produce one's identity as a neighbor. In Michel de Certeau's study of everyday life in a neighborhood of Paris, France, "propriety" describes the behaviors of neighbors that create belonging by defining who is an insider and who is an outsider to the neighborhood.[17] Likewise, participation in mahalle life expresses one's identity as Kuzguncuklu and thus defines others as outsiders. The cultural practices that create mahalle space identify those who perform actions or receive them as neighbors, as insiders, by creating a vocabulary of tanımak. This knowing indicates a familiarity of shared connections articulated through conformative and expected social actions as a neighbor that continually retrace neighbor relationships. In de Certeau's terms, this knowing is sustained by propriety, the code of behavior for the neighborhood that is performed for the purpose of the expected benefit of belonging. In the Turkish mahalle, this knowing goes beyond the patronage of local corner grocers and other local businesses and the walking along the main street discussed in de Certeau's study of Paris, though these are also important elements of mahalle life. The knowing between neighbors is most directly created, in Kuzguncuk, by neighboring among women.

In de Certeau's study, the French neighborhood is an extension of the private into the public sphere. However, this extension of the private illustrated by that context does not describe the kind of fluid boundaries between the inside of homes and the street that is created by the continual daily visiting in the Turkish mahalle.[18] Women who are always at home and who watch the residential street from the window participate in the control of this space not only by visiting with neighbor women but also by a kind of policing that creates safety for children and makes known any presence of strangers as well as any deviant activity. The knowing created by this observation and the sharing of information between women in ongoing neighboring practices occupy a delicate balance between creating familiarity and invading private boundaries of space and knowledge.[19]

Changing notions of privacy have begun to influence the desires of Istanbul people of younger generations, as some young women cite the invasion of privacy as a reason to leave the mahalle.[20]

The closeness of mahalle life, while it creates a space of safety and familiarity, also includes the potential for a negative neighbor to abuse the connected neighborhood space and violate delicate norms by spreading private information or manipulating others. This potential makes cultural propriety, and conforming to the neighborhood practice, very important. Christa Salamandra, in her work on Damascus, argues that ethnographies of societies in the Middle East (with rare exceptions) have tended to romanticize the bonds between women. Salamandra describes relationships among women of the Damascus elite as an "emotive power struggle" and "sociability tinged with hostility," arguing that the competition between women results not only from fear of falling social status but also from a patriarchal social structure.[21] In Kuzguncuk, women's relationships can thus be imbued with both negativity and support. I witnessed neighbor women supporting each other emotionally and materially, by reading fal, for example, and I also heard sharp gossip and open criticism, as in the case of neighbors telling stories about fellow neighbor Gönül Teyze.

Propriety, Belonging, and Silence

Neighbors warned me about Gönül Teyze, a neighbor who watched the street from her window and commented frequently on the comings and goings of other neighbors. Zeynep often complained that Gönül Teyze visited too often, stayed too long, and asked too personal questions. I heard gossip about Gönül Teyze's involvement in the affairs of another neighbor's private financial situation and stories about her invasions of others' privacy. The notion of propriety discussed in de Certeau's work suggests that Gönül Teyze was insensitive to the unstated conventions of neighborhood life that balance the connection of private space and the protection of privacy. This propriety maintains that homes always be open to visitors. It would have been unthinkably impolite for Zeynep not to invite Gönül Teyze in for visits in spite of her unpleasant behavior.

The actions that regulate conforming mahalle behavior (the practices of propriety) in Kuzguncuk can cause frustration for women. This became particularly visible during one group interview with older neighbors in which the group collectively lectured me on the propriety of neighborhood life. While we were speaking, the daughter-in-law of one of my informants came in and was invited to join us for tea. When she realized that I wanted to hear about mahalle life, she sat next to me and began to complain about the lack of privacy in the neighborhood. She was born in Kuzguncuk and married someone also born in Kuzguncuk, and she plans to live in the neighborhood all her life. However, she said that because everyone knows everything, there is no private life.

> Because we're all in the same place, the neighbor across from me knows everything about me, like my financial situation, or what my kids do. If you lose your job everyone knows about it and that's annoying. I have two small children and if one of them does even the smallest thing I hear about it immediately. Everyone will tell me. You're always under observation and you have to always be careful about your behavior. For example, I can't wear shorts in Kuzguncuk because it's like a village. When I go to visit my friend in Göztepe, though, I can wear them over there.

She told me that during the two years she dated her husband before they got married they were careful not to be seen walking or talking together because it would create rumors and problems for her and her family. Gossip ("information tinged with judgment") was a constitutive part of her social environment and, as such, it conditioned her behavior.[22]

Her words caused a reaction on the part of the older women in the group, who joined in together to talk about the positive elements of Kuzguncuk life. One of them explained,

> For example, if you don't have money on hand you can still pick up things at the corner store or get a ride in the local taxi. When someone dies everyone learns about it because the imam reads the prayer for the dead over the mosque speakers and people come down to the boat station to see the name posted there. Because everyone knows their neighbors, everyone attends the funeral. People who visit Kuzguncuk are very surprised by this because they don't know their neighbors at all.

This interview was a deliberate narration of what neighbors wanted me to know and hear about Kuzguncuk. As a group, neighbors' stories confirmed and reinforced each other. This kind of censoring of dissonant information is important for preserving community and making the system of perceived equality in mahalle life work. As such, it is one of the "miniscule oppressions" of propriety.[23] This method works to silence a gossiper like the neighbor mentioned earlier, and it was being employed here toward me to silence any potential negative things I might mention about Kuzguncuk as I wrote about my research. As they shared their hospitality with me as a neighbor, they were ensuring my compliance with propriety.

As a foreigner, and especially as a researcher, I could potentially threaten the mahalle by betraying its secrets. Marcy Brink-Danan describes similar experiences during her fieldwork among Turkish Jews in Istanbul, where people told her directly that she must never write about "certain things" for reasons of "security." In Brink-Danan's interactions with Turkish Jews, their exercise of propriety was meant to contain community secrets and was one of several Jewish practices of silencing difference in the public sphere or of hiding any tensions regarding being Jewish in Turkey.[24] This pressure to conform, and to keep secrets, lies at the core of the larger issue of exerting power through discourses of silence and codes of proper behavior, and protecting the ideals of the state and society. This is the same propriety that protects the collective memory of neighborhood life and the cultural memory of the tolerant cosmopolitan past. The process of propriety works at multiple scales, from the living room through the city, and explains the silence and reluctance of everyone, Turks and minorities alike, to address tension and violence of the past. The miniscule oppressions of propriety are the price of belonging to community in Istanbul, whatever community that might be.

In a fascinating conversation during our interview, the women in the group used the example of a recent book about Kuzguncuk, written by a man who grew up in the neighborhood, to warn me not to breach propriety. A member of the group brought out the book by Mehmet Ünver released several months before. As I discuss briefly in chapter 2, one of the themes Ünver explores in his book is the migration of rural people to Kuzguncuk in the 1960s and their rural lifestyles. He remembers, for example, the fact that girls used to be able to walk from their houses to the beach in their swimsuits because everyone knew them, but that when rural men with moustaches started hanging around and watching them, they became uncomfortable.[25] During the conversation, one of the neighbors asked me directly, "Do you know what 'speaking too openly' (*fazla açık konuşmak*) means?" She said the author wrote about things that should not have been said, that he should have written "closed," but he did not. His work should not have been advertised as a book about Kuzguncuk, but as a book specifically about Ünver's own private life, because of the things he said that he should not have discussed publicly. These neighbors were enforcing, with me, the same policing of knowledge the younger woman had complained about earlier. The control of information and the group censoring of nonconforming ideas is one of the ways mahalle space is made known and familiar. Being a neighbor and known means restricting deviance and protecting the collectivity.

While the practices that create this interconnection and knowing are sometimes a source of frustration for residents like the young woman described earlier, they are always valued as typical of mahalle life. Even the young woman acknowledged later that the safety and belonging of "everyone knowing everyone else" is too valuable for her ever to move away from Kuzguncuk: "All my close women friends are people I've known all my life, and I haven't made a new friend in the last fifteen years because I haven't felt a need to." While some long-term Kuzguncuk residents describe the familiarity of the neighborhood by saying, "It takes me half an hour to get down the street because everyone comes out, and I have to say hello to them" and "My kids are safe because everyone knows them and looks after them on the street," others say "It's changed; no one knows me when I go back" or "I don't know anyone anymore."

New Neighbors in Kuzguncuk

The mahalle as it is practiced among people and in places such as the older communities of Kuzguncuk still exists in traces throughout Istanbul, even in newer areas, in the practice of knowing a certain corner store or occasionally helping one's nearby neighbors. However, even these relationships have become unusual, and there are parts of the city where they are not present at all (Kuzguncuk is an obvious exception). The close-knit geographically small area with neighbors who perform the cultural practices of mahalle life is now fairly rare, but it remains an important, present idea in popular culture. While traditional neighboring is performed in Kuzguncuk among some of its long-term residents, mahalle life has become the subject of much nostalgia, paradoxically, among those whose more modern lifestyles are made possible by its passing. Kuzguncuk attracts people who want to live in and re-create mahalle life. Yet incoming women, because of their different socioeconomic status or notions of privacy, are not easily accepted in the mahalle and occupy an ambivalent stance regarding the spatialization of gender roles in the neighborhood.

The actions of tanımak, of everyone knowing everyone else, depend partly on lived relationships to place over time. Many people on the particular residential street Zeynep lives on were born in the neighborhood, or married other people whose families are also from the neighborhood. Mahalle life in Kuzguncuk belongs to the older communities, the few non-Muslims who remain in Kuzguncuk, as well as the families of people who migrated fifty or sixty years ago. The long habitation in place and the practices that continuously form connections between neighbors creates difficulty for newcomers in acquiring the status of a neighbor. In this context, foreigners are very visible as outsiders. People were especially curious about me because of my status as a national foreigner and a woman living alone, and this curiosity probably played a significant part in my own success in neighboring among some Kuzguncuk residents. New people in the mahalle, whether they are Turkish or national foreigners like myself, are sometimes the object of suspicion. Being foreign to the neighborhood, then, reflects elements of difference that are articulated through lack of identification with place, although they also signify socioeconomic and cultural difference. Just as the creation of tanımak through komşuluk is dependent on the cultural practices of women, it is the women who perform nontraditional gender roles (including working outside the home and/or living alone or being divorced) who suffer the most from lack of membership in the mahalle. One group considered outsiders to the mahalle by the longer-term residents is the diverse group of people who began gentrification in Kuzguncuk.

One man I interviewed identifies himself as one of the earliest people to move to Kuzguncuk to renovate a wooden house. He moved to Kuzguncuk in the mid-1980s. He is a well-educated professional with a family. He explained that he is still an outsider in Kuzguncuk because other residents have had lifelong experience or family in the neighborhood, and he does not. When I expressed surprise that he would still feel an outsider in spite of being in Kuzguncuk for almost twenty years, he said that it not only takes time but that he is also socially different because of some of his ideas (he thinks smoking is offensive, for example, and has asked people not to smoke around him, which others find unusual). He and his wife moved to Kuzguncuk, he said, because they lived in a newer neighborhood where an important element of Turkish culture had been lost. He explained what this element was by saying that when he passes through a village, he is always asked to stop by for dinner. He said that this could not happen in the city, that manners and ways in cities are different. According to him, Kuzguncuk retains some of this special element, and this is why he and his wife moved there.

Indeed, not all women who were part of the economic and cultural elite in Kuzguncuk desired traditional close mahalle relationships. Some women moved to Kuzguncuk because they already had friends there, and they were content to rely on those relationships. I also met women who enjoy living in Kuzguncuk but who rely on old friendships with women in other neighborhoods for community support. As Ebru said (see chapter 2), she moved to Kuzguncuk to escape the city crowds and to live in a house, but she does not do komşuluk with her neighbors because she works and goes out in the evening, and those kinds of relationships would be invasive to her privacy.

These narratives suggest that participating in neighboring, whether desired or not, depends on a neighbor's relative socioeconomic status and family status in relationship to other women. In this way, for all the reputation of Kuzguncuk as a neighborhood of especially close neighborly relationships, matters of class and identity segment social relations just as socioeconomic status fragments Istanbul society on a larger scale. Women who identify with modern ideals of a single-family home or an elite lifestyle, or who transgress traditional home-family boundaries as produced through the gender roles of older, long-term residents, may be threatened with isolation in Kuzguncuk if they do not find connections to others like themselves. Kuzguncuk is a mahalle (in terms of neighboring practice) primarily for its oldest communities, and so some of those women who move to Kuzguncuk because they desire the close life of a traditional mahalle find this life to be inaccessible. The mahalle, as an abstract cultural idea, thus attracts people to older neighborhoods precisely when urbanization and changes in gendered social roles have disrupted traditional ways of relating to place. The mahalle becomes a collective memory of communitarian social life in a city where that life is eroded by social change. And yet because of the ways it is threatened by new urban lifestyles, the mahalle has become exclusive, a space for those who already belong or for those who move there through previous friendships: it is not an inclusive community for otherwise disconnected newcomers.

The Kuzguncuk Neighborhood Association: Desire for Neighboring

The Kuzguncuk Neighborhood Association, founded in the early 1990s, offers a space for forming connections as an alternative to traditional neighboring. Its membership between 2000 and 2003 included a significant group of core members who were single, professional women.[26] The majority of the most involved activists in the early effort to protect the market garden were also women. Although the membership in the neighborhood association is not exclusive to new social actors (single women, economic elites, intellectuals, and artists), they predominate in its membership. During the time of my regular participation in association meetings and activities, I observed that while the association did provide alternative means of connecting for women not otherwise part of the neighborhood community, the association had mixed success in terms of providing the kinds of support found in traditional mahalle neighboring practices. First, participation in the association waxed and waned dramatically according to whether or not the association needed to perform a specific activity regarding the green-space project and whether or not key members were attending meetings. Other activities, such as earthquake preparedness, did not create sustained member activity. Sometimes several weeks would pass with successive meetings canceled for lack of attendance. Second, the strongest connections between members were naturally among those who had sustaining friendships outside the organization. The association was not necessarily successful for other women as a vehicle for forming new strong and lasting friendships.

Arzu, a woman I met at the neighborhood organization, appeared to face a problem with forming neighboring relationships in Kuzguncuk.

She was eager to make connections, and when she heard I was interviewing Kuzguncuk residents, she wanted to talk to me. Her husband has a well-paid professional job, and while she used to work outside the home, she retired in her midforties to pursue personal interests. Her family had moved to Kuzguncuk in the previous year. They restored their house, adding an extra floor and a new kitchen. They had hobbies—including painting landscapes along with Bob Ross's old 1970s PBS shows—that they did in the added room upstairs. Having hobbies in a segregated part of the house is unusual in Istanbul and indicates enough wealth to provide space and time alone. Arzu's family's nontraditional use of space is indicative of their nontraditional lifestyle.

In spite of her house, which affords individual privacy, community is very important to Arzu. She said that when she lived in an apartment in Etiler (an elite neighborhood of Istanbul), neighbor relationships never went beyond simple greetings. "Komşuluk," she said, "exists a little bit more in these older neighborhoods, and Kuzguncuk especially has better komşuluk than other places." One day, as I walked by Arzu's house, she was in her garden and she waved me over to have tea. When I told her I was interviewing elderly non-Muslim people of Kuzguncuk, Arzu told me that her house once belonged to a Jewish family (though it had an intermediate Muslim owner from whom they purchased it). She said that her next-door neighbor might be Jewish, because there was a foreign name on the electric and water bills. I was surprised that after living in Kuzguncuk for over a year, Arzu still did not know her neighbor. She told me that in the former Yugoslavia, where she had traveled, people sat outside at night in the summer, visiting with their neighbors. I said that elderly people told me that this used to be a common practice in Kuzguncuk as well. Arzu wanted to reinvigorate this lost neighborhood practice and suggested that the neighborhood association meet at the local café on the first of each month to get to know other people in the neighborhood.

It appears that Arzu, who moved to Kuzguncuk to be part of neighborhood life and who claims that Kuzguncuk has more of a neighborhood quality than other parts of the city, is missing neighborhood community. Her private single-family home with a gate and a garden, the fact that her children are grown and so she does not know neighboring mothers, and her experience working outside the home and living in an income bracket where she no longer needs to work make her different from the neighbors around her. She lives within two blocks of Zeynep and the neighbors that visit each other daily but she has never met any of them.

Nil is another woman I met at the neighborhood organization who joined the group to form neighboring relationships, because traditional ways of participating in neighborhood life were closed to her. She was not a member of the intellectual/professional community moving to the neighborhood to purchase a home: she was a single woman who migrated to Istanbul to seek education. Nil moved to Kuzguncuk because she had heard of its mahalle closeness and wanted to participate in the intellectual and art culture there. Nil lived by herself, and her migration as a young woman to the city alone from the village where she grew up was unusual. Remaining unmarried differentiated her from the other (predominantly older) women on her street, though not from the women in the more elite artist community or from some of the younger members of the neighborhood association. She was not in the same financial or professional class as the artists in the neighborhood, however, and lived in a modest basement apartment on a side street.[27] She thought it would be in a place like Kuzguncuk where she could be accepted as a single person and find community, yet she appeared to be unable to make meaningful connections.

Female members of the new and gentrifying community of Kuzguncuk are ambivalent regarding mahalle life. Their lifestyles are in some ways incompatible with the roles that have created mahalle space in the past, and yet they are also producing new neighborhood spaces through activities such as participation in the neighborhood association. These complicated genderings of a no-longer traditional space raise questions regarding changing gender roles for women, the effects of gentrification on community, and options for women to form meaningful connections in changing urban spaces. The ambivalence that desires and yet rejects traditional mahalle life reflects the complex debate concerning what it means to be a woman, and the nature of belonging, in Turkey.

Modernity, Tradition, and the Loss of Mahalle

While mahalle practices support women in their roles as wife and mother, they cause tension for women who occupy nontraditional gender roles. Increasing freedom of choice in profession and lifestyle has not brought a corresponding new social system of support for women, and women are still expected to bear primary responsibility as reproducers of family. While the changes of gender roles and their effects on traditional neighborhood life are similar to the changes in neighborhood life brought by modernization in other parts of the Middle East, women's experiences concerning mahalle life in Kuzguncuk are particular to contemporary culture in Istanbul and what it means to be both Turkish and female.

Women with increased education or financial independence cannot access the daily networks of support that are part of gender-divided daily life in the mahalle; while they may experience a greater physical mobility, their social relationships in the space of daily life are confined.[28] Furthermore, many desire modern individual privacy in the home, drawing sharper boundaries between private home space and the public space of the street and rejecting the fluid private/public, home/street boundaries of traditional mahalle life. The current nostalgia for mahalle life thus reflects not only the fragmentation of community in urban space but also tension regarding the places of women and family in the locality. Although Kuzguncuk is one mahalle where traditional practices are retained among some neighbors, paradoxically, the people who maintain its exceptional image and preserve its nostalgic landscape are part of the very transformation that is fragmenting the social cohesion of the mahalle.[29] Furthermore, they do not desire the mahalle constraints of life they view as nonmodern. The residential street of the mahalle is in various turns, in different moments and for different women, a more private or more public space. While the gendered terms of belonging in community are being redefined and contested in Turkey, visions of what it means to be a woman continue to be articulated in relationship to the spaces of collective memory, just as notions of national cultural identity are negotiated through the cultural memory of the city.

Identity in Shifting Spaces

As Linda McDowell writes, "It is socio-spatial practices that define places and these practices result in overlapping and intersecting places with multiple and changing boundaries, constituted and maintained by social relations of power and exclusion . . . These boundaries are both social and spatial—they define who belongs to a place and who may be excluded, as well as the location or site of the experience."[30] Identities are multiple and constituted together with other dimensions of social difference through social space.

Women who are intermarried, non-Muslim, and poor have noncon- formist identities so beyond the norm for the neighborhood and for their religious communities alike that they have become nearly invisible in aca- demic studies of Istanbul's minorities, in conversations concerning minor- ity history and social relations in the neighborhood, and in the dominant social networks of minority religious communities themselves.[31] Their identities are often hidden from surrounding neighbors or known but not acknowledged. What spaces do these women create as they negotiate their multiple identities as "other" through spaces of belonging in the mahalle?

As I discuss in more detail in the next chapter, after the departure of most of Istanbul's non-Muslim minorities, remaining Greeks, Armenians, and Jews relocated from old minority neighborhoods to new areas, re- clustering together with other minorities. The Greek Orthodox Church, Armenian Orthodox Church, and the synagogue are filled on weekend services with people who come to Kuzguncuk from other neighborhoods. The minorities who return on weekends to maintain the religious buildings have a complicated relationship with the remaining minorities who could not afford to move to areas with higher property values and social status and who are predominantly women and mostly intermarried to Muslims. They attend church and synagogue but in their everyday social circles they have little to do with the wealthier, dominant members of their religious communities. They neighbor with nearby rural Muslim migrants who are frequently also poor and sometimes marginalized.

Intermarriage appears to have been a fact of life in Kuzguncuk over the last several generations, although the issue of intermarriage seems to have become increasingly tense for minority communities since their numbers have dwindled so significantly that their existence is threatened and the search for marriage partners with whom they may preserve their ethnic-religious identity has become more difficult. The nonconformity of intermarriage is reinforced by the social norms that dictate the terms of belonging in the nation and in the neighborhood, and the maintenance of this propriety means not breaking the norms that define marriage as within one's religious group.[32]

The subject of intermarriage emerged as a taboo topic during my research. One Jewish woman who works closely with the chief rabbinate in Istanbul said that official positions on intermarriage are increasingly conservative because the community fears total assimilation; children of intermarried Jews, she said, are not allowed in some of the Jewish youth groups. An elderly Jewish man I met, born to a Greek mother, concealed his mother's identity and the difficulties this caused him during his childhood. An Armenian woman told me that it has become increasingly difficult for young people to meet suitable marriage partners in Istanbul and so they work through friends of family to find marriage partners abroad. A Greek Orthodox woman cautioned a friend of mine "never to take a Turk." Just as the Turkish nation is gendered, minority women, too, are the bearers of family and those who preserve minority ethnic identity. They use neighboring to create alternative spaces of belonging when they are excluded from normative neighborhood space and church or synagogue spaces.

In this excerpt from her memoir, Zakire Büyükfırat writes about her friendship with a boy growing up in Kuzguncuk. She is Muslim, and her friend is Christian.

> "Korni," I said, one day. "If only you were a Turk." He was three or four years older than I was.
>
> "Me," he said. "I am a Turk."
>
> "Noooo. That's not what I mean." He looked at me strangely and then said, "I understand." He continued, "Okay, would you be a Christian?"
>
> "Ohhh, as if that were possible," I said.
>
> "So, why would I be a Muslim?" he said.
>
> Muslim, Greek Orthodox, Turk. I learned these three categories for the first time from Korni, and I was embarrassed. The next day I said, "Korni. Even if you aren't a Muslim I still love you."
>
> And after that day we never spoke about such topics again.[33]

In Büyükfırat's story, the boundaries of belonging, of being a Turk, hinge on ethnic-religious identity. Boundaries that define being a Muslim and being a minority may not impinge on friendships or neighborly relationships but when it comes to intimacy and marriage, they are firm. I heard a few stories in Kuzguncuk of how these boundaries became tragic when lovers couldn't marry or when antiminority events such as the 1955 riots or the 1964 deportation of Greeks forced a loved one, unmarried, to leave Kuzguncuk forever. Discussions of intermarriage were fairly rare but revealed the ways in which the teller perceived ethnic-religious identity differences. For example, a Turkish woman told me that the famous writer Nazim Hikmet had an aunt Sara who lived in Kuzguncuk. While several people told me this, she was the only one to say that Sara was a Jewish woman who came from Hungary and that she married a Turk because there was no conflict in terms of religious difference, from the perspective of Jews. She contrasted what she believed to be a Jewish perspective with that of Greeks, to say that a Greek-Turkish marriage would be impossible because the Greek family would never allow it.

One elderly Jewish man told me,

> Today in Kuzguncuk there are thirteen remaining Jewish families. This
> includes an older man who lives alone, and one other family whose
> mother is in ill health. The other families are all mixed . . . There's
> one Greek, the remaining all Muslim . . . [I ask him if intermarriage
> is a new thing.] There were intermarriages before, but not that many.
> There were many Jews, and so a girl could find a man. Families helped
> each other . . . And now a girl comes to sixteen to seventeen years
> old. She lives in a house in Kuzguncuk. Her friends are all Muslim,
> school friends Muslim, they come to the house—there's no one. What
> happens, there's a boyfriend.

He continues with some language that reflects his patriarchal attitude, which reveals that for him, women's bodies are the bearers of honor and the preservers of ethnic-religious community identity:

> When they [Muslims] take a [Jewish] woman it's worth like ten
> Muslim women. Because of that, they're still begging for our women.
> They know our value, to be precise . . . With the words "I love you,"
> those words, the women have to go. These guys know that really well.
> We're not obstinate, but today everywhere there's intermarriage, but
> there's more of it here. If you ask me, my daughter died. Because I
> don't know half of her.

His daughter is one of the remaining Jewish women in Kuzguncuk married to a Muslim. What are the spaces created by the boundaries of belonging and exclusion so visible in diverse narratives about intermarriage? What spaces of belonging do intermarried women create for themselves?

Nadalia Teyze is a Christian woman who calls herself the last remaining one of her community. She is in her sixties and was once married to a Muslim but now lives alone. On the day I met her she was on the way to the local weekly market with her neighbor, a covered Muslim woman. She told me later that all her neighbors are Muslim now. When I came back later, another female Muslim neighbor was out on the street waiting for us to arrive so she could tell Nadalia Teyze. During our visit a vegetable seller was passing by, crying out the kinds of vegetables he sells, and she poked her head out of the window and told him to bring some vegetables down to her elderly lady neighbor because she doesn't hear. She explained that she and her neighbors help each other all the time, which was obvious. Nadalia Teyze is poor. Her house is, she says, nearly two hundred years old. It's made of wood and it's falling down. There are holes in the walls and the floors are sagging. She was trying to sell it.

During our visit, the difficulties she experienced as a minority emerged as a primary theme. Like the other people I interviewed, she remembered aloud all the minority residents who owned the shops on the main street and listed off their Greek, Armenian, and Jewish names. She was very sad that they left after the riots in 1955. She said that during those riots their churches burned and the rioters cried, "Death to the heathens!" The following year her own son returned from his military service and her family put out a Turkish flag in front of their house to celebrate his return. Neighbors came to tell them, "Take that flag down right away; it's not appropriate for you." She said in the past that the churches were open to anyone and no one bothered anyone else, but that after the 1955 riots everyone left and the neighborhood became filled with rural migrants from Inebolu and Rize, cities in the Black Sea region. She said that afterward the neighborhood culture changed. She said that neighborly relationships were always very good between Christians but less so with Muslims, that their women were covered—they were good people, but covered. At another point in the conversation she said that Muslims tend to gossip. Yet I observed that her immediate neighboring relationships of daily company and help were with women of this very same migrant community. Nadalia Teyze's daily social practices—of looking out for and being looked out for by the women around her—that create her belonging in neighborhood space were with her actual neighbors.

A Jewish woman called Mimi Abla, like Nadalia Teyze, is also intermarried and in her sixties. During our first visit, she told me that her life was like a soap opera and that if she told me her life story it would take hours and it would make me cry. All her family, except for her, emigrated to Israel. She raised her daughter in another religion. She told me how she met her husband on the ferryboat, how she used to admire how handsome he was when he walked by, how she found out who he was, how they fell in love. She didn't tell me what it was like for her to decide to marry him and what her family's reaction was, but she left me to imagine it, saying many other times that her marriage and her life have been very difficult.

Mimi Abla lives in a house built by her great-grandfather near some squatter settlements built in the 1970s and 1980s by rural migrants. Her neighbors are thus other intermarried families and rural Muslim migrants. All are women she depends on, as she is illiterate, and her neighbors read her bills and pay them for her at the post office. I got to know those women as well, because they were people I met many times over the course of my ongoing neighboring visits. Like Nadalia Teyze, Mimi Abla's daily interactions of neighboring that create a social space of belonging are with those whose identities are beyond the boundaries of her religious community.

She told me stories about the antiminority property taxes of 1942–43 in Kuzguncuk, about the riots of 1955, and about the changes in the neighborhood after so many rural migrants came. She told me not to talk about these events with Muslim friends and cautioned me not to trust Turks completely with information about myself either. I sometimes asked her about other Jewish people I was meeting, wealthier people who lived in other neighborhoods now but who grew up in Kuzguncuk in the years that she did, and she didn't know them. She says she has experienced discrimination from other Jews because she married someone who isn't Jewish. I was with her at the Jewish cemetery when the caretaker there told her, after her complaint that her plot was no longer marked and set aside as it had been, that she should be buried with her husband instead of in that cemetery.

Intermarried women use neighboring practices to form bonds with Muslim neighbor women, and yet at other moments they exclude those neighbors from knowledge of their minority identities. While they attend church and synagogue, they are not fully integrated members. In conversations about Kuzguncuk and about cosmopolitan social life they are invisible, even while the current nostalgia for this past emphasizes the tolerant mixing of religious groups. Nostalgia's rosy facade thus also conceals the bitter experiences of intermarried minority women, who create alternate and shifting spaces of belonging, at turns expressing some facets of their identities while hiding others. In this way, the conceptual boundaries of belonging and exclusion in the nation become real boundaries in everyday life when they inscribe markers of identity in the neighborhood.

In this chapter, I examine the roles of women in creating the mahalle as a space of belonging and familiarity and the rules of propriety that govern neighboring practices and that are the price of belonging. Propriety silences transgressive behavior in the mahalle, including telling stories that would betray the positive and cohesive collective image of Kuzguncuk. As such, the rules of propriety that govern neighboring practices can be seen as "established codes of behavior [that] have often served in unacknowledged ways as checks against a fully democratic order and in support of special interests, institutions of privilege, and structures of domination."[34]

A study that offers a fascinating comparative context is Tone Bringa's ethnographic research among Catholic and Muslim women in a Bosnian village before its disintegration in the civil war. The interethnic relationships in Bosnia that she studied provide a valuable comparison for examining similar relationships in an Istanbul neighborhood, as the ethnic complexities of both places result from their shared Ottoman heritage. The problems of state-authored nationalism also proved similarly destructive for interethnic relationships in both places, although through very different processes. We can see the extent of the cultural similarity through the linguistic terms Bringa explains in her study, as Bosnian hamlets within a village were called *mahala*, and the neighborhood within a hamlet was called *komšiluk*. These Bosnian terms are similar to the modern Turkish words mahalle and komşuluk, and thus they reveal the links Bosnia and Turkey share to the Ottoman past, in spite of the fact that these places are now located in what are nationally very different spaces.[35]

In the Bosnian village, as in Kuzguncuk, coffee visits provided the main social activity among married women, and neighboring played a crucial integrating role for Muslim and Christian communities. Coffee visits were but one of a variety of social practices among men and women in the village that together constituted a system of ongoing social exchange. As in the mahalle of Kuzguncuk, coffee visits articulated a sense of shared Bosnian identity because they reinforced the cultural value of hospitality and reproduced a shared cultural code. Bringa also notes, however, the ways in which women observed and commented on the similarities and differences between groups as reflected in their different customs, "with some customs being described as practiced 'among you' . . . or 'among us' . . . or being 'yours' or 'ours.'"[36] Neighboring was governed by the same rules of social conduct that created belonging in the village while, at the same time, marking a distinction between ethnic-religious groups.[37] While villagers *shared* a discourse of difference about their village, a discourse they used to distinguish their village from other villages, *within* the village each distinct ethnic-religious community constructed parallel, distinct ideas about the place.

Bringa conducted her research in the late 1980s, and her rich ethnography details the complex relationships between ethnic-religious groups there in the context of efforts by the Yugoslav state to define and create a nation-state in this mixed territory. Chillingly, the village in which Bringa conducted her research collapsed in 1992, as neighbors joined outsiders in killing Muslims and burning their houses. We thus read her ethnography with the knowledge of what would happen to destroy the society she describes, where villagers created bonds of belonging while they also maintained distinct ethnic-religious identities. During Bringa's research, villagers referred to a common "Bosnian" identity to describe what they shared in common with other people in Bosnia.[38] Yet this shared sense of being Bosnian did not prevent conflict among neighbors and the destruction of multiethnic villages in rural areas outside Sarajevo. As I examine in the next and last chapter, Kuzguncuklu Jews constitute their distinct cultural and ethnic-religious identities through their historical, and remembered, relationships to Kuzguncuk as a "Jewish neighborhood"; yet they also recall a shared sense of being "Kuzguncuklu" with non-Jewish neighbors. These memories are told, however, from the contemporary moment in Istanbul where interethnic neighborly relationships in everyday life have become an exception. Although cosmopolitan neighborhood life was not destroyed by a civil war as it was in Bosnia, Kuzguncuk's multiethnic sociality has been lost to rural-urban migration and state-authored ethnic nationalism.

6 Jacob Street
Jewish Identity in Place

I met an elderly Jewish man in his office, in an old building in the European side of Istanbul. I was introduced to him by his son, and it was our first and only meeting.[1] Throughout our conversation, which he consented to my recording, businessmen wandered in and out, and he paused to greet them or to exchange a note or a document. Our interview took place in a semipublic place, and his words were on record: his narrative can thus be interpreted as part of the outwardly focused discourse produced by Turkish Jews in Istanbul, of which tolerance among Jews and Turks is an important constitutive element.[2] This is an excerpt from what he told me:

> That place we grew up, it was the place we lived, our place, our
> citizens, from local Greeks, Armenians, with Turkish citizens, all of us
> there were like siblings . . . We had a beautiful life . . . We were all like
> siblings; we had no problems . . . All of us there never argued; all of

us, from poor to rich we loved each other very much; there were never any divisions, no divisions like, "I'm rich; you're poor." We lived such a life in Kuzguncuk, though now of course, I don't know . . . I left Kuzguncuk thirty-five years ago . . . I grew up there and still until now I can speak Greek, rather a lot . . . because I would go out and we had friendships with Greeks . . . The Muslims there would even speak our language, you know. They spoke Spanish; it was such a beautiful life, Ottoman times I can say. I don't remember the Ottoman city; I didn't grow up in Ottoman times, but what remains there of the Ottomans is very beautiful . . . Because we are Kuzguncuklu Jews our Muslims over there loved us very much. Loved us very much.

In his memory, the friendship and siblinghood among Greeks, Armenians, and Turks is embedded in the culture of the neighborhood itself. Being Kuzguncuklu transcended any difference between neighbors that might have been based on religion or ethnicity: "*Because we are Kuzguncuklu Jews our Muslims over there loved us very much.*" He explained that he, as a Sephardic Jew, knew some Greek because he grew up with Greeks in Kuzguncuk and said that Muslims would even speak the language of the Jews. His mention of having shared different languages with his neighbors stands out, to me, in sharp contrast to the reality of today's Istanbul. Because speaking Ladino in public spaces was something that marked Jews as different, and even became grounds for anti-Jewish violence in 1930s Istanbul, the pressures to assimilate have meant that Ladino has largely been lost among young generations today. His memory of *Muslims speaking Ladino* as a result of close neighborly relationships is even more striking, as it is impossible to imagine a Muslim Turk growing up in today's Istanbul speaking, as a reflection of the culture of her neighborhood, any language other than Turkish. By emphasizing the cultural blending and closeness of Kuzguncuk's multiethnic past, this man marked it as exceptional. And as I examine the points he emphasized, I also try to understand the silences that lie in between, to see them as shadows that illuminate the contours of present-day Kuzguncuk. Although this man did not discuss life in contemporary, overurbanized Istanbul, where ethnic Turkish nationalism occasionally produces antiminority violence and where Jews are extremely cautious, this is the geographic context and discursive field that conditions this man's cultural memory of cosmopolitanism in Kuzguncuk.

Subtle signs of a Jewish past are present in Kuzguncuk's landscape, but they are hard to see. On the main street the entrance to the large synagogue Beth Yaakov is not visible from the sidewalk but obscured by walls and very high doors that enclose an inner courtyard. A stranger to Kuzguncuk, in the effort to negotiate the busy narrow sidewalk, could easily pass the doors without knowing what they conceal or whether the space behind them is lived and inhabited. The other synagogue in Kuzguncuk, Beth Nisim (also known as the Virane Synagogue), is located on Jacob (Yakup) Street, a side street much farther away from the coast road. While a Star of David is visible on the outside wall, and Hebrew is written over the main doors, its walls are modest and do not call attention to its status as an important historical religious building.

One of the most significant traces in the landscape of Kuzguncuk's identity as a historical Jewish neighborhood is the Jewish cemetery. The cemetery is far from the center of the neighborhood, however. The creek that once flowed down the center of Kuzguncuk's valley began at a place along the hillside, at the northeastern interior end of the neighborhood. The cemetery lies even farther beyond this point, at the hill's summit. The small part of the cemetery that is still in use is accessible only from a gate on a very narrow side street located on the farthest edge of the neighborhood. Because Jewish places in Istanbul have in recent decades been the target of violent attacks, their entrances are monitored and tucked away from public view; safety has demanded invisibility. "The Jews' constant suppression of outward Jewish identity demands symbolic erasure work through unmarked public buildings," among other practices.[3] Jewish landscapes represent and contain, in their material form, the same emphases and silences woven through my interview with the elderly man.

For any Jewish person from Istanbul, however, the Kuzguncuk cemetery is well known. Kuzguncuk is famous for being, like Balat and Hasköy, one of Istanbul's oldest Jewish neighborhoods. By the turn of the twentieth century, Jewish families and communities had become richly interconnected through Jewish migration to and from particular mahalles in the city. The sense of Kuzguncuk as a Jewish neighborhood was the reason why some Jews migrating to Istanbul—from Thrace, for example, after the pogroms there in 1934—would come to Kuzguncuk. Jewish people from other parts of Istanbul were also moving to Kuzguncuk, because of the large number of Jews already living there or because of social or marriage connections they made to people in Kuzguncuk through the larger Jewish community in Istanbul. Jews moved away from Kuzguncuk as well, to new neighborhoods on the European side. Those new neighborhoods, such as Kuledibi and Galata, emerged as intracity migration destinations as Istanbul became segregated by class and new areas became known for their elite social status and as spaces through which to gain upward social mobility.

In the ensuing few decades, however, Turkification resulted in massive minority, including Jewish, emigration; this emigration combined with an enormous wave of Turkish-Muslim, rural-urban migration to Istanbul to cause, for its remaining Jewish residents, a total loss of Kuzguncuk's identity, or atmosphere, as Jewish. Those Jews who remained in Istanbul left Kuzguncuk for still newer Jewish neighborhoods. Galata and Kuledibi were no longer growing but had been replaced as target migration areas by other European neighborhoods such as Şişli, Asian-side neighborhoods along Bağdat Street such as Göztepe and Caddebostan, and later by still newer neighborhoods on the European side such as Gayrettepe. Through the early and mid-twentieth century, migration from old Jewish mahalles to new neighborhoods became increasingly related to a desire to live among other Jews. Although issues of status and upward mobility continued to be important, they were part of a larger concern to maintain community cohesion and identity, to blend in, and to feel safe. Jewish mahalles have been—and *continue* to be—spaces through which Turkish Jews negotiate being Turkish and being Jewish in Istanbul.

Kuzguncuk's landscape today is marked by visible traces of the major shifts that have changed the cultural landscape of Istanbul in the last several decades, as old Jewish neighborhoods lost their historical communities. For a while, the Jewish cemetery lay in ruins, the gravestones in indistinguishable heaps and piles, half-buried and obscured by overgrown thistles and other weeds. It was nearly totally destroyed by earthquakes and other environmental factors, years of neglect, and then by a squatter settlement built by rural migrants.[4] Some of the headstones were used in building houses, and others are visible in walls belatedly erected to surround and protect the remaining area. The destruction of the cemetery can be read as a landscape of symbolic violence against this community and their deep historical claims to place in Kuzguncuk.

Today, part of the cemetery is carefully guarded and maintained, and it is actively being used for burials. It has seen renewed attention not only

Figure 6. Squatter settlement on the Jewish cemetery. Author's photo.

because of the larger Istanbul community's recent efforts to preserve and celebrate Kuzguncuk's Jewish history but because another large Jewish cemetery in Şişli is becoming full. Jews from other neighborhoods, many of them with family roots in Kuzguncuk, return to the Beth Yaakov Synagogue on the weekends and the building has been beautifully restored. The central courtyard has new stones and a star-shaped fountain, which was given to the synagogue as a gift from a Muslim friend. Kuzguncuk has regained contemporary importance as people preserve and perform important community rituals in its historical structures, although Kuzguncuk is no longer a Jewish neighborhood in the lived sense, for only a few Jews live there today.

One aim of this chapter is to examine the role of the neighborhood in constructing and maintaining Jewish identity, both for individuals who lived there in the past and for those who work to preserve Jewish community identity in Istanbul from assimilation.[5] This approach builds on geographic research on identity that foregrounds the relationship between place and identity and views them as coconstitutive. As locations (such as the Beth Yaakov Synagogue) gather meaning through narratives, rituals, and remembrances, Jewish identity is performed. It *takes place*. Because the processes that create place are dependent both on the place's past and its interconnection with other places, understanding the local sociospatial relationships involved in sustaining ethnic-religious identity involves seeing their links to processes occurring beyond the local, to urban and national scales. Examining identity through place is also important because contested meanings of place reveal contested aspects of Jewish identity: how and what Jewish Kuzguncuklu people remember aloud about Kuzguncuk's past illuminates the nature of their relationships in the present, both to other Kuzguncuklu Jews and also to other actors in the mahalle and in the broader social context.

A second important contribution of this chapter is to reveal the ways in which national and minority religious or ethnic identity is produced through spatial practices of living in, moving through, and creating particular landscapes and places of belonging in the city. The Kuzguncuklu Jewish community—and thus, the mahalle—is not self-contained but rather is interdependent on other communities in Istanbul and to migration origins and destination points far beyond the city. This chapter thus extends the analysis begun in chapter 1, which emphasizes the fluid and continually reconstructed quality of neighborhood spaces and of community identities.

A third aim of this chapter is to complement the previous work in this book that contrasts Kuzguncuk's identity as a place with a romanticized cosmopolitan identity with its reality as a predominantly Turkish-Muslim, gentrifying neighborhood. I use Jewish place narratives to examine more closely *why* Kuzguncuk no longer has a vibrant, living Jewish community located in the mahalle. Interviews in Istanbul explain a decline of the Jewish population and a loss of urban or cosmopolitan culture that prompted Jews to leave the mahalle for other parts of the city. Interviews in Tel Aviv describe an emerging ethno-religious and minority national identity occurring within a context of increasing ethnic Turkish nationalism in the city. Together these themes illuminate the realities of minority experiences in Istanbul, which are obscured by silence and the seeming truths of the nostalgia for cosmopolitanism.

I begin the chapter by introducing the complex situation of Jews in Istanbul who maintain both a distinct religious-ethnic identity as well as a social and cultural membership in Turkish society that involves assimilation. I then describe my entrance into meeting Kuzguncuklu Jews and the ways in which the cultural politics of doing research and the hesitance of Jews in Istanbul to talk about the past shaped my research methods and the information I gathered. I continue by examining the historical cultural geography of Kuzguncuk's Jewish community to understand the interconnected relationships between mahalles and to understand Jewish memories of this particular neighborhood within their larger urban and national contexts. I continue with a close look at memories that describe, or silence, difficult moments in Kuzguncuk's past, such as the Wealth Tax, and memories that describe changes in Jewish life in Kuzguncuk in the context of increasing rural urban (Turkish Muslim) migration and the emigration of Istanbul's minorities.

Between Being Turkish and Being Jewish

When older Jews in Istanbul, such as the man whose story introduces this chapter, avoid mention of nationalist events and instead emphasize the positive aspects of the historical cosmopolitan past, they maintain what one anonymous Turkish Jewish author describes as the "delicate balance" Turkish Jews perform in Turkish society, a reflection of what Leyla Neyzi describes as their "ambiguous and ambivalent relationship to Turkishness."[6] An interviewee for a research project on Turkish Jews and citizenship described his identity in this way: "In terms of identity, our situation is more complex than other ordinary Turkish citizens. I'm a Turkish citizen but one with a Jewish origin. I think I'm not alone in this feeling of divided identity."[7] Marcy Brink-Danan exposes the linguistic and social strategies employed in maintaining a dual, divided, or ambivalent identity: among themselves, Jews acknowledge and even joke about the tension and fear they feel in Istanbul, while in public they participate in a positive discourse of tolerance and often conceal signs of Jewish identity in interactions with Turks.[8]

An important aspect of this delicate balance is the strong, positive, and public relationship between official spokespeople for the community and the Turkish government.[9] The community representatives, who maintain this positive public face for the community, are members of its elite.[10] Connections between the Turkish government and Jewish community leadership coalesced in 1992, when the government gave the Jewish Quincentennial Foundation funds to support their commemoration of the Ottoman Empire's invitation to exiled Jews in 1492. The Quincentennial Foundation also founded the Zulfaris Jewish Museum of Tolerance, which, Brink-Danan argues, similarly employs a representational frame of tolerance, a strategy that simultaneously erases Jewish difference while representing Jewish love for the Turkish nation.[11] The oligarchic structure and insularity of the community prohibits the expression of dissenting opinions, either of the Quincentennial Foundation or of the relationship between the Turkish state and its Jewish citizens.[12]

A complicating factor for the Turkish Jewish community is the relationship with Israel. This relationship occurs officially, as representatives from the leadership of the Jewish community help maintain harmonious economic and political relations between Turkey and Israel at the state level. I also perceived a personally felt significance for Israel among some interviewees. One person explained when we were introduced that because he was born on the day Israel was declared a state, his middle name is "Siyon," reflecting his connection to Israel through the moment of his birth. Another man, much older, remembered the day Israel was founded as among the most vivid memories of his life. In 1948 he was fifteen or sixteen years old. "I heard that they were going to hang a flag for the Israeli consulate. At the Holland consulate they were going to hang a flag. I went, and no one believed it; the street was filled with thousands of Jews, all speaking different languages, Turkish, Ladino, Hebrew, French, but all crying." Both Jewish official and personal identification with Israel contributes to Jews' sense of insecurity in Turkey because of the fact that, in Turkey, ethnicity and national identity are linked.

Turks perceive local non-Muslim minorities as having a natural affinity for and identification with other nation-states: Greeks, Armenians, and Jews are understood to be representatives of Greece, Armenia, and Israel.[13] Therefore, by virtue of having a non-Muslim religious and cultural identity, the loyalty of Jews, Greeks, and Armenians to the Turkish state is placed under suspicion, in a way that it is not for Muslim Turks, and many people perceive non-Muslims as untrustworthy and as "infidels."[14]

The relationship to Israel further places Turkish Jews in a difficult position because of Turkish popular support for the Palestinian cause. For example, at an art exhibit at the Istanbul Jewish Cultural Center in 2001, which displayed photographs of the Auschwitz death camp, a majority of visitors who wrote comments in an album likened Israeli treatment of Palestinians in the second intifada to the Holocaust.[15] This situation has become strained in recent years under the Justice and Development Party leadership, which has been readier than its predecessor to criticize Israel for its treatment of the Palestinians, particularly regarding Israel's winter 2008 bombing of Gaza. Because of the ways in which Jewish religious identity and Israeli state Zionism are often problematically tied in Turkey, political criticism of Israel extends into anti-Semitic rhetoric in the press and in periodic violence against the Jewish community. This violence affects all Turkish Jews, including Jews in Kuzguncuk; several told me about the death of one of their community members in the 1986 bombing of the Neve Şalom Synagogue in Galata. This situation has become more serious in recent years with increasing Islamist political and cultural rhetoric in popular media and more frequent attacks against Jews and synagogues in Turkey, including two synagogue attacks in 2003.

Another dimension of the delicate balance is that Jews perceive historical and institutional discrimination, such as in the belief that they are prevented from attaining very high positions in the military or in the state administration.[16] In Istanbul, many Jews maintain that anti-Semitism is not institutionalized and that state policies that have affected minorities, such as the Wealth Tax, were not directed specifically against minorities or against Jews. In Şule Toktaş's research on citizenship, and in a few of my interviews, people said that prejudice is not widespread, although it exists among individuals in Turkish society.[17] In contrast, many of the Kuzguncuklus who emigrated to Israel view such events as reflections of anti-Semitism among state-level decision makers. In general, Jews (and, in my research experience, to a much greater extent Greeks and Armenians) believe that to talk about past negative events may increase the community's vulnerability, which explains why Jews in Istanbul deflect attention away from the role of the state in anti-Semitism and claim, rather, that it is a phenomenon among particular individual Turks.

The result of vulnerability is that while Jews maintain a positive public presence and disguise their distinction from others in broader Turkish society, community leadership is also keen to preserve Jewish identity and to prevent complete assimilation. The leadership promotes activities such as encouraging youth to socialize in Jewish clubs so they can meet eligible Jewish marriage partners, for marriages with non-Jews have been increasing in numbers in recent years.[18] The rabbinate also mandates education on religious practices before all Jewish marriages.[19]

Practices to maintain distance and distinction also shape personal social life. Although they may prefer doing business with other Jews, Turkish Jews are generally comfortable integrating with Muslims in professional life.[20] Yet this integration depends on concealing open expressions of their Jewish identity in mixed spaces, as in the case of three male professionals I met, all of whom were over forty years old. One interviewee, for example, introduced himself to me by his given first name. At the conclusion of our interview, when he gave me his business card and invited me to contact him if I had further questions, he explained that I should use his Turkish name if I ask for him at his workplace, because people there didn't know him by his Jewish name. I witnessed another man being called by two different names, by one name when we were in Istanbul and by another name when he traveled to Tel Aviv to attend the Kuzguncuklu reunion. Another man I met has a distinctly Turkish name and told me he didn't think all of his colleagues knew he was Jewish. Names and language signal difference; most Turkish Jews of younger generations have Turkish names and have assimilated into secular middle-class Turkish culture, and Ladino and French (previously signifying lower- or upper-class Jewish identity, respectively) have been replaced by the Turkish language.[21] Jews may feel comfortable, on one level, with integration even while they may not feel comfortable publicly displaying this integration to other Jews, thus positioning themselves in different ways depending on the sociospatial context. As one woman describes the situation, "For example, while I am as comfortable with my Muslim friends as I am with my Jewish friends, I am not comfortable enough to blend them. When I invite friends to my house, I take care not to mix the two groups together. Thus, even if I consider myself integrated into the larger Turkish society, I don't contribute to the integration of my Jewish and non-Jewish friends."[22] The issue of tension between maintaining a balance between Jewish and Turkish identities, and concealing or revealing Jewish identity, thus had an important impact on the number of people I was able to interview and the information I gathered.

Methods and Encounters

In spite of the fact that, compared with Greeks, Jews were *far* more open to my research (which is why I devote an entire chapter to Jewish Kuzguncuklu identity and lack enough similar information to write so deeply about Kuzguncuklu Greeks or Armenians), I had a great deal of difficulty using a snowball effect to gain increasing numbers of interviews through primary contacts. While individuals may have felt comfortable speaking with me individually, community pressures meant that individual comfort did not necessarily extend to individuals being open about their participation in my research with other Jews or to using their social connections to help me find more interviews in the broader Jewish community (by contrast, the snowball strategy worked easily with secular Muslim Turks).[23]

During my first few months living in Kuzguncuk, as I began developing relationships with people in the neighborhood, I was introduced to Mimi Abla, the middle-aged, intermarried Jewish woman introduced in the last chapter. I visited her countless times on neighboring visits, and I was able to witness her relationships with the other people in her part of the neighborhood, as well as her relationships with some of the people who attend the synagogue. She introduced me in passing to some of the other intermarried Jewish women in the neighborhood, people whom I came to know well enough by sight to greet on the street. However, she did not invite them to her home to meet me, they did not express interested in being interviewed, nor did they invite me to their homes for visiting. At an early stage, my friend told me she would bring me to the synagogue but that she would lie and say that I was Jewish and a relative of some of her extended family in Israel. I did not agree to this situation and understood that she felt that introducing me as a non-Jewish foreigner was an uncomfortable risk.

An academic colleague in Istanbul happened to have a personal friend whose family is from Kuzguncuk and introduced me to him. This man, in turn, invited me to his house to introduce me to his mother, his wife, and his closest friend. He also brought me to the synagogue, twice, although no one we met there agreed to be interviewed. Our relationship also did not extend into other interviews through his friend or through other personal connections. Much later, in 2006 the same colleague, when learning that I was planning to travel to Tel Aviv, gave me the e-mail address of a man who leads the Association of Turkish Jews in Tel Aviv. This person sent a notice to their Listserv regarding my research and my planned visit to Israel. A Kuzguncuklu man in Tel Aviv named David Angel contacted me and volunteered to arrange some interviews with Kuzguncuklu people in Tel Aviv. David Angel comes from a fairly well-known family in Kuzguncuk, and it was my contact with him, and the Istanbul contacts I received from him and from the association in Tel Aviv, that produced more interview connections back in Istanbul in 2006. These contacts led to the leadership of the Kuzguncuk synagogue, which led to interviews with some of the men who visit most frequently and help take care of the building. However, the connections back to Istanbul did not lead to home visits, nor did they lead to any interviews with women. I did, however, visit the Kuzguncuk synagogue a few more times and attempt to meet people there after services. I was also invited to distribute a survey, and although I distributed sixty surveys (requesting, anonymously, such information as length of residence in Kuzguncuk and current neighborhood of residence) on two different visits, I received only four responses from new contacts (a previously known contact completed a fifth).

By contrast, in Tel Aviv, David Angel was able to either coordinate interviews or to give me phone numbers of more than a dozen people who were immediately interested in being interviewed. All of those visits involved invitations to meet people in their homes, including to a family Shabbat meal, something I consider an unusual expression of interest and trust because I am not Jewish. The number of interviews I could do in Tel Aviv was limited only by my time and my capacity to travel around the city during my short visit, not by hesitance among people there to participate in my research (only one person declined to be interviewed). David also initiated and organized a reunion of Kuzguncuklu Jews there, the first one they have ever held, where he invited me to show slides of the neighborhood as it looks today and to talk a little bit about Kuzguncuk and my research. I distributed a survey and received thirty responses at the reunion, although this relatively low response was probably conditioned by extenuating circumstances other than a lack of desire to participate.[24] This reunion led quickly to many personal home visits in Tel Aviv.

I remember my interviews and visits in Tel Aviv as exceptionally rich and personal experiences in contrast to those I conducted with Jews in Istanbul, as people were much more willing to share personal stories with me than the people I met in Turkey. During a Friday dinner, the brother and sisters of one family recounted stories of Kuzguncuk and sang songs they knew as children. During other interviews, people laughed and cried while telling stories. One man spoke for four hours about Kuzguncuk without being prompted with questions. I also saw, at the reunion, the emotional attachments people still have to the neighborhood of their childhoods and young adult lives. People exclaimed when they saw childhood friends for the first time in decades and walked to the front of the audience to talk about what they remember of Kuzguncuk and how they felt to be attending the reunion. The enthusiasm among Kuzguncuklus in Tel Aviv for participating in my research and attending the reunion reflects, I believe, that people maintain a continued personal attachment to Kuzguncuk. This is in spite of the fact that many of them do not continue to socialize regularly with Kuzguncuklu people in Tel Aviv, although many return to Kuzguncuk periodically to visit the old mahalle.

One of the main differences between the narratives gathered in Kuzguncuk and those in Tel Aviv was that interviewees from Tel Aviv described in frank detail the antiminority events experienced in Turkey, particularly before and during World War II. They recounted not only fear and persecution by the state and the resulting loss of property or safety in Kuzguncuk but also perceptions of social difference as Jews vis-à-vis other minorities and Muslim Turks. The mention of these details in Tel Aviv indicates that silencing does occur regarding these events in Istanbul and sheds light on what is normally never told in Istanbul. The narratives illustrate a picture of early and midcentury Kuzguncuk as a place torn apart by nationalist imaginaries at work from the scale of the state, through the city, and among people in the neighborhood.

Jewish Geographies

One important theme that emerges in Jewish narratives of Kuzguncuk is that although the Jewish community relies on particular Jewish neighborhoods, such as Kuzguncuk, for the reproduction of its social connections, the Kuzguncuklu community is in fact also produced through its interconnections to other places in the city and beyond. Being Kuzguncuklu does not represent a static and rooted relationship of a single family origin in one place, as Kuzguncuklu families have roots in many neighborhoods. Rather, *being* Kuzguncuklu comes from a cultural memory of sharing community, knowing particular families, or having witnessed important characteristics or events in the neighborhood.

Second, there was indeed a gradual decline of the Jewish population of Kuzguncuk commensurate with the larger waves of emigration from old neighborhoods and from Turkey to Israel, beginning in the early twentieth century and markedly increasing during the 1940s, after 1948, again after the 1955 riots, during the political turmoil in Turkey in the 1970s, and through the 1990s. However, even during this long decline some Jews continued to move to Kuzguncuk, while other families moved away and then returned. The impact of emigration on Kuzguncuk's community was thus complex. In general, as minorities left Istanbul, remaining minorities continued to move away from their old mahalles to new neighborhoods, and yet the fact that Kuzguncuk had long been an important Jewish neighborhood meant that many people continued to have ties there that drew some back even during the decline of the community there. Many factors combined to cause emigration from Kuzguncuk and from Turkey to Israel, and these processes are intertwined. Important themes from the oral histories are events and experiences related to Turkish nationalism and urbanization (including perceptions of the relative lack of security and uncomfortable cultural change); the personal circumstances of particular families (including, for example, educational opportunities or medical needs); and Kuzguncuk's relative status as a fairly poor neighborhood compared with other areas of the city.

Early Places

One of the women I met in Tel Aviv gave David Angel and me a copy of a large family tree.[25] The family tree traces her family back to Salonica, to Manuel Saporta who was born there in 1791. Salonica was the largest Jewish city in Southeastern Europe, and Jews constituted the majority of its population at that time.[26] Manuel Saporta's is the earliest birth recorded on the tree; the most recent took place in 2004 in Tel Aviv. The names of seven generations of people appear on the tree, which also provides most of the places of births and deaths, and the names and places of origin of marriage partners. I read the tree as a crude map of the family's connections, through the generations, to the cities of Salonica, Tel Aviv, and Rio de Janeiro; the countries of Canada, France, Italy, Germany, and South Africa; and the Turkish cities of Çanakkale, Edirne, and, most prevalently, Istanbul. Kuzguncuk frequently appears, as do the neighborhoods of Balat and Ortaköy. Many entries simply list "Istanbul" with no neighborhood identified. Most of the people on the family tree have Sephardic names.

Istanbul had a historical local Jewish community before Sephardic migration impacted the city's demography. Ottoman Romaniot Jews were local Jews who had, for centuries, lived under Roman and Byzantine rule. They used Greek in their secular communication and were proud of their Greek heritage, and viewed themselves as distinct from Jewish immigrants from Europe. They lived primarily in areas on the old historical peninsula of Istanbul and in Galata.[27] After the Ottoman conquest they were moved from Galata to areas around Eminönü, under the policy of *sürgün* (forced migration), whereby Mehmet II repopulated Istanbul (Constantinople) after the conquest in 1453, as part of its transformation into the imperial capital.[28] Jews from other parts of the empire were also transferred to Istanbul because of sürgün at this time and became the third largest group in the city after Turks and Greeks.[29] Settlement under this policy meant that arrivals were located in predetermined areas according to their places of origin and were not permitted to move.[30] Ottoman authorities demonstrated their preference for repopulating Istanbul with Jews rather than Christians by allowing Jews to build new synagogues in the city, a violation of Holy Law and in contrast to the fact that many churches were closed after the city's conquest.[31]

Sephardic Jews, those who migrated to the Ottoman Empire from Spain after 1492, eventually became the most dominant Jewish group in Istanbul. Most of the Jews coming in the decades after 1492 from Spain and Italy settled near Eminönü; fewer went also to Balat and Hasköy.[32] Istanbul also had a population of Ashkenazi Jews who had fled persecution from western, central, and northern Europe and whose legal and religious practices differed from Sephardic and Romaniot Jews. Ashkenazi Jews coming from Germany in the 1470s settled in Hasköy, while later immigrating Ashkenazi Jews would settle near Balat.[33] Karaites, a distinct community that relied on the Bible for religious law and denied Talmudic-rabbinic tradition, also lived in Istanbul. They maintained separate beliefs and practices and lived in relative isolation, although their shared plight under sürgün meant that Karaites eventually came to be influenced in their traditions by Rabbinic Jews.[34]

The Jewish community in Istanbul was thus relatively less unified in leadership in comparison to Greeks and Armenians.[35] This situation was due in part to the fact that Jews migrating from a particular place outside Istanbul arrived together and maintained these ties within the mahalle. Migrant communities prayed together in specific synagogues, which would form the center of the community. (The Hebrew term for a Jewish mahalle community sharing a place of origin is *kahal* or *qahal,* plural *kehalim.*)[36] A Jewish mahalle community was "a group of people who originated from the same place, prayed in the same synagogue, and followed the same leaders; the people were not simply residents of the same geographical area of Istanbul."[37] Jews also tended to organize themselves into fairly separate residential areas for the purposes of maintaining community traditions. Neighborhoods changed over time, however, as Jews would leave their qahal to move to other areas.[38] Minna Rozen argues that one of the reasons why people would leave kehalim was that the congregation was the only sphere in which Jews could express social or political ambitions, and so someone unable to realize those ambitions in one community would have to move to another congregation, or gather others and form a new congregation entirely.[39] As the city of Istanbul became more integrated, the interconnections among predominantly Jewish mahalles would multiply, and the distinctive nature of particular kehalim would erode.

During the sixteenth century, Portuguese Jews began to settle in new areas of the city, not only in Galata (reflecting their role in trade with European Christians), but also along the Bosphorus, including in Kuzguncuk.[40] By the sixteenth century, the area surrounding Eminönü had become crowded and frequently subject to fires, which also prompted Jews to move from that area to other parts of Istanbul. Many Jews were living in homes rented on a permanent basis from Muslim trust endowments, and after fires some trustees decided to use the land for other purposes rather than to rebuild houses for Jewish tenants. Those families simply moved away, or exchanged their rights to a ruined house for another house in a different part of the city. Jewish communities from different origins began to blend and integrate as families moved from their original mahalles to new ones during this period.[41] Although Kuzguncuk had become a growing area of Jewish settlement by the end of the sixteenth century, as its earliest Jewish grave dates from 1562, its Jewish population constituted less than 2 percent of Istanbul's total Jewish population at that time.[42]

Kuzguncuk's Jewish population would grow during the seventeenth century. After an enormous fire in Istanbul in 1660 that destroyed several neighborhoods near Eminönü and many Christian and Jewish houses of worship, the Ottoman administration employed restrictive Islamic law in their rebuilding policies of this area, effectively Islamizing the area and symbolizing this achievement in the construction of the New Mosque (Yeni Cami).[43] Displaced Istanbuli Jews from these areas near Eminönü moved to Balat and Hasköy and to Kuzguncuk, Üsküdar, and Kadıköy.[44] Kuzguncuk was thus among the neighborhoods that became major areas of Jewish settlement at that time, together with Galata, where the Jewish population also grew during the seventeenth century.[45] Jews moved for other reasons in addition to restrictive policies, such as the large group of Jews who left Galata for Üsküdar in 1618 to escape a plague outbreak.[46] One result of these migrations was that, during the seventeenth century, the Jewish neighborhoods of Balat, Hasköy, and Ortaköy had become stratified by class. Ortaköy was the wealthiest neighborhood, where some Jews lived in waterfront mansions alongside Muslims and Greeks. Jews in Hasköy, by contrast, were predominantly poor, while the community in Balat was even poorer. Jews in Hasköy also lived alongside Greeks and Armenians, although there were Jewish enclaves within the larger mahalle. These Jewish neighborhoods were characterized by a high population density and multistory buildings.[47] This situation created a fire risk, as demonstrated by the major fires of 1740 and 1744, which caused hundreds of Jews to move to Kuzguncuk and Üsküdar.[48]

If we return back to the Saporta family tree, we see that three of Manuel Saporta's four children, all of whom were born in Salonica, eventually migrated to Istanbul. The eldest daughter died in Kuzguncuk in 1913 and is the ancestor of the woman who gave me the family tree in Tel Aviv. The second daughter stayed in Salonica, where she married and eventually died. (Her son migrated to Istanbul, however, where he married and died.) The third child, another daughter, married a man born in Istanbul and they lived and died in Istanbul; their daughter was born in Kuzguncuk. The fourth child, a son, also migrated and bore four children before he died in Istanbul. So, three children from Salonica at the turn of the eighteenth century ended their lives in Istanbul. One of them bore a child in Kuzguncuk, and another died there.

By the end of the nineteenth century, "the larger neighborhood had replaced the congregation in Jewish social life."[49] According to Stanford Shaw, this is when the neighborhoods of Galata and Beyoğlu, Ortaköy and Arnavutköy, and Kadıköy and Kuzguncuk became important centers of Jewish society.[50] Kuzguncuk's Alliance Israelite Universelle, the French-Jewish educational foundation, founded a school in 1895, although Kuzguncuk's wealthier Jewish population began to decline around this time as they moved to other areas of the city.[51] Jews continued to move among Jewish neighborhoods in the city, and fires, exacerbated by population density, continued to be a major cause of intracity migration. Late nineteenth-century European travel narratives describing Jewish life in Balat, for example, emphasize crowded conditions and the lack of air and light.[52] Balat and Hasköy suffered several major fires, and Kuzguncuk also experienced huge fires in 1874 (1,740 people were affected) and again in 1911 (91 people were affected).[53]

The vibrancy of Istanbul's Jewish neighborhoods and persecution against Jews combined to pull migrants from regional cities to Istanbul. During the nineteenth century, in the Balkans and in Anatolia, anti-Semitism developed among Christian bankers and traders who felt threatened by Jewish economic competition, and these tensions turned into religious hostility.[54] Jews became afraid of being attacked by Greeks and Armenians on the street and left for Jewish neighborhoods in Istanbul where they would feel safer.[55] This was even the case in Salonica, where Christians attacked Jews or accused them of ritual murder. (Muslim neighborhoods in Salonica were perceived as safer for Jews than Christian neighborhoods.)[56] One Turkish source published by the Hemdat Israel Synagogue Foundation, associated with the synagogue in Istanbul's neighborhood of Kadıköy, states that Jews seeking refuge from anti-Semitism in cities such as Samsun, Izmit, and Bursa migrated to Haydarpaşa (in Kadıköy).[57] Kuzguncuk's Jewish population was growing during this period, which is when Manuel Saporta's descendants also arrived in Kuzguncuk. His descendants may have been among the new congregation of Beth Yaakov, Kuzguncuk's larger synagogue. This synagogue, close to the sea, was probably constructed by the wealthier of Kuzguncuk's Jews, including rich merchants and businesspeople who owned costal properties surrounding the jetty next to wealthy Armenians and Muslims.[58]

It is difficult to determine from the secondary sources exactly when Kuzguncuk's two synagogues were built, and the dates available suggest that both the smaller Virane (Beth Nisim) Synagogue and the larger Beth Yaakov Synagogue were built in the nineteenth century. The Beth Yaakov Synagogue was built perhaps in 1846 or 1878.[59] The Virane Synagogue might have been built in 1886 or earlier, around 1840.[60] This focus on the nineteenth century suggests that much of the information has been lost, because contrasting evidence describing vibrant Jewish society in Kuzguncuk as early as the sixteenth and seventeenth centuries (cited in the previous several pages of this chapter) suggests there was once a much older synagogue in Kuzguncuk, perhaps located where the Beth Yaakov Synagogue is today.[61]

By the early twentieth century, most of the historical local Romaniot and Ashkenazi Jewish communities had been absorbed and the larger Istanbul Jewish community had become predominantly Sephardic, although the Sephardim had achieved relative hegemony over Romaniot communities by the seventeenth century.[62] This Sephardic identity, which locates origins in Spain, is important to many Kuzguncuklus. As an elderly man explained to me, "My father was Kuzguncuklu; my grandfather was Kuzguncuklu; since we came from Spain our family has roots in Kuzguncuk. Five hundred years, five hundred ten years we are Kuzguncuklu; over there we were born, my grandfather's grandfather's grandfather was born there." Another senior man, when we met, asked me if I spoke Spanish and then explained that he was originally from Spain, although he was born in Kuzguncuk. Those who remain connected to the neighborhood today are Sephardic, and the older members speak Ladino and, some of them, French.

Intracity Migration and Jewish Life in
the Early Twentieth Century

The eldest daughter of the Salonican Manuel Saporta, the daughter who died in Kuzguncuk in 1905, married a man who was also born in Salonica. They (presumably) migrated together and had four children: a first son (this son eventually fathered a daughter who died in Kuzguncuk in 1963); a second son, about whom no information is given; a third child, a daughter, who married a man from Balat; and a fourth daughter who also married and who died in Kuzguncuk in 1957. The youngest daughter's granddaughter was born in Kuzguncuk, and this granddaughter eventually married someone from Haydarpaşa. The granddaughter also had a brother born in Kuzguncuk, and the two siblings had several cousins in Kuzguncuk. By the 1920s and 1930s, several branches of the family lived in Kuzguncuk and were connected to several other neighborhoods of the city through marriages.

Connections between mahalles were facilitated, in part, by the improved transportation infrastructure that increased the geographic interlinking of the city. As discussed in chapter 1, in the late nineteenth and early twentieth century the steamboat integrated Kuzguncuk into Istanbul's urban fabric. Jews from other Istanbul neighborhoods moved to Kuzguncuk because of social ties to it through education, profession, or marriage and because of its status as a Jewish neighborhood.[63] Chief Rabbi Mose ha-Levi Efendi founded Jewish primary schools in Hasköy, Kuzguncuk, and Dağhamamı in 1893. Alliance Israelite Universelle operated French-language boys' and girls' schools in Kuzguncuk, and Jewish children were still attending mixed boys and girls Jewish schools in Kuzguncuk in the 1920s and 1930s.[64] Jewish schools were important because Christian missionary activity in schools attended by Jewish children was considered a problem.[65] One interviewee from Tel Aviv, over ninety years old, remembers attending a school in upper Kuzguncuk in the 1920s, where he was taught by French Christians and where he would recite Christian prayers in the morning.

A French traveler to Constantinople in 1918 identified the main Jewish centers of Istanbul at that time as Balat, Hasköy, Ortaköy, and Kuzguncuk and characterized all of them that year as pitiful suburbs where lower classes lived in makeshift shelters of squalor.[66] Kuzguncuk's Jews were of mixed economic classes, although many were relatively poor, and a Jewish charity, La Unyon, provided aid to the poorest residents.

Fires and personal tragedies continued to impact intracity migration in the early decades of the twentieth century.[67] One interviewee in Tel Aviv remembered Jews who suffered a fire in Balat in 1904 or 1905 coming to Kuzguncuk.[68] He continued to explain that when there was a large fire in Kuzguncuk later, some of the Jews went to Galata. The fire in the early

1920s in nearby Dağhamamı is remembered as a very significant event that affected many families and ultimately led to the end of the Jewish community in that area.[69] One interviewee in Tel Aviv recalled hearing his mother's story about her life as a child in Dağhamamı, of her helping a neighbor move things out of the house during a big fire and learning from a different neighbor that her own house was burning too. The fire spread very quickly and damaged many houses; several who lost their homes moved down the street to Kuzguncuk.[70] The choice of where to migrate after losing a home in the fire would depend on a variety of factors: one married couple who left Dağhamamı after the fire moved to Haydarpaşa, near Kadıköy, because the wife's family had lived in Haydarpaşa for several generations, and she had grown up there. He had himself migrated to Dağhamamı directly from Edirne, where he was born.[71]

As modernization impacted the geographic and social structure of Istanbul, mahalles began to increasingly stratify by class. Wealthier Kuzguncuklu Jews began moving to newer, more elite minority neighborhoods on the European side, such as Galata or Kuledibi, to achieve higher social status, as these areas were the most European parts of the city. As the residential neighborhoods of foreigners, they were also home to Istanbul's local elite.[72] This migration parallels what was occurring in Arab cities in the late nineteenth century, as affluent Jews moved away from Jewish quarters and to other quarters of Cairo, Tunis, Tripoli, and Jerusalem, for example, as a result of the increasing presence of European powers in those cities.[73] Galata had expanded with the arrival of Jews from central Europe, and these new Jewish neighborhoods on the European side "represented modernity," the ascension of social class, and the acquisition of status as modern.[74]

The personal history of one elderly woman I interviewed is typical of early intracity neighborhood migrations away from Kuzguncuk to elite neighborhoods. This woman was born in Kuzguncuk in the 1920s and lived on the main street. She attended St. Benoit Lise, a French school on the European side. Her father was from Hasköy, but his family was originally from Kuzguncuk. She left Kuzguncuk in the early fifties when she got married at twenty-six years old and moved to Kuledibi, on the European side. Her sister was married and moved to Galata. Today, however, she lives in Caddebostan and her sister lives in Osmanbey.

Her move away from Kuzguncuk reflects its relatively decreasing social status in comparison to the emerging European neighborhoods. Indeed,

Kuzguncuk was home to many of the poor. One man, for example, describes this area during his childhood in the 1930s:

> Over there was our mahalle, called the *dere içi* [the area by the creek]. All those buildings you see were where all our Jewish citizens lived, poor, rich, all of them mixed. There wasn't any kind of separation, segregation over there . . . At the end of Kuzguncuk's central street . . . who lived there? Koen lived there.

Later he explains their family's situation:

> My father was a tailor and also sold secondhand things; we were a family that encountered a lot of difficulty. We lived in an old house. When it snowed . . . it was a house that my father inherited from his father, an old house. We didn't have any opportunity to go anywhere better; we knew what poverty meant. On holidays we'd have chicken to eat; sometimes we went hungry. We didn't have stuff in the refrigerator. When I wouldn't be full from two meatballs [during the day], only that much, my mother would say what are you going to eat this evening? Only that much. In the evening there'd be nothing. We couldn't get new socks until they had been repaired twenty times. Shoes were repaired three or four times; then we'd wear them until they fell apart. Clothes were like that too. But we were clean. My mother kept us very clean. That's all we could do.

Two related points from his narrative are important: first is the poverty he experienced as a child and the second is his emphasis on the social equality among Jews of different economic groups. This theme emerged in other interviews as well and is another dimension of the propriety that regulates the ways in which Jews protect a positive image of their community. As Marie-Christine Bornes-Varol argues, regarding cultural memories of Balat, the perception of equality, or the practice of ignoring social differences among Jews, comes from a "constant concern for maintaining the community's unity and cohesiveness."[75] And yet social difference among Jews was among the push-and-pull factors for intracity migration in Istanbul.

The importance of community unity continued to draw immigrating Jews to Jewish neighborhoods in Istanbul, but what community unity meant and how it was felt and expressed began to change in the nationalist atmosphere of the 1930s and 1940s in Istanbul. Jewish identity became increasingly politicized in the city even while, at the same time, memories of Jewish life during this period describe a sense of belonging among other non-Jewish neighbors in the mahalle.

Kuzguncuk became a receiving neighborhood for Jews from Thrace who left the cities of Edirne, Tekirdağ, Kırklareli, and Çanakkale after the Thrace events of 1934.[76] At that time, the Turkish government was trying to move Jews from this border region, which was also heavily populated with Greeks and Bulgarians. Jews were perceived as a particular problem because of their economic dominance in those cities. Pograms were organized, in which local Muslims, fellow residents and neighbors of Jews, participated in stoning houses and shops. These actions, following official and unofficial boycotts of Jewish businesses, provoked a great deal of fear among Jewish families and had the intended effect of causing their migration from Thrace in huge numbers, many of them to Istanbul.[77] The Thrace events were similar to the later 1955 riots in Istanbul in that they targeted the wealth and property of non-Muslim minorities and were state-organized but perpetrated by locals.[78] And so, although the events took place in Thrace, they became an important part of cultural memory among Jews in Istanbul, and in Kuzguncuk, who received people fleeing from the violence. State-led and locally enacted ethnic Turkish nationalism thus began to contribute to a larger perception of nationalist anti-Semitism and the potential role of neighbors in violence against non-Muslim minorities.

Kuzguncuklus, such as this man from Istanbul, remembered the arrival of people from Thrace:

> There was a migration, from Edirne, Thrace, I don't know; from
> there rather a lot of Edirneli people came to Kuzguncuk. And we
> continued our life with them together. Like . . . we taught them our
> traditions, and our Edirneli friends are now many here. From Edirne,
> Thrace, Tekirdağ . . . many people, I mean, our Jewish citizens, came
> to Kuzguncuk. There was a big settlement. But they didn't come
> to Kuzguncuk from Balat, from Hasköy, from Ortaköy. They went

more often from Kuzguncuk to Balat, Hasköy, and more to Şişli; they started [going] over there . . . They wanted a more luxurious life there. Because of that Kuzguncuk is empty until now. I don't know why.

This man remembers the arrival of people in Kuzguncuk from outside the city and contrasts this to how people who were already in Istanbul did not view Kuzguncuk as a destination because of their desire for luxury. My research suggests that the appeal of a safer and more comfortable neighborhood dominated by minorities and closer to the urban core also motivated intracity migration away from Kuzguncuk.[79] Like other narratives conditioned by propriety, this teller is willing to acknowledge nationalist anti-Semitism outside of Istanbul but deflects attention away from this issue toward class when he mentions Kuzguncuk. And yet the issue of safety was heightened as a nationalist atmosphere began to make Jews feel uncomfortable in daily life. In the 1930s, while the Thrace events were taking place in Edirne, Istanbul's non-Muslim minorities were affected by the Citizen, Speak Turkish campaign and economic policies that banned certain minority-dominated professions from minorities.[80]

One of the most interesting dimensions of narratives of the 1930s from Tel Aviv is the ways in which they describe nationalism, social difference, and discrimination against Jews operating alongside, even as part of, an urban culture where the teller also felt a sense of belonging with non-Jews as a Kuzguncuklu. The 1930s was a period during which the Zionist movement in Istanbul was growing, and the city became a transit point for illegal Jewish immigration from Europe to Palestine. In the following excerpt, a man from Tel Aviv shares his memories of ethnic difference and strong neighborhood ties in the context of emerging Turkish nationalism:

When we [Jewish youth] had a football team, in 1938, they wanted to have a game with us; in Beylerbeyi we had a match. After the match, I don't know what happened. I went to Istanbul by ferryboat. The Turks won the match, but we also scored a few goals, and they came on [to the boat]; they came, eight or ten guys walking around [the ferry] . . . When they found a guy from our team they'd start to beat him . . . After the match I went to Istanbul, and I'm coming out from the ferry station [returning to Kuzguncuk]. They're coming out from the ferry; the station was like this [he shows me]. I couldn't escape; they caught me. They were about to beat me but my friend [Mehmet], he was a bit slow but a good kid, they used to call me Moise . . . "Moise! I won't let them get you! I'll beat you all!" he said. He saved me. He loved me a lot. He saved me. They were fighting with us . . . But generally, it was good, between us. Later, I don't know.

This story of how a Turkish Muslim friend from the mahalle protected a Jewish friend against hooligans from another neighborhood both links and contrasts experiences of social discrimination and shared neighborhood belonging in a single moment. Shared belonging comes through in excerpts from another interview about the 1930s, in which an elderly Jewish woman describes the predominantly Jewish and yet mixed quality of the neighborhood: "At that time all the nearby buildings were Jewish. When someone had a wedding, all Kuzguncuk would come. It was like that. There were many Jews. Also Rum. Jews spoke Greek; Greeks spoke Jewish (Musevice). There was a lot of neighboring." Later, she continued. "My mother spoke a lot of Greek with us. Rum women would watch the children, before going to school, like a day care, and they taught me Greek over there, when I was small. I forgot it, but sometimes I remember."

There are many ways to interpret Jewish narratives that nostalgically recall friendships and neighboring between Jews and non-Jews. These two narratives were told in Tel Aviv, not in Istanbul, and so they are not a product of the same conspiracy of silence among Turkish Jews in Istanbul that elides social difference and promotes tolerance discourse in the public sphere. These tellers describe, together with multiethnic social relationships, moments of difference, tension, and violence. In the next section of this chapter I begin to examine memories of antiminority nationalist events in Istanbul. Alongside the critical stories that expose histories silenced in Istanbul are stories of being saved by Turkish neighbors. What emerges from these Jewish oral histories, in combination with those told in Istanbul, is a picture of midcentury mahalle life increasingly becoming impacted by a nationalist discourse that eventually came to structure individual actions and to define belonging and exclusion along ethnic-religious terms.

The seemingly top-down, state-authored definitions of Turk and minority had come to penetrate daily life and to determine the actions of people both in daily situations and in crises. What emerges as a growing, personally felt awareness of national difference at the social level can also be viewed as the process of blending and intertwining state-authored nationalist ideals and personal identity. Even while nationalist imaginaries of who belonged and who should be excluded were increasingly creating an atmosphere of intolerance and persecution, at moments of crisis mahalle interactions between individuals could be complex and unpredictable, sometimes resulting in discrimination and sometimes in acts of protection. Both are flip sides of the same coin, however, as neighbors negotiated with national imaginaries in daily actions that reflected notions of who was, or who couldn't be, a neighbor.

The Saporta family tree shows that by the 1940s no one connected to the family was being born in Kuzguncuk anymore, and by the 1970s and 1980s several members of the family were being born in Israel. The migration of this family to Kuzguncuk, their significant presence there for several decades, and their eventual migration away from Kuzguncuk illustrates in actual terms the changing ways in which one extended family negotiated their social status, religious identity, and personal opportunities in a changing national and urban context, through links across Istanbul and to cities beyond Turkey.

World War II in Turkey and the Wealth Tax

During World War II, increasing ethnic Turkish nationalism combined with Jewish fears that Nazis might occupy Turkey to make Istanbul's Jews feel increasingly vulnerable. Jewish perceptions of state anti-Semitism were fueled by the circumstances of the 1942–43 Wealth Tax, which was levied most heavily against the non-Muslim minorities of Istanbul and most especially on Jews. Kuzguncuk was directly affected by the tax, in spite of the fact that most Jews of Kuzguncuk were not particularly wealthy, a situation that contradicts Turkish claims that only the wealthy were taxed and that ethnic identity played no role in taxation.

The minority practice of silencing any talk of antiminority experiences significantly conditions what people in Istanbul discuss regarding the Wealth Tax. While several Kuzguncuklu Jews I interviewed in Israel told examples of how they were affected by the tax, very few in Istanbul volunteered to talk about it or would explain it if I asked. One middle-aged woman in Istanbul, whose family no longer lives in Kuzguncuk and whom I met through academic connections, spoke with me fairly openly about political events that affected the Jewish community in Istanbul in general. As she had just revealed to me that part of her family was from Kuzguncuk, I asked her whether her family was affected personally by the tax. While she said that her grandfather lost his business because of the tax, she didn't elaborate and did not discuss anything more personal or specific about his business or her family's history, thus refusing to personally identify with the political circumstances she could discuss in nonspecific terms. Another Kuzguncuklu woman in her early sixties recalled an emotional memory of the police coming to the family's house next door to take their things because they couldn't pay the tax, and they emptied a candy dish of its contents to take the dish. She didn't tell me whether or how her own family was affected, however. One older Kuzguncuklu male interviewee told me how his brother lost his business because of the tax and they went into a wholesale business together afterward but did not want to discuss anything specific regarding his own situation or the mechanism of the tax. Another man, who invited me to interview his mother, who had grown up in Kuzguncuk, warned me that she, like others of her generation, would not ever talk about any negative events from the past, and so I didn't ask her about it.

It is thus very difficult to gather information about how this event affected people in Kuzguncuk. Historian Ayhan Aktar published an analysis of the impact of the tax on the European side of the city through a detailed examination of property records for some of the most affected mahalles, records that are now closed.[81] Rıfat Bali has written the tax into the larger history of the relationships between the Jewish community and the Turkish state and has relied on, among other sources, reports of foreign ambassadors and of the Jewish community to foreign leaders. He has also reprinted several anti-Semitic cartoons from the Turkish press during the time of the tax, which suggest that the tax was an extension of serious anti-Jewish sentiment already circulating in broader popular culture.[82]

The tax is considered the major cause of Jewish emigration from Istanbul after the foundation of the state of Israel in 1948.[83] Emigration of Kuzguncuklus to Israel happened over a longer period and for several reasons: many were very poor and seeking economic opportunity, some were very politically active in the Zionist movement, and others perceived an insecure future in Turkey because of the political climate. These factors give contours to the cultural and political dimensions affecting people's choices to leave Kuzguncuk for other parts of Istanbul, in which the tax played a crucial role.

One woman in Tel Aviv told me about what it was like to live as a child during the Wealth Tax. She linked the national context directly to her family's experience and her personal decision to emigrate from Kuzguncuk. "During the Wealth Tax, they took my father to the military; they took all the men in my family to Aşkale . . . We remained with no food, no money—these things really scared me; I put it in my mind that one day I'd go to Israel. After I came here, the rest of my family moved from Kuzguncuk to Galata."

She was seven years old during the Wealth Tax and didn't emigrate until she was in her twenties. In her narrative, the taxes had a dire impact on her family and the events were a significant part of her thinking about emigrating to Israel.[84] She left after the large wave of Jewish emigration from Turkey to Israel after 1948, and after many other Jews and also many Greeks (who departed in large numbers after the 1955 riots) emigrated.[85] Her family's move to Galata took place during a period when minority families in old neighborhoods were moving across the city to regroup with other minorities in new neighborhoods. She told me, however, that the reason her family moved at that time was because her father got a job at the Neve Şhalom Synagogue in Galata, and they needed to be within walking distance of the synagogue because they couldn't use transportation on Shabbat.

In another narrative of the tax, a woman described how her family's experience with the tax depended on their personal relationships in the mahalle:

About the Wealth Tax . . . I was born in 1937; in 1939 the Germans came out, until 1945. Turkey didn't enter the war, but Turkey was getting ready. In Balat they built crematory ovens.[86] In 1940, my mother would tell me to turn off the lights. To turn on the lights we'd hang a blanket on the window so the light wouldn't be seen. We had no bread, no sugar. [The government] did it to show the Turkish people, because there was anti-Semitism. And they wanted money. Those who couldn't pay the tax were sent to Aşkale. My aunt's husband went to Aşkale. My father . . . had a shop selling printed scarves and fabric. He had to pay the tax. He came to an agreement with the muhtar who adjusted the tax so he could pay. My father was respected and he knew the muhtar. We lived in a two-floor house, lived on one floor and rented the other. We rented the shop, and my father paid the tax. If he'd been young, or had nothing to give, he would have gone to Aşkale too . . . When we were growing up in Kuzguncuk, we had Turkish teachers at school, and they knew who was Jewish; there was anti-Semitism. Jews, Greeks, Turks, some of the teachers were good; some were anti-Semitic.

Although national categories of belonging as Turk or minority were produced at the level of the state—through the tax and other policies—these stories reveal how the categories came to have meaning for individual people when neighbors in Kuzguncuk began to have the power to reinforce or intervene in the imagining of the nationalist boundaries of belonging as a Turk or minority. Sometimes this was positive, like the memory of the boy being saved by his Turkish neighbor from bullies or the woman whose father knew the muhtar, so he was able to pay a feasible tax. Sometimes this was negative, however, as when this woman's teachers knew who was Jewish, and she felt discrimination as a student.

For some people, during this period of Turkish nationalism (the late 1930s and 1940s also witnessed the first significant wave of rural-urban Turkish Muslim migration to Kuzguncuk), one could hold seemingly contradictory identities: Kuzguncuklu, with Turkish friends; Jewish, a religious and not necessarily political identity; and Zionist, an explicitly political identity seemingly at odds with the sense of belonging as Kuzguncuklu. In the following excerpt, this elderly man (the same man who told the story of being saved by a bully) described his memories of the tax, together with his political activities in a context of increasing pressure against Jews in Istanbul:

During the Wealth Tax, my uncle went to Sivrihisar. My wife's father was sent to Aşkale. They had shops but the tax that was levied on them was to the extent they couldn't pay it . . . During the Second World War, at that time . . . sugar, foodstuffs were going from the storage to the Germans. That's why the Germans didn't enter Turkey. The government was supporting the Germans. They'd give us a quarter loaf of bread. It was, excuse me, like mud. All the wheat was going to the Germans. On one hand it was a good thing. Germany didn't enter Turkey but, at that time, because of the Germans, anti-Semitism really increased in Turkey . . . At that time, I was in the first year of university, 1942, 1943 . . . When I was in university I was working, and studying. I was also working [in the Zionist youth group] Ne'emanei Zion and in Aliyat Hanoar . . . In Çamlica we'd go for walks; later the youth would come, from Czechoslovakia, Hungary, Romania. We'd meet them at Sirkeci [train station] and invite them as guests. I didn't go to the Sirkeci station; I didn't have a lot of time. We'd invite them up to a hotel called Mado Palas in Moda; we'd invite them there and take them to Haydarpaşa [train station] on their way [to Palestine], and they'd go from there by train.[87]

Here, the story of Kuzguncuk becomes situated within the nationalist context in Turkey and bound together with the teller's identity and experiences as a young, bright student involved in Zionist youth groups.[88] This man is connected through Zionist youth groups to other Jews in Istanbul, and so his narrative of Kuzguncuk is thus also a Jewish narrative. He was both a Kuzguncuklu and a young man with an emerging Jewish political consciousness linked to people across the city who would eventually emigrate to Israel.

Another Tel Aviv interviewee's family was involved in Zionist activity in Istanbul, something that played a part in their move from Kuzguncuk to Kuledibi (near Galata) in the 1940s. Her family had origins in Italy and was known as Italian in Kuzguncuk. She explained that her father didn't want them to move to another neighborhood where they'd be known as Italian, so they moved near Galata so they could blend in with other Jews. Her father was a machinist, who also manufactured fake documents (such as visas or other certificates) to facilitate illegal emigration to Palestine or to change the birth dates of Jewish boys who didn't want to serve in the mandatory Turkish military service. She said that secret police dressed in plainclothes would linger around their front door. Her brother became one of the founders of the Zionist organization Pioneer, or Chaluz. She explained that this was a youth movement active in Galata that split from another Zionist movement, Manetzion. It was formed by Jewish youth who wanted to escape Turkey and go to Israel. They helped emigrating Jews leave from Galata in small boats. Her brother escaped through the Syrian border, which was still under the French Mandate at that time. He helped establish the kibbutz Hagoshrim, established by Turkish Jews in response, she said, to the fact that other kibbutzim didn't want Turks because they were "Eastern Jews." Her brother also fought in the 1948 brigades, in the same unit in which Ariel Sharon was an officer.

The declaration of Israel's statehood in 1948 caused the largest emigration of Jews from Turkey to Israel and directly impacted Kuzguncuk.[89] As an elderly woman described, "A lot of people went to Israel when it was founded." "Did a lot of our neighbors leave?" asked her son. "There was a grocer; the grocer's siblings all went. A lot of people went. Of course, they were poor." Most of the emigrants who left at this time were from lower socioeconomic classes and spoke Ladino. Not everyone wanted to leave, however, and not everyone who wanted to could. As one man explained, he didn't go because he had just married. He didn't speak Hebrew and would have encountered a lot of difficulty there. But his father-in-law, brother, nieces, and nephews are all in Israel. He explained, "I went to Israel a lot, traveled around there a lot; it's a beautiful place, wonderful people, country. I like it, but not once have I thought of going over there and settling down. We have no complaint here; no one ever gives anyone any trouble."

While emigration to Israel meant a loss of much of Kuzguncuk's Jewish population and while issues of upward mobility or desires to be with other Jews in new Jewish neighborhoods meant that many of those remaining were moving to other neighborhoods, some Jews were still moving to Kuzguncuk in the middle of the century. One man, born in Kuzguncuk in 1925, was married to a woman from Kadıköy in 1950. They met on the European side, where they were both working in the same neighborhood. After their marriage they settled in Kuzguncuk. They lived there until the 1980s, when they moved back to Kadıköy and later to Caddebostan, where they live now. In another example, a man from Ortaköy who married in the early 1960s met and married a woman from Kuzguncuk through an arranged marriage. She was from a poor family and worked in a factory, and after they were married, he forbade her to work outside the home but gave her the equivalent of the salary she had been earning in the factory. They lived first in Ortaköy but then moved to Kuzguncuk. He explained that there wasn't a lot of water in Ortaköy, and they were coming to Kuzguncuk every week to visit family. Then they moved and he bought his house from a Greek carpenter who was emigrating to Greece. They lived for nineteen years in Kuzguncuk, before they moved later to Göztepe in the early 1980s, where they live now. Moves to and from Kuzguncuk would continue to fluctuate, although ensuing events in the 1950s and 1960s meant that Kuzguncuk's Jewish population continued to decrease overall. The city's Jewish population fluctuations also reflected larger movements nationally, because Jewish mass emigration from Turkey caused remaining Jews to move to Istanbul, where Jewish communities remained.[90] Yet the majority of Turkey's Jews came to live not in traditional mahalles but in newer neighborhoods of Istanbul.

Emigrating from Kuzguncuk after the 1955 Riots

As I discuss in chapter 4, one of the most important events to impact minority emigration from Istanbul, and from Kuzguncuk, was the riots of 6–7 September 1955. Like in the stories recounted in that chapter, Kuzguncuklus in Tel Aviv also describe instances of their Muslim neighbors protecting Jewish neighbors in Kuzguncuk, and tellers emphasize the siblinghood between Kuzguncuklular of different ethnic-religious origins.

> There, in 1955, [19]56, the 6–7 September events happened. Turks against the Greeks, all the Greek places, their houses, they stole a lot; it was a big event. Turkish families protected the Jewish families. Turks at that time said, "gayrımüslim" [non-Muslim]; they confused people [meaning that rioters didn't know who was Greek versus Jewish or Armenian]. The Turks really protected us. One night, after 1955, was it 1962, 1963?—a different time, whenever it was that they started to attack, another time. Again it was Turks doing it, again from outside [Kuzguncuk]. There was a grandmother; she lived over on Garden Street; everyone called her "grandmother." Grandmother said, "No Greeks here!" and saved us.

A similar story is recounted by this woman in Tel Aviv: "The 6–7 September events happened, two years before I left, against the Greeks and

Armenians and the Jews. They went out; they burned the houses; they threw things out of the windows. It happened in all of Istanbul; it happened in Kuzguncuk too. Our good Turkish neighbors hid us."

By 1955 Kuzguncuk's demography had already begun to change radically with the arrival of large numbers of rural Turkish migrants—this is the context in which these memories of Turkish neighbors protecting Jews come across as exceptional. And, as discussed in chapter 4, many people remember that it was not local Kuzguncuklu Turks who participated in the riots but rather rural migrants who came on boats from other parts of the city during the riots. It was in this context of rural-urban migration that religious identity increasingly became a matter of assimilation versus otherness, of inclusion or exclusion from the larger sociality of the mahalle.

Memories of this period, particularly in one oral history of a man I'll refer to as Robert, illustrate the importance of the synagogue and of religious life in maintaining Jewish community relationships during that time, even for people who weren't religiously conservative. From the earliest histories of Jews in Istanbul, the synagogue traditionally played a very important role in the everyday life of a mahalle's Jewish community.[91] Robert's focus on the synagogue and on religious life reveals the fact that intracity migration, the loss of old communities, and the assimilation of Jews into neighborhoods most defined by secular, middle- and upper-middle-class life had come to change the nature of Jewish life in the mahalle. Although he described himself as not religious, as "not having looked warmly on religion" as a young person, he expressed nostalgia for the synagogue, for the special foods and events of religious holidays, and for family times shared with other Jews.

> There were two synagogues; how full they were on Saturdays, that
> they had a first and second service . . . Saturday was a typical Shabbat.
> Those who went to the first service were people who had to work
> later on in the day. The others, I'll give you an example, a worker in
> a factory, on Saturday . . . On Saturday we went to school [Hebrew
> school], after school straight to my maternal grandmother's; they
> were just coming home from synagogue. It was a holiday atmosphere;
> special foods were made, pastries and such; the best food was made
> that day. Saturdays were like a holiday for all the Jewish people of
> Kuzguncuk.

Later, he describes how, on

Friday afternoon, women would be at home preparing the table for
Shabbat. Women were working at home. Pastries and other foods were
prepared. At that time there was no oven at home. There was an oven
in Kuzguncuk but it wasn't for bread; it was for family foods. They'd
prepare a pan of what was to be baked, like pastries, and send their
sons with the pans to the oven. I would bring the food to the oven,
and they'd be ready at a certain time. Fridays were more when the
Jews' baking was done at the oven. In every house there were pastries.
Friday night the favorite foods would be eaten. Unleavened bread was
made at a place associated with the chief rabbi and was distributed at a
central location.

Socializing with family was important for Robert's family and, it seems
from his story, for Kuzguncuklu Jews in the 1960s:

In my childhood, you know, it was a different society. Women
generally sat at home. Women would gather together and visit. There
were a lot of neighborly relationships . . . I had a good friend (a
Muslim man), who was a policeman, and I used to go to his house . . .
He had a wife; over there we'd drink tea; they'd come to us; we'd go
to them.

Later, he says,

We were [with Muslims] in the same school, the same classes; we had
a lot of friends; this was real. But another reality—between family
visits, between couples, if we were going to the movies, or if there was
neighboring between families, of course it was more between Jewish
and Jewish families, or Greek and Greek families. It is true that we
went to the same cinema, for example, but if Muslim Turks and Jews
would go together, Jews would go more often with Jews, Greeks more
often with other Greeks . . . My father would tell me . . . "In our
time Kuzguncuk was all Jewish, us," he'd say . . . "At that time, more
accurately, we couldn't even speak Turkish," he said. In Kuzguncuk it
was always Jewish, Ladino, that was spoken. On the streets, even. Most
of us didn't know Turkish; there were that many of us.

In his memory of Kuzguncuk as a young boy, several decades after the turn of the century and of ethnic Turkish national events in Istanbul, so many Jews still lived in Kuzguncuk that he recalls that most of them didn't speak Turkish (or if they did, they didn't need to do so in public spaces). And yet his story also shows divisions between minority groups in social spaces and in interactions in social life.[92] As he says, his friendship with a Muslim was real, but he mostly socialized with other Jews.[93] Robert's narrative also describes the ways in which Jews sometimes dominated the main public social spaces of the neighborhood, as in the following excerpt:

> Spring and summer months, synagogues were full. When the people left synagogue, they went to a really nice cafeteria on the seaside. Everyone filled the cafeteria; of course the weather was beautiful. Tea, conversation until one or two. The whole cafeteria would be filled with Jews, women with men, with children. Young, old. Tea. The weather was beautiful; of course then the Bosphorus was much more beautiful. Now there's air pollution, traffic, natural areas covered with cement; the Bosphorus then was completely green. Jews would leave synagogue and sit. I'd be next to my paternal and maternal grandmothers, my uncle, passing time, children playing.

The synagogue was also an important place where he socialized with his friends:

> We children, Jewish children . . . of course in those times it was more religious; of course Kuzguncuk was a small place. In the afternoons children went to synagogue for religious education, especially when classes were closed, more especially in the summer; we gathered with the rabbi to read, learn prayers and Hebrew. I was the worst student. I never looked that warmly at religion . . . The rabbi especially in the summer months would try to get us more interested and would get us ice cream, ice cream for the ones who said their prayers well. In summer of course ice cream was our favorite thing; everyone would get an ice cream, how wonderful. Of course when there was no class we'd play in the synagogue garden, ball, or a game, these things too. We lived beautiful childhoods there.

These memories are similar to those of Balat, where "The informants spoke with an air of nostalgia about a quarter that had been huddled around its synagogues, where life flowed according to the rhythms of Jewish festivals and religious beliefs, whatever might be the degree of fortune of its inhabitants."[94] The centrality of the synagogue in daily local mahalle life and the public socializing of Jews in the mahalle is something that has eroded since the time of Robert's childhood.

Urbanization and Cultural Change

After the 1960s rural migration began to impact Kuzguncuk. Open areas along the main street, away from the coast road, began to be built with squatter settlements. A Jewish woman who was a child at this time told me about a new fountain that was installed in this area, close to where she lived, in the late 1960s. She said there had been two fountains, one by the sea, which had the best water, and a second fountain much farther up, near the corner of Icadiye Hamam Street. She said they used to bring water from there in buckets, water for drinking, washing, cooking, and everything. Then she said later they put in a third fountain, very close to where she lived, although it turned out to be dirty and have mosquitoes, and her mother didn't like her to get water from that fountain. The new fountain would have met the needs of the new Turkish, Muslim migrant population growing along Kuzguncuk's peripheral area. It's possible that my friend's mother might not have wanted her daughter to get water from this nearby fountain because of mixing with migrants.

The area she lived in was called the upper neighborhood, by the creek, which was also referred to in Ladino as Bella Vista (Beautiful View) or La Vinya (The Vineyard). This area of open space was used for gardening and picnicking and remained largely undeveloped until rural migrants began to establish squatter settlements there. As Tone Bringa explains, regarding sociospatial differentiation in a Bosnian village, in a statement that holds very true for midcentury Kuzguncuk as well, "the upper and lower part of the village occupied different ends of what we can call a hierarchy of culturedness, which is closely associated with the rural-urban divide."[95] By the 1960s social classes in Kuzguncuk continued to mix, although a sense of social and spatial differentiation by economic status had emerged, which would cause emigration of minorities and upper classes from Kuzguncuk.

In my childhood [early 1960s] there were also differences within Kuzguncuk. People closer to the sea were more wealthy. Middle people were more up the road. Poor people lived at the very end of the street, where a creek flowed; there was no road then. Now there's a road; cars go over it, but then it was a small dirt path. There were the poorer people. Then with time as the city grew and people got richer, then they moved to other neighborhoods.

An elderly Jewish man whose family is originally from Diyarbakir but who has been in Kuzguncuk all his life (he still lives there now) talked with me in front of a coffee shop on Icadiye Street, where he was sitting and drinking tea, waiting for the Saturday morning service to begin. As we spoke, he greeted Jews walking by who were going to services. He said to me, "There used to be so many Jews in Kuzguncuk; it was full of Jews, but now they come from other places to the synagogue, from Caddebostan. If they didn't come it would be just three families, no one left. Nothing of the old times is left here; they all went. After 1948 they went to Israel." I asked why people from Caddebostan come to Kuzguncuk's synagogue, and he said simply that "they come." I asked why would people leave Kuzguncuk and he said, "Caddebostan is a nice place; there are lots of them there." He said his brother went to Israel and is still there. His own family died, his wife and children, young. He couldn't go to Israel. He said at that time they'd give you a house and a job; it wasn't difficult. But still, "It's hard to settle in a new country." He doesn't know Hebrew. "In synagogue they use Hebrew, and I don't understand it," he said. He talked about a professor who bought their old house and filled it with books. He explained that it was sold cheaply and doesn't know why his father sold it [or he didn't want to tell me]. His father had been a construction worker. The departure of Jews from Kuzguncuk, combined with the arrival of rural migrants, was a theme of many other interviews, as seen in these excerpts:

Our family moved to Kadıköy in 1967; three to five years later an unbelievable decrease of Jews in Kuzguncuk happened. They went to places like Kadıköy, Bostancı, Caddebostan, Kurtuluş, Şişli, and by the middle of the 1970s or so only ten families or so remained in Kuzguncuk. People began to come from other places to fill the synagogues in Kuzguncuk. If you go on a Saturday, you'll see it full but all those people come from other neighborhoods. They come to keep the synagogue open. They are mostly those born in Kuzguncuk, but there are some who aren't. If the synagogue goes unused it will be closed, and the foundation will go to the state. To prevent this from happening, every Saturday there's a service.

And,

After 1965 the Greeks left. Then 1971 came. Greeks were in the back mahalle, about thirty people, ten to twelve families. Jews were forty to fifty families. Armenians were more up the street (near Bağlarbaşı and Dağhamamı) . . . Here was Jewish until 1975, when many families went to Caddebostan, to Şişli. Then the Anatolians came; with their families, they came.

One man, born in the early 1940s, who responded to a survey I distributed at the Kuzguncuk synagogue, wrote that he left Kuzguncuk in 1969 to move to Suadiye when he got married. He went to Suadiye because "at the time I bought my house the atmosphere was like that of Kuzguncuk." He also wrote that he still visits his old Kuzguncuklu friends, but that they live in Moda, Caddebostan, and Şişli. Another respondent, also born in the early 1940s, lives in Caddebostan. He moved there in 1962 because of the "large presence of Jews" there. He also visits old Kuzguncuklu friends, some in Kuzguncuk, some in Caddebostan, and sees them at their workplaces in various parts of the city. Another respondent, also born in the early 1940s, now lives in Göztepe. He didn't move there until 2000 and still goes to Kuzguncuk every day to visit friends, writing that "I don't return home until I've first gone to Kuzguncuk." He continues to visit old Kuzguncuklu friends in other neighborhoods around Kadıköy. Another resident, born in the early 1950s, left Kuzguncuk in 1970 for Istinye. He wrote that none of his old friends or neighbors remain in Kuzguncuk, but he's been returning to the synagogue since 1988.

The nature of the decline of cosmopolitan culture, that the departure of minorities happened together with the arrival of rural migrants, came up in Robert's narrative. He argued that the rural/urban difference is at the root of current issues in Istanbul, rather than a difference between Muslims and non-Muslims.

What can I explain about Kuzguncuk before I came into the world? . . . In the 1930s it was mostly Jews, Greeks, Armenians, not too many Muslims . . . In my childhood it began to change. Why? In the 1950s in Turkey urbanization started, from villages, migration to cities. Kuzguncuk was . . . influenced of course, definitely. The Black Sea people, and the people from Anatolia, they came to Kuzguncuk, Muslim Turks . . . In my childhood there was still a population of Greeks, Armenians, Jews, but not the majority; the majority were Turks. The foundation of Israel in 1948 caused Jewish emigration. Jewish people in Kuzguncuk also moved to more upper-class neighborhoods in Istanbul . . . By the middle of the 1970s only ten families or so remained in Kuzguncuk. People began to come from other places to fill the synagogues in Kuzguncuk . . . There were clear cultural differences. Cultural and life differences between city people and newcomers. The problems maybe come from these differences, maybe from village and city difference more than religious difference. All the Jews, Armenians, Greeks, Muslims in the city had lived among each other sharing the same culture; there was no big cultural difference. They were all city people.

In his narrative, he described how minorities were leaving as rural migrants arrived in Kuzguncuk. He mentions only that Jews emigrated after 1948 and omits any discussion of the larger national or sociopolitical context that shaped migration decisions at that time.

One elderly Jewish woman I met migrated from Kuzguncuk to the European side in the late forties, and then in the late sixties she moved again to live in Gayrettepe. She told me about life in Kuzguncuk in the thirties and forties; for her, the changing ethnic-religious composition of the neighborhood was clearly an important element in her experience and perception, and she contrasted the pleasant cosmopolitan past with a different view of what Kuzguncuk is like today: "Sometimes I go back to Kuzguncuk, to the synagogue, to look at the house. Once I knocked on the door, a covered woman came to the door. I said, 'I was born here, born in this house. Can I come in?' She said, 'Welcome, welcome.' She was a good woman. But . . . her head was covered. In my time we were so modern; we would ride bicycles, go swimming."

Her story reveals what she thinks is an important cultural change, as she compares the woman's covered dress with the modernity she experienced riding bicycles and swimming as a young girl. The fluency of Kuzguncuk-lus with a diversity of languages and cultures in the past is contrasted with the rurality, or relative nonmodernity, of a rural migrant Turk in a head scarf. Secularism and modernity are notions she relates to as a Turkish Jewish woman, and as she invokes the link between these two through the re-telling of this memory, she aligns her personal identity with the dominant secularist discourse of the state.[96]

Her movement from an old neighborhood to new neighborhoods became important, perhaps, for moving up in the internal hierarchy of the larger Jewish community, together with general economic success, education, and other signs of modern, integrated Turkish identity.[97] Her memories of Kuzguncuk's multilingual and diverse past also suggest, however, that for her, cosmopolitanism is a sign of modernity and that this modernity is urban, secular, and no longer located in Kuzguncuk.

The Jewish Neighborhood Is Lost

For other remaining Jews in Istanbul, describing the loss of Kuzguncuk's cosmopolitanism is less about aligning oneself with modernist discourse and more directly about articulating identity as a minority, as in the following narrative. This woman describes the pain of having lost her community in Kuzguncuk (and does not describe exactly what happened). Our interview took place after she took me on a tour of Kuzguncuk to show me all the houses that were homes to Jewish families when she was a child.

> Husbands would come from the ferry station. There were a lot of Jews here; many, many Jews were here. After that the Jews went here and there. Before they left, the Jews, everyone in the evening would wait for their husbands at the ferry station down below. They'd dress up, the women, and when their husbands would get off the ferry, they'd walk

with them arm in arm. There were restaurants with music and outside tables and chairs, and there they'd sit, and they'd eat. There was a synagogue, and they'd go to the cinema . . . Everyone could wear their bathing suit and walk down to the sea with their bathing suits; then it was so free that no one would look at anyone else and they'd wear their bathing suits and go into the sea . . . Of course I wore my bathing suit and went to the sea, everyone did . . . Amy, we had a beautiful life, until '65, here, until '65. Yes. [I asked her, "What happened in 1965?"] Then, things happened; I won't say what, and the Jews left. They sold their houses . . . Ayyyy, there's so much to say, but I've lost my head; I'm upset. Everyone went; everyone scattered; everyone sold their house. You understand? For one lira, for eighty kuruş, they sold their houses, the whole Jewish community. After that Kuzguncuk was finished.

The memory of being together with other Jews on the main street and in Kuzguncuk's public spaces is also recalled in this person's story: "Kuzguncuk is a beautiful place . . . There is Balat, and Hasköy, but our little place on the Bosphorus was Kuzguncuk. The life we lived there was like nowhere else . . . When we went out, from the lower synagogue, from the upper synagogue, we'd gather together, that crowd; we'd walk along the main street. An amazing togetherness, an amazing togetherness, a big crowd, an amazing togetherness, like, happiness." This sense of togetherness in public space contrasts with the ways in which Kuzguncuklu Jews today are fairly circumspect about displaying their identities, a consequence of the increasingly Turkish-Muslim character of the neighborhood in the context of an ever more nationalist and Muslim Istanbul.

By the late 1980s, the majority of Istanbul's Jews had come to live on its European side, in the area north of Taksim.[98] One elderly man explained the transformation of the neighborhood fabric after Jews left. His story describes a later phase of change in the neighborhood, when it had become truly transformed by increasing and continued rural migration and by the final loss of the Greek and Jewish community.

Before [in the early seventies] every four out of ten houses was Jewish. The neighbor next door was Muslim; he had his own house. The other house was Jewish, but he emigrates, marries, sells the house, that house becomes Muslim. It was all mixed. For example, here [in the synagogue] there's a Greek caretaker, an Armenian caretaker; it's all changed. In Kuzguncuk it's all mixed people. Here my brother was living in a five-story building, one floor was Jewish. They emigrated, sold it to a Muslim. It's mixed everywhere.

He said in one case a family left Kuzguncuk because of intolerance from the increasing number of Muslim Turks in the neighborhood: "There was a house; they lived on the main street. She was a tailor; her husband made pajamas. During the Cyprus events, they threw rocks at her house, at their own neighbor's house. They broke everything. They moved to Kadıköy, and then they went to Greece." He described what life in Kuzguncuk was like in the 1970s, saying,

> There were more Jews than Greeks then. This place was Jewish until
> 1975; then most of us went to Israel, Caddebostan, Şişli; this is how the
> emigration went. The Greeks left after 1965. It started to become like
> it is now, with the people who came from Anatolia with their families
> and friends . . . When I was a child in Ortaköy, there were about eighty
> Jewish families there, many related. Most of them are now in Israel.

One of the elements at work in the migration of Jews from historical mahalles is their identity as urban. For these later intracity emigrants from Kuzguncuk, the reason for moving to new Jewish neighborhoods was not to seek elite social status. Rather, Kuzguncuk had lost its cosmopolitan and diverse social character because of a shift toward a less socially and politically tolerant and more homogeneously Muslim, Turkish, rural migrant culture. In this way, nationalism and urbanization were not separate processes but, rather, *worked together* with urbanization to transform the social spaces of urban life. Symbols of Muslim, Turkish identity came to signify cultural conservatism in social spaces, together with Jewish perceptions of migrants' lack of familiarity with non-Muslims' liberal, urban ways of life. Jewish emigration to new neighborhoods was thus very similar to the movement of other non-Muslim minorities through the city and also to the movement of the Turkish cultural and economic elite to new expensive neighborhoods. This process continues as gated communities and exclusive neighborhoods blossom in the city and in its periphery. However, for minorities, these issues are not separate from issues of national identity, as issues of cultural change and rural-urban migration reverberate together with minority memories of Turkish nationalist events and intolerance of minority languages and ways of life in the past. As this occurred, Jews continued to move through various neighborhoods in the city in a spatial practice to protect and maintain their identity, and old neighborhoods such as Kuzguncuk lost their minority communities. Thus, as the city was Turkified through state policies against minorities, the urbanization of Istanbul effectively meant a Turkification of Istanbul's urban culture. Minorities view themselves—and are viewed by the Turks whose families were of Istanbul for several generations—as the holders of a true Istanbul culture, because they embody its past.

The perception among Jewish community leadership that assimilation is a problem has meant increasing attention to preserving Jewish history. In this context, old neighborhoods become symbolic places through which the larger Istanbul Jewish community maintains its heritage and identity, although very few Jews live in the old mahalles today. Today, the people managing the synagogue and the majority of people who attend Saturday services in Kuzguncuk come from other neighborhoods. During my field-work in 2001 and 2002, plans were underway by staff at the Jewish news-paper Şalom to hold the Jewish cultural day of the year in Kuzguncuk in June 2002. Community members were collecting photographs, artifacts, documents, and other memorabilia to display at a street fair in front of the synagogue in Kuzguncuk to celebrate the Jewish history of that commu-nity. The materials were gathered, although the event itself was canceled because of security concerns. The larger Jewish community thus maintains its relationship to Kuzguncuk from a distance, through the past.

Geographies of Memory

The geography of memory—that is, the social space through and on which memory is constructed—is complex and constituted together with the production of memory itself. Memory and narrative are always grounded in locality. The ways in which we imagine, narrate, and practice the social relationships that make up who we are always occur in specific places; thus the relationship to place is constitutive of identity. As I demonstrate in this chapter, the geography of memory for minority narratives told in Istanbul is the larger nationalist context in Turkey. While minority narratives told in Turkey avoid describing contentious political events and feelings of persecution, stories told in Israel tell of antiminority events as they happened at the state level and in personal experience.

In this chapter I examine how minority perspectives reveal that the state-authored nationalism that produced the categories of Turk and minority did indeed operate through urban space. Oral histories and migration flows illuminate the discursive field in which notions of national belonging and ethnic difference came to have meaning for ordinary residents, and they raise serious questions regarding the emphases and silences surrounding the nostalgic cultural memory of Kuzguncuk's cosmopolitanism. These stories reveal, in contrast, that the mahalle was transformed through nationalist discourse and antiminority events into a space through which minority identity, and difference, was reproduced. Ordinary residents, with their words and actions in the mahalle, sometimes reinforced and sometimes reinterpreted the categories Turk and minority as terms of belonging or exclusion, thus coming to have power as individuals to sustain or dismantle the power of nationalist ideology. Examining the ways in which ideology comes to have meaning through the interactions between people in local places such as Kuzguncuk complicates our understanding of the primacy of the state in producing the nation.

Conclusion

Nostalgia for Cosmopolitanism in Istanbul

Streets of Memory investigates the tensions, silences, and absences surrounding Istanbul's minority past, a past that is, paradoxically, constantly being recalled, represented, and made visible in the present. Contradictions imbue the mahalle with a beguiling mystery surrounding what was, and what is, really there. In memories of Kuzguncuklu residents, "such a thing never could have happened in Kuzguncuk" (but it did); "Kuzguncuk has better neighboring than other parts of Istanbul" (but no one knows each other anymore). In a further irony, Istanbul's past minorities are represented by the landscape, while current minorities are absent from the scene.[1] In the search to understand Kuzguncuk, *Streets of Memory* uncovers many truths embedded in landscapes of the cosmopolitan past.

I began the book by examining a particular cultural memory of a tolerant, multicultural past circulating through Istanbul through its cultural media and through the narratives of residents. In this cultural memory, there was no difference between neighbors on the basis of religion. Greeks, Jews, Armenians, and Muslims shared food and religious celebrations. The pace of life was gentler, and people were more respectful of each other. This cultural memory seems, to people in Istanbul, to be particularly true for Kuzguncuk. And so I examined the ways in which the narratives that construct this memory acquire authority in Kuzguncuk by relying on particular landscapes, such as the mosque and church together, as evidence of their truth. I also unfolded the most significant dimension of this process: the ways in which the value-laden cultural image in material form conceals the historical processes that created it by guiding our gaze to only that which the image is intended to represent. To expose this work of the landscape, I shared some of the stories that are obscured by the landscape's powerful nostalgic image. I related the story of the Greek woman and the state confiscation of her family's market garden property; the narratives of many older Kuzguncuklu people of all stripes who described a cultural shift in neighborhood life brought by rural-urban Turkish migration; stories from Kuzguncuklu Jews in Israel who described their experiences in Turkey of anti-Semitism and being targeted by the Wealth Tax; and the narrative told by the minority woman whose son was returning from his military service and whose neighbors told her she had no right to fly the Turkish flag . . . these and other stories are concealed by the nostalgic cultural memory of a cosmopolitan past where everyone belonged in, and to, the city.

What does this study of nostalgia for Istanbul's minority peoples and places tell us about the life and culture of the city? The nostalgia I studied in *Streets of Memory* is yet another dimension of what other scholars have argued is a particular intertwining of state and society in Turkey to the extent that not only are state and society not distinct but they are indeed mutually interdependent. In *Nostalgia for the Modern*, for example, Esra Özyürek argues that nostalgia for Atatürk and for the early years of the republic became commodified, privatized, and personalized in the 1990s. During that period in Istanbul, a cultural and personal embracing of state ideology arose, she says, in response to the failure of the state.[2] In the context of frustration with state corruption, the disempowerment of the old secular elite, and the rise in Islamist politics that challenged the nature of Turkish national identity, people began to participate in practices such as purchasing and displaying images of Atatürk. The commodified nostalgia for Atatürk demonstrated a personal identification with the modern, secular ideals that were symbolized by his memory but that many people felt had been disastrously betrayed by subsequent leaders.

In an urban context where the head scarf became a political sign, pictures of Atatürk and other symbols of Kemalist ideology also became tools for enacting the cultural politics of the secular nature of the Turkish state. The nostalgia for the cosmopolitan past discussed in *Streets of Memory* has also become commodified and privatized through the gentrification of historical minority mahalles. The nostalgia for cosmopolitanism, however, is related to a different facet of the state's identity than the nostalgia Özyürek studied, for it responds more directly to the ethnic-national dimension of the state's identity and the failed promise of the nation to be inclusive of all local ethnic groups.[3] The cultural politics of ethnic national identity are negotiated through nostalgia for the cosmopolitan past through symbols, memories, emotions, and stories, and, most importantly for this book, through the representation and reproduction of cultural landscapes such as the mahalle landscape of Kuzguncuk.

The processes through which state and society in Turkey are intertwined thus have an important geographic dimension. The landscapes of the city are not merely the palimpsest on which symbols of ethnic-religious identity or ideologies of nationalism, cosmopolitanism, and secularism are represented or inscribed. Rather, the cultural politics of identity *work through the urban landscape*, which thus plays an integral role in the reproduction and contestation of national imaginaries. The landscape should be viewed first as a medium through which identity politics are articulated and negotiated. It is also, however, unlike other cultural media, a constitutive player in this process because of its materiality and representative power. The notion that the Armenian Orthodox Church in Kuzguncuk gave land to the mosque appears as a natural truth because the church and mosque actually, physically, stand side by side; they seem, incontrovertibly, to be evidence of a historical truth of siblinghood. We can see the church and mosque. We cannot doubt that they stand together. The landscape is not only a standing materiality, however, but also a *way of seeing*: the conditions in Istanbul at the turn of the millennium that produce this way of seeing mean that this narrative of multiethnic tolerance, this cultural memory, acquires the veneer and the cultural-political authority of truth. This powerful narrative image draws more people to consume and reproduce the seemingly historical mahalle.

The landscapes representing the cultural memory of cosmopolitanism in Istanbul are, like cultural memory, continually being re-created in the present. The landscape itself becomes a constitutive part of the processes of imagining and making real both inclusion and exclusion from the neighborhood social space and the nation. Nationalist ideologies are not merely produced by the state and adopted by urban residents; the landscape, through its production, commodification, and interpretation, becomes a medium through which nationalist ideology is made meaningful, in multiple and sometimes unintended ways, just as state secularism became personal. The urban landscape is the physical, cultural, geographic dimension of the intertwining of state and society in Turkey. This is why, perhaps, that Istanbul, the city itself, is such a constant subject of representation, meditation, love, longing, and debate in Turkish culture.

Whose cultural politics does the nostalgia for Istanbul's cosmopolitanism serve: what does this nostalgia *do*? The nostalgia that foregrounds tolerance in interethnic relationships obscures the tensions and violence of the processes through which the cosmopolitan city became nationally Turkish. By appearing to be real, by the ways in which the materiality of landscapes seem to authentically represent a tolerant multicultural past, this nostalgia preserves the illusions of the state, illusions that the nation is inclusive, that it does or can exist for all. Like the nostalgia for the modern, this nostalgia for equality and tolerance occurs in a time and place that the state is threatened, and state/social (they are not separate) intolerance is so acutely experienced. The nostalgia for cosmopolitanism is thus, in part, also a privatization of a state narrative.

But why do non-Muslim minorities become the subject of nostalgia? As I demonstrate in chapters 2 and 4, the nostalgic emphasis on minority cultures in Istanbul is a way of reinforcing a sense of cultural and social difference, a way of othering, that ultimately works to co-opt minorities back into the predominantly Turkish imagination of the city. Thus nostalgia embraces and reinforces a nationalist context that defines social difference (without which, there perhaps wouldn't *be* social difference) along ethnic and religious lines. If we interrogate the cultural politics of this nostalgia, we see that nostalgia constitutes the flip side of silence. By focusing on the dimensions of interethnic neighborhood social life that emphasize togetherness and sharing, nostalgia erases fissures and difference. In chapter 4, I discuss how nostalgic memories of life on the main street smooth over the violence of particular antiminority events in Kuzguncuk: the erasures accomplished by nostalgia actually reify the ideology behind the dominant national narrative, that Turkey is an inherently Turkish nation. Nostalgia for cosmopolitanism, by sustaining the erasure of difference, writes minorities back into a seamless collective, and so nostalgia for minority places and people is part of the discursive field that dispossesses minorities of place. Minorities comply by maintaining silence regarding their experiences of Turkish nationalist discrimination and by assimilating, thereby ensuring their safety. In this way, the primary function of the nostalgia for cosmopolitanism is to sustain and mediate social and personal experiences of ethnic Turkish nationalism. The conclusion is that in Istanbul, cosmopolitanism is imagined locally in ways that perpetuate the notions of social difference and inequality that cosmopolitanism, as an ideal, claims to transcend.

The Cultural Politics of Writing Cosmopolitanism

As in so many other places in the world, nostalgic cultural memories in Istanbul function to obscure difficult tensions of the past. What is less obvious are the ways in which this process depends on an unstated agreement by everyone, Turks and minorities alike, to comply with a code of belonging, an agreement that is not entirely succeeding. No one, I think, is comfortable with the price of belonging, which involves upholding mahalle propriety, including limitations regarding proper behavior for women and for neighbors; proper mores that dictate "not speaking too openly"; and restrictions among minorities not to discuss their past and present experiences of fear and discrimination as a result of Turkish nationalism to others outside their private inner circles.

The price of belonging, in Turkey, comes at a cost—the forgetting of particular histories at the expense of the frequent retelling of others and the silencing of particular memories that cannot entirely be repressed. Everywhere, just as nostalgic cultural memorabilia proliferate, as seemingly historical landscapes become commodified, as people are drawn to live in, eat at, and buy postcards of old minority places and watch television shows that romanticize the past, we can also see the signs that, in Istanbul, the propriety that conspires to forget/remember history in particular ways is breaking down. Witness the social changes that have become increasingly visible in Istanbul since the 1990s: the rise of virulent ethnic Turkish nationalism; the surge in Islamist cultural and political symbols and power; the widespread cultural representation and consumerism surrounding Atatürk; the strong political movement to advance Kurdish and other minority human rights; the growth of personal and place-based history projects among university faculty, students, and ordinary residents; the growing voices of critical Turkish historians and sociologists interrogating the secrets of the state; and the vocal, authoritative response of historians who support the state narrative. This is the larger context in which the complicated, silence-filled, nostalgic stories of Kuzguncuk are told, and the landscapes that recall a sense of history are re-created. Istanbul, and Istanbullus, are negotiating the terms of belonging through a transformative cultural moment, and yet they do so within a social context conditioned by factors far more complex than a binary distinction between Turkish and minority identities, or between cosmopolitanism and nationalism.

Every discussion regarding minorities in Turkey becomes polarizing, whether among residents, pundits, politicians, or researchers, whether Turkish, European, or American. This binary way of understanding place and history is not unique to minority issues in Turkey but is related to the position of Turkey in the Middle East and to global cultural political discourse surrounding Muslim and non-Muslim social life in general. See, for example, what Yoram Bilu and Andre Levy write regarding research on the historical Jewish community of Morocco:

> The scholarship on the Jewish-Muslim encounter in Morocco has
> been dominated by two contrasting approaches. Some researchers
> have chosen to describe Jewish existence amid the Muslim majority as
> basically peaceful, emphasizing, among other factors, the important
> role of personal ties and dyadic arrangements between individuals
> from the two sectors in regulating relations and neutralizing potential
> tensions. As against this "harmony" position, other scholars have
> espoused a "conflict" approach, which takes special note of the
> suppression and humiliation that were the lot of the Jews in the
> Muslim orbit and of their inferior legal-religious status as *dhimmi*. The
> fact that such radically divergent conclusions could be derived from
> studies dealing with the same subject matter is in itself an indication

of the complexity and multidimensionality inherent in Jewish-Muslim relations in Morocco.[4]

Christine Philliou makes a similar point regarding Ottoman historiography, which has viewed the "Ottoman legacy" as one of either authoritarianism and ethnic strife or of cosmopolitan multiconfessionality. Her research on the centrality of Orthodox Christians to nineteenth-century Ottoman administration reveals layer on layer of paradoxes. These contradictions are only paradoxical, however, because of the ways in which we impose our own imagined but rigid boundaries between ethnic and social groups. We do so, she argues, because we always study the Ottoman past from our own national present.[5]

This situation raises complicated questions regarding how we understand oral histories of the cosmopolitan past in Kuzguncuk, because we read about and study contemporary Turkey, too, from our own national present. This national present, like landscapes of cosmopolitanism, occludes a real understanding of interethnic neighborhood life. Throughout *Streets of Memory* I have written about the ways in which nostalgia serves to silence critical perspectives on the state. However, my research suggests that there was also—*together with* the process of Turkification and nationalism—a shared neighborhood practice where belonging as Kuzguncuklu transcended national/minority social difference. It does seem that neighbors cared about each other and shared many rituals and practices of ordinary daily life, even while some of them also sometimes articulated prejudice or discrimination. During the process of rural-urban migration, some neighbors dispossessed each other of their property or benefited from the sale and abandonment of minority properties, even while they may also have protected their neighbors during the moments of crisis that led to their emigration. Some of this complexity is nostalgically remembered in oral histories, and some of it is silenced by nostalgia. In midcentury Istanbul, cosmopolitan social relations *existed alongside* a process of nationalization of urban space and culture, and eventually were destroyed by the ways in which nationalism and urbanization coincided, as nationalist ideals became more widespread and minorities left, which is why cosmopolitanism is the subject of so much nostalgia today.

Joelle Bahloul arrives at a similar question regarding the ways in which all Jewish and Muslim memories of interethnic life in midcentury colonial

Algeria stressed the harmony of neighborly relationships between Jews and Muslims. She wonders "whether it was not just another aspect of the heroizing effect inscribed in memory or . . . a matter of my hosts' telling me what they thought I wanted to hear." Her suspicions were challenged, however, by the host of specific details Jews and Muslims remembered, and by the fact that she was spontaneously very warmly welcomed, as the descendant of a Jewish family, by the Muslim neighbors who remembered her relatives. Bahloul argues that memories of harmony are a strategy for coping with what were historical tensions and describes the relationships between these groups as one of "distinction without hostility."[6]

In midcentury Istanbul, as ethnic nationalism was promoted by the state and as minorities emigrated, was it not possible that there were some individual neighborhood friendships and local neighboring practices that survived? What is there to make of Turkish-Israeli Jews who remember friendships with Greek, Armenian, and Muslim neighbors and who go back to Istanbul to visit, or Turks in Istanbul who maintain long-distance relationships with their former Greek neighbors, or the kinds of relationships and friendships between Jewish and secular Muslim Turks in Istanbul now? Are they only possible through a distance, facilitated through silence or the years and miles traversed since emigration? Or is it possible that this distance is a recent outcome of a long period of urban nationalism during which Turkish, Jewish, and Greek neighbors indeed shared a respectful awareness of (and took pleasure in) social difference in the neighborhood? In this case, can we say that Kuzguncuk *was* cosmopolitan?

A shared relationship to locality is indeed something that brought Christians, Jews, and Muslims together in Turkey to share a place-based identity. This is why rural-urban migration, which broke apart lived relationships to place over time, played such an important role in processes of urban Turkish nationalism in destroying cosmopolitan local life. We can see this place-based cosmopolitanism in many different recent studies of Turkish minority identities. In novels about the Greek-Turkish population exchange, for example, authors portray a "culture of coexistence where Anatolia does not signify a national territory but rather a soil that organically relates individuals to each other."[7] In another example, Rum identity on the (formerly Greek and now Turkish) island of Imbros/Gökçeada is constructed through memory of, and attachment to, place rather than through national ethnic-religious frameworks.[8] Shared relationships to place are so important for Rum Istanbullu emigrants in Athens that they share a distinctive identity in many ways closer to other Istanbullus, even to Turks, than to other Greeks in Athens.[9]

Interethnic relationships in Istanbul continue to create important cultural forms even now, such as Turkish Jewish music, for example. Historically, Ottoman Jewish religious music was produced through networks of social relationships occurring in multiethnic social spaces and neighborhoods of Istanbul.[10] Interethnic relationships continue to sustain Turkish Jewish religious music making in Istanbul today, in spite of the fact that minority communities have almost disappeared and are in many ways assimilated or hidden.[11] As I demonstrate in chapter 5, minority intermarried women and Turkish Muslim women employ complex strategies of concealing and revealing particular aspects of identity as they neighbor and depend on each other in daily life. To what extent do their practices reflect a historical culture of interethnic relations in urban daily life: can we think of *them* as cosmopolitan?

As we should be suspicious of the narratives landscapes tell, we should also be very cautious of claiming or seeking any one particular truth regarding cosmopolitanism. We need to interrogate why cosmopolitanism is such a salient topic of current academic study and political debate and what our expectations are when we encounter research on, or memories of, interethnic relationships. Oral histories of Kuzguncuk suggest that there is no one "truth" regarding the historical or contemporary existence of cosmopolitanism in Istanbul. Every person of Istanbul experiences and remembers the city from a partial, contextual, positioned reality. There are thus many truths.

The issues of polarization in thinking about national identities and minority histories in Turkey arise from the larger global context that sees cosmopolitanism as a Western inheritance and thus assumes an either/or set of possibilities.[12] Discussing, researching, and writing about cosmopolitanism in Turkey takes place in this same global context; it, too, has a cultural politics. As Turkey seeks accession to the European Union, for example, the state negotiates improvements regarding minority human rights locally in the context of its ongoing international political relationship with Europe. Minorities in Istanbul become caught in the crosshairs as Turkey feels itself to be in a position of defending its sovereignty and legitimacy against a body that had once attempted to occupy it, even while it wants to position itself favorably with regard to economic and political ties with Europe and the United States. In this context, what does it *do* to argue that Istanbul, that largest city in predominantly Muslim Turkey, was, or could be, cosmopolitan? What does it *mean* to argue that life in Istanbul involved—and continues to mean—a careful negotiation of multiple identities in daily life?

Right now there is ample evidence that not only nationalist, ethnic violence is increasing in Istanbul but antiminority rhetoric is also on the rise, especially among secular right-wing nationalists and in the Islamist press. Minorities are increasingly silent, and silenced. And yet there is, too, an increasing curiosity and desire among Turkish citizens to learn more about places and pasts in Turkey, including the possibility that minority histories exist, heretofore forgotten, in personal family histories and in the histories of neighborhoods. And so although in Istanbul nostalgia largely functions to obscure history, it is also possible that interest in cosmopolitanism may indicate a shift, an increasing awareness of minority positions and experiences. Is increasing ethnic-nationalist intolerance and violence a sign that rigid nationalist definitions of the nation can no longer contain the future? What would a transition from a discursive field dominated by nationalism to one conditioned by a sense of awareness of a multifarious, complicated urbanity look like? Oral histories and observations of Kuzguncuk today suggest that tolerance and intolerance together structured complicated mahalle relationships in daily life. Is this what it means to see cosmopolitanism inhabited in reality?

If nationalist, secularist, and Islamist intolerance is ever to subside in Istanbul, people must openly perceive that antiminority discrimination and oppression is a problem and must also imagine a peaceful, shared diversity to be possible. Imagining that a multiethnic, multireligious, diverse urban life happened in the past, by looking at the places where it happened, must occur together with a critical look at how and why those places were transformed and why non-Muslim minorities are now, mostly, gone. The church and the mosque must not merely be taken for granted as "proof" that tolerance existed. Similarly, oral histories that recall a shared neighborhood life cannot be seen as simply reproducing a nostalgic discourse. Rather, memories of cosmopolitanism must be examined for how they speak of loss and betrayal, and how they articulate a stake in the future of the city. As the process of Turkish nationalism occurred through Istanbul, it transformed—and was transformed by—the city's multiethnic mahalles in various and in complicated ways, producing memories of both tolerance and of violence, remembered and untold. These stories must be brought together, through the places where they originated. That has been the aim of this book.

NOTES

Introduction

1. I use the word "Turk" to describe a Muslim citizen of Turkey because this is over-whelmingly how people, regardless of religion, refer to Muslims. Jews and Christians, however, are not usually referred to primarily as Turks, but with words that identify their religion or ethnicity. This language reveals the significance of the relationship between Muslim identity and Turkish ethnicity, and how the commonplace notion of belonging in Turkey is defined in ethnic and religious terms.

2. See Özbek, "Arabesk Culture." For a discussion of the negotiation between rural and urban identities in Ankara, see Nalbantoğlu, "Silent Interruptions."

3. Hebbert, "Street as Locus," 581.

4. Ibid., 592.

5. In the preface of their edited volume dedicated to Spiro Kostof, authors Çelik, Favro, and Ingersoll analyze the architectural characteristics of particular streets in diverse international cities within their social contexts. Their work is inspired by Kostof's own attention to issues of vernacular architecture and multiculturalism, themes important also for this book. See, for example, Kostof, *History of Architecture*.

6. Bahloul, "Architecture," 10.

7. See Slyomovics, *Object of Memory*.

8. İçduygu, "Anatomy of Civil Society." See also Committee against Racism and Discrimination, *Review of Minority Rights*; U.S. Bureau of Democracy, Human Rights, and Labor, "Human Rights Practices"; and Commission of the European Communities, *Progress Report*.

9. Penal Code 301, instituted in June 2005, is a law prohibiting the insult of Turkey, of Turkish ethnicity, or the Turkish state. Until reform of the law in 2008, the law prohibited "insulting Turkishness." The law was revised in an attempt to prohibit its abuse by ultranationalist lawyers who have attempted to prosecute famous authors, editors, and journalists who write openly about minority perspectives on contentious political issues in Turkey.

10. Haluk Şahin, "Türkiyeli, Türk, Alt-kimlik, Üst-kimlik" [Of Turkey, Turk, Underlying Identity, Overarching Identity], *Radikal*, 22 October 2004.

11. Meijer, *Cosmopolitanism, Identity and Authenticity*. See also my discussion in chapter 1.

12. Zürcher, *Turkey*.

13. Bauman, *Culture as Praxis*, xxx. The process of defining ethnic Turkishness relied primarily on linguistic distinction, an emphasis that excluded non–Turkish-speaking (including non-Muslim) minorities. See Bali, "Politics of Turkification," and Çağaptay, "Passage to Turkishness," 64.

14. Göçek, "Dangerous Underbelly."

15. For nationalism in the built environment, see Bozdoğan, *Modernism and Nation-Building*; Sargın, "Displaced Memories"; Wilson, "Mausoleum"; and Meeker, "Once There Was." For nationalism in urban life, see Çınar, *Modernity*; Öncu, "Ideal Home"; Keyder, *Global and the Local*; Navaro-Yashin, *Faces of the State*; and Özyürek, *Nostalgia for the Modern*. Because I focus on the role of ordinary citizens in national identity politics, I set aside a discussion of the ways in which counternarratives to state ideology are promoted by official groups in the public sphere, in contrast to, for example, Çınar's discussion of the ways in which the Islamist political party in power in the Istanbul municipality in the 1990s articulated a modern Islamic identity through urban projects in the city (*Modernity*).

16. Timothy Mitchell, *Colonising Egypt*; Çelik, *Urban Forms, Empire*; Wright, *Politics of Design*.

17. Makdisi and Silverstein, introduction, *Memory and Violence*.

18. Salamandra, *New Old Damascus*.

19. Neuwirth and Pflitsch, "Crisis and Memory."

20. Ibid., 17.

21. Meijer, *Cosmopolitanism, Identity and Authenticity*.

22. Bali, *Adventure in Turkification*, 196.

23. Grigoriadis, "Turk or Türkiyeli?"

24. Like the secular cultural memories that are the focus of my study, Islamist representations of Turkey's Ottoman heritage also idealized a past multiculturalism but did so within a Islamic religious framework in which non-Muslims were protected within an Islamic state. Both broad strains of cultural memory can be seen as challenging the strained secular, ethnically Turkish identity for Turkey authored by the secular, military, ruling elite. See Çolak, "Ottomanism vs. Kemalism."

25. Key works in this field are Renan, "What Is a Nation?"; Elie Kedourie, *Nationalism*; Smith, *Theories of Nationalism*; Breuilly, *Nationalism and the State*; Gellner, *Nations and Nationalism*; Anderson, *Imagined Communities*; Smith, *Ethnic Origins of Nations*; and Greenfeld, *Nationalism*.

26. See Smith, "Ethno-Symbolism."

27. Brubaker, *Nationalism Reframed*, 7.

28. Anderson, *Imagined Communities*.

29. For a regional example of this approach, see Davis's work on the Baathist regime's production of Iraqi history and heritage for the purposes of suppressing cultural pluralism and political dissent (*Memories of State*). For a focus on the failures of this project, see Simon, "Imposition of Nationalism."

30. Göçek, "Dangerous Underbelly." For Mardin (writing in 1997), Turkish social science has been characterized by a framework that understands social change in terms

of top-down projects, which may explain why much of the focus has been on the state's imagining of the nation rather than a ground-up investigation on how people themselves make meaning of this process ("Projects as Methodology").

31. Çağaptay, "Passage to Turkishness," 63–64.

32. Gür, "Stories in Three Dimensions"; Wilson, "Mausoleum"; Inan, "Lectures and Courses"; Burris, "Other from Within."

33. Bhabha, introduction, *Nation and Narration*.

34. Lockman, "Arab Workers," 254. A similarly complex portrait of identity emerges in Stein's research on Ottoman Jewry; see "Permeable Boundaries."

35. See also Khalidi, "Formation of Palestinian Identity," and Budeiri, "Palestinians."

36. A recent work frames the identity question in Turkey as "post-nationalist" and gathers several critical essays focusing on state Turkification and Jewish, Armenian, Sabbataean, and Alevi minority histories, as well as on Islamist and Kurdish conflicts in Turkey. See Kieser, *Turkey beyond Nationalism*.

37. These works, in general, also share the concern for multiplicity and complexity. See, for example, Billig, *Banal Nationalism*; Herzfeld, *Cultural Intimacy*; Brubaker and others, *Nationalist Politics*; Gülalp, *Citizenship and Ethnic Conflict*; Migdal, *Boundaries and Belonging*; and Guibernau, *Identity of Nations*.

38. See the works of Smith and Elie Kedourie, for example. See also Chatterjee, *Nationalist Thought*, "Whose Imagined Community?" For works on nationalism in the Middle East and Southwest Asia, see Jankowski and Gershoni, *Rethinking Nationalism*; Leoussi and Grosby, *Nationality and Nationalism*; and Shatzmiller, *Nationalism and Minority Identities*.

39. Alonso, "Space, Time, and Substance."

40. Herzfeld, *Cultural Intimacy*, 10.

41. Brubaker and others, *Nationalist Politics*, 11; Bringa, *Being Muslim*.

42. The pioneering work in this field is Bozdoğan and Kasaba, *Rethinking Modernity*. Similar issues are addressed in Kandiyoti and Saktanber, *Fragments of Culture*. See also Özyürek, *Nostalgia for the Modern*, and Keyder, *Global and the Local*. A significant area of focus has been on the study of modern Islamist cultural and political identities. See White, *Islamist Mobilization*; Yavuz, *Islamic Political Identity*; Çınar, *Modernity*; and Turam, *Between Islam and the State*.

43. See, for example, Secor, "There Is an Istanbul"; Başdaş, "Cosmopolitanism in Istanbul"; Üstündağ, "Turkish Republican Citizenship"; and Gökariksel, "Feminist Geography of Veiling."

44. Navaro-Yashin, for example, argues that the state and society are not separate but are embedded within one another (*Faces of the State*). Secor's research with Kurdish migrants and lower-class Turkish residents in Istanbul demonstrates the ways in which citizenship and identity are produced through daily spatial practices and everyday experiences with the state ("Between Longing and Despair").

45. See the introduction to Brubaker and others for a similar discussion regarding the dangers of scholarship on nationalism that, by assuming ethnic-group labeling

to reflect a truly bounded sense of identity, unknowingly adopts nationalist categories or assumes the nation itself to be a homogeneous category, thereby overlooking the cultural and political discursive processes through which categories come to have meaning (*Nationalist Politics*).

46. Hobsbawm and Ranger, *Invention of Tradition*; Hodgkin and Radstone, *Contested Pasts*; Bal, Crewe, and Spitzer, *Acts of Memory*; Pennebaker, Paez, and Rime, *Political Events*. Le Goff makes a distinction between memory and history. Memory is the source material for history as written by historians. History, as a discipline, nourishes the social processes of memory and forgetting but is also based on an understanding that there does exist historical "truth" (*History and Memory*). See also Lowenthal, *Foreign Country*.

47. Nora, *Realms of Memory*; Halbwachs, *Collective Memory*. The terms "cultural memory," "social memory," and "historical memory" are used interchangeably in literature on memory and nation (Till, "Memory Studies"). I use primarily "cultural memory" to refer to the dominant, imagined national memory. I study cultural forms—including narratives and their embodiment in landscapes—as the media through which cultural memory happens.

48. Nicola King, *Memory, Narrative, Identity*; Fentress and Wickham, *Social Memory*; Bal, Crewe, and Spitzer, *Acts of Memory*; Hodgkin and Radstone, *Contested Pasts*.

49. Eber and Neal, *Memory and Representation*, 5.

50. Bal, Crewe, and Spitzer, *Acts of Memory*, vii.

51. Lowenthal, *Foreign Country*. See also Boyer, *City of Collective Memory*.

52. Bal, introduction, *Acts of Memory*, xi.

53. Herzfeld, *Cultural Intimacy*, 118.

54. Bal, Crewe, and Spitzer, *Acts of Memory*, viii.

55. Özyürek, *Public Memory*.

56. Till, "Memory Studies"; Duncan, "Sites of Representation"; Jackson and Penrose, *Race, Place, Nation*. See also Spitzer, "Back through the Future," and Bardenstein, "Collective Memory."

57. Hoelscher, "Making Place," 661. See also Hoelscher and Alderman, "Memory and Place," and Nuala Johnson, *Geography of Remembrance*.

58. Blunt, "Productive Nostalgia"; Massey, "Places and Their Pasts"; Bastea, *Memory and Architecture*.

59. Savage, *Standing Soldiers, Kneeling Slaves*; Hoelscher, *Heritage on Stage*.

60. Schein, "Place of Landscape."

61. Much of the discussion that follows in this section is drawn from Mills, "Narratives in City Landscapes."

62. Sauer wrote about the cultural imprint ("Morphology of Landscape") and Lewis about the unwitting autobiography ("Axioms," 12).

63. Duncan and Duncan, "(Re)reading the Landscape"; Duncan, *City as Text*; Barnes and Duncan, *Writing Worlds*. The text metaphor was an important intervention in the "cultural turn" in geography, which first became visible in cultural landscape

studies in Cosgrove, *Social Formation*. The text metaphor was later criticized for paying insufficient attention to the real materiality of landscapes and their consequences for social life (e.g., Don Mitchell, review of *Writing Worlds*; Peet, review of *City as Text*). For studies of symbolism in landscapes, see Cosgrove and Daniels, *Iconography of Landscape*.

64. Duncan and Duncan, "(Re)reading the Landscape," 117.

65. Don Mitchell, *Lie of the Land*; Duncan and Duncan, *Landscapes of Privilege*; Hoelscher, "Making Place"; Schein, *Landscape and Race*; Rose, *Feminism and Geography*.

66. For a discussion of landscape as "discourse materialized," see Schein, "Place of Landscape," 663. Recent commentaries on landscape studies continue to reflect the tension between issues of ideology and materiality inherent in landscape studies. See Don Mitchell, "Cultural Landscapes."

67. Cosgrove, *Social Formation*.

68. Handler and Gable, *New History*; DeLyser, "Authenticity on the Ground"; Hoelscher, "Making Place."

69. Don Mitchell, *Lie of the Land*.

70. Nicola King, *Memory, Narrative, Identity*, 28.

71. Bal, Crewe, and Spitzer, *Acts of Memory*, vii.

72. Till, *New Berlin*.

73. The phrase *lieux de memoire* originated in Nora, *Realms of Memory*.

74. Baban, "Public Sphere."

75. Neyzi, "Remembering to Forget," 138.

76. Özyürek, introduction, *Public Memory*; For a discussion of how this took place with regard to the Alevi community and the Turkish-Greek population exchange, respectively, see Poyraz, "Turkish State and Alevis," and Iğsız, "Geographic Kinship." See also the works on the Muslims exchanged from Greece into Turkey in 1923, cited in Hirschon, *Crossing the Aegean*, 19: Yorulmaz, *Children of the War*; Yalçın, *Entrusted Trousseau*; Yildirim, "Diplomats and Refugees"; Köker, "Lessons in Refugeehood"; and Koufopoulou, "Muslim Cretans in Turkey."

77. Some researchers and booksellers in Istanbul argued, in conversations with me, that the increasing number of these publications does not necessarily reflect a larger shift toward thinking critically about minority history, because the production and consumption of these books remains limited to a very small cultural elite. At the same time, I have observed, however, there is increasing popular interest in minority oral histories at a popular level. The Economic and Social History Foundation of Turkey has sponsored many projects on local oral histories over the last fifteen years. In 2009 the Ottoman Bank Museum held a workshop to teach local people how to conduct their own oral histories. Two hundred residents from across Turkey, many of them from places with complex minority histories, attended.

78. Akar, *Passengers to Aşkale*; Bali, *Adventure in Turkification*; Aktar, *Wealth Tax*; Güven, *September Events*; Demir and Akar, *Istanbul's Last Exiles*; Bali, *Moses's Sons*; Gedik, *Old Istanbul Life*.

79. See Türker's books on former minority neighborhoods of Istanbul, for example, *Corner of Ottoman Istanbul*. For works on minority human rights, see Oran, *Minorities in Turkey*, and Kaya and Tarhanlı, *Majority and Minority Politics*.

80. Neyzi, *Forgetting in Istanbul*; Özyürek, *Remembering and Forgetting*. For important works in English, see Neyzi, "Remembering to Forget"; Özyürek, *Public Memory*; and Türköz, "Surname Narratives." See also the special issue dedicated to "Social Memory," Ahıska and Kırlı, *New Perspectives on Turkey*. This issue includes relevant articles by Ahıska, "Occidentalism"; Sırman, "Public Emotions"; Babül, "Claiming a Place"; Bilal, "Lost Lullaby"; and Öztürkmen, "Remembering Conflicts."

81. Examples of memoirs include Tunç, *If It's Convenient*, and Boysan, *Where Did Istanbul Go?* For examinations of the role of literature in cultural memory, see Evin, "Novelists," and Bertram, *Turkish House*.

82. Karakoyunlu, *Salkım Hanım's Necklace*.

83. Çelik, "Urban Preservation"; Mills, "Narratives in City Landscapes."

84. Bali, *Style of Life*, 134–41.

85. Mills, "Narratives in City Landscapes."

86. Bertram, *Turkish House*.

87. A very small *mescit* (a small mosque or place of prayer for individuals that has no minbar or place from which an imam may lead a formal Friday prayer gathering of Muslims) was built for Kuzguncuk's Muslim elite, however, in the late nineteenth century (Akın, "Kuzguncuk," 145).

88. Bal, Crewe, and Spitzer, *Acts of Memory*, viii.

89. Bal, "Memories in the Museum," 180.

90. Nicola King, *Memory, Narrative, Identity*, 1–2.

91. In this way *Streets of Memory* contributes to recent research that examines how discourses of tolerance are produced by majorities. In this literature, discourses of tolerance are revealed to sustain unequal power relations, because majorities define what tolerance is, and minorities are excluded from that process (see Galeotti, *Toleration as Recognition*, 227). Questions such as "who should be tolerant of what, or of whom, and why?" are embedded throughout my analysis. After the completion of the manuscript, the press and I added the word "tolerance" to the subtitle because it expresses an important dimension of the subject of the book, even though tolerance wasn't an organizing paradigm for my work during the writing process. I hope this book will contribute to that literature, particularly regarding research on tolerance discourse (see also Germann and Gibson, *Mobilizing Hospitality*).

92. De Certeau, *Practice of Everyday Life*.

93. I lived in Istanbul with few breaks between June 2001 and August 2003. I lived in Kuzguncuk for about seventeen months of this time, between October 2001 and March 2003, when I left the mahalle and moved to the European side of the city. I returned to Istanbul in February 2005 and June 2006 and traveled to Tel Aviv, Israel, in July 2006 to interview Kuzguncuklu people who emigrated to Israel. Throughout this book I use pseudonyms to conceal the identities of specific Kuzguncuklu people. All translations from Turkish are my own unless otherwise indicated.

94. An anthropologist who conducted research in Kuzguncuk interviewed people he met in the male spaces of the coffee shops, and he wrote about political Islam and Kurdish issues as reflected in Kuzguncuk and the larger area of Üsküdar (Houston, *Turkish Nation State*).

95. Moss, *Feminist Geography in Practice*.

96. See Mahtani's discussion of Gillian Rose's work in "Racial ReMappings."

97. I focus on Kuzguncuk's Jewish history and memory (rather than Rum) because Kuzguncuk was one of very few historically significant Jewish neighborhoods in the city. It is also true, however, that the remaining Kuzguncuk Greek community (with a few important exceptions), the leadership of the Greek Orthodox Church in Kuzguncuk, and the administration of the Patriarchate was extremely closed in terms of sharing any information, documents, or opinions. I met several people in the larger Armenian community in Istanbul who were willing to discuss various issues with me and who brought me to visit several churches and congregations, including to the Armenian church in Kuzguncuk. However, they possessed almost no knowledge of Kuzguncuk and seemed disconnected to the three elderly Armenians I knew who remained in the mahalle (one of whom I interviewed) and so could contribute only the most general information for my particular study.

98. Anthony King, *Spaces of Global Cultures*, 30–32. See, for example, Poppi, "Wider Horizons."

99. These quotes are from interviews with residents. For Mignolo, cosmopolitanism negotiates the coloniality of power and imagines a conviviality across religious and racial divides ("Many Faces of Cosmo-polis").

100. Kant, *Political Writings*. See Harvey's extensive discussion of the geographic structure and assumptions of Kant's cosmopolitanism in Harvey, "Banality of Geographical Evils."

101. Harvey, "Banality of Geographical Evils," 530.

102. El Kadi and Elkerdany, "Belle-epoque Cairo"; della Dora, "Rhetoric of Nostalgia"; Salamandra, *New Old Damascus*; Porter, "Unwitting Actors." See Söderström, "Cosmopolitan Landscapes," for how notions of cosmopolitanism shape urban landscapes in Beijing.

103. Özür Diliyorum, http://www.ozurdiliyoruz.com.

104. Singerman and Amar, "Contesting Myths," 30.

105. A body of scholarship has emerged that examines the social, political, cultural, and ultimately geographic processes that produced cosmopolitanisms in specific historical contexts. See, for example, volume 16 of *History and Anthropology*, including the following papers: Polycandrioti, "Literary Quests"; Sifneos, "Greek Commercial Diaspora"; and Driessen, "Mediterranean Port Cities." See also the papers in Keyder, Özveren, and Quataert, "Port Cities"; Ilbert, Yannakakis and Hassoun, *Alexandria*; and Cartier, "Maritime World City."

106. Sifneos, "Greek Commercial Diaspora."

107. Pollack and others, "Cosmopolitanisms," 3.

108. For example, most of the essays in Cheah and Robbins's *Cosmopolitics* and

in Pollock and others' *Cosmopolitanism* deal with places and issues of contemporary internationalism and globalization. See also Brennan, *Home in the World*; Schueth and O'Loughlin, "Belonging to the World"; Isin, *Global City*; and Nijman, "Locals, Exiles and Cosmopolitans."

109. Robbins, "Actually Existing Cosmopolitanism," 2. See also Robbins's review of Kwame Anthony Appiah's contention that cosmopolitanism and patriotism are not necessarily incompatible ("Cosmopolitanism").

110. Robbins, "Actually Existing Cosmopolitanism," 2–3. See Malcomson in this volume.

111. Philliou, "Paradox of Perceptions."

112. Harvey, "Banality of Geographical Evils," 543.

113. Singerman and Amar, "Contesting Myths," 29.

114. Ibid., 25.

115. Pollack and others, "Cosmopolitanisms," 1.

116. See Popke, "Geography and Ethics," for a review of the ways in which urban space has been taken for granted as the ideal locus of cosmopolitanism.

Chapter One. *The Turkish Nation in the Urban Landscape*

1. Ebcim, *Kuzguncuk*, 13.

2. See, for example, Akşin, *Turkey*. This book was first published in Turkish in 1996 for a Turkish audience and was also printed in the daily newspaper *Cumhuriyet*. Historical research has also idealized relations between non-Muslims and Muslims in Turkey as exceptionally tolerant (Bali, *Adventure in Turkification*). Critical research on these topics in Turkey has been prohibitively difficult for various reasons, including censorship, closure of archives, denial of research permission, and the change in the methods by which census information was collected, which by 1964 had completely obscured the actual decline of non-Muslim populations.

3. Lefebvre's conceptual triad describes the interrelationships between planned and built, and imagined and practiced, urban space. Planned aspects of urban space have been an important site of study for scholars of Turkey interested in the roles of architecture and urban planning, for example, in the articulation of state power and the production of national identity. Symbolic monuments, architecture, or urban plans are *conceived space*, "the space of scientists, planners, urbanists, technocratic subdividers and social engineers" (*Production of Space*, 38). I am interested, rather, in focusing on other dimensions of urban space that are deeply related to the built environment but that involve the agency and nonmaterial actions of residents who are not in a position of power as planners or architects. I focus on the uses and meanings of otherwise unremarkable economic and residential spaces of daily urban life, what Lefebvre would describe as *spatial practice*, which "embraces production and reproduction, and the particular locations and spatial sets characteristic of each social formation. Spatial practice ensures continuity and some degree of cohesion" (33).

4. The millet "was a form of organisation and legal status arising from the submis-

sion of followers of monotheistic religions (ehl-I zimmet) to the authority of Islam after the annexation of a region to the Empire, under an ahidname or treaty granting protection" (Ortayli, *Ottoman Studies*, 19). An extensive literature describes the millet system. See, for example, Clogg, "Millet within a Millet," and Kastoryano, "From Millet to Community."

5. A more developed discussion of this idea appears in chapters 2 and 5, and also in Mills, "Boundaries of the Nation."

6. There is extensive literature on millets and mahalles as coconstitutive sociospatial forms. See Behar, *Neighborhood*; Bierman, Abou-El-Haj, and Preziosi, *Ottoman City*; and Mardin, "Religion and Secularism," 368. As a subject of study, the mahalle has a complicated historiography as part of Orientalist studies of the "Islamic City" and was considered an integral element of that city type (Abu-Lughod, "Islamic City"). For example, see Lapidus, "Traditional Muslim Cities."

7. Meijer, introduction, *Cosmopolitanism*, 1. Emphasis mine.

8. Clogg, "Millet within a Millet," 117.

9. Behar, *Neighborhood*.

10. Riedler, "Armenian Labour Migration," 6.

11. See the church inscriptions in Kuzguncuk. These communities were interlinked perhaps because Christians from this area were Karamanlı, or Turcophone, which might explain why they migrated to the same mahalle of Istanbul. See Necipoğlu, *Age of Sinan*, 129–30. Thanks to Christine Philliou for this information.

12. Behar, *Neighborhood*, 4.

13. Keyder, "Consequences," 41. On coffeehouses, see Örs, "Coffeehouses."

14. Barnai, "History of the Jews," 32.

15. Mardin, "Religion and Secularism," 368.

16. Behar, *Neighborhood*, 5. See also Tamdoğan-Abel, "Our Mahalle."

17. Tamdoğan-Abel, "Our Mahalle."

18. In spite of striking temporal and geographic differences, the close social ties of Istanbul mahalles resemble those in other parts of the Middle East, such as in the *darb* (neighborhood) of Morocco (Eickelman, "Islamic City") and the *murabba'* (square) in Cairo (Ghannam, *Remaking the Modern*).

19. The precise history of Kuzguncuk is unknown. I use two kinds of sources to write the sketch in this chapter: one is the secondary literature in Turkish on Bosphorus and Istanbul history, and the other is travel narratives written by foreign visitors. Neither type of source can be considered definitively accurate. No one yet done the necessary archival research that would provide exact information. Most secondary histories date the social geography of Kuzguncuk's various ethnic-religious groups according to the construction of religious buildings, and I take a similar strategy in my own historical sketch in this chapter. However, even the construction dates of Kuzguncuk's churches and synagogues are contested in the secondary literature. One dimension of this problem is that secondary historical sources in Turkish (even very recent ones) do not give references for where they get information regarding building construction, making it impossible to determine the relative accuracy of different

historical claims. As a result, my own historical sketch may unintentionally replicate historiographic inaccuracies.

20. Solmaz, *Asia's Door throughout History*, 11, quoted in Bektaş, "Kuzguncuk," 106. See Bektaş for a discussion of how Chrysokeramos may have referred to the nearby mahalles of Beylerbeyi or Çengelköy. Another source gives different dates for this gold-tiled church, built during Justinian's rule between 565–578 (Akın, "Kuzguncuk," 145).

21. P. Ğ. Inciciyan, *18th Century*, 133. Thanks to Christine Philliou for the insight regarding the possible linguistic—and therefore ethnic—roots of this name.

22. Deleon, *Bosphorus*, 127; Ayverdi, *History on the Bosphorus*, 376; Talas and Dinç, *Istanbul*, 104.

23. Deleon, *Bosphorus*, 86.

24. Kastoryano, "From Millet to Community"; Shaw, *Ottoman Empire*.

25. Aksoy and Yalçintan, "Holy Land."

26. P. Ğ. Inciciyan, *18th Century*, 133, quoted in Bektaş, "Kuzguncuk," 107.

27. Ghukas Inciciyan, *Bosphorus Villas*, 151.

28. Banoğlu, *Istanbul with Its History*, 81.

29. See Başbakanlık Arşivi, Cevdet Adliye #1073 23 Ş 1287 (1870), Prime Ministry State Ottoman Archive, Istanbul, Turkey. Interviews indicate that Jews continued to live in this area until the 1950s in the small houses that stand there today, which were built by Jewish families in the early 1900s. Thanks to Christine Philliou for identifying this document.

30. Most sources indicate that the currently existing synagogue buildings were built sometime in the nineteenth century, and it seems that the location and construction date for the neighborhood's first synagogue is not definitively known. See chapter 6 regarding the problems with dating Jewish history in Kuzguncuk.

31. Banoğlu, *Istanbul with Its History*, 81.

32. Clay, "Labour Migration," 14.

33. Ibid., 5. For a discussion of the restrictions Armenian businesspeople faced after the 1890s in Istanbul, see Riedler, "Armenian Labour Migration."

34. Riedler, "Armenian Labour Migration," 9–10.

35. Ibid., 2.

36. Census data for Kuzguncuk is not available. It is collected only by the local *muhtar* and his records are closed. The municipal district census information for Üsküdar, of which Kuzguncuk is a part, does not break down population data by mahalle.

37. Clay, "Labour Migration," 5; Riedler, "Armenian Labour Migration," 2.

38. The population breakdown for Üsküdar in 1885 was 52,805 Muslims; 10,046 Greek Orthodox; 22,160 Armenian Orthodox; and 5,197 Jews, out of a total of 95, 667 (Shaw, "Population of Istanbul," 268).

39. Augustinos, *Greeks of Asia Minor*, 39.

40. Tuğlacı, *Istanbul's Armenian Churches*, 169.

41. See Başbakanlık Arşivi, Cevdet Adliye #2000 16 M 1284 (1868), Prime Ministry State Ottoman Archive, Istanbul, Turkey. Thanks to Christine Philliou for identifying and translating this document.

42. This information is from church inscriptions that identify people from Sinason and Serafion, Kesarin [Kayseri]. Thanks to Christine Philliou for reading and translating all of the inscriptions.

43. Akın, "Kuzguncuk," 146.

44. See the church inscriptions.

45. Çelik, *Remaking of Istanbul.*

46. Banoğlu, *Istanbul with Its History,* 81.

47. Clay, "Labour Migration," 11. The Armenian population was perhaps affected by the day Talat Pasha ordered Armenian clerics and notables in Istanbul to be killed and by events surrounding the commemoration of this day. See Riedler, "Armenian Labour Migration." The Armenians who care for and maintain the church in Kuzguncuk have no knowledge of Armenian Kuzguncuklu history. Armenians remain today in nearby Bağlarbaşı and Üsküdar.

48. Clarence Richard Johnson, *Constantinople Today,* 133–34.

49. This period emerges as very significant in Jewish narratives of Kuzguncuk discussed in chapter 6.

50. Kaygılı, *İstanbul's Nooks and Crannies,* quoted in Ebcim, *Kuzguncuk,* 61.

51. Bektaş, "Kuzguncuk."

52. Local folklore cites the presence of this mosque next to the Armenian church as physical evidence of exceptional tolerance, because the church "gave" the land for the mosque to be built. Such a transfer of property would have been legally impossible. In fact, a Jewish family owned three houses along the coast road there (see Rozen, "Fishermen's Guilds"), and this property was sold to a Muslim, who donated or sold it to provide space for the mosque. In 1952 the priest of the church gave five hundred Turkish lira to the mosque (Çakil, "Little Paris," 25).

53. Ebcim, *Kuzguncuk,* 265.

54. Banoğlu, *Istanbul with Its History,* 81.

55. Ayverdi, *History on the Bosphorus,* 377.

56. Bektaş, "Kuzguncuk," 108.

57. Ebcim, *Kuzguncuk,* 23. Bektaş cites a 1992 population of twenty-five Greeks, seventeen Jews, and six Armenians ("Kuzguncuk," 108). Most of the remaining non-Muslims are intermarried and many of their children are not raised in the same religious traditions as minority parents. Both of these authors live in Kuzguncuk, reflecting their relationships to the local muhtar and thus the availability of census information that is otherwise closed to researchers.

58. For historian Bali, Turkification refers explicitly to the policies of the 1920s and 1930s that aimed to turn Christians and Jews into Turkish citizens through the promotion of the Turkish language, for example. He contrasts this to the perspective of Turkish academics who view those policies together with later, distinct events, such as the Wealth Tax and the 1955 riots, as evidence of a long-term program of nationalist Turkification to purge Turkey of its non-Muslim minorities. For Bali, those events should be viewed within their distinct temporal contexts. For the purposes of my research, I adopt the second perspective on Turkification and link these events together,

because they were narrated together by people describing their perceptions of cultural change and individual experience in Kuzguncuk, and they are *perceived* by many as constituting a broader Muslim, Turkish, nationalist project. See Bali, "1934 Thrace Events," pars. 44–47.

59. According to Shaw, Greek and Armenians resisted Jewish competition during the Tanzimat reforms by purchasing foreign citizenship and foreign protection in an effort to squeeze out Muslim and Jewish presence in business and government service (*Ottoman Empire*, 176–77).

60. Schroeter, "Changing Relationship."

61. Augustinos, *Greeks of Asia Minor*, 38; İçduygu and Soner, "Turkish Minority Rights," 449.

62. Hanioğlu, "Turkism," 5.

63. Mardin "Patriotism and Nationalism."

64. Hanioğlu, "Turkism."

65. Kechriotis, "Modernization," 54.

66. For a thorough discussion of the period between the Young Turk Revolution in 1908 and the foundation of the Turkish Republic in 1923, see chapter 3 in Ahmad, *Making of Modern Turkey*. For a detailed and richly documented explanation of the links between nationality conflicts in the fragmenting empire, the relationships between European states and the Ottoman administration, and the ways in which this resulted in widespread massacres of Armenians before and after the turn of the century, see Dadrian, *Armenian Genocide*. Dadrian discusses massacres of Armenians on the streets of Istanbul that took place in 1895 after Armenians marched to the Ottoman government to deliver a protest regarding the Armenian massacre at Sassoun (120–21). See also Akçam, *Empire to Republic*.

67. Çağaptay, "Passage to Turkishness."

68. Şeker, "Demographic Engineering."

69. Aktar, "Homogenising the Nation," 80.

70. Hirschon, *Crossing the Aegean*, 15.

71. Vryonis, *Mechanism of Catastrophe*. See also Hirschon, *Crossing the Aegean*.

72. Oran, "Those Who Stayed," 110.

73. Hirschon, *Crossing the Aegean*, 16.

74. Hirschon, *Crossing the Aegean*.

75. İçduygu and Soner, "Turkish Minority Rights," 453.

76. The identity of Kurds as an ethnic minority was completely denied by a nationalist narrative that described them as actually Turkish, qualifying their difference by calling them "mountain Turks." It was during the 1990s, during an opening of discussion regarding minorities in Turkey (brought about in part by the work of Kurdish activists and others after the war between the Turkish army and the Kurdistan Workers' Party in the southeast), that Kurds and other groups began to claim a minority status and thus expose their collective oppression by the state.

77. Atatürk was inspired by Mehmet Ziya Gökalp, who differentiates between culture and civilization, separating the values of a community from the system of knowl-

edge that governs it. Gökalp argues that the Turkish nation had its own strong culture, but that it had been submerged in an Islamic/Arab and partly Byzantine civilization (Zürcher, *Turkey*, 136). See Gökalp, *Turkish Nationalism*.

78. Bauman, relying on the work of Barth (*Ethnic Groups*), links the category of ethnicity to the problem of identity as a member of the nation. The nation created an "ethnic category" to legitimize its own existence by marking the terms of exclusion and thus making the nation the preferable category of identity (*Culture as Praxis*, xxx).

79. İçduygu and Soner, "Turkish Minority Rights."

80. Bali, *Adventure in Turkification*, 196.

81. Shaw provides the following information on the population of Istanbul by religion from the official census: In 1885, 1906, and 1914, Muslims grew from 44.06 percent, to 49.93 percent, to become 61.59 percent of the city's population. For the same years, the Greek Orthodox population grew from 17.48 percent, to 20.41 percent, to 22.57 percent. Armenian Gregorians experienced the most significant change in numbers. In 1885 they were 17.12 percent, but by 1906 they were 7.14 percent, and in 1914 they were 8.02 percent of the city's population. The Jewish proportion of the population remained fairly stable, they were 5.08 percent in 1885, 5.53 percent in 1906, and 5.73 percent in 1914 ("Population of Istanbul"). The dramatic decrease in the Armenian population was possibly a result of the riots and massacres in Istanbul after Armenians protested at the Ottoman Bank building (see Riedler, "Armenian Labour Migration").

82. Shaw, "Population of Istanbul," 277.

83. Aktar, "Homogenising the Nation," 81.

84. Guttstadt, "Depriving Non-Muslims," 51.

85. Neyzi, "Strong as Steel."

86. Ibid., 170.

87. Bali, "1934 Thrace Events."

88. Toktaş, "Conduct of Citizenship," 123. I discuss the complexity of Turkey's Jewish community in much more detail in chapter 6.

89. Kastoryano, "From Millet to Community," 267.

90. Jews were particularly vulnerable in this situation because they spoke Ladino and French, the language of the Jewish Alliance Israelite Universelle schools. If they had spoken Hebrew they could have argued that they were entitled to continue to speak it and teach it freely under the protection of the Lausanne Treaty (Bali, "Politics of Turkification," 45).

91. İçduygu and Soner, "Turkish Minority Rights," 459; Bali, *Adventure in Turkification*.

92. Aslan, "Citizen, Speak Turkish!" 253–54.

93. Aktar, "Homogenising the Nation," 92. See also Bali, *Adventure in Turkification*.

94. Bali, "Politics of Turkification," 47.

95. Aktar, *Wealth Tax*, 60, 56.

96. Bali, *Adventure in Turkification*, 211, 214, 228.

97. Alexandris, "Religion or Ethnicity," 119. See also Bali, *Adventure in Turkification*, and Aktar, *Wealth Tax*.

98. Aktar, *Wealth Tax*.

99. Ibid., 135.

100. Ökte, *Tragedy*.

101. Aktar, *Wealth Tax*, 154.

102. Akar, *Passengers to Aşkale*, 108.

103. Bali, *Adventure in Turkification*, 455, 437, 444.

104. Aktar, *Wealth Tax*.

105. Oran, "Those Who Stayed," 101, 103. Cyprus has a historical Greek population, in addition to a Turkish population, that dates from the sixteenth-century Ottoman conquest of the island. Britain took control over Cyprus in 1878 and initially promised it would remain Ottoman territory. The British revoked that promise when the Ottomans entered World War I, and Cyprus became a British colonial possession. The British then promised Cyprus to the Greeks in return for Greek support during the war. This promise greatly encouraged the patriotism of Greeks on the island who had, since the nineteenth century, desired reunification with mainland Greece. A Greek Cypriot revolution in 1931 attempted to overthrow British rule, although the British remained powerful in Cyprus. Conflicts between Greek and Turkish residents of Cyprus, and Greek and Turkish national sentiment regarding the territorial identity of the island, resulted in ongoing tension between Turkey and Greece regarding the future of Cyprus.

106. Oran writes that this event was "originally a display of anti-Rum feeling organized by the Cyprus Is Turkish Association," which was tacitly approved by the government ("Those Who Stayed," 104n21).

107. Bahcheli, *Greek-Turkish Relations*, 174. According to Oran, thirteen thousand Greek citizens living and working in Istanbul were deported, including both Greeks who came from Greece to work in Turkey under the provisions of the 1930 convention and local Rum who had Greek citizenship ("Those Who Stayed," 104).

108. Pope and Pope, *Turkey Unveiled*, 116.

109. Oran, "Those Who Stayed," 104.

110. Demir and Akar, *Istanbul's Last Exiles*, 190.

111. Bahcheli, *Greek-Turkish Relations*, 174.

112. Pope and Pope, *Turkey Unveiled*, 116.

113. Alexandris, "Religion or Ethnicity," 119.

114. The Turkish government exercised tight control of Greek church–owned property; for example, the Greek Orthodox patriarchate wasn't able to secure permission to repair damage done in a 1941 fire until 1987 (Pope and Pope, *Turkey Unveiled*, 117).

115. Bahcheli, *Greek-Turkish Relations*, 175. However, today negotiations are underway for a peaceful resolution to the conflict and to bring both parts of Cyprus into membership in the European Union. Turkey is eager to be conciliatory, with hopes of also joining the European Union.

116. For a discussion on the general complexities of determining property owner-ship in Turkey, see Demir and Çoruhlu, "Determining the Property Ownership."

117. Keyder explains the legislation regulating individual property ownership in the late nineteenth century and the ways in which Armenian and Greek properties abandoned in the 1910s were taken over by the Turkish political elite, issues that con-stitute a historical background for minority property rights later ("Consequences," 45). Aktar describes how Greek properties abandoned in Cesme in 1914 were plundered by the local population or taken by Rumelian refugees from Salonica, in spite of a lo-cal governor's effort to redistribute property ("Homogenising the Nation," 84). Oran discusses the problem of property rights regarding the emigrants of the 1923 popula-tion exchange and their resolution by the Ankara Convention in 1930 ("Those Who Stayed," 101).

118. Demir and Akar, *Istanbul's Last Exiles*, 160.

119. Lekka, "Legislative Provisions," 148.

120. Ibid., 149–53.

121. Oran, "Those Who Stayed," 108.

122. The landscapes of neighborhoods (e.g., Tepebaşi, Galata) that were primarily Greek reflect this ambiguous legal status, as many empty buildings continue to stand unrenovated, unable to be purchased or sold because owners are resident in Greece or are untraceable.

123. Istanbul's Greek (Rum) population has diminished from more than 100,000 in 1923 to approximately 2,500 today (Oran, "Those Who Stayed," 101). Greeks are esti-mated at around 2,500 to 3,000, and Armenians at approximately 60,000 (Karimova and Devereli, *Minorities in Turkey*).

124. Aktar, *Wealth Tax*, 208.

125. Oran "Those Who Stayed," 108.

126. Ibid.

127. Bonine, *Population, Poverty and Politics*, and Keyder, *Global and the Local*.

Chapter Two. Uryanizade Street

1. *Radikal*, "Kuzguncuk Semt Mi, Set Mi?" [Is Kuzguncuk a Neighborhood or a Film Set?], 25 November 2007.

2. Kanal Bir, http://www.kanalı.com.

3. This quotation is from a description on diziler.com, which disseminates informa-tion about Turkish television series (Diziler.com, http://www.diziler.com).

4. Çelik, "Urban Preservation," 89. Kuzguncuk was featured in a tourism bulletin as early as 1975. See Erdem Yücel, "Kuzguncuk."

5. The resident architects and intellectuals of this street rejected a name change in favor of recognizing the television show, and so the neighboring street was renamed.

6. Anılarım, http://www.anilarim.net.

7. Baudrillard describes the "successive phases of the image: it is the reflection of

a basic reality; it masks and perverts a basic reality; it masks the absence of a basic reality; it bears no relation to any reality whatsoever: it is its own pure simulacrum" (*Simulations*, 11).

8. For a discussion of the symbolic meanings of landscapes, see Cosgrove and Daniels, *Iconography of Landscape*, and Duncan and Duncan, "(Re)reading the Landscape." For studies interrogating the ways in which material forms create an aura of authenticity for constructed histories, see Handler and Gable, *New History*, and DeLyser, "Authenticity on the Ground."

9. Tanrıöver, "Family, Neighborhood, and Community."

10. Don Mitchell, *Lie of the Land*, 2.

11. Representational space, "embod[ies] complex symbolisms, sometimes coded, sometimes not, linked to the clandestine or underground side of social life" (Lefebvre, *Production of Space*, 33). Representational space is also understood as *lived space*, "space as directly lived through its associated images and symbols, and hence the space of 'inhabitants' and 'users.'" (39).

12. Tunç, *If It's Convenient*, 13.

13. Ibid., 20–22, 35, 291–93.

14. "Bizim zamanımızda . . . güzel sohbet vardı, güzel komşuluk vardı . . . şimdi nerede, nerede?"

15. Boyer, *City of Collective Memory*.

16. Bali, *Style of Life*, 134–41.

17. Lowenthal, *Foreign Country*, *Possessed by the Past*.

18. Massey, "Places and Their Pasts."

19. Tanrıöver, "Family, Neighborhood, and Community," 94.

20. Ibid., 94, 95.

21. Ibid., 95.

22. Don Mitchell, *Lie of the Land*, 1.

23. See Bektaş, "Public Participation," and Height, "Cengiz Bektaş."

24. Bektaş, *Other Name for Tolerance*.

25. The 1983 Bosphorus laws regarding the classification and preservation of structures in historical areas meant that the facades of a building must be retained to preserve the historical fabric. In practice, however, the facades sometimes differed if a building was rebuilt slightly taller or if less attention was paid to exactly reproducing the facade. Furthermore, the historical houses were largely unpainted and so, before renovation, were the color of old wood. After renovation the houses are usually brightly painted in a move that calls attention to the restoration rather than attempting to blend the structure into the existing landscape. See Parlak, *Urban Law*.

26. These projects are described in Bektaş, *Take a Neighbor*.

27. Bektaş, *Other Name for Tolerance*, 94.

28. Bektaş, "Urban Projects."

29. Bektaş, *Other Name for Tolerance*, 94.

30. Bektaş's unpublished writings quoted in Aksoy and Yalçintan, "Holy Land," 38.

31. Bektaş, *Other Name for Tolerance*, 34.

32. Ibid., 28.

33. Aksoy and Yalçintan, "Holy Land," 38. See also this typical example of nostalgic representations of Kuzguncuk in news media: Hande Bayındir, "En Popüler İstanbul Köyü" [The Most Popular Istanbul Village], *Milliyet*, 18 May 2001, real estate sec. 3.

34. Aksoy and Yalçintan, "Holy Land," 40.

35. Aynur Gürsoy, "Istanbul'daki Son Cennet: Kuzguncuk" [The Last Heaven in Istanbul: Kuzguncuk], *Hürriyet Magazine*, 8 January 1992.

36. Çakil, "Little Paris," 25.

37. Ibid.

38. Ibid., quote on 26, 28.

39. Daniş and Değer, "Empty Space."

40. Karaçizmeli, "Uğur Yücel," 13.

41. Kuzguncuk had an ample supply of old housing stock because it had never been a wealthy area, and so it was comparatively less vulnerable to the real estate speculation during the 1960s and 1970s that resulted in replacing houses with apartments. In 1983 new legislation concerning the historical areas along the Bosphorus required the protection of building facades and the prohibition of new construction in these areas. The new legislation ensured that after 1983, Kuzguncuk's landscape would be maintained within certain parameters. Although Bektaş's early renovation project worked with repairing existing structures, most of the later "restoration" has meant tearing down and rebuilding "historical" homes in concrete with painted wooden facades. Several such concrete houses were created during my fieldwork. They characterize gentrification in the area during the 1990s.

42. The most popular mahalle television serials, for example, have boosted gentrification in the old neighborhoods where they take place, not only in Kuzguncuk, but also in Çengelköy (the set for *Süper Baba*, or Super Dad), Emirgan (set for *Babaevi*, or Father's House), and Samatya (set for *İkinci Bahar*, or Second Spring). See Tanrıöver, "Family, Neighborhood, and Community," 95.

43. Historical renovation in Kuzguncuk follows some of the social and economic patterns identified in North American and European literature on gentrification (Uzun, *Gentrification in Istanbul*, 19). See also "Impact of Urban Renewal."

44. Uzun, *Gentrification in Istanbul*, 24, 130–31, 137–47, quote on 150.

45. Uzun argues that artists in Istanbul have a special identity that is most compatible with living in gentrified neighborhoods of the city (*Gentrification in Istanbul*).

46. Ibid., quote on 24, 122.

47. The migration of a wealthier elite into this neighborhood caused an increase in property values. See Bayındir, "Most Popular Istanbul Village."

48. Akay, "Mahalle Construction," 78.

49. *Turkish Daily News*, "Kuzguncuk for all Seasons: Part 2," 13 January 2002.

50. Local real estate agents acknowledge that rents went up significantly since the late 1980s, that houses for sale are very hard to come by because of the tight market and high demand, and that rents are often demanded in Euros or U.S. dollars. See

"Flat with a Bosphorus View at Üsküdar for $15,000 a Month," *Turkish Daily News*, 11 September 2007.

51. Houston's work on the Islamic political movements in Istanbul is founded in fieldwork in Kuzguncuk with members of the local Islamist group. He argues that this group is engaged in the project of creating an "alternative locality" in the neighborhood. They meet to read the Koran together and refuse to go to the local mosque. Their identity exists in opposition to the larger Islamist party in power in the Üsküdar municipality, as well as to the other social groups in Kuzguncuk, including the community of artists and intellectuals (Houston, *Turkish Nation State*).

52. Ramazan Yazgan, "Perran Kutman Görse Üzülürdü" [If Perran Kutman Saw It, She'd Be Saddened], *Hurriyet*, 8 June 1999, sec. 3.

53. The title, *A 'Kuzgun' Summer*, plays on the name of Kuzguncuk, which means "little crow." The word for crow also means dark or black (Ünver, *Dark Summer*).

54. Nalan Barbarosoğlu, "Kanatsiz Kuzgunlar" [Wingless Crows], review of *Kuzgun Bir Yaz* [A Dark Summer] by Mehmet Ünver, *Radikal*, 22 March 2002, book sec., 10.

55. Mehmet Ünver, "Anılarda Kalan Kuzguncuk" [Kuzguncuk in Memory], interview with Nena Çalidis, *Cumhuriyet*, 12 February 2002.

56. His concerns echo those written much earlier by famous author Salah Birsel, who wrote in 1982 about the minorities who made Kuzguncuk so special and about the danger of the destruction of the neighborhood. He refers to the loud singing and noise made by Black Sea migrants who kept others up at night (*Diamond Bosphorus*, 313–14).

57. Don Mitchell, *Lie of the Land*, 6.

58. Halbwachs, *Collective Memory*, 131–32.

Chapter Three. Garden Street

1. The association's struggle has not been easy. In the words of Kuzguncuk Neighborhood Association members and on their Web site, "Kuzguncuk halkı karşı cıktı" (the people of Kuzguncuk came out in resistance), implying that the struggle was unified from the beginning (Kuzguncuklular Derneği, http://www.kuzguncuk.org). In fact, not everyone came out in protest at first. Some were afraid of political action because of what happened to one resident who openly opposed an illegal parking lot in Kuzguncuk and was badly beaten, allegedly by the mafia (Efe Erdem, "Davam Sürecek" [My Case Will Continue], *Milliyet*, 28 April 1999). Other residents resisted joining the association for other reasons. Shop owners hoped their stores would benefit from the development, although they later joined the association's cause (Tankuter, "Interview," 6). Even today some people view any political activity as dangerous and undesirable. In 2001 an association member said that when he distributed fliers about the community garden project, an old friend accused him of being communist. Such a perception is extremely negative in Turkey, because of political violence during the 1970s that polarized communities in Istanbul. Neighborhood organizations continue to face these perceptions. The Kuzguncuk Neighborhood Association membership remains

fairly small. Most meetings had no more than five members, and the largest meeting I witnessed had approximately twenty members. Often the meetings were cancelled because no one attended. Official membership, however, was eighty in 2003.

2. Cresswell, *In Place*; Keith and Pile, *Politics of Identity*; Jackson and Penrose, *Race, Place, Nation*; Hoelscher, "Making Place"; Rose, "Cultural Politics"; Tuan, "Language."

3. Till, *New Berlin*.

4. Throughout the book, I refer to neighbors with pseudonymous first names to reflect the names I used with people in Kuzguncuk, and which indicate the degree of friendship, familiarity, and closeness I actually experienced with them. Most of the people in this book who appear only by first name are women; this reflects the degree of familiarity I developed with the women I knew (in contrast to men). People regularly use terms such as "Sister" (Abla) and "Aunt" (Teyze), or "Brother" (Abi) and "Uncle" (Amca) for men, to recognize relationships of seniority, even among people who aren't truly blood relatives. These are also terms of respect. Some of the people I knew well I called by first name only; with others I used terms such as "Sister" or "Aunt." Other people I met only a few times and always referred to as "Mr." (Bey) or "Mrs." (Hanim) in the most polite of terms.

5. 2960 Sayılı Boğaziçi Kanunu, Yeşil Alanlar, Madde 5 (Bosphorus Law 2960, Green Spaces, Section 5). For a discussion of efforts and laws to protect historical and green spaces in Istanbul, see Parlak, *Urban Law*.

6. Kira Kontratosu (Rental Contract), 25 March 1992 to 29 February 2002, no. 14785, İstanbul Vakıflar Bölge Müdürlüğü (Foundations Area Ministry, Istanbul), Türkiye Organ Nakli ve Yanık Tedavi Vakfı (Turkish Organ Donation and Burn Treatment Foundation), Özel Şartlar Bölümünde (Special Requirements Section), Arsa (Land).

7. The proposed school was two blocks away from the existing school in Kuzguncuk, which consistently ran under capacity. The school was not necessary and would not have benefited the neighborhood.

8. For more on post-1990 neighborhood associations in Turkey, see Erman and Coşkun-Yıldar, "Emergent Local Initiative."

9. Kuzguncuk Neighborhood Association, pamphlet, 2000.

10. Can Yücel, "Lullaby." "Dandini Dandini Dasdana" refers to a children's lullaby.

11. Uğur Tandoğan, "Dünya" [World], *Istanbul*, 2 June 2000.

12. Ibid.

13. Daniş and Değer, "Empty Space," 42.

14. Behice Özden, "Hrisokeramas'tan Kuzguncuk'a" [From Hrisokeramas to Kuzguncuk], *Radikal*, 9 July 2000, 13.

15. Kaynar, "Organ Donation."

16. Daniş and Değer, "Empty Space," 42.

17. Kuzguncuklular Derneği, http://www.kuzguncuk.org.

18. I attended a service at the synagogue, where I heard a discussion about earthquake preparedness. The Kuzguncuk Neighborhood Association has focused on

earthquake preparedness for the neighborhood since 1999. These communities don't join forces in community initiatives.

19. These sources included photocopies of the property deed, a description of the deed along with other information explaining how the property was lost, the relevant laws and regulations pertaining to the property, the rental contract, and correspondence from Haberal's Foundation to the Turkish Engineering and Architectural Association. They are stored in the office of the Kuzguncuk Neighborhood Association.

20. The most significant difficulty in researching the actual processes through which minority properties were lost is the lack of documentation, partly because local people (in my experience, especially Rum) are very protective of this information.

21. Özden, "From Hrisokeramas."

22. Ibid.

23. This law, first written in 1915 (numbered 13.9.1331) and amended in 1923 (numbered 15.4.1339), states that the property belonging to "firari" individuals would transfer to the Hazine, the Treasury, and in the case of Foundation properties, to the Foundations Ministry, and that even if the property deed was registered to a person's name, this would not constitute claim to ownership of the property. It further states that those who can prove that the property was in their hands on 6 August 1924 can claim ownership of the property and those who couldn't would forfeit rights to the property. The reference to this law on a deed in 1977 is thus clearly inappropriate. The definitions of firari are (1) fugitive, runaway, escapee; (2) someone who has slipped off; (3) deserter; (4) defector; and (5) truant (*Redhouse Turkish-English Dictionary*, 5th ed., s.v. "firari"). This law was written explicitly to address Armenian property "abandoned" after 1915. For a detailed discussion of this issue, see Lekka, "Legislative Provisions," 138–39.

24. I extend my sincerest thanks to this lawyer for his help and support throughout my research.

25. For information on non-Muslim minority foundation property histories, legal status, and rights, see Turkish Economic and Social Studies Foundation, *Foundations Legal Proposal*; Oran, "Non-Muslim Pious Foundations"; Reyna and Zonana, *Community Foundations*; and Öztürk, *Minority Foundations*, 65–170.

26. Massey, "Places and Their Pasts," 184–85.

27. Dilmen, *Kuzguncuk Folk Song*, 68–69.

Chapter Four. Icadiye Street

1. Büyükfırat, *Kuzguncuk*. This memoir was shared with me in its unpublished form by some people I interviewed at the Greek Orthodox Church.

2. Boym, *Future of Nostalgia*, 8.

3. Icadiye is the mahalle next to Kuzguncuk, and Icadiye Creek, named for that mahalle, once flowed down from the hill near that neighborhood through the center of Kuzguncuk. The creek has been channeled and paved over; its old course is now the street called Icadiye.

4. Hebbert, "Street as Locus," 592.

5. Dilmen, *Kuzguncuk Folk Song*, 30.

6. Örs describes the suppression of memories of these riots among some Rum who now live in Athens, Greece, as a strategy for dealing with the pain of having suffered these traumatic events ("Last of the Cosmopolitans," 207).

7. Brison, "Trauma Narratives," 41.

8. Makdisi and Silverstein, introduction, *Memory and Violence*, 1.

9. See Legg, "Contesting and Surviving Memory," 490.

10. Collective memory narratives reinforce a perspective on history agreed on by a cultural group (Fentress and Wickham, *Social Memory*).

11. Bal, introduction, *Acts of Memory*, ix.

12. Stewart, "Nostalgia."

13. Nicola King, *Memory, Narrative, Identity*, 2.

14. Here the narrator refers to the Struma incident. In December 1941 a ship from Romania, bound for Palestine, was carrying Jewish refugees who lacked immigration papers. While awaiting repairs, the boat was stopped by Turkish authorities in the Black Sea. The British, determined to restrict Jewish immigration to Palestine, pressured the Turkish government to deny the Jews entry into Turkey. Over two months later, the boat exploded and more than seven hundred passengers died.

15. Bektaş does not describe what happened but instead tells how people of four faiths continue to live in Kuzguncuk and how he successfully restored, through his oral history project, tolerant community life ("Kuzguncuk," 110–111). These issues explored more fully in chapter 2.

16. Güven, *September Events*, 55–56, 20–23.

17. *London Times*, "Demonstration in Istanbul," 7 September 1955.

18. A. C. Sedgwick, "Athens Protests Turkish Violence," *New York Times*, 8 September 1955.

19. News in Pictures, "Blitz Night in Istanbul," *Time Magazine*, 10 October 1955.

20. Michael Hoffman, "Rioting in Turkey Called Danger Sign" *New York Times*, 17 September 1955.

21. Vryonis, *Mechanism of Catastrophe*, xviii.

22. Ibid., 17–24.

23. Güven, *September Events*.

24. Stamatopoulos, *E Teleutaia Analampe*, 291, quoted in Vryonis, *Mechanism of Catastrophe*, 176.

25. Vryonis *Mechanism of Catastrophe*, 176–81, 104, 180.

26. See Nicola King's discussion of Primo Levi in *Memory, Narrative, Identity*, 25.

27. Benjamin, "Berlin Chronicle," 303, quoted in Nicola King, *Memory, Narrative, Identity*, 26.

28. Neyzi "Strong as Steel," 168.

29. Dilmen, *Kuzguncuk Folk Song*, 29.

30. Ibid., 54.

31. See Örs, "Last of the Cosmopolitans," 189.

32. The character Saranda utters these words at the beginning of an extended scene in which Greek, Armenian, and Jewish properties are haggled over at cheap prices, and Turkish neighbors begin to scramble for a stake in the new market of minority properties made available as minorities emigrated after the riots (Dilmen, *Kuzguncuk Folk Song*, 56).

33. Ibid., 66.

34. The Laz, an ethnic group from the Black Sea region, are sometimes the subject of jokes or discrimination in Istanbul.

35. Pennebaker and Banasik, "Creation and Maintenance," 10.

36. Paez, Basabe, and Gonzalez, "Social Processes," 147.

37. Ibid., 148.

38. Andre Levy remarks, regarding his research on the Jewish community of Morocco, "researchers in all social sciences generally tend to neglect studying the effects of emigration on those who stay behind" ("Jewish-Muslim Relationships," 365). His work involves a very similar mass emigration of Jews from Morocco between the 1950s and the 1970s.

39. Excerpts from Gökdel, *My Friend*, 122–26.

40. Kritzman, "In Remembrance," ix.

41. See Örs's discussion of how Rum people and places embody contemporary nostalgia for old Istanbul ("Last of the Cosmopolitans," ch. 7).

42. İleri, *I Didn't Forget You*, 14.

43. Chakrabarty, *Habitations of Modernity*, 136–37. Emphasis mine.

44. Boyer, *City of Collective Memory*, 5.

Chapter Five. New Day Street

1. Much of the material in this chapter also appears in Mills, "Space in Istanbul."

2. An extensive literature on the changing sociopolitical context in Istanbul and the ideal status and roles of women as symbols of Turkish modernity exists, demonstrating the contested nature of what it means to be a Turkish woman in Istanbul. For just a few sources, see Özbay, "Changes in Women's Activities"; Arat, "Project of Modernity"; Navaro-Yasin, "Historical Construction"; and Arat, "Women's Movement."

3. Tamdoğan-Abel, "Our Mahalle."

4. Erman has observed a similar extension of home space into street space through women's visiting inside and in nearby outside spaces in a squatter settlement in Ankara ("Housing Environment"). Visiting among women also takes place in suburban areas of Ankara, although Ayata notes the prevalence of other activities and spaces for socializing among women, including playing tennis, participating in bridge clubs, or going to shopping malls, which, in my observation, were less frequent in Kuzguncuk ("New Middle Class").

5. De Certeau, *Practice of Everyday Life*.

6. Staeheli and Kofman, "Mapping Gender," 10. See also Nagar, "Mapping Feminisms"; Fincher, "Dualisms to Multiplicities"; and Cope, "Gendered Political Acts."

7. I use a first name for her pseudonym here to express the important dimensions of friendship and personal connection that characterized our relationship, although in this chapter I write about the things I learned from this relationship that pertained to my larger research interests.

8. Ghannam's ethnography of Cairo makes a similar claim about the gendered nature of spatial practices in everyday life. Women in the popular quarter she studied also prefer to be with other people rather than to spend time alone (*Remaking the Modern*). The space of nearby apartments in the development in Cairo is an intimate one, much like the Turkish mahalle.

9. Uzun, *Gentrification in Istanbul*, 146.

10. See Tanrıöver for a discussion of the mahalle and feelings of belonging and familiarity associated with this cultural space ("Family, Neighborhood, and Community"). Advertising for new gated communities in Istanbul also invokes the desire for a place where people know each other, where families visit each other, and where people greet each other; these gated communities are described as having similar characteristics of mahalles. Importantly, however, these gated communities are not inclusive but are, predictably, limited to the upper class (Bartu, "Exclusionary Concept").

11. In linking secularism and modernity in my description of Zeynep I employ a historical and cultural identification of the secular as modern, which is rooted in the early foundations of the Turkish Republic (see Özyürek, *Nostalgia for the Modern*). I use these terms here, however, because they are Zeynep's as well.

12. I became a *tanıdık*, or one who is known: a neighbor.

13. Navaro-Yashin, *Faces of the State*, 69–70.

14. Many Jews in Istanbul also regularly participate in looking at coffee fortunes and yet avoid this activity on holy days (Brink-Danan, "Reference Points," 205–6).

15. See Herzfeld's discussion of hospitality and social boundaries in "Your Own House."

16. See Erman, "Housing Environment," 772. Similarly, Bosnian women practiced ongoing neighboring visits to find among other women the support they couldn't obtain from their husbands' families (Bringa, *Being Muslim*, 92). Jewish and Muslim women in colonial Algeria visited and shared information, goods, and services in galleries of courtyard houses, which were "an intermediate space between individual families and the domestic community as a whole" (Bahloul, *Architecture*, 41).

17. De Certeau, *Practice of Everyday Life*, 15–23.

18. In her article interrogating the lineage of the idea of an Islamic city, Abu-Lughod describes a sense of otherness she feels walking along a residential street of a historically Muslim city in India. For her, streets in that city have a semiprivate quality not characteristic of the French neighborhood of Mayol's study ("Islamic City").

19. Bringa explains, similarly, how villagers in a Bosnian village employed moral values to control women's spatial movement. Women who "go about the village too much" were castigated; Bringa explains that this reflects fear regarding a woman who would go outside the moral control of her household and neighbors (*Being Muslim*, 88–89).

20. Ghannam describes the difficulty of explaining how privacy works in Cairo, for example, where a cultural practice excludes an understanding of privacy as it is understood in the U.S. context (*Remaking the Modern*). In Istanbul in 2001, a radio talk show hosted by two women and whose callers were all women was devoted to the topic of the advantages of the single-family private home. The most desired aspect of the home was the ability to live according to one's desires and not have to think about neighbors' perceptions and judgments. This notion of private space is derived from a U.S. ideal; single-family homes in Istanbul are extremely unusual and accessible only to the elite (see Öncu, "Ideal Home").

21. Salamandra, *New Old Damascus*, 60–70. See also Elie, "Harem Syndrome."

22. Hansen, *Very Social Time*, 115. Thanks to Leon Jackson for suggesting this and other sources on gossip and secrets in U.S. contexts.

23. De Certeau, *Practice of Everyday Life*, 17.

24. Brink-Danan, "Reference Points," 108. See chapter 2 for a broader discussion of Jewish strategies of invisibility in Istanbul society. Thanks to a helpful and anonymous press reader of my manuscript for directing me to Brink-Danan's work.

25. Ünver, *Dark Summer*.

26. For a discussion of socioeconomic status and neighborhood associations in Turkey, see Erman and Coşkun-Yıldar, "Emergent Local Initiative."

27. Gentrification, and a corresponding elevation of property value and rents, is happening throughout Kuzguncuk. However, while prices are also rising for rents in 1950s- and 1960s-era apartment buildings on side streets that are yet to be renovated, these rents are not yet as high as the rents in buildings that have been renovated or that have exclusive views or prime locations. For a discussion of the case of Kuzguncuk as not one of true gentrification, because of the integrating role of the neighborhood association, see Morgül, "Confused Essay."

28. Marouli cites a similar phenomenon in Athens, where an increase in class status in neighborhoods correlates to the loss of semiprivate residential space, as well as of systems of support among women ("Women Resisting").

29. See Erman and Coşkun-Yıldar, "Emergent Local Initiative."

30. McDowell, *Gender, Identity, and Place*, 4.

31. In contrast, intermarriage among Jews in North Africa has taken place to such an extent that the family and community intervene to prevent the total loss of Jewish identity among children of intermarried couples, who "develop a strong entrenchment in Jewish ritual and in Jewishness, through extended family socialization" (Bahloul, "Sephardi Family," 317).

32. Bringa describes, similarly, how Catholic and Muslim women in a Bosnian village enjoyed neighborly relationships but were unwilling to accept a bride from outside the family's ethnic-religious community. As one Catholic man's mother stated, "We get along well and we have a good time together, but this is one thing. It is another to have somebody from a different religion together with you in the kitchen. When two who prepare different foods and keep different holy days share the same house many problems arise" (*Being Muslim*, 80; see also 149–54).

33. Büyükfırat, *Kuzguncuk*, 19–20.
34. Kasson, *Rudeness and Civility*, 3.
35. Bringa, *Being Muslim*, 54.
36. Ibid., 67.
37. See, comparatively, Bahloul's discussion of social relations among Muslim and Jewish neighbors in colonial Algeria that were grounded in the space of the courtyard house and that both reinscribed relationships as neighbors and circumscribed social and ethnic-religious difference (*Architecture*).
38. Bringa, *Being Muslim*, xi, 66.

Chapter Six. Jacob Street

1. Much of the text and analysis in this chapter was published in Mills, "Identity in the Nation." However, the argument and the historical analysis in this chapter are slightly different, and more developed, than in the article.
2. Brink-Danan, "Reference Points."
3. Ibid., 96.
4. According to people I spoke with who live in the *gecekondu* (squatter settlements) and to some Turkish residents in the historical core, the migrants came from villages near the city of Sivas. Jewish informants told me that the community in Kuzguncuk at the time (sometime around the 1950s and 1960s) was politically weak as well as extremely cautious and couldn't raise effective complaints to the municipality, and this is why it took so long to stop the gecekondu. Eventually members of the synagogue built walls around the cemetery to try and protect what remained; the cement walls themselves contain jumbled pieces of gravestones. Apparently the neighborhood administrator did not intervene to prevent this illegal development and, indeed, during that period much of the land along the upper length of Kuzguncuk's main street was also developed with gecekondus, which remain today.
5. The urban quarter has historically played an important role in maintaining Jewish identity for Jews in Arab-Islamic cities and has been a focus of scholarship in Jewish history and in urban Islamic studies. See, for example, Hirschberg, "Jewish Quarter"; Schroeter, "Moroccan City" and Schroeter, "Arab-Islamic Cities." I discuss this topic in more detail with regard to Istanbul in a later section of this chapter.
6. "Jewish Life," 34. The fact that this paper was written anonymously indicates that writing with that degree of frankness is something the author does not feel comfortable doing openly: she herself maintains a careful balance (Neyzi, "Strong as Steel," 168).
7. Toktaş, "Conduct of Citizenship," 128.
8. Brink-Danan, "Reference Points."
9. For further discussion of the social and political factors that contribute to the Jewish community's positive relations with the Turkish state, see Bali, *Adventure in Turkification*, 20–28.
10. Toktaş, "Perceptions of Anti-Semitism," 204.

11. Brink-Danan, "Reference Points," 150–55.

12. Neyzi, "Strong as Steel," 174.

13. Toktaş, "Perceptions of Anti-Semitism," 206.

14. In 2001 a well-known Jewish man was murdered. In the media coverage in the wake of the event, a prominent Turkish businessperson commented, "Although he was a Jew, Mr. Garih loved Turkey." The media admonished the speaker but, for Jews, it was evidence that Muslims aren't completely accepting of Jews ("Jewish Life," 34). See also Bali, "1934 Thrace Events," par. 55.

15. "Jewish Life," 33.

16. While it is not true that Jews are legally barred from those jobs, some people believe this to be the case. Others simply cite the absence of Jews in such positions as evidence that they are unattainable (Toktaş, "Perceptions of Anti-Semitism," 215).

17. Ibid., 211.

18. Kastoryano, "From Millet to Community," 263.

19. Brink-Danan, "Reference Points," 142–45. Brink-Danan interprets these required marriage lessons, conducted by three rabbis and a male lay educator, as a kind of "salvage performance, aimed at resurrecting a lost cultural form" (145). In several unpublished papers at a conference on Jewish Turkish women, authors wrote about personal experiences with, and research surveys on, the community pressure on women to marry other Jews and maintain their traditions. These papers were not published, however, testifying perhaps to the sensitive nature of making these kinds of claims as a Turkish, Jewish woman (see Brandeis University, "Jewish Women in Turkey").

20. Kastoryano, "From Millet to Community," 262; "Jewish Life." Landau writes that Jewish and non-Jewish relationships toward the end of the Ottoman Empire existed primarily within the sphere of business and not in other arenas of social life ("Relations," 543).

21. The Turkish language and Turkish names have been used by Turkish Jews as vehicles of protective assimilation (Brink-Danan, "Reference Points"; Neyzi, "Strong as Steel"; cf. Toktaş, "Conduct of Citizenship").

22. "Jewish Life," 34.

23. Kastoryano argues that "behind the shifting boundaries of the group, the 'individual becomes the collectivity'; individual actions have a collective consequence in terms of their own representation within both the interior of the group as well as within the larger society" ("From Millet to Community," 271). For one individual to introduce me to another individual would thus immediately bring that individual's relationship with me to the attention of the whole community. The collective community pressure to regulate information by attempting to control any outside threat to the community, such as a researcher, that may betray its secrets (see Brink-Danan, "Reference Points") would mean unwanted attention toward any member of the community who might be involved in bringing in an outsider. The reluctance of anyone to introduce me to anyone else is, for these reasons, very understandable.

24. Nearly one hundred people planned to attend the reunion, although only fifty actually came, as the 2006 summer Israeli bombing of Beirut began after my arrival,

and many people coming from Haifa feared their safety amid ongoing rocket attacks and stayed home.

25. This family tree illustrates seven generations of the family linked back to this primary ancestor. I describe the paths of successive family members and generations through various places based on my reading of the family tree, but aside from the name of this primary ancestor, I do not give the names of any specific people for the sake of protecting their privacy, as they may still be alive or may remain in the living memories of people who reside in Kuzguncuk today.

26. Shaw, *Ottoman Empire*, 38. Salonica was also the base for the Ottoman Sabbatean community. Members of this Jewish messianic sect concealed their identity and maintained a public Muslim identity. See Neyzi, "Remembering to Forget."

27. Shaw, *Ottoman Empire*, 49.

28. The policy also included forcibly moving specific populations around the empire for the purposes of controlling or colonizing territory.

29. Rozen, "Public Space," 332; Avigdor Levy, *Sephardim*, 22.

30. Hacker, "Sürgün System," 6.

31. Avigdor Levy, *Sephardim*, 22.

32. Rozen, "Public Space," 334.

33. Ibid., 333; Shaw, *Ottoman Empire*, 49.

34. Shaw, *Ottoman Empire*, 49–51; Hacker, "Sürgün System," 11.

35. Shaw, *Ottoman Empire*, 48, 170–71.

36. Rozen "Public Space," 338; Shaw, *Ottoman Empire*, 48–49.

37. Rozen, *Jewish Community*, 65.

38. Barnai, "History of the Jews," 24.

39. Rozen, *Jewish Community*, 82.

40. Ibid., 60; Rozen, "Public Space," 334.

41. Rozen, "Public Space," 334–35, 336.

42. Rozen, *Jewish Community*, 61; Galante, *History of Turkish Jews*, 1, 305, quoted in Rozen, "Public Space," 334n16, 337.

43. For a thorough discussion on the Islamization of this landscape, and the disparate Ottoman administrative treatment of Jews in comparison to Christians, see Baer, "Great Fire of 1660."

44. For a reference to migration to Balat and Hasköy, see Rozen, "Public Space," 337. For discussion to migration to the Asian side, see Kadıköy, *Haydarpaşa*, 5.

45. Rozen "Public Space," 336.

46. Kadıköy, *Haydarpaşa*, 5.

47. Rozen "Public Space," 341, 344.

48. Kadıköy, *Haydarpaşa*, 5.

49. Rozen, "Fishermen's Guilds," 75.

50. Shaw, *Ottoman Empire*.

51. Rodrigue, *French Jews*, 91.

52. Bornes-Varol, "Balat Quarter," 633.

53. Kadıköy, *Haydarpaşa*, 8.

54. Barnai, "History of the Jews," 28. Landau describes this economic rivalry as the result of Jews moving into new professions ("Relations," 541).

55. Kadıköy, *Haydarpaşa*, 11.

56. Avigdor Levy, *Sephardim*, 40.

57. Kadıköy, *Haydarpaşa*, 11.

58. Rozen, "Fishermen's Guilds," 77–79.

59. For the 1846 date, see Banoğlu, *Istanbul with Its History*, 81, and Akın, "Kuzguncuk," 146; for 1878, see Güleryüz, *Synagogues*, 107.

60. Bektaş claims 1886 ("Kuzguncuk," 110), while Güleryüz states 1840 (*Synagogues*, 113). None of the sources regarding the dates for these synagogues' completions cite any original primary sources for determining the dates they claim.

61. Güleryüz (*Synagogues*, 107) states that the Beth Yaakov Synagogue was built on the foundation of an older synagogue, Etz Ahayim, which had repairs in 1801, 1825, and 1861. No earlier information regarding the original construction date for this older synagogue is available, however.

62. Kastoryano, "From Millet to Community," 255; Barnai, "History of the Jews," 20. Barnai's book includes a photograph of the house once occupied by the rabbi of Kuzguncuk, indicating the degree to which Kuzguncuk's landscape is regarded as an important remnant of the Sephardic material culture of the region (23).

63. According to Shaw, Kuzguncuk was considered the most elegant Jewish neighborhood in the 1920s (*Ottoman Empire*, 246), although this contrasts with other perspectives mentioned in this chapter, suggesting that neighborhoods on the European side such as Galata were considered more fashionable by that time.

64. Shaw, *Ottoman Empire*, 250.

65. Kadıköy, *Haydarpaşa*, 8.

66. Bareilles, *Constantinople*, 307, quoted in Bornes-Varol, "Balat Quarter," 634.

67. Kastoryano, "From Millet to Community," 257.

68. Shaw explains that fires in Balat in 1910 destroyed Jewish Alliance schools there, causing Jews to leave the neighborhood (*Ottoman Empire*, 247).

69. Kadıköy, *Haydarpaşa*, 5.

70. Kastoryano, "From Millet to Community," 257. See the example of a family that moved from Dağhamami to Kuzguncuk and then to Ortaköy in Kastoryano ("Jews of Istanbul," 661).

71. Kadıköy, *Haydarpaşa*, 11.

72. Kastoryano, "From Millet to Community," 258.

73. See Schroeter, "Arab-Islamic Cities," 295n60, where he cites sources for Cairo, Tunis, Tripoli, and Jerusalem.

74. Kastoryano "Jews of Istanbul," 660, "From Millet to Community," 259.

75. Bornes-Varol, "Balat Quarter," 639.

76. See Kastoryano, "From Millet to Community," 256–57.

77. Karabatak, "Thrace Events"; Neyzi, "Strong as Steel," 172; Bali, "1934 Thrace Events."

78. Bali, "1934 Thrace Events," pars. 28–32.

79. Kastoryano makes the point that families would follow the general pattern of Jewish migration across the city from historical to new, modern mahalles to prevent feeling excluded from the larger community ("From Millet to Community," 258).

80. Bali, *Adventure in Turkification*.

81. Aktar, *Wealth Tax*.

82. Bali, *Adventure in Turkification*; Bali, *Varlik Vergisi*.

83. Bali, *Republican Years*.

84. Toktaş, "Immigration to Israel," 508.

85. Toktaş, "Immigration to Israel"; Bali, *Republican Years*.

86. This widespread rumor, although untrue, caused many to feel a dire fear that the Nazis would soon occupy Turkey and that Jews there would face the Holocaust (Bali, "Talat Pasha's Bones," 45).

87. This man explained later that he encountered a lot of anti-Turkish sentiment in Israel. He decided in 1948 that he was interested in going to Israel but was engaged and wanted to know more about the situation there, so he worked, six times, on boats that carried Turkish Jews to Israel. He said that when they reached the shore and the doctor there would ask for information regarding the presence of diseases on the boat and the origin of the boat's passengers, inevitably the Israeli doctor would curse at the information that the boat was coming from Turkey.

88. Benbassa explains that Zionist associations before World War I appealed to young people in populist neighborhoods such as Balat, and perhaps in Kuzguncuk ("Associational Strategies," 468, 471).

89. Toktaş, "Immigration to Israel."

90. Similarly, as Jews emigrated from Morocco overall, remaining Jews increasingly concentrated in Casablanca (Andre Levy, "Jewish-Muslim Relationships," 370).

91. Barnai, "History of the Jews," 24.

92. See Schulze, *Jews of Lebanon*, 6, 37–38, for mention of Jewish memories of daily life with Muslims and Christians in Lebanon.

93. Landau writes that Jews living in mixed neighborhoods in the early twentieth century were "mostly active in their own circles" ("Relations," 543). Similarly, Bahloul states that Jews and Muslims in colonial Algeria "say that they lived in happy cohesion" but were "significantly differentiated on a daily basis." Jews had closest relationships with other Jews (*Architecture*, 40).

94. Bornes-Varol, "Balat Quarter," 636.

95. Bringa, *Being Muslim*, 58. See also 58–65, where Bringa discusses the ways in which Catholics, the minority, imagined themselves as relatively more cultured in comparison to Muslims, whom they imagined as uncultured.

96. Özyürek, *Nostalgia for the Modern*.

97. Kastoryano, "From Millet to Community," 263.

98. In 1987 these neighborhoods were Şişli (31 percent), Gayrettepe (25 percent), Nişantaşı (17 percent), and Kurtuluş (6 percent); on the Anatolian side, Göztepe (5 percent), Caddebostan (5 percent), and Suadiye (3 percent). The remainder (13 percent) lived in other areas, including in Kuzguncuk (Shaw, *Ottoman Empire*, 262).

Conclusion

1. Andre Levy writes, regarding Morocco, "There is an irony here, in that Morocco's Jewish absentees remain present in the landscape, whereas present-day Jews appear to be absent" ("Jewish-Muslim Relationships," 366). The situation is remarkably similar to that of Istanbul.

2. See Akçam's discussion of the ways in which the state crushed the groups that opposed it, while paradoxically making itself more vulnerable to future challenges. He argues that state oppression actually resulted in breaking down sociopolitical norms that had made the struggle against the state a taboo in the first place and writes that this situation has resulted in a fragmented process of democratization and what he terms a stalemate between the state and civil society (*Empire to Republic*, 27–30).

3. The nostalgia for cosmopolitanism is part of the same discursive field that responds to the failure of secular modernist ideals and sees non-Muslim minorities as the bearers of a more urban, secular, and modern culture.

4. Bilu and Levy, "Nostalgia and Ambivalence," 291.

5. See Philliou, *Biography of Empire*.

6. Bahloul, *Architecture*, quote on 81, 81–82, quote on 83.

7. Iğsız, "Geographic Kinship," 174.

8. Babül, "Claiming a Place."

9. Örs, "Last of the Cosmopolitans."

10. Jackson, "Crossing Musical Worlds." Musical Jewish families in Balat, in the early twentieth century, for example, learned and played Sephardic songs, Hebrew classical music, Turkish art music, and European classical music (*Mixing Musics*, ch. 3).

11. Jackson, "Crossing Musical Worlds."

12. See Marc Baer's discussion of the role of the *dönme*, a small minority, in creating cosmopolitanism in Salonica, a marginal city of the former Ottoman Empire. He describes how minority peoples and places are written out of the larger Western-oriented literature on cosmopolitanism ("Globalization").

BIBLIOGRAPHY

Abasıyanık, Sait Faik. *Mahalle Kahvesi* [Mahalle Coffeehouse]. Istanbul: Yapı Kredi, 2002.

Abu-Lughod, Janet. "The Islamic City—Historic Myth, Islamic Essence and Contemporary Relevance." *International Journal of Middle East Studies* 19 (1987): 155–76.

Ahıska, Meltem. "Occidentalism and Registers of Truth: The Politics of Archives in Turkey." *New Perspectives on Turkey* 34 (2006): 9–30.

Ahıska, Meltem, and Biray Kolluoğlu Kırlı, eds. "Social Memory." Special issue, *New Perspectives on Turkey* 34 (2006).

Ahmad, Feroz. *The Making of Modern Turkey*. New York: Routledge, 1993.

Akar, Rıdvan. *Aşkale Yolcuları: Varlık Vergisi ve Çalışma Kampları* [Passengers to Aşkale: The Wealth Tax and Labor Camps]. Istanbul: İletişim, 1998.

Akay, Ali. "Bir Mahalle İnşası" [A Mahalle Construction]. *Istanbul Dergisi* 40 (2002): 78–80.

Akçam, Taner. *From Empire to Republic: Turkish Nationalism and the Armenian Genocide*. New York: Zed Books, 2004.

Akın, Nur. "Kuzguncuk." In Dünden Bügüne İstanbul Ansiklopedisi [Istanbul Encyclopedia from Yesterday to Today], 5:145–46. Istanbul: Tarih Vakfı, 1994.

Akşin, Sina. *Turkey: From Empire to Revolutionary Republic; The Emergence of the Turkish Nation from 1789 to the Present*. New York: New York University Press, 2007.

Aksoy, Yasemin, and Murat C. Yalçıntan. "Kutsal Topraklara Varmadan Önceki Son Durak: Kuzguncuk" [The Last Stop before Reaching the Holy Land]. *Kent Gündemi* 1 (1997): 37–40.

Aktar, Ayhan. "Homogenising the Nation: Turkifying the Economy." In Hirschon, *Crossing the Aegean*, 79–96.

———. *Varlık Vergisi ve Türkleştirme Politikaları* [The Wealth Tax and Turkification Politics]. Istanbul: İletişim, 2000.

Alexandris, Alexis. "Religion or Ethnicity: Identity of the Minorities." In Hirschon, *Crossing the Aegean*, 117–43.

Alonso, Ana Maria. "The Politics of Space, Time, and Substance: State Formation, Nationalism, and Ethnicity." *Annual Review of Anthropology* 23 (1994): 379–405.

Anderson, Benedict. *Imagined Communities: Reflections on the Origin and Spread of Nationalism.* New York: Verso, 1983.

Anılarım [My Memories]. Links to music, film, magazines, electronic games, and television series from the 1980s and 1990s. http://www.anilarim.net/mazi/konu _oku.asp?konu=perihan%20abla (accessed 10 September 2007).

Arat, Yeşim. "The Project of Modernity and Women in Turkey." In Bozdoğan and Kasaba, *Rethinking Modernity,* 95–112.

———. "Women's Movement of the 1980s in Turkey: Radical Outcome of Liberal Kemalism?" In *Reconstructing Gender in the Middle East,* edited by Fatma Müge Göçek and Shirin Balaghi, 100–112. New York: Columbia University Press, 1994.

Aslan, Senem. "'Citizen, Speak Turkish!' A Nation in the Making." *Nationalism and Ethnic Politics* 13, no. 2 (2007): 245–72.

Atabaki, Touraj, ed. *The State and the Subaltern: Modernization, Society and the State in Turkey and Iran.* New York: Tauris, 2007.

Augustinos, Gerasimos. *The Greeks of Asia Minor: Confession, Community and Ethnicity in the Nineteenth Century.* Kent, Ohio: Kent State University Press, 1992.

Ayata, Sencer. "The New Middle Class and the Joys of Suburbia." In *Fragments of Culture: The Everyday of Modern Turkey,* edited by Deniz Kandiyoti and Ayşe Saktanber, 25–42. New York: Tauris, 2002.

Ayverdi, Samiha. *Boğaziçi'nde Tarih* [History on the Bosphorus]. Istanbul: Baha, 1976.

Baban, Feyzi. "The Public Sphere and the Question of Identity in Turkey." In Keyman, *Remaking Turkey,* 75–99.

Babül, Elif. "Claiming a Place through Memories of Belonging: Politics of Recognition on the Island of Imbros." *New Perspectives on Turkey* 34 (2006): 47–66.

Baer, Marc David. "Globalization, Cosmopolitanism, and the Dönme in Ottoman Salonica and Turkish Istanbul." *Journal of World History* 18, no. 2 (2007): 141–69.

———. "The Great Fire of 1660 and the Islamization of Christian and Jewish Space in Istanbul." *International Journal of Middle East Studies* 36 (2004): 159–81.

Bahcheli, Tozun. *Greek-Turkish Relations since 1955.* Boulder, Colo.: Westview, 1990.

Bahloul, Joelle. *The Architecture of Memory: A Jewish-Muslim Household in Colonial Algeria, 1937–1962.* Translated by Catherine Du Peloux Ménagé. New York: Cambridge University Press, 1996.

———. "The Sephardi Family and the Challenge of Assimilation: Family Ritual and Ethnic Reproduction." In Goldberg, *Sephardi and Middle Eastern Jewries,* 312–24.

Bal, Mieke. Introduction. In Bal, Crewe, and Spitzer, *Acts of Memory,* vii–xvii.

———. "Memories in the Museum: Preposterous Histories for Today." In Bal, Crewe, and Spitzer, *Acts of Memory,* 171–90.

Bal, Mieke, Jonathan Crewe, and Leo Spitzer, eds. *Acts of Memory: Cultural Recall in the Present.* Hanover, N.H.: University Press of New England, 1999.

Bali, Rıfat. "The 1934 Thrace Events: Continuity and Change within Turkish State Policies regarding Non-Muslim Minorities. Interview." *European Journal of Turkish Studies* 7 (2008). http://www.ejts.org/document2903.html (accessed 15 February 2009).

———. *Bir Türkleştirme Serüveni 1923–1945* [An Adventure in Turkification: 1923–1945]. Istanbul: İletişim, 1999.

———. *Cumhuriyet Yıllarında Türkiye Yahudileri: Aliya, bir Toplu Göçun Öyküsü 1946–1949* [Turkish Jews in the Republican Years: Aliya, the Story of a Mass Migration; 1946–1949]. Istanbul: İletişim, 2002.

———. *Musa'nın Evlatları Cumhuriyet'in Yurttaşları* [Moses's Sons: Citizens of the Republic]. Istanbul: İletişim, 2001.

———. "The Politics of Turkification during the Single Party Period." In Kieser, *Turkey beyond Nationalism*, 43–49.

———. "Talat Paşa'nın Kemiklerini Mi Nazi Fırınları Mı?" [Talat Pasha's Bones or Nazi Ovens?]. *Toplumsal Tarih* 150 (2006): 42–47.

———. *Tarz-ı Hayat'tan Life Style'a: Yeni Seçkinler, Yeni Mekanlar, Yeni Yaşamlar* [From Style of Life to Lifestyle: New Elites, New Places, New Lives]. Istanbul: İletişim, 2002.

———. *The "Varlik Vergisi" Affair: A Study on Its Legacy; Selected Documents.* Istanbul: Isis, 2005.

Banoğlu, Niyazi Ahmet. *Tarih ve Efsaneleri ile İstanbul* [Istanbul with Its History and Its Legends]. Istanbul: Ak, 1966.

Bardenstein, Carol. "Trees, Forests, and the Shaping of Palestinian and Israeli Collective Memory." In Bal, Crewe, and Spitzer, *Acts of Memory*, 148–70.

Bareilles, Bertrand. *Constantinople: Ses Cites Franques et Levantines* [Constantinople: Its French and Levantine Sites]. Paris: Bossard, 1918.

Barnai, Jacob. "On the History of the Jews in the Ottoman Empire." In *Sephardi Jews in the Ottoman Empire: Aspects of Material Culture*, edited by Esther Juhasz, 19–34. Jerusalem: Israel Museum, 1990.

Barnes, Trevor, and James S. Duncan. *Writing Worlds: Discourse, Text, and Metaphor in the Representation of Landscape.* New York: Routledge, 1992.

Barth, Fredrik, ed. *Ethnic Groups and Boundaries: The Social Organization of Cultural Difference.* London: Allen and Unwin, 1969.

Bartu, Ayfer. "Dışlayıcı bir Kavram Olarak 'Mahalle'" ["Mahalle" as an Exclusionary Concept]. *Istanbul Dergisi* 40 (2002): 84–86.

Başdaş, Begum. "Cosmopolitanism in Istanbul: Everyday Claims to Bodies, Sexualities and Mobility in the City." PhD diss., University of California, Los Angeles, 2007.

Bastea, Eleni, ed. *Memory and Architecture.* Albuquerque: University of New Mexico Press, 2004.

Baudrillard, Jean. *Simulations.* Translated by Paul Foss, Paul Patton, and Philip Beitchman. New York: Semiotext(e), 1983.

Bauman, Zygmunt. *Culture as Praxis.* London: Sage, 1999.

Behar, Cem. *A Neighborhood in Ottoman Istanbul: Fruit Vendors and Civil Servants in the Kasap Ilyas Mahalle.* Albany, N.Y.: SUNY Press, 2003.

Bektaş, Cengiz. *Ev Alma, Komşu Al* [Don't Take a House, Take a Neighbor]. Istanbul: Tasarım, 1996.

———. *Hoşgörünün Öteki Adı: Kuzguncuk* [The Other Name for Tolerance: Kuzguncuk]. Istanbul: Tasarım Yayın Grubu, 1996.

———. "Kuzguncuk." *Istanbul Dergisi* 2 (1993): 105–15.

———. "Public Participation in the Rejuvenation of the Old Fabric of Cities." In *Proceedings, International Conference on the Revitalisation of Historic Cities.* UN Development Programme, USAID, Nicosia, Cyprus, 20–22 May 1999.

———. "Urban Projects and Planning Initiatives against Gentrification" workshop. Discussion participant. Symposium on Applying Gentrification Theories to Istanbul, Kadir Has University, Istanbul, 20 May 2003.

Benbassa, Esther. "Associational Strategies in Ottoman Jewish Society in the Nineteenth and Twentieth Centuries." In Levy, *Jews of the Ottoman Empire,* 457–84.

Benjamin, Walter. "A Berlin Chronicle." In *One Way Street and Other Writings.* Translated by Edmund Jephcott and Kingsley Shorter, 293–346. 1932. Reprint, London: New Left Books, 1979.

Bertram, Carel. *Imagining the Turkish House: Collective Visions of Home.* Austin: University of Texas Press, 2008.

Bhabha, Homi. Introduction. In Bhabha, *Nation and Narration,* 1–7.

———. *Nation and Narration.* 1882. Reprint, New York: Routledge, 1990.

Bierman, Irene, Rifa'at Ali Abou-El-Haj, and Donald Preziosi, eds. *The Ottoman City and Its Parts: Urban Structure and Social Order.* New Rochelle, N.Y.: Caratzas, 1991.

Bilal, Melissa. "The Lost Lullaby and Other Stories about Being an Armenian in Turkey." *New Perspectives on Turkey* 34 (2006): 67–92.

Billig, Michael. *Banal Nationalism.* Thousand Oaks, Calif.: Sage, 1995.

Bilu, Yoram, and Andre Levy. "Nostalgia and Ambivalence: The Reconstruction of Jewish-Muslim Relations in Oulad Mansour." In Goldberg, *Sephardi and Middle Eastern Jewries,* 288–311.

Birsel, Salah. *Sergüzeşt-i Nono Bey ve Elmas Boğaziçi* [Mr. Nono the Adventurer and the Diamond Bosphorus]. Ankara, Turkey: Türkiye İş Bankası, 1982.

Blunt, Alison. "Collective Memory and Productive Nostalgia: Anglo-Indian Homemaking at McCluskieganj." *Environment and Planning D: Society and Space* 21, no. 6 (2003): 717–38.

Bonine, Michael. *Population, Poverty and Politics in Middle East Cities.* Gainesville: Florida University Press, 1997.

Bornes-Varol, Marie-Christine. "The Balat Quarter and Its Image: A Study of a Jewish Neighborhood in Istanbul." In Levy, *Jews of the Ottoman Empire,* 633–45.

Boyer, M. Christine. *City of Collective Memory: Its Historical Imagery and Architectural Entertainments.* Cambridge: MIT Press, 1996.

Boym, Svetlana. *The Future of Nostalgia*. New York: Basic Books, 2001.

Boysan, Aydın. *Nereye Gitti İstanbul? Yaşantı* [Where Did Istanbul Go? A Memoir]. Istanbul: Yapı Kredi, 2004.

Bozdoğan, Sibel. *Modernism and Nation-Building: Turkish Architectural Culture in the Early Republic*. Seattle: University of Washington Press, 2002.

Bozdoğan, Sibel, and Reşat Kasaba, eds. *Rethinking Modernity and National Identity in Turkey*. Seattle: University of Washington Press, 1997.

Brandeis University, Hadassah International Research Institute on Jewish Women. Unpublished papers from "Jewish Women in Turkey: Living in Multiple Worlds" conference, Waltham, Mass., 9 December 2002.

Brennan, Timothy. *At Home in the World: Cosmopolitanism Now*. Cambridge, Mass.: Harvard University Press, 1997.

Breuilly, John. *Nationalism and the State*. Manchester, UK: Manchester University Press, 1982.

Bringa, Tone. *Being Muslim the Bosnian Way*. Princeton, N.J.: Princeton University Press, 1995.

Brink-Danan, Marcy. "Reference Points: Text, Context and Change in Definitions of Turkish-Jewish Identity." PhD diss., Stanford University, 2005.

Brison, Susan J. "Trauma Narratives and the Remaking of the Self." In Bal, Crewe, and Spitzer, *Acts of Memory*, 39–54.

Brubaker, Rogers. *Nationalism Reframed: Nationhood and the National Question in the New Europe*. New York: Cambridge University Press, 1996.

Brubaker, Rogers, Margit Feischmidt, Jon Fox, and Liana Grancea. *Nationalist Politics and Everyday Ethnicity in a Transylvanian Town*. Princeton, N.J.: Princeton University Press, 2006.

Budeiri, Musa. "The Palestinians: Tensions between Nationalist and Religious Identities." In Jankowski and Gershoni, *Rethinking Nationalism*, 191–206.

Burris, Gregory A. "The Other from Within: Pan-Turkist Mythmaking and the Expulsion of the Turkish Left." *Middle Eastern Studies* 43, no. 4 (2007): 611–24.

Büyükfırat, Zakire. *Kuzguncuk: Bella Vista Hoşçakal* [Kuzguncuk: Goodbye, Beautiful View]. Istanbul: Sone, 2005.

Çağaptay, Soner. "Passage to Turkishness: Immigration and Religion in Modern Turkey." In *Citizenship and Ethnic Conflict*, edited by Haldun Gülalp, 61–82. New York: Routledge, 2006.

Çakil, Dila. "Istanbul'da Kucuk bir Paris: Kuzguncuk" [A Little Paris in Istanbul: Kuzguncuk]. *Akademist* 1, no. 3 (2002): 24–29.

Cartier, Carolyn. "Cosmopolitics and the Maritime World City." *Geographical Review* 89, no. 2 (1999): 278–89.

Çelik, Zeynep. *Empire, Architecture, and the City: French-Ottoman Encounters, 1830–1914*. Seattle: University of Washington Press, 2008.

———. *The Remaking of Istanbul: Portrait of an Ottoman City in the Nineteenth Century*. Seattle: University of Washington Press, 1986.

————. *Urban Forms and Colonial Confrontations: Algiers under French Rule.* Berkeley: University of California Press, 1997.

————. "Urban Preservation as Theme Park: The Case of Soğukçesme Street." In Çelik, Favro, and Ingersoll, *Streets*, 83–94.

Çelik, Zeynep, Diane Favro, and Richard Ingersoll. Preface. In Çelik, Favro, and Ingersoll, *Streets*, 1–7.

————, eds. *Streets: Critical Perspectives on Public Space.* Berkeley: University of California Press, 1994.

Chakrabarty, Dipesh. *Habitations of Modernity: Essays in the Wake of Subaltern Studies.* Chicago: Chicago University Press, 2002.

Chatterjee, Partha. *Nationalist Thought and the Colonial World: A Derivative Discourse?* Minneapolis: University of Minnesota Press, 1993.

————. "Whose Imagined Community?" In *Mapping the Nation*, edited by Gopal Balakrishnan, 214–25. New York: Verso, 1996.

Cheah, Peng, and Bruce Robbins, eds. *Cosmopolitics: Thinking and Feeling beyond the Nation.* Minneapolis: Minnesota University Press, 1998.

Çınar, Alev. *Modernity, Islam, and Secularism in Turkey: Bodies, Places, Time.* Minneapolis: University of Minnesota Press, 2005.

Clay, Christopher. "Labour Migration and Economic Conditions in Nineteenth Century Anatolia." In *Turkey Before and After Ataturk: Internal and External Affairs*, edited by Sylvia Kedourie, 1–32. Portland, Ore.: Cass, 1999.

Clogg, Richard. "A Millet within a Millet: The Karamanlides." In *Ottoman Greeks in the Age of Nationalism: Politics, Economy and Society in the Nineteenth Century*, edited by Dimitri Gondicas and Charles Issawi, 115–42. Princeton, N.J.: Darwin, 1999.

Çolak, Yılmaz. "Ottomanism vs. Kemalism: Collective Memory and Cultural Pluralism in 1990s Turkey." *Middle Eastern Studies* 42, no. 4 (2006): 587–602.

Commission of the European Communities. "Turkey 2008 Progress Report." Commission Staff working document, SEC (2008) 2699 final, Brussels, 5 November 2008. http://64.233.169.104/search?q=cache:tCGSXQ3G0UQJ: www.abgs.gov.tr/files/AB_Iliskileri/Tur_En_Realitons/Progress/turkey _progress_report_2008.pdf+review+of+minority+rights+environment+in +turkey+2008&hl=en&ct=clnk&cd=19&gl=us&client=firefox-a (accessed 13 November 2008).

Committee against Racism and Discrimination. *Review of Minority Rights Environment in Turkey.* Istanbul Branch: Human Rights Association, January– July 2005.

Cope, Meghan. "Placing Gendered Political Acts." In Staeheli, Kofman, and Peake, *Mapping Women, Making Politics*, 71–86.

Cosgrove, Denis. *Social Formation and Symbolic Landscape.* Madison: University of Wisconsin Press, 1998.

Cosgrove, Denis, and Stephen Daniels, eds. *The Iconography of Landscape: Essays on the Symbolic Representation, Design and Use of Past Environments.* New York: Cambridge University Press, 1989.

Cresswell, Timothy. *In Place/Out of Place.* Minneapolis: University of Minnesota Press, 1996.

Dadrian, Vahakn N. *The History of the Armenian Genocide: Ethnic Conflict from the Balkans to Anatolia to the Caucasus.* Oxford: Berghahn Books, 1995.

Daniş, Timur, and Alican Değer. "Boş Arazi Mi Bulamamışlar!" [Couldn't They Find an Empty Space?]. *Nokta* 14 (June 1992): 42–43.

Davis, Eric. *Memories of State: Politics, History, and Collective Identity in Modern Iraq.* Berkeley: University of California Press, 2005.

De Certeau, Michel. *Practice of Everyday Life.* Vol. 2, *Living and Cooking.* Minneapolis: University of Minnesota Press, 1998.

Deleon, Jak. *The Bosphorus: A Historical Guide.* Translated by Mary Berkman. Istanbul: InterMedia, 1999.

Della Dora, Veronica. "The Rhetoric of Nostalgia: Postcolonial Alexandria between Uncanny Memories and Global Geographies." *Cultural Geographies* 13 (2006): 207–38.

DeLyser, Dydia. "Authenticity on the Ground: Engaging the Past in a California Ghost Town." *Annals of the Association of American Geographers* 89, no. 4 (1999): 602–32.

Demir, Hülya, and Rıdvan Akar. *İstanbul'un Son Sürgünleri* [Istanbul's Last Exiles]. Istanbul: Belge, 1994.

Demir, Osman, and Yakup Emre Çoruhlu. "Determining the Property Ownership on Cadastral Works in Turkey." *Land Use Policy* 26 (2008): 112–20.

Dilmen, Güngör. *Kuzguncuk Türküsü* [Kuzguncuk Folk Song]. Istanbul: Mitos Boyut Tiyatro, 2000.

Diziler.com [Series.com]. Schedules, links, and forums for Turkish television series. http://www.diziler.com/index.php?page=shows&id=1058 (accessed 10 September 2007).

Driessen, Henk. "Mediterranean Port Cities: Cosmopolitanism Reconsidered." *History and Anthropology* 16 (2005): 129–41.

Duncan, James S. *The City as Text: The Politics of Landscape Interpretation in the Kandyan Kingdom.* New York: Cambridge University Press, 1990.

———. "Sites of Representation: Place, Time and the Discourse of the Other." In *Place/Culture/Representation,* edited by James S. Duncan and David Ley, 39–56. New York: Routledge, 1993.

Duncan, James S., and Nancy Duncan. *Landscapes of Privilege: The Politics of the Aesthetic in an American Suburb.* New York: Routledge, 2003.

———. "(Re)reading the Landscape." *Environment and Planning D: Society and Space* 6, no. 2 (1988): 117–26.

Ebcim, Nedret. *Üç Dinin ve Ünlülerin Buluştuğu Semt: Kuzguncuk* [Kuzguncuk: The Neighborhood Where Three Religions and Their Famous People Meet]. Istanbul: İleri, 2005.

Eber, Dena, and Arthur Neal. *Memory and Representation: Constructed Truths, Competing Realities.* Bowling Green, Ohio: Bowling Green State University Popular Press, 2001.

Eickelman, Dale. "Is There an Islamic City? The Making of a Quarter in a Moroccan Town." *International Journal of Middle East Studies* 5 (1974): 274–94.

Elie, Serge. "The Harem Syndrome: Moving beyond Anthropology's Discursive Colonization of Gender in the Middle East." *Alternatives* 29 (2004): 139–68.

El Kadi, Galila, and Dalia Elkerdany. "Belle-epoque Cairo: The Politics of Refurbishing the Downtown Business District." In Singerman and Amar, *Cairo Cosmopolitan,* 345–71.

Erman, Tahire. "Women and the Housing Environment: The Experiences of Turkish Migrant Women in Squatter (*Gecekondu*) and Apartment Housing." *Environment and Behavior* 28, no. 6 (1996): 764–98.

Erman, Tahire, and Meliha Coşkun-Yıldar. "Emergent Local Initiative and the City: The Case of Neighbourhood Associations of the Better-off Classes in Post-1990 Urban Turkey." *Urban Studies* 44, no. 13 (2007): 2547–66.

Evin, Ahmet O. "Novelists: New Cosmopolitanism versus Social Pluralism." In *Turkey and the West: Changing Political and Cultural Identities,* edited by Metin Heper, Ayşe Öncu, and Heinz Kramer, 92–115. New York: Tauris, 1993.

Fentress, James, and Chris Wickham. *Social Memory.* Cambridge, Mass.: Blackwell, 1992.

Fincher, Ruth. "From Dualisms to Multiplicities: Gendered Political Practices." In Staeheli, Kofman, and Peake, *Mapping Women, Making Politics,* 49–70.

Galante, Avram. *Histoire des Juifs de Turquie* [History of Turkish Jews]. Istanbul: Isis, n.d.

Galeotti, Anna E. *Toleration as Recognition.* New York: Cambridge University Press, 2002.

Gedik, Betül. *Eski İstanbul Hayatı ve İstanbul Yahudileri* [Old Istanbul Life and Istanbul's Jews]. Istanbul: Pera Orient, 1996.

Gellner, Ernest. *Nations and Nationalism.* Ithaca, N.Y.: Cornell University Press, 1983.

Ghannam, Farha. *Remaking the Modern: Space, Relocation and the Politics of Identity in a Global Cairo.* Berkeley: University of California Press, 2002.

Gilmartin, Mary, and Lawrence D. Berg. "Locating Postcolonialism." *Area* 39, no. 1 (2007): 120–24.

Göçek, Fatma Müge. "Nationalism as the Dangerous Underbelly of the Modern Turkish Republic." In *Nationalism in Contemporary Europe,* edited by I. Pawel Karolewski and A. Marcin Suzycki, 167–79. London: Continuum, 2007.

Gökalp, Ziya. *Turkish Nationalism and Western Civilization: Selected Essays by Ziya Gökalp.* Edited and translated by Niyazi Berkes. New York: Columbia University Press, 1959.

Gökariksel, Banu. "A Feminist Geography of Veiling: Gender, Class and Religion in the Making of Modern Spaces and Subjects in Istanbul." In *Women, Religion, and Space*, edited by Karen Morin and Jeanne Kay Guelke, 61–80. Syracuse, N.Y.: Syracuse University Press, 2007.

Gökdel, Reza Suat. *Dostum* [My Friend]. Istanbul: Kastas, 1991.

Goldberg, Harvey E. *Sephardi and Middle Eastern Jewries: History and Culture in the Modern Era*. Bloomington: Indiana University Press.

Greenfeld, Liah. *Nationalism: Five Roads to Modernity*. Cambridge, Mass.: Harvard University Press, 1992.

Gregory, Derek. *The Colonial Present: Afghanistan, Palestine, Iraq*. Cambridge, Mass.: Blackwell, 2004.

Grigoriadis, Ioannis N. "Turk or Türkiyeli? The Reform of Turkey's Minority Legislation and the Rediscovery of Ottomanism." *Middle Eastern Studies* 43, no. 3 (2007): 423–38.

Guibernau, Montserrat. *The Identity of Nations*. Malden, Mass.: Polity, 2007.

Gülalp, Haldun, ed. *Citizenship and Ethnic Conflict: Challenging the Nation-State*. New York: Routledge, 2006.

Güleryüz, Naim A. *The Synagogues of Istanbul*. Istanbul: Gözlem Gazetecilik, 2008.

Gür, Asli. "Stories in Three Dimensions: Narratives of the Nation and the Anatolian Civilizations Museum." In Özyürek, *Public Memory*, 40–69.

Guttstadt, Corinna Görgü. "Depriving Non-Muslims of Citizenship as Part of the Turkification Policy in the Early Years of the Turkish Republic: The Case of Turkish Jews and Its Consequences during the Holocaust." In Kieser, *Turkey beyond Nationalism*, 50–56.

Güven, Dilek. *Cumhuriyet Dönemi Azınlık Politikaları Bağlamında 6–7 Eylül Olayları* [The 6–7 September Events as Tied to Minority Politics during the Republican Period]. Istanbul: Tarih Vakfı, 2005.

Hacker, Joseph. "The Sürgün System and Jewish Society in the Ottoman Empire." In Rodrigue, *Ottoman and Turkish Jewry*, 1–66.

Halbwachs, Maurice. *The Collective Memory*. Translated by Francis J. Ditter Jr. and Vida Yazdi Ditter. New York: Harper Colophon Books, 1980.

Handler, Richard, and Eric Gable. *The New History in an Old Museum: Creating the Past at Colonial Williamsburg*. Durham, N.C.: Duke University Press, 1997.

Hanioğlu, M. Şükrü. "Turkism and the Young Turks 1889–1908." In Kieser, *Turkey beyond Nationalism*, 3–19.

Hansen, Karen V. *A Very Social Time: Crafting Community in Antebellum New England*. Berkeley: University of California Press, 1994.

Harvey, David. "Cosmopolitanism and the Banality of Geographical Evils." *Public Culture* 12, no. 2 (2000): 529–64.

———. *Cosmopolitanism and the Geographies of Freedom*. New York: Columbia University Press, 2009.

Hebbert, Michael. "The Street as Locus of Collective Memory." *Environment and Planning D: Society and Space* 23 (2005): 581–96.

Height, David. "Cengiz Bektas and the Community of Kuzguncuk in Istanbul." *Architectural Design* 75, no. 5 (2006): 44–49.

Herzfeld, Michael. "'As in Your Own House': Hospitality, Ethnography, and the Stereotype of Mediterranean Society." In *Honor and Shame and the Unity of the Mediterranean*, special pub. 22, edited by David D. Gilmore, 75–89. Washington, D.C.: American Anthropological Association, 1987.

———. *Cultural Intimacy: Social Poetics in the Nation-State*. New York: Routledge, 1997.

Hirschberg, Haim Z. "The Jewish Quarter in Muslim Cities and Berber Areas." *Judaism* 17, no. 4 (1968): 405–21.

Hirschon, Renee, ed. *Crossing the Aegean: An Appraisal of the 1923 Compulsory Population Exchange between Greece and Turkey*. New York: Berghahn Books, 2003.

Hobsbawm, Eric, and Terence Ranger, eds. *The Invention of Tradition*. Cambridge: Cambridge University Press, 1983.

Hodgkin, Katharine, and Susannah Radstone, eds. *Contested Pasts: The Politics of Memory*. New York: Routledge, 2003.

Hoelscher, Steven. *Heritage on Stage: The Invention of Ethnic Place in America's Little Switzerland*. Madison: University of Wisconsin Press, 1998.

———. "Making Place, Making Race: Performances of Whiteness in the Jim Crow South." *Annals of the Association of American Geographers* 93, no. 3 (2003): 657–86.

Hoelscher, Steven, and Derek Alderman. "Memory and Place: Geographies of a Critical Relationship." *Social and Cultural Geography* 5, no. 3 (2004): 347–55.

Houston, Christopher. *Islam, Kurds, and the Turkish Nation State*. Oxford: Berg, 2003.

İçduygu, Ahmet. "The Anatomy of Civil Society in Turkey: Toward a Transformation." In Keyman, *Remaking Turkey*, 179–97.

İçduygu, Ahmet, and B. Ali Soner. "Turkish Minority Rights Regime: Between Difference and Equality." *Middle Eastern Studies* 42, no. 3 (2006): 447–68.

Iğsız, Aslı. "Polyphony and Geographic Kinship in Anatolia: Framing the Turkish-Greek Compulsory Population Exchange." In Özyürek, *Public Memory*, 162–87.

Ilbert, Robert, and Ilios Yannakakis, with Jacques Hassoun. *Alexandria 1860–1960: The Brief Life of a Cosmopolitan Community*. Translated by Colin Clement. Alexandria, Egypt: Harpocrates, 1997.

Ileri, Selim. *İstanbul Seni Unutmadım* [Istanbul, I Didn't Forget You]. Istanbul: Oğlak, İstanbul Kitapları, 2001.

Inan, Süleyman. "The First 'History of the Turkish Revolution' Lectures and Courses in Turkish Universities (1934–42)." *Middle Eastern Studies* 43, no. 4 (2007): 593–609.

Inciciyan, Ghukas V. *Boğaziçi Sayfiyeleri* [Bosphorus Villas]. Edited by Orhan Duru. Istanbul: Eren, 2000.

Inciciyan, P. Ğ. *18. Asırda Istanbul* [Istanbul in the 18th Century]. Istanbul: İstanbul Enstitüsü, 1976.

Isin, Engin, ed. *Democracy, Citizenship and the Global City*. New York: Routledge, 2000.

Jackson, Maureen. "Crossing Musical Worlds: Jews Making Ottoman and Turkish Classical Music." Second-place prize, Sakip Sabanci International Research Award, Brookings Institution and Sabanci University, Istanbul, 2008.

———. "Mixing Musics: The Urban Landscape of Late Ottoman and Turkish Syagogue Music." PhD diss., University of Washington, 2008.

Jackson, Peter, and Jan Penrose, eds. *Constructions of Race, Place, Nation*. London: University College London Press, 1993.

Jankowski, James, and Israel Gershoni, eds. *Rethinking Nationalism in the Arab Middle East*. New York: Columbia University Press, 1997.

"Jewish Life in Turkey Today." In *Jewish Women from Muslim Societies Speak*, edited by Susan M. Kahm, Nancy F. Vineberg, and Sarah Silberstein Swartz, 32–34. Waltham, Mass.: Brandeis University, American Sephardi Federation and Hadassah International Research Institution on Women, 2003.

Johnson, Clarence Richard. *Constantinople Today; or, The Pathfinder Survey of Constantinople: A Study in Oriental Social Life*. New York: Macmillan, 1922.

Johnson, Nuala. *Ireland, the Great War, and the Geography of Remembrance*. New York: Cambridge University Press, 2003.

Kadıköy Hemdat İsrael Sinagogu Vakfı (Foundation of the Hemdat Israel Synagogue of Kadıköy). *Haydarpaşada Geçen 100 Yılımız* [Our Past 100 Years in Haydarpaşa]. Istanbul: Gözlem, 1999.

Kanal Bir [Channel One]. *Ekmek Teknesi* program description and photo of actors. http://www.kanalı.com.tr/progr.ekmek_teknesi_1,29696.html (accessed 10 September 2007).

Kandiyoti, Deniz, and Ayşe Saktanber, eds. *Fragments of Culture: The Everyday of Modern Turkey*. New Brunswick, N.J.: Rutgers University Press, 2002.

Kant, Immanuel. *Kant: Political Writings*. Edited by H. S. Reiss. Cambridge: Cambridge University Press, 1991.

Karabatak, Haluk. "1934 Trakya Olaylari ve Yahudiler" [Jews and the 1934 Thrace Events]. *Tarih ve Toplum* 146 (1996): 68–80.

Karaçizmeli, Gülseren. "Uğur Yücel'i Köyünde Ağırlamak!" [Recognizing Uğur Yücel in His Village]. *Mülkiyeliler Mektubu* 77 (2002): 12–13. Mülkiyeliler Birliği, İstanbul Şubesi.

Karakoyunlu, Yılmaz. *Salkım Hanımın Taneleri* [Salkım Hanım's Necklace]. Istanbul: Doğan Kitapçilik, 1990.

Karimova, Nigar, and Edward Devereli. *Minorities in Turkey*. Occasional Paper 19. Stockholm: Swedish Institute of International Affairs, 2001.

Kasson, John F. *Rudeness and Civility: Manners in Nineteenth-Century America*. New York: Hill and Wang, 1990.

Kastoryano, Riva. "From Millet to Community: The Jews of Istanbul." In Rodrigue, *Ottoman and Turkish Jewry*, 253–77.

————. "Trajectoires dans la ville: Les Juifs à Istanbul" [The Jews of Istanbul: Study of an Urban Population]. *Critique* 48, no. 543–44 (1992): 657–70.

Kaya, Ayhan, and Turgut Tarhanlı, eds. *Türkiye de Çoğunluk ve Azınlık Politikaları: AB Sürecinde Yurttaşlık Tartışmaları* [Majority and Minority Politics in Turkey: Citizenship Struggles in the EU Process]. Istanbul: Tesev, 2005.

Kaygılı, Osman Cemal. *Köşe Bucak İstanbul* [Istanbul's Nooks and Crannies]. 1931. Reprint, Istanbul: Selis, 2003.

Kaynar, Sevda. "Organ Nakline Evet Doğa Katline Hayır" [Yes to Organ Donation, No to Environmental Destruction]. *Hey Girl*, August 1992.

Kechriotis, Vangelis. "The Modernization of the Empire and the Community 'Privileges': Greek Orthodox Responses to Young Turk Policies." In *The State and the Subaltern: Modernization, Society and the State in Turkey and Iran*, edited by Touraj Atabaki, 53–70. New York: Tauris.

Kedourie, Elie. *Nationalism*. London: Hutchinson, 1960.

Kedourie, Sylvia, ed. *Turkey Before and After Ataturk: Internal and External Affairs*. Portland, Ore.: Cass, 1999.

Keith, Michael, and Steve Pile. *Place and the Politics of Identity*. London: Routledge, 1993.

Keyder, Çağlar. "The Consequences of the Exchange of Populations for Turkey." In Hirschon, *Crossing the Aegean*, 39–52.

————. *Istanbul between the Global and the Local*. New York: Rowman and Littlefield, 1999.

Keyder, Çağlar, Y. Eyüp Özveren, and Donald Quataert, eds. "Port Cities of the Eastern Mediterranean, 1800–1914." Special issue, *Review* 16, no. 4 (1993).

Keyman, E. Fuat, ed. *Remaking Turkey: Globalization, Alternative Modernities, and Democracy*. New York: Lexington Books, 2007.

Khalidi, Rashid. "The Formation of Palestinian Identity: The Critical Years: 1917–1923." In Jankowski and Gershoni, *Rethinking Nationalism*, 171–90.

Kieser, Hans-Lukas, ed. *Turkey beyond Nationalism: Towards Post-Nationalist Identities*. New York: Tauris, 2006.

King, Anthony D. *Spaces of Global Cultures: Architecture, Urbanism, Identity*. New York: Routledge, 2004.

King, Nicola. *Memory, Narrative, Identity: Remembering the Self*. Edinburgh, Scotland: Edinburgh University Press, 2000.

Köker, Tolga, with Leyla Keskiner. "Lessons in Refugeehood: The Experience of Forced Migrants in Turkey." In Hirschon, *Crossing the Aegean*, 193–208.

Kostof, Spiro. *A History of Architecture Settings and Rituals*. New York: Oxford University Press, 1985.

Koufopoulou, Sophia. "Muslim Cretans in Turkey: The Reformulation of Ethnic Identity in an Aegean Community." In Hirschon, *Crossing the Aegean*, 209–20.

Kritzman, Lawrence. "In Remembrance of Things French." Foreword. In *Realms of Memory: The Construction of the French Past*, by Pierre Nora, 1:ix–xiv. Edited by

Lawrence Kritzman. Translated by Arthur Goldhammer. New York: Columbia University Press, 1998.

Kuzguncuklular Derneği [Kuzguncuk Neighborhood Association]. Official Web site with history and goals. http://www.kuzguncuk.org (accessed 2 May 2002).

Landau, Jacob M. "Relations between Jews and Non-Jews in the Late Ottoman Empire: Some Characteristics." In Levy, *Jews of the Ottoman Empire*, 539–46.

Lapidus, Ira. "Traditional Muslim Cities: Structure and Change." In *From Madina to Metropolis: Heritage and Change in the Near Eastern City*, edited by L. Carl Brown, 51–72. Princeton, N.J.: Darwin, 1973.

Lefebvre, Henri. *The Production of Space*. Cambridge, Mass.: Blackwell, 1991.

Legg, Stephen. "Contesting and Surviving Memory: Space, Nation, and Nostalgia in *Les Lieux de Memoire*." *Environment and Planning D: Society and Space* 23 (2005): 481–504.

Le Goff, Jacques. *History and Memory*. Translated by Steven Rendall and Elizabeth Claman. New York: Columbia University Press, 1992.

Lekka, Anastasia. "Legislative Provisions of the Ottoman/Turkish Governments regarding Minorities and Their Properties." *Mediterranean Quarterly* 18 (2007): 135–54.

Leoussi, Athena S., and Steven Grosby, eds. *Nationality and Nationalism*. Vol. 3, *Area and Period Studies: Modern Middle East, Asia, Africa, the Americas, Australia*. New York: Tauris, 2004.

Levy, Andre. "Notes on Jewish-Muslim Relationships: Revisiting the Vanishing Moroccan Jewish Community." *Cultural Anthropology* 18, no. 3 (2003): 365–97.

Levy, Avigdor. *The Jews of the Ottoman Empire*. Princeton, N.J.: Darwin.

———, ed. *Jews, Turks, Ottomans: A Shared History, Fifteenth through the Twentieth Century*. Syracuse, N.Y.: Syracuse University Press, 2002.

———. *The Sephardim in the Ottoman Empire*. Princeton, N.J.: Darwin, 1992.

Lewis, Pierce. "Axioms for Reading the Landscape." In *The Interpretation of Ordinary Landscapes*, edited by Donald Meinig, 11–32. New York: Oxford University Press, 1979.

Lockman, Zachary. "Arab Workers and Arab Nationalism in Palestine: A View from Below." In Jankowski and Gershoni, *Rethinking Nationalism*, 249–72.

Lowenthal, David. *The Past Is a Foreign Country*. New York: Cambridge University Press, 1985.

———. *Possessed by the Past: The Heritage Crusade and the Spoils of History*. New York: Free Press, 1996.

Mahtani, Minelle. "Racial ReMappings: The Potential of Paradoxical Space." *Gender, Place and Culture* 8, no. 3 (2001): 299–305.

Makdisi, Ussama, and Paul Silverstein. Introduction. In *Memory and Violence in the Middle East and North Africa*, edited by Ussama Makdisi and Paul Silverstein, 1–26. Bloomington: Indiana University Press, 2006.

Malcomson, Scott L. "The Varieties of Cosmopolitan Experience." In *Cosmopolitics:*

Thinking and Feeling beyond the Nation, edited by Peng Cheah and Bruce Robbins, 233–45. Minneapolis: Minnesota University Press, 1998.

Mardin, Şerif. "Patriotism and Nationalism in Turkey." In Leoussi and Grosby, *Nationality and Nationalism*, 12–29.

———. "Projects as Methodology: Some Thoughts on Modern Turkish Social Science." In Bozdoğan and Kasaba, *Rethinking Modernity*, 64–80.

———. "Religion and Secularism in Turkey." In *The Modern Middle East*, edited by Albert Hourani, Philip Khoury, and Mary Wilson, 347–74. Berkeley: University of California Press, 1993.

Marouli, Christina. "Women Resisting (in) the City: Struggles, Gender, Class and Space in Athens." *International Journal of Urban and Regional Research* 19, no. 4 (1995): 534–48.

Massey, Doreen. "Places and Their Pasts." *History Workshop Journal* 39, no. 1 (1995): 182–92.

McDowell, Linda. *Gender, Identity, and Place: Understanding Feminist Geographies*. Minneapolis: University of Minnesota Press, 1999.

Meeker, Michael. "Once There Was, Once There Wasn't: National Monuments and Interpersonal Exchange." In Bozdoğan and Kasaba, *Rethinking Modernity*, 157–91.

Meijer, Roel, ed. *Cosmopolitanism, Identity and Authenticity in the Middle East*. Surrey, England: Routledge Curzon, 1999.

Migdal, Joel S., ed. *Boundaries and Belonging: States and Societies in the Struggle to Shape Identities and Local Practices*. New York: Cambridge University Press, 2004.

Mignolo, Walter D. "The Many Faces of Cosmo-polis: Border Thinking and Critical Cosmopolitanism." In Pollock et al., *Cosmopolitanism*, 157–88.

Mills, Amy. "Boundaries of the Nation in the Space of the Urban: Memory and Landscape in Istanbul." *Cultural Geographies* 13, no. 3 (2006): 367–94.

———. "Gender and *Mahalle* (Neighbourhood) Space in Istanbul." *Gender, Place, and Culture* 14, no. 3 (2007): 335–54.

———. "Narratives in City Landscapes: Cultural Identity in Istanbul." *Geographical Review* 95, no. 3 (2005): 441–62.

———. "The Place of Locality for Identity in the Nation: Minority Narratives of Cosmopolitan Istanbul." *International Journal of Middle East Studies* 40, no. 3 (2008): 383–401.

Mitchell, Don. "Cultural Landscapes: Just Landscapes or Landscapes of Justice?" *Progress in Human Geography* 27, no. 6 (2003): 787–96.

———. *The Lie of the Land: Migrant Workers and the California Landscape*. Minneapolis: Minnesota University Press, 1996.

———. Review of *Writing Worlds: Discourse, Text, and Metaphor in the Representation of Landscape*, by Trevor Barnes and James S. Duncan. *Professional Geographer* 45, no. 4 (1993): 474–75.

Mitchell, Timothy. *Colonising Egypt*. Berkeley: University of California Press, 1991.

Moltz, Jennie Germann, and Sarah Gibson, eds. *Mobilizing Hospitality: The Ethics of Social Relations in a Mobile World*. Burlington, Vt.: Ashgate, 2007.

Morgül, Tan. "Kuzguncuk üzerine Kafa Karışık bir Deneme" [A Confused Essay on Kuzguncuk]. *Mimarist* 21: (2006).

Morin, Karen, and Jeanne Kay Guelke, eds. *Women, Religion, and Space*. Syracuse, N.Y.: Syracuse University Press, 2007.

Moss, Pamela, ed. *Feminist Geography in Practice: Research and Methods*. Malden, Mass.: Blackwell, 2002.

Nagar, Richa. "Mapping Feminisms and Difference." In Staeheli, Kofman, and Peake, *Mapping Women, Making Politics*, 31–48.

Nalbantoğlu, Gülsüm Baydar. "Silent Interruptions: Urban Encounters with Rural Turkey." In Bozdoğan and Kasaba, *Rethinking Modernity*, 192–210.

Navaro-Yashin, Yael. *Faces of the State: Secularism and Public Life in Turkey*. Princeton, N.J.: Princeton University Press, 2003.

Navaro-Yasin, Yael. "The Historical Construction of Local Culture: Gender and Identity in the Politics of Secularism versus Islam." In *Istanbul: Between the Global and the Local*, edited by Çağlar Keyder, 59–75. Lanham, Md.: Rowman and Littlefield, 1999.

Necipoğlu, Gülru. *The Age of Sinan: Architectural Culture in the Ottoman Empire*. Princeton, N.J.: Princeton University Press, 2005.

Neuwirth, Angelika, and Andreas Pflitsch. "Crisis and Memory: Dimensions of Their Relationship." Introduction. In *Crisis and Memory in Islamic Societies*, edited by Angelika Neuwirth and Andreas Pflitsch, 1–17. Proceedings of the Third Summer Academy of the Working Group Modernity and Islam. Beirut, Lebanon: Orient Institute of the German Oriental Society in Beirut, 1998.

Neyzi, Leyla. *İstanbul'da Hatırlamak ve Unutmak* [Remembering and Forgetting in Istanbul]. Istanbul: Yurt, 1999.

———. "Remembering to Forget: Sabbateanism, National Identity and Subjectivity in Turkey." *Comparative Studies in Society and History* 44, no. 1 (2002): 137–58.

———. "Strong as Steel, Fragile as a Rose: A Turkish Jewish Witness to the Twentieth Century." *Jewish Social Studies* 12, no. 1 (2005): 167–89.

Nijman, Jan. "Locals, Exiles and Cosmopolitans: A Theoretical Argument about Identity and Place in Miami." *Tijdschrift voor Economische en Sociale Geografie* 98, no. 2 (2007): 176–87.

Nora, Pierre. *Realms of Memory: Rethinking the French Past*, edited by Lawrence Kritzman. New York: Columbia University Press, 1996.

Ökte, Faik. *The Tragedy of the Turkish Capital Tax*. Translated by Geoffrey Cox. 1951. Reprint, Wolfboro, N.H.: Croom Helm, 1987.

Öncu, Ayşe. "The Myth of the 'Ideal Home': Travels across Cultural Borders to Istanbul." In *Space, Culture and Power: New Identities in Globalizing Cities*, edited by Ayşe Öncu and Petra Weyland, 56–72. London: Zed Books, 1997.

Oran, Baskin. "The Non-Muslim Pious Foundations and the Declarations of 1936." Paper presented at the "Istanbul: Present and Future" conference, Istanbul, 30 June 2006.

―――. "Those Who Stayed." In Hirschon, *Crossing the Aegean*, 97–116.

―――. *Türkiye'de Azınlıklar* [Minorities in Turkey]. Istanbul: İletişim, 2004.

Örs, Ilay. "Coffeehouses, Cosmopolitanism, and Pluralizing Modernities in Istanbul." *Journal of Mediterranean Studies* 12, no. 1 (2002): 119–45.

―――. "The Last of the Cosmopolitans? Rum Polites of Istanbul in Athens: Exploring the Identity of the City." PhD diss., Harvard University, 2006.

Ortayli, Ilber. *Ottoman Studies*. Istanbul: Bilgi University Press, 2004.

Özbay, Ferhunde. "Changes in Women's Activities Both Inside and Outside the Home." In *Women in Modern Turkish Society*, edited by Şirin Tekeli, 89–111. London: Zed Books, 1991.

Özbek, Meral. "Arabesk Culture: A Case of Modernization and Popular Identity." In Bozdoğan and Kasaba, *Rethinking Modernity*, 211–32.

Öztürk, Nazif. *Azınlık Vakıfları* [Minority Foundations]. Ankara, Turkey: Altınküre, 2003.

Öztürkmen, Arzu. "Remembering Conflicts in a Black Sea Town: A Multi-Sited Ethnography of Memory." *New Perspectives on Turkey* 34 (2006): 93–115.

Özür Diliyorum [I'm Sorry]. Signatures of Turkish people who express empathy and pain regarding the massacres of Armenians in 1915. http://www.ozurdiliyoruz. com (accessed 28 July 2009).

Özyürek, Esra. Introduction. In Özyürek, *Public Memory*, 1–15.

―――. *Nostalgia for the Modern: State Secularism and Everyday Politics in Turkey*. Durham, N.C.: Duke University Press, 2006.

―――. *The Politics of Public Memory in Turkey*. Syracuse, N.Y.: Syracuse University Press, 2007.

―――. *Türkiyenin Toplumsal Hafızası: Hatırdıklarlıyla ve Unuttuklarıyla* [Remembering and Forgetting: Social Memory in Turkey]. Istanbul: İletişim, 2001.

Paez, Dario, Nekane Basabe, and Jose Luis Gonzalez. "Social Processes and Collective Memory: A Cross-Cultural Approach to Remembering Political Events." In Pennebaker, Paez, and Rime, *Political Events*, 147–74.

Parlak, Derviş. *Şehrin Hukuku: Çevre ve Kültür Değerlerinin Korunmasında bir Karşı Saldırı Aracı Olarak Hukuk* [Urban Law: Law in the Service of a Counterattack in the Protection of Environmental and Cultural Values]. Istanbul: Kanat Kitap, 2007.

Peet, Richard. Review of *The City as Text: The Politics of Landscape Interpretation in the Kandyan Kingdom*, by James S. Duncan. *Annals of the Association of American Geographers* 83, no. 1 (1993): 184–87.

Pennebaker, James W., and Becky Banasik. "On the Creation and Maintenance of Collective Memories: History as Social Psychology." In Pennebaker, Paez, and Rime, *Political Events*, 3–20.

Pennebaker, James W., Dario Paez, and Bernard Rime, eds. *Collective Memory of Political Events: Social Psychological Perspectives.* Mahwah, N.J.: Erlbaum, 1997.

Philliou, Christine. *A Biography of Empire: Governing Ottoman Christians in an Age of Revolution.* Berkeley: University of California Press, forthcoming.

———. "The Paradox of Perceptions: Interpreting the Ottoman Past through the National Present." *Middle Eastern Studies* 44, no. 5 (2008): 661–75.

Pollock, Sheldon, Homi Bhabha, Carol Breckenridge, and Dipesh Chakrabarty, eds. *Cosmopolitanism.* Durham, N.C.: Duke University Press, 2002.

———. "Cosmopolitanisms." In Pollock et al., *Cosmopolitanism,* 1–14.

Polycandrioti, Ourania. "Literary Quests in the Aegean (1840–1940): Identity and Cosmopolitanism." *History and Anthropology* 16 (2005): 113–27.

Pope, Nicole, and Hugh Pope. *Turkey Unveiled: Ataturk and After.* London: Murray, 1997.

Popke, Jeff. "Geography and Ethics: Spaces of Cosmopolitan Responsibility." *Progress in Human Geography* 31, no. 4 (2007): 509–18.

Poppi, Cesare. "Wider Horizons with Larger Details: Subjectivity, Ethnicity, and Globalization." In *The Limits of Globalization: Cases and Arguments,* edited by Alan Scott, 284–305. New York: Routledge, 1997.

Porter, Geoff D. "Unwitting Actors: The Preservation of Fez's Cultural Heritage." *Radical History Review* 86 (2003): 123–48.

Poyraz, Bedriye. "The Turkish State and Alevis: Changing Parameters of an Uneasy Relationship." *Middle Eastern Studies* 41, no. 4 (2005): 503–16.

Renan, Ernest. "What Is a Nation?" Translated by Martin Thom. In Bhabha, *Nation and Narration,* 8–22.

Reyna, Yuda, and Ester Moreno Zonana. *Son Yasal Düzenlemelere Göre Cemaat Vakıfları* [Community Foundations according to Recent Adjustments]. Istanbul: Gözlem Gazetecilik, 2003.

Riedler, Florian. "Armenian Labour Migration to Istanbul and the Migration Crisis of the 1890s." Paper presented at the "Migration and Urban Institutions in the Late Ottoman Reform Period" workshop, Zentrum Moderner Orient, Berlin, May 2007.

Robbins, Bruce. "Actually Existing Cosmopolitanism." Introduction, part 1. In *Cosmopolitics: Thinking and Feeling beyond the Nation,* edited by Peng Cheah and Bruce Robbins, 1–19. Minneapolis: Minnesota University Press, 1998.

———. "Cosmopolitanism: New and Newer." *Boundary 2* 34, no. 3 (2007): 47–60.

Rodrigue, Aron. *French Jews, Turkish Jews: The Alliance Israelite Universelle and the Politics of Jewish Schooling in Turkey 1860–1925.* Bloomington: Indiana University Press, 1990.

———. *Ottoman and Turkish Jewry: Community and Leadership.* Bloomington: Indiana University Turkish Studies, 1992.

Rose, Gillian. "The Cultural Politics of Place: Local Representation and Oppositional Discourse in Two Films." *Transactions of the Institute of British Geographers* 19 (1994): 46–60.

———. *Feminism and Geography: The Limits of Geographical Knowledge.* Minneapolis: University of Minnesota Press, 1993.

Rozen, Minna. "Boatmen's and Fishermen's Guilds in Nineteenth-Century Istanbul." *Mediterranean Historical Review* 15, no. 1 (2000): 72–93.

———. *A History of the Jewish Community in Istanbul: The Formative Years, 1453–15.* Leiden, Netherlands: Brill, 2002.

———. "Public Space and Private Space among the Jews of Istanbul in the Sixteenth and Seventeenth Centuries." *Turcica* 30 (1998): 331–46.

Salamandra, Christa. *A New Old Damascus: Authenticity and Distinction in Urban Syria.* Bloomington: Indiana University Press, 2004.

Sargın, Güven Arıf. "Displaced Memories, or the Architecture of Forgetting and Remembrance." *Environment and Planning D: Society and Space* 22, no. 5 (2004): 659–80.

Sauer, Carl. "The Morphology of Landscape." In *Land and Life: A Selection of Writings of Carl Ortwin Sauer,* edited by John Leighly, 315–50. 1925. Reprint, Berkeley: University of California Press, 1963.

Savage, Kirk. *Standing Soldiers, Kneeling Slaves: Race, War, and Monument in Nineteenth-Century America.* Princeton, N.J.: Princeton University Press, 1997.

Schein, Richard, ed. *Landscape and Race in the United States.* New York: Routledge, 2006.

———. "The Place of Landscape: A Conceptual Framework for Interpreting the American Scene." *Annals of the Association of American Geographers* 87 (1997): 660–80.

Schroeter, David. "The Changing Relationship between the Jews of the Arab Middle East and the Ottoman State in the Nineteenth Century." In *Jews, Turks, Ottomans: A Shared History, Fifteenth through the Twentieth Century,* edited by Avigdor Levy, 88–107. Syracuse, N.Y.: Syracuse University Press, 2002.

———. "The Jewish Quarter and the Moroccan City." In *New Horizons in Sephardic Studies,* edited by Yedida K. Stillman and George K. Zucker, 67–81. Albany, N.Y.: SUNY Press, 1993.

———. "Jewish Quarters in the Arab-Islamic Cities of the Ottoman Empire." In Levy, *Jews of the Ottoman Empire,* 287–300.

Schueth, Sam, and John O'Loughlin. "Belonging to the World: Cosmopolitanism in Geographic Contexts." *Geoforum* 39 (2008): 926–41.

Schulze, Kirsten E. *The Jews of Lebanon: Between Coexistence and Conflict.* Brighton, UK: Sussex Academic Press, 2001.

Secor, Anna. "Between Longing and Despair: State, Space, and Subjectivity in Turkey." *Environment and Planning D: Society and Space* 25, no. 1 (2007): 33–52.

———. "'There Is an Istanbul That Belongs to Me': Citizenship, Space, and Identity in the City." *Annals of the Association of American Geographers.* 94, no. 2 (2004): 352–68.

Şeker, Nesim. "Demographic Engineering in the Late Ottoman Empire and the Armenians." *Middle Eastern Studies* 43, no. 3 (2007): 461–74.

Shatzmiller, Maya, ed. *Nationalism and Minority Identities in Islamic Societies.* Montreal: McGill-Queen's University Press, 2005.

Shaw, Stanford. *Jews of the Ottoman Empire and the Turkish Republic.* London: Macmillan, 1991.

———. "The Population of Istanbul in the Nineteenth Century." *International Journal of Middle East Studies* 10, no. 2 (1979): 265–77.

Sifneos, Evridiki. "'Cosmopolitanism' as a Feature of the Greek Commercial Diaspora." *History and Anthropology* 16 (2005): 97–111.

Simon, Reeva. "The Imposition of Nationalism in a Non-Nation State: The Case of Iraq during the Interwar Period: 1921–1941." In Jankowski and Gershoni, *Rethinking Nationalism,* 87–104.

Singerman, Diane, and Paul Amar, eds. *Cairo Cosmopolitan: Politics, Culture, and Urban Space in the New Globalized Middle East.* New York: American University in Cairo Press, 2006.

———. "Contesting Myths, Critiquing Cosmopolitanism, and Creating the New Cairo School of Urban Studies." In Singerman and Amar, *Cairo Cosmopolitan,* 1–46.

Sırman, Nükhet. "Constituting Public Emotions through Memory: Interviewing Witnesses." *New Perspectives on Turkey* 34 (2006): 31–46.

Slyomovics, Susan. *The Object of Memory: Arab and Jew Narrate the Palestinian Village.* Philadelphia: University of Pennsylvania Press, 1998.

Smith, Anthony D. *The Ethnic Origins of Nations.* Oxford: Blackwell, 1986.

———. "Ethno-Symbolism and the Study of Nationalism." Introduction. In *Myths and Memories of the Nation,* edited by Anthony D. Smith, 3–28. New York: Oxford University Press, 1999.

———. *Theories of Nationalism.* New York: Harper and Row, 1971.

Söderström, Ola. "Studying Cosmopolitan Landscapes." *Progress in Human Geography* 30, no. 5 (2006): 553–58.

Solmaz, Mehmet. *Tarih Boyunca Asya'nın Kapısı: Her Yönüyle Üsküdar* [Asia's Door throughout History: Üsküdar from Every Side]. Istanbul: Zafar, 1982.

Spitzer, Leo. "Back through the Future: Nostalgic Memory and Critical Memory in a Refuge from Nazism." In Bal, Crewe, and Spitzer, *Acts of Memory,* 87–104.

Staeheli, Lynn, and Eleonore Kofman. "Mapping Gender, Making Politics: Towards Feminist Political Geographies." In Staeheli, Kofman, and Peake, *Mapping Women, Making Politics,* 1–13.

Staeheli, Lynn, Eleonore Kofman, and Linda J. Peake, eds. *Mapping Women, Making Politics: Feminist Perspectives on Political Geography.* New York: Routledge, 2004.

Stamatopoulos, Kostas. *E Teleutaia Analampe: E Konstantinoupolitike Romiosyne Sta Chronia 1948-1955.* Athens, 1996.

Stein, Sarah Abrevaya. "The Permeable Boundaries of Ottoman Jewry." In *Boundaries and Belonging: States and Societies in the Struggle to Shape Identities and Local Practices,* edited by Joel S. Migdal, 49–72. New York: Cambridge University Press, 2004.

Stewart, Kathleen. "Nostalgia—a Polemic." *Cultural Anthropology* 3, no. 3 (1998): 227–41.

Talas, I. Hakkı, and Sitki Dinç. *İstanbul: Kısaca Tarihi, Coğrafyası, Suları, Semtleri ve Anıtları ile* [Istanbul: Its Brief History, Geography, Waters, Neighborhoods, and Monuments]. Istanbul: Suhulet, 1948.

Tamdoğan-Abel, Işık. "Osmanlı Döneminden Günümüz Türkiye'sine 'Bizim Mahalle'" ["Our Mahalle" from Ottoman Times to Today's Turkey]. *Istanbul Dergisi* 40 (2002): 66–70.

Tankuter, Korkut. "Interview with Güler Yücel." *Çevre*, July 1992.

Tanrıöver, Hülya. "Türk Televizyon Dizilerinde Aile, Mahalle ve Cemaat Yaşamı" [Family, Neighborhood, and Community Life in Turkish Television Serials]. *Istanbul Dergisi* 40 (2002): 93–96.

Tekeli, Şirin, ed. *Women in Modern Turkish Society*. London: Zed Books, 1991.

Till, Karen. "Memory Studies." *History Workshop Journal* 62, no. 1 (2006): 325–41.

———. *The New Berlin: Memory, Politics, Place*. Minneapolis: Minnesota University Press, 2005.

Toktaş, Şule. "The Conduct of Citizenship in the Case of Turkey's Jewish Minority: Legal Status, Identity, and Civic Virtue Aspects." *Comparative Studies of South Asia, Africa and the Middle East* 26, no. 1 (2006): 121–33.

———. "Perceptions of Anti-Semitism among Turkish Jews." *Turkish Studies* 7, no. 2 (2006): 203–23.

———. "Turkey's Jews and Their Immigration to Israel." *Middle Eastern Studies* 42, no. 3 (2006): 505–19.

Tuan, Yi-Fu. "Language and the Making of Place: A Narrative-Descriptive Approach." *Annals of the Association of American Geographers* 81, no. 4 (1991): 684–96.

Tuğlacı, Pars. *İstanbul Ermeni Kiliseleri* [Istanbul's Armenian Churches]. Istanbul: Pars, 1991.

Tunç, Ayfer. *Bir Maniniz Yoksa Annemler Size Gelecek: 70'li Yıllarda Hayatımız* [If It's Convenient My Mom Will Visit: Our Lives in the 1970's. Istanbul: Yapı Kredı, 2001.

Turam, Berna. *Between Islam and the State: The Politics of Engagement*. Stanford, Calif.: Stanford University Press, 2007.

Türker, Orhan. *Osmanlı İstanbulu'ndan bir Köşe: Tatavla* [A Corner of Ottoman Istanbul: Tatavla]. Istanbul: Sel, 1998.

Turkish Economic and Social Studies Foundation. *Vakıflar Kanunu Tasarısı'nın Cemaat Vakıflarını İlgilendiren Hükümleri Üzerine* [Report regarding the Laws Related to Community Foundations in the Foundation Legal Proposal]. Istanbul: Turkish Economic and Social Studies Foundation, 2004.

Türköz, Meltem. "Surname Narratives and the State-Society Boundary: Memories of Turkey's Family Name Law of 1934." *Middle Eastern Studies* 43, no. 6 (2007): 893–908.

Ünver, Mehmet. *Kuzgun bir Yaz* [A Dark Summer]. Istanbul: Okuyan Us, 2002.

U.S. Bureau of Democracy, Human Rights, and Labor. "Country Reports on Human Rights Practices: Turkey, 2007." U.S. Department of State. http://www .state.gov/g/drl/rls/hrrpt/2007/100589.htm (accessed 25 September 2009).

Üstündağ, Ebru. "Turkish Republican Citizenship and Rights to the City." PhD diss., York University, 2005.

Uzun, C. Nil. *Gentrification in Istanbul: A Diagnostic Study.* Nederlandse Geografische Studies 285. Utrecht, Netherlands: Universiteit Utrecht, 2001.

———. "The Impact of Urban Renewal and Gentrification on Urban Fabric: Three Cases in Turkey." *Tijdschrift voor Economische en Sociale Geografie* 94, no. 3 (2003): 363–75.

Uzuner, Buket. *Kumral Ada, Mavi Tuna* [*Mediterranean Waltz*]. Istanbul: Everest, 2002.

Vryonis, Speros, Jr. *The Mechanism of Catastrophe: The Turkish Pogrom of September 6–7 1955 and the Destruction of the Greek Community of Istanbul.* New York: Greekworks.com, 2005.

White, Jenny. *Islamist Mobilization in Turkey: A Study in Vernacular Politics.* Seattle: University of Washington Press, 2003.

Wilson, Christopher S. "The Persistence of the Turkish Nation in the Mausoleum of Mustafa Kemal Atatürk." In *Nationalism in a Global Era: The Persistence of Nations,* edited by Mitchell Young, Eric Zuelow, and Andreas Sturm, 93–114. New York: Routledge, 2007.

Wright, Gwendolyn. *The Politics of Design in French Colonial Urbanism.* Chicago: University of Chicago Press, 1991.

Yalçın Kemal. *Emanet Çeyiz: Mübadele İnsanları* [Entrusted Trousseau: The People of the Exchange]. Istanbul: Belge, 1998.

Yavuz, M. Hakan. *Islamic Political Identity in Turkey.* New York: Oxford University Press, 2003.

Yildirim, Onur. "Diplomats and Refugees: Mapping the Turco-Greek Exchange of Populations, 1922–1934." PhD diss., Princeton University, 2002.

Yorulmaz, Ahmet. *Savaşın Cocukları* [Children of the War]. Istanbul: Bilge, 1997.

Yücel, Can. "Dandini Dandini Dasdana" [Lullaby]. *İkibin'e Doğru,* August 1992, 37.

Yücel, Erdem. "Kuzguncuk." *Türkiye Turing ve Otomobil Kurumu Belleteni* 50, no. 329 (1975): 5–11.

Zubaida, Sami. "Cosmopolitanism and the Middle East." In *Cosmopolitanism, Identity and Authenticity in the Middle East,* edited by Roel Meijer, 15–34. Surrey, England: Curzon, 1999.

Zürcher, Erik. *Turkey: A Modern History.* New York: Tauris, 1995.

INDEX

Aşkale (Turkey), 20, 53, 190–91
assimilation, 51, 156, 164, 167, 169, 172, 195, 205, 211, 215
Association of Turkish Jews (Tel Aviv), 174
Atatürk, Mustafa Kemal: alleged bombing of birthplace of, 54, 119, 120; as founder of Turkish Republic, 7–8, 31, 50; nostalgia for, 208–9, 212
Ayata, Sencer, 240n4
Ayios Panteleymon Church (Kuzguncuk), 43, 123
Ayios Yeoryios Church (Kuzguncuk), 43

Baer, Marc, 248n12
Bağlarbaşı (Istanbul neighborhood), 42, 43, 229n47
Bahloul, Joelle, 6, 213–14, 243n37
Balat (Istanbul neighborhood), 20, 190; as Jewish neighborhood, 165, 177, 179, 180, 182, 184, 185–86, 198, 203
Bali, Rıfat, 189, 229n58
Balkans, 48, 180
Barnai, Jacob, 38, 246n62
Barth, Fredrik, 231n78
bathing suits, 114, 202, 203
Baudrillard, Jean, 233n7
Bauman, Zygmunt, 231n78
Beirut (Lebanon), 9, 33, 37, 244n24
Bektaş, Cengiz: as character in a play, 104; on destruction of cosmopolitanism in Kuzguncuk, 118–19; and Kuzguncuk gentrification, 5, 70–72, 76, 78–79, 82, 235n41; and Kuzguncuk Neighborhood Association, 5; on size of Kuzguncuk's minority population, 229n57
belonging: gender and, 28, 137, 153, 154–60; in Kuzguncuk, 112, 117, 127–34, 136–38, 140, 141, 144–62, 185–87, 209–10; mahalle life and national, 22–26, 30–34, 39, 57, 61, 63–64, 67, 71, 107, 109–10, 112–17,

125; and neighboring in the mahalle, 27, 39, 67, 112, 134, 136–38, 140, 141, 144–62, 187, 213; propriety as price of, in the mahalle, 134, 136, 144–46, 148, 160, 211–12; question of national, among minorities, 24–26, 30, 46–58, 87, 107, 109–10, 117, 128–34, 136–38, 140, 155–60, 170–72, 187–88, 191, 201–6, 208, 209–10, 219n1. See also citizenship; identity: of Kuzguncuk people; national identity
Benbassa, Esther, 247n88
Beth Nisim (Virane) Synagogue (Kuzguncuk), 41, 165, 181
Beth Yaakov Synagogue (Kuzguncuk), 41, 165, 167, 168, 180–81
Beylerbeyi (Istanbul neighborhood), 24, 42, 45, 67, 82, 102, 186, 228n20
Beyoğlu (Istanbul neighborhood): on European side of Istanbul, 20; film production in, 66, 77; minority dominance in, 9, 21, 52, 67, 180; riots of 1955, 119, 120, 124, 126
Bhabha, Homi, 12, 34
Bilu, Yoram, 212–13
Bir Maniniz Yoksa Annemler Size Gelecek (Tunç), 64–65
Birsel, Salah, 236n56
Bornes-Varol, Marie-Christine, 184
Bosnia, 13, 160–62, 198, 241n16, 241n19, 242n32
Bosphorus Law 2960, 89
Bosphorus Planning Bureau, 89
Bosphorus Sea, 3, 39–40, 43, 72
Bostancı (Istanbul neighborhood), 46, 118, 199
Boyer, Christine, 76
Boym, Svetlana, 107, 108
Breckenridge, Carol, 34
Bringa, Tone, 160–62, 198, 241n19, 242n32
Brink-Danan, Marcy, 147, 169, 170, 244n19

Brubaker, Rogers, 11
Bulgarians, 53, 185
Bursa (Turkey), 180
Büyükfırat, Zakire, 106–7, 109, 156

Caddebostan (Istanbul neighborhood), 46, 166, 183, 193, 199, 200, 204, 247n98; as elite neighborhood, 65; minority neighborhoods in, 227n18
Cairo (Egypt), 31, 183, 241n8, 242n20
Çamlıca (Turkey), 192
Çanakkale (Turkey), 177, 185
Çelik, Zeynep, 219n5
Çengelköy (Istanbul neighborhood), 60, 67, 96, 101, 102, 121, 228n20, 235n42
censorship (Turkish): activists opposed to, 31; and difficulty of doing research on Turkish minorities, 46, 82, 226n2; of Istanbul's multicultural history, 7, 19, 20; by media during 1955 riots, 119–20; of non-Turkish languages and cultures, 50, 52; about Turkish nationalist antiminority policies, 36, 147–48. See also silence
Certeau, Michel de, 144–45
Chakrabarty, Dipesh, 34, 133
Christians: anti-Semitism among, 180; in Bosnia, 13, 160–62; decline of population of, in contemporary Kuzguncuk, 46, 78, 109, 119, 128, 132, 158–59; decline of population of, in contemporary Turkey, 2, 10, 49, 207, 226n2; discrimination against, 10, 177; as having dominated Istanbul's culture at one time, 2, 9–10, 21, 33, 47, 51, 114; mixed marriages among, 46, 55, 215, 229n57; in Ottoman Empire, 9, 213. See also Armenians; churches; Greeks; minorities
churches: destruction of, in 1955 riots, 109, 119–21, 124, 158; in Kuzguncuk, 16, 23–24, 40, 42–44, 46, 72, 73, 74, 81–83, 99, 113, 115, 117–18, 155,

160, 209, 216, 227n19, 229n47; and Kuzguncuk Neighborhood Association, 86, 94
Cihangir (Istanbul neighborhood), 2, 75
Çınar, Alev, 220n15
Çınaraltı Café, 23, 110
Citizen, Speak Turkish campaign, 10, 36, 52, 186, 231n90
citizenship: Lausanne Treaty's guarantee of, for minorities in Turkey, 49, 53, 55, 231n90; minorities' insecurity about their, 128, 169–71, 175, 176, 185–88, 198–200, 203, 205; minority groups' contention over, 230n59; removing of Turkish, from Turkish Jews in Europe, 51
class: and gender identity, 137–38, 150; gentrification tensions related to, 27, 63–64, 70–72, 74, 76–83, 86, 88, 138–39, 141, 149–53, 199; Istanbul neighborhoods associated with elite, 65, 183, 204; Jewish neighborhoods stratified by, 179, 183, 185–86, 201; in Kuzguncuk, 27, 43, 44, 63, 70–72, 74, 76–83, 86, 88, 136–39, 149–53, 164, 176, 182, 183–84, 188, 193, 198–99; and Kuzguncuk identity, 4; as linked to Turkish national identity, 28, 30–31; of Muslim elites, 30–31, 33, 204; and neighboring practices, 138, 150, 153–55; of Perihan Abla characters, 69; Turkish perceptions of minorities', 53
coffee fortune readings, 140–45, 161, 241n14
coffeehouses, 27, 38, 39, 45, 139
collective memory (historical memory; social memory): adopting, 129–30; defined, 14, 222n47; forgetting's role in, 130, 132, 211–12; of historical multiethnic tolerance in Kuzguncuk, 6, 25–26, 30, 35, 62, 71–72, 74, 78, 82–83, 93, 95, 100, 102–4, 107–10,

collective memory (*continued*)
113–19, 122, 126, 129, 131–32, 134, 141, 147, 163–64, 187, 196, 201, 203–4, 206, 207–9, 214; vs. history, 14, 59–84, 106–34, 216–17, 222n46, 239n10; vs. individual memory, 6, 14, 15, 25, 29, 107, 111, 112, 125; mahalles as places of, 36–37, 58, 64–84, 132, 136, 137, 151, 154, 160, 176; narratives of, 111–32; and national identity politics, 14–16, 106–34, 154; and remembering and forgetting minorities, 6–7, 9, 19–22, 25–26, 64–67, 82, 100–101, 104–5, 109–27, 130–31, 207–12; streets as locus of, 6, 62, 219n5; of violence against minorities in Kuzguncuk, 25, 118–34. *See also* cultural memory; landscapes; nostalgia
community(-ies): Bektaş' efforts to create, in Kuzguncuk, 70–71; gated, 77, 204, 241n10; imagined, 2, 3, 8–16, 18, 22, 26, 28–32, 34, 36, 50, 132, 209; Kuzguncuk as ideal, 78. *See also* mahalles; memory
Constantinople. *See* Istanbul
corruption, 91–92, 98, 208
cosmopolitanism: "actually existing," 33; current academic focus on, 215–16; elites' perception of, 31; historical, 37; loss of, in Kuzguncuk, 29, 83, 100, 109, 113–30, 166, 198–205, 214; mahalles' role in, 46–47; memories of, 10, 18–22, 28–36, 43–44, 64, 112–34; minorities' association with, 7, 21, 67, 107, 118–19, 122–23, 126, 128–29, 201–2, 204–6, 214, 248n3; vs. nationalism, 30–34, 46–58, 118–19, 122, 168, 203–4, 206–17; nostalgia for, 9, 20–22, 36, 57–58, 62, 67, 168, 207–11; seen as Western influence, 215; Turkish state's destruction of, 30–34, 46–58, 118–22, 204–17; and urbanization, 7, 38. *See also* mi-

norities; modernization; tolerance; urbanization
Çukurcuma (Istanbul neighborhood), 20
cultural geography. *See* landscapes; place
cultural memory: defined, 222n47; of minorities in Turkey, 2, 6, 10, 18–26, 30, 34, 35–36, 57–58, 71–72, 95–100, 102–4, 107–10, 113–19, 122, 126, 129, 131–32, 147, 163–65, 187; as obscuring historical tensions, 61–62, 64, 81–84, 87, 110, 111, 210–11, 214. *See also* collective memory
Culture and Nature Preservation Committee (Turkey), 89
Cyprus: issues relating to, affecting Greek-Turkish relations, 54–55, 99, 119–21, 204, 232n105; Turks' emigration from, 48

Dadrian, Vahakn N., 230n66
Dağhamamı (Istanbul neighborhood), 182, 183
Damascus (Syria), 9, 31, 145
Demir, Hülya, 56
difference (social). *See* class; ethnic identity; gender; minorities; national identity; "other"; place of origin; religious identity
Dilmen, Güngör, 104, 107–8, 127–28
disaster-preparedness. *See* earthquake-preparedness
discrimination. *See* minorities: human rights violations against, in Turkey
Diyarbakır (Turkey), 2, 199

earthquake-preparedness, 4, 90–91, 95, 151
Ebcim, Nedret, 35, 46
Economic and Social History Foundation of Turkey, 223n77
Edirne (Turkey), 177, 183, 185, 186
Ekmek Teknesi (television show), 59–61, 61, 62, 81

gentrification (*continued*)
77, 79, 81, 99, 235nn47, 50; women involved in, 141, 150. *See also* class; housing; property

Germans. *See* Nazis

Ghannam, Farha, 241n8, 242n20

globalization: of capitalism, 30–31; discourses associated with, 9, 14, 32, 33; gentrification as driven by, 75–76; and transnationalization of identity, 30, 215–16

Gökalp, Mehmet Ziya, 230n77

Gökdel, Reza Suat, 131–32

gossip, 145–47, 158

Göztepe (Istanbul neighborhood), 65, 146, 166, 194, 200, 247n98

Greece: Turkish Greeks' links to, 170; Turkish population exchange with, 48, 49; Turkish territorial disputes with, 47, 54. *See also* Greeks

Greek language, 21, 29, 39, 164, 177

Greeks (Rum): churches of, 40, 43; departure of, from Turkey, 10, 19, 36, 54–58, 98, 99, 102, 109, 114, 118, 123, 132, 134, 157, 194, 200, 204, 232n107; gentrification of landscapes associated with, 20, 77; identity of, on Imbros/Gökçeada, 214–15; in Istanbul, 18, 21, 27–29, 49–51, 94, 177, 178, 180; in Kuzguncuk, 25, 38, 40–41, 43, 44, 71, 74, 87, 88, 95–100, 113–16, 120–23, 194–98, 200, 201, 207–8; no place for, in contemporary Turkey, 78, 104–5, 132; as original owners of Kuzguncuk garden, 4, 5, 24–25, 87, 88, 93, 95–102, 129, 208; in Ottoman Empire, 7, 37; population statistics on, 43, 46, 48–51, 54–55, 102, 121–22, 207, 231n81, 233n123; as research subjects, 27, 51, 171, 173, 225n97; riots of 1955 directed at, 54, 99, 109, 119–26, 194; schools for, in Kuzguncuk, 44; Turkish discrimination against, 53, 87;

Turkish perceptions of, 51–52, 170. *See also* Christians; cosmopolitanism; Greece; minorities; property; riots (of September 1955)

Güler, Ara, 21

Güleryüz, Naim, 246n61

Güven, Dilek, 121

Haberal, Mehmet, 88–90, 92, 95

Hagoshrim (kibbutz), 193

Halbwachs, Maurice, 83–84

Hasköy (Istanbul neighborhood), 165, 177, 179, 180, 182, 183, 185–86, 203

Hatay (Turkey), 48

Haydarpaşa (Istanbul neighborhood), 180, 182, 183, 192

head scarves (among Muslim women), 129, 147–48, 158, 201–2, 209

Hebrew language, 193, 199, 231n90

Hemdat Israel Synagogue Foundation, 180

heritage, 67. *See also* history; nostalgia

Herzfeld, Michael, 13

Hikmet, Nazim, 157

history: collective memory vs., 14, 59–84, 106–34, 216–17, 222n46, 239n10; of minorities in Turkey, 19, 31, 82, 118–19; nostalgia as obscuring, 9, 15, 33, 36, 81–84, 87, 104–5, 118–19, 133–34, 168, 208, 210–11, 213, 216; silenced moments of, 121; sources for, 44, 226n2, 227n19; state versions of, 10–13, 17, 19, 36, 212. *See also* censorship; landscapes; memory; minorities; silence

Holy Trinity Church (Kuzguncuk), 42

Hoşgörünün Öteki Adı: Kuzguncuk (Bektaş), 104

housing (in Kuzguncuk): history revealed in cultural landscapes associated with, 16; of Istanbul elites, 43; Ottoman, 4, 22, 23, 61, 62; "restoration" of Ottoman, 70, 74, 77, 78,

83, 234n25, 235n41; set-apart, 76–77; single-family, 242n20; in squatter settlements, 45–46, 129, 159, 166, *167*, 198, 243n4. *See also* gentrification; mahalles; property

Houston, Christopher, 236n51

Icadiye (Istanbul neighborhood), 45, 76, 238n3

Icadiye Creek, 40, 45, 99, 114, 117, 165, 238n3

Icadiye Street (Kuzguncuk), *108*; churches and synagogues on, 41, 43; description of, 3, 45, 238n3; memories of, 25, 72, 99, 105, 106–34; neighborliness on, 6, 130; shops on, 3, 6, 23, 41, 44, 45, 57, 59, 61, 62, 67, 99, 107; television film sets on, 59–62

identity: author's, 21, 27, 147, 149, 173, 174; contested nature of Turkish, 1–2, 6–15, 17, 24–26, 30–34, 47–58, 87, 107, 109–10, 117, 136–38, 140, 155–60, 170–72, 187–88, 191, 201–6, 208–10, 219n1; cultural and political, 86, 209–10; gendered, 136–38, 144 (*see also* women); individual, as multiple, 14, 26, 28–30, 37–38, 137, 139, 140, 155, 160, 191; Jewish, in Turkey, 14, 163–206; of Kuzguncuk people (Kuzguncuklus), 3, 28–29, 71, 75, 86–87, 95–103, 109–10, 112–16, 125, 129–34, 144, 161–62, 174–76, 181, 186, 191, 192, 213; lifestyle, 76; modern, 38–39; place's association with, 1, 3, 29–30, 37, 39, 67, 86–87, 93–105, 168, 176, 214–17; sociocultural, of Istanbul neighborhoods, 2–3; transnationalization of, through globalization, 30; trauma's effect on, 109–10; Turkish, as created by the state, 8–11, 13, 47–50, 162, 209–10, 214, 220n13, 231n78. *See also* belonging; ethnic identity; family identity; gender; minorities; national

identity; place of origin; religious identity; *specific identities*

ideology: as embedded in cultural landscapes, 8, 17, 83, 105, 209–11. *See also* collective memory; nationalism; nostalgia

Ikinci Bahar (television series), 74–75

İleri, Selim, 132

Imagined Communities (Anderson), 11

imperialism, 8, 30–33. *See also* Ottoman Empire

Inciciyan, P. Ğ., 40–41

individual memory: vs. collective memory, 6, 14, 15, 25, 29, 107, 111, 112, 125; of multiethnic harmony in Kuzguncuk, 6, 25, 107–8, 113–18, 122–26, 131–32, 163–64, 187, 194–96, 201, 203–4, 214; of violence against minorities in Kuzguncuk, 26, 119–27

Ingersoll, Richard, 219n5

investments. *See* gentrification

Iran, 48

Iraq, 48

Işık, Hasan Esat, 55

Islam. *See* Islamists; Muslims

Islamists: antiminority views among, 171, 216; and cultural memory of Ottoman past, 10, 220n24; on gentrification, 80; in Kuzguncuk, 236n51; mahalles identified with, 2–3; not among interviewees, 27; rise of, 208, 212; urban projects associated with, 220n15

Israel: Beirut bombing by, 244n24; discrimination against Turkish Jews in, 193, 247n87; interviews with Jews from Kuzguncuk now in, 27, 29, 168, 171–75, 182–83, 186–88, 190–95, 206, 208, 224n93; migration of Turkish Jews to, 54, 118, 123, 124, 159, 176, 188–90, 192–93, 199, 201, 204; Turkish Jews' relationship to, 170–71. *See also* Jerusalem; Zionism

Istanbul (formerly Constantinople):
Asian side of, 96, 121, 166; author in,
224n93; European side of, 3, 20, 44,
52, 60, 95, 163, 166, 183, 189, 193, 201,
203, 247n98; former cosmopolitanism of, 7, 18–22, 32–33, 35, 37–38, 50,
216; intracity migration in, 36, 38,
40, 51, 94, 99, 118, 155, 165–66, 176,
178–88, 190, 192, 193–95, 199–202,
204–5; language diversity in historical, 7, 37–39; minorities as having
dominated, at one time, 2, 8–10, 21,
33, 46, 47, 50–58, 114, 161, 165–66,
177–85, 194; neighborhoods of, 2–3,
247n98; nostalgia for mahalles in, 14,
59–84; as Ottoman Empire's capital,
9, 18, 32, 33, 36, 164; population of,
2, 9–10, 41–42, 50, 51, 53, 54–55, 57,
201, 231n81; transformation of, to
Turkish city, 32, 33, 35, 50–58, 201.
See also cosmopolitanism; mahalles;
migration; minorities; Turkification;
urbanization; *specific neighborhoods,
especially Kuzguncuk*
Istanbul Dergisi (magazine), 19
Istanbul Jewish Cultural Center, 171
Istinye (Istanbul neighborhood), 200
Italy, 53, 177, 192
Izmir (Turkey), 47, 120
Izmit (Turkey), 180

Jerusalem, 40, 41, 183
Jewish cemetery (in Kuzguncuk), 40, 41,
45, 159, 165–67, *167*, 179
Jewish Quincentennial Foundation, 170
Jews, 163–206; Ashkenazi, 37–38, 177,
181; departure of, from Turkey, 10,
21, 53–55, 67, 78, 117, 118, 124, 129,
132, 159, 166, 174–76, 188–90, 193–94,
198–201, 203, 208; as having dominated Istanbul's culture at one time,
2, 8–10, 21, 33, 51–54, 114, 177–85;
insecurity of, in Turkey, 169–71,

175, 176, 185–88, 198–200, 203, 205;
intracity migration by, in Istanbul,
38, 51, 94, 118, 155, 165–66, 176,
178–88, 190, 192–95, 199–202, 204–5;
as Israeli interviewees, 27, 29, 168,
171–75, 182–83, 186–88, 190–95, 206,
208, 224n93; as Istanbul interviewees,
27, 127, 147, 163–65, 168, 169, 174–75,
187, 188–89, 202–3, 206; in Kuzguncuk, 6–7, 25, 29, 32–33, 40–41, 43, 71,
74, 88, 113–17, 122–23, 126–27, 129,
157–59, 163–205, 207–8; and mixed
marriages, 46, 156–60, 172, 173, 215,
229n57, 242n31; in Morocco, 212–13;
no place for, in contemporary Turkey,
104–5, 132, 168; and other minorities
in Istanbul, 18–21, 67; in Ottoman
Empire, 7, 9, 37; population of, in
Kuzguncuk, 42, 43, 46, 78, 94, 119,
128, 132, 168, 176, 199–205; population of, in Turkey, 2, 10, 49, 168, 176,
207, 226n2, 231n81; and riots of 1955,
54, 107, 109, 158, 194–95; Romaniot,
177, 181; schools for, in Kuzguncuk,
43–44, 180, 182, 231n90; Sephardic,
37–40, 164, 176–81; and Turkish
assimilation, 51, 156, 164, 167, 169,
172, 195, 205, 211, 215. *See also* anti-
Semitism; cosmopolitanism; millet
system; minorities; synagogues; violence: against minorities; Wealth Tax
Judeo-Spanish language. *See* Ladino
language

Kadıköy (Istanbul neighborhood), 39,
40, 121, 179, 180, 193, 199, 200, 204
Kaloumenos, Demetrios, 120–21
Kant, Immanuel, 30
Karaites, 177–78
Kastoryano, Riva, 52, 244n23, 247n79
Kayseri (Turkey), 2, 42–43
Kemalist movement, 51. *See also* Atatürk,
Mustafa Kemal

Keyder, Çağlar, 233n117
King, Nicola, 18
Kırklareli (Turkey), 185
knowing (tanımak), 39, 140–41, 143–49
Kohen, Moiz, 51
komşuluk. *See* neighboring
Kostof, Spiro, 219n5
Kuledibi (Istanbul neighborhood), 166, 183, 192
Kumral Ada, Mavi Tuna (Uzuner), 19–20
Kurds: conflicts between Turkish state and, 19, 212, 230n76; forcible relocation of, in Turkey, 48; not among research interviewees, 27; as part of rural-urban migration to Istanbul, 10, 19, 20; status of, in Turkey, 48, 50
Kurtuluş (Istanbul neighborhood), 199, 247n98
Kutman, Perran, 60, 80
Kuzgun Baba, 40
Kuzgun Bir Yaz (Ünver), 81
Kuzguncuk (Istanbul neighborhood): Armenians in, 24, 38, 40–43, 52, 71, 74, 88, 102, 107, 131, 200, 201, 204; churches in, 16, 23–24, 40, 42–44, 46, 72, *73*, 74, 81–83, 99, 113, 115, 117–18, 155, 160, 209, 216, 227n19, 229n47; cinema in, 58, 66, 110–11, 139, 196, 203; class in, 27, 43, 44, 63, 70–72, 74, 76–83, 86, 88, 136–39, 141, 149–53, 164, 176, 182, 183–84, 188, 193, 198–99; coastal road to, 24, 40, 65; corruption in, 91–92, 98; creek in, 40, 45, 99, 114, 117, 165, 238n3; ferry station in, 6, 24, 72, 182, 186–87, 202–3; garden issues in, 3–5, 24–25, 85–105, *91*, 130, 151; gentrification in, 5, 58, 60–61, 63, *63*, 64, 70–83, 86, 99, 138–39, 141, 168, 235n41; Greeks in, 4, 5, 24–25, 38, 40–41, 43, 44, 71, 74, 87, 88, 93, 95–102, 113–16, 120–23, 129, 194–98, 200, 201, 207–8; history of, 40, 227n19; intimate social

character of, 3–4, 6, 15, 23–24, 30, 45, 74–75, 78, 107–8, 110–11, 113, 131, 202–3; issues of belonging to, 112, 117, 127–34, 136–38, 140, 141, 144–62, 185–87, 209–10; Jews once dominant minority in, 46, 161, 165–66, 169, 176, 178–85, 196–97, 199, 202–4, 225n97, 246n63; language diversity in historical, 44, 164, 187, 202; loss of cosmopolitanism in, 29, 83, 100, 109, 113–30, 166, 198–205, 214; migration of rural Turks to, 24, 45–46, 57, 74, 79, 81, 117–19, 123, 126, 128–29, 133–34, 139, 147, 148, 155, 158–59, 162, 166, 169, 191, 195, 198–205, 208, 213, 214, 236n56, 243n4; migrations to, 38, 86, 95, 100–102, 169, 182–85, 193–94; multiethnic history of, 3, 6, 7, 15, 22–26, 30, 35, 40–45, 62, 71–72, 74, 78, 88, 93–100, 102–4, 107–10, 113–19, 122, 126, 129, 131–32, 134, 141, 147, 162–65, 187, 194–96, 201, 203–4, 209, 214; Muslims as currently dominating Kuzguncuk, 131, 158–59, 201–4, 208; Muslims in, 24, 42, 43, 45–46, 57, 74, 81, 101–2, 117–19, 123, 126, 128–29, 133–34, 137–39, 147, 148, 155–62, 166, 168, 169, 195, 198–205, 208, 213, 214, 236n56, 243n4; name origins of, 40, 99, 236n53; nostalgia for, 59–84, 95–100, 106–34, 163–64, 168; people identifying with (Kuzguncuklus), 3, 4, 28–29, 33, 71, 75, 86–87, 95–103, 109–10, 112–16, 125, 129–34, 144, 161–62, 174–76, 181, 186, 191, 192, 213; population statistics about, 43, 46, 102, 128, 179, 194, 229n57, 247n98; as retaining old-fashioned mahalle characteristics, 3, 22, 61; riots of 1955 in, 36, 71, 74, 107, 109, 110, 118–27, 134, 194–95; schools in, 43–44, 180, 182, 231n90; silence about violence against minorities in, 10, 25, 36, 100–101,

Kuzguncuk (*continued*)
109–10, 112, 114, 121, 122, 125–27, 130, 136, 159, 175, 203–4, 212; social geography of, 39–46; synagogues in, 23, 27, 41, 46, 86, 94, 99, 115, 117–18, 155, 160, 165, 167, 168, 173, 174, 180–81, 195–201, 203, 205, 208, 227n19, 246n61; as television series setting, 6, 21, 24, 58, 59–62, *61*, 64, 67–70, 77, 80–81, 235n42. *See also* gentrification; housing; Kuzguncuk Neighborhood Association; migration; streets
Kuzguncuk Neighborhood Association, 3, 4–5, 27, 60, 79, 85–105, *91*, 139, 141; as alternative to traditional neighboring, 151–53; resistance to, 86, 94–97, 236n1

Ladino language, 37–39, 164, 172, 181, 193, 196, 198, 231n90
Landau, Jacob, 244n20, 246n54
landscapes: author's emphasis on, 13–14; cultural, 16–18, 57–58, 64–70, 74, 209–10; everyday, 6, 13, 16–17; historical, 71–72, 83–84, 165, 207–8; ideology as embedded in cultural, 8, 17, 83, 105, 209–11; Jewish, 175–76; memory as embedded in cultural, 16–18, 34, 74, 81–82, 222n47; naturalizing of social inequalities by, 17–18, 25–26; nostalgia for cultural, 59–84, 104; symbols in, 17, 23–24, 62, 72, 74, 81–84, 93, 119, 205–6; Turkification of cultural, 54, 56–58. *See also* gentrification; history; mahalles; place; streets; urbanization
language(s): as a basis of Turkish national identity, 220n13; and "everyday ethnicity," 13; historical diversity of, among Jews, 51, 170, 172; historical diversity of, in Istanbul, 7, 37–39; historical diversity of, in Kuzguncuk, 44, 164, 187, 202; Turkification's ef-

fects on, 9, 10, 36, 48, 51–52, 164, 186, 205, 220n13, 229n58, 231n90. *See also specific languages*
La Unyon (Jewish charity), 182
Lausanne Treaty (1923), 48–49, 53, 55, 231n90
Lebanon. *See* Beirut; Tripoli
Le Goff, Jacques, 222n46
Levy, Andre, 212–13, 240n38, 248n1
"Little Paris," 30, 74, 94
locality. *See* place
Lockman, Zachary, 12–13
Lowenthal, David, 67

Mahalle Kahvesi (Abasıyanık), 65–66
mahalles (neighborhoods): abandoned properties in, 20, 55–58, 98, 233n122, 238n23; "belonging" in, 27, 39, 67, 112–16, 134, 136–38, 140, 141, 144–62, 187, 213; blending of private and public space in, 62, 67–70, 79–80, 136, 139, 143–44, 154, 240n4; characteristics associated with, 3–4, 6, 15, 22–24, 26, 39, 59, 61–63, 67–70, 78, 80, 93, 107, 113, 139–41, 145–48, 153; class differences in gentrified, 63–64, 76–83, 138–39, 141; fracturing of, in recent years, 10, 63, 77–80, 82, 109–10, 117, 128, 130, 134, 136, 137, 154, 206, 209–15; gated communities likened to, 241n10; in Istanbul, 2–3; minorities no longer residents of certain, 78, 82–83, 132, 165–66, 201–6; nostalgia for, 15, 21–22, 24–26, 59–84, 93, 95, 104–34, 141, 163–64, 205–17; as Ottoman urban form, 10, 22, 36–39, 46–47; as place of historical multiethnic harmony, 3, 6, 22, 26, 43, 63, 107–8, 110, 113–19, 122, 129, 134, 141, 147, 163–64, 187, 196, 209, 214; as places of collective memory, 36–37, 58, 64–84, 132, 136, 137, 151, 154, 160, 176; as places of religious harmony,

15, 25, 29, 30, 32, 35, 44, 72, 74, 102, 107–8, 112, 113–18, 122, 125–27, 164, 187, 196, 208; relationships in, likened to siblings, 22, 28, 30, 35, 57, 72, 107, 109, 126, 127, 130, 133, 139–40, 163–64, 194, 209; Turkification's effects on minority, 46, 50–58, 204–5, 213; women's ambivalence toward, 76–77, 138–39, 141, 145–48, 153–54. *See also* cosmopolitanism; gentrification; migration; millet system; minorities; neighboring; violence; *names of specific mahalles, especially Kuzguncuk*

Manetzion (Zionist organization), 192
Mardin, Şerif, 220n30
Marouli, Christina, 242n28
Massey, Doreen, 103–4
McDowell, Linda, 154–55
media: anti-Semitism in, 171; on Kuzguncuk garden controversy, 90–93; on Kuzguncuk gentrification, 70; on Kuzguncuk property formerly owned by minorities, 97; nostalgia for mahalle life in, 59–67, 72, 74–75, 77–78, 80–81, 104, 207
Mediterranean Waltz (Uzuner), 19–20
Mehmet II (Sultan), 40, 177
Meijer, Roel, 37, 47
memory: defined, 15; geography of, 205–6; historical, vs. collective memory, 80–84, 106–34, 216–17, 222n46, 239n10; individual vs. collective, 6, 14, 15, 25, 29, 107, 111, 112, 125; national, 14–16, 19; of place, 18–19, 205–6, 214–17; and remembering and forgetting minorities, 6–7, 9, 19–22, 25–26, 64–67, 82, 100–101, 104–5, 109–27, 130–31, 207–12; shame and, 130; Turkish crises of, 10. *See also* collective memory; cultural memory; history; identity; individual memory; nostalgia; place; silence

migration: from Black Sea area, 26–29, 41–42, 44, 63, 79, 86, 95, 100–103, 113, 137–39, 149, 158, 201, 236n56; forced, of minorities in Ottoman Empire (sürgün), 42, 177–78; of Greeks from Turkey, 10, 19, 36, 54–58, 98, 99, 102, 109, 114, 118, 123, 132, 134, 157, 194, 200, 204, 232n107; intercity, 36, 38, 40, 165, 180, 185–86; intracity, 36, 38, 40, 51, 94, 99, 118, 155, 165–66, 176, 178–88, 190, 192–95, 199–202, 204–5; of minorities from Turkey, 8, 10, 19, 21, 24, 25, 36, 43, 48, 49, 51, 53–57, 63, 67, 71, 78, 82–83, 98, 99, 102, 109, 111, 114, 116–19, 122–29, 132, 134, 155, 157–59, 166, 169, 174–76, 185, 188–90, 192–94, 198–204, 208, 213, 216, 232n107; of Muslims from around the world to Turkey, 48; rural-urban, as having negative effect on minorities in Turkey, 7, 201–5; rural-urban, in Lebanon, 9; rural-urban, in Turkey, 2, 7, 10, 15, 24, 45–46, 57, 66, 74, 81, 100, 111, 117, 118–19, 123–26, 128–29, 131–32, 134, 139, 147–48, 155, 158–59, 162, 166, 169, 191, 195, 198–205, 208, 213, 214, 243n4; of Salonica Jews to places around the world, 177; of Spanish Jews to Ottoman Empire, 170; to squatter settlements, 45–46, 129, 159, 166, 167, 198, 243n4; of Turkish tribes from Central Asia, 11
military service (Turkish), 51, 158, 190, 208
millet system, 10, 36–38, 42, 43, 47–50. *See also* mahalles; minorities
Ministry of Foundations (Turkey), 87–90, 96–98
minorities: cosmopolitanism, civilization, and urbanism associated with, 7, 21, 67, 107, 118–19, 122–23, 126, 128–29, 201–2, 204–6, 214, 248n3;

minorities (*continued*)
defined as not ethnically Turkish and not Muslim, 8, 87, 128, 131, 204–5; difficulty of doing research on Turkish, 46, 82, 226n2; European associations with, 20, 21, 47; as having dominated Istanbul's culture at one time, 2, 9–10, 21, 33, 46, 47, 51–53, 114, 130, 161, 177, 205; human rights violations against, in Turkey, 6–8, 10, 19, 25, 28, 29, 36, 49, 50–59, 71, 74, 87, 97–101, 104, 107, 109–10, 118–27, 130–34, 136, 147, 159, 165, 168, 169, 171, 175, 176, 185–89, 194–95, 202–7, 211, 215, 216, 229n58; Kurds as, 230n76; in Kuzguncuk, 39–46, 82, 87, 93, 94–95, 101–2, 111, 113–27, 131–33, 136, 149, 163–69, 176, 185–86, 201–5; many mahalles as no longer including, 78, 82–83, 132, 165–66, 201–6; migration of, from Turkey, 8, 10, 19, 21, 24, 25, 36, 48, 49, 53–57, 63, 67, 71, 78, 82–83, 98, 99, 102, 109, 111, 114, 116–19, 122–29, 132, 134, 155, 157–59, 166, 169, 176, 185, 189–90, 192–94, 199–204, 208, 213, 216, 232n107; mixed-marriages among, 27, 46, 55, 137, 138–39, 155–60, 172, 173, 215, 229n57, 242n31; and national belonging, 24–26, 30, 46–58, 87, 107, 109–10, 117, 128–34, 136–38, 140, 155–60, 170–72, 187–88, 191, 201–6, 208, 209–10, 219n1; nostalgia for, in Istanbul, 20–22, 24, 25, 36, 57–84, 102, 106, 112–27, 131–34, 158, 210–12; as not supporting Kuzguncuk Neighborhood Association, 94–95; in Ottoman Empire, 7–10, 22, 36–39, 47, 49–50, 131, 160, 179, 213, 214, 244n20; property formerly owned by, 4, 5, 9–10, 20, 24–25, 29, 53–57, 77, 82, 87, 95–101, 103, 117, 123, 152, 194, 199, 208, 209, 211, 213, 233n117; remem-
bering and forgetting, 6–7, 9, 19–22, 25–26, 64–67, 82, 100–101, 104–5, 109–27, 130–31, 207–12; rights for, in Turkey, 8, 27, 31, 49, 53, 55, 231n90; seen as "other," 30, 131–34, 155–206, 210; Turkish work camps for, 20, 53, 190–91; Wealth Tax's effects on, 10, 19–20, 28, 53–54, 57, 98, 159, 169, 171, 188–94, 208. *See also* Armenians; assimilation; Christians; Greeks; Jews; Kurds; migration; millet system; property; silence; Turkification
Mitchell, Don, 83
Moda (Istanbul neighborhood), 192, 200
modernization: and class stratification, 183; contemporary women's view of, 13, 31, 38–39, 47, 50, 154; Jews' association with, 183, 201–2, 248n3; nostalgia for days before, 65, 210; and Turkish Republic, 7, 13, 31, 38–39, 47, 50, 208–9, 241n11. *See also* cosmopolitanism
Morocco, 31, 212–13, 227n18, 248n1
mosques: in Istanbul, 179; in Kuzguncuk, 23, 24, 44, 45, 72, 73, 74, 83, 113, 115, 208, 209, 216, 224n87, 227n19, 229n52; workers on, 42
Muslims: arrival of, in Kuzguncuk, 24, 43, 113, 201; in Bosnia, 13, 160–62; conservative, 129, 143, 147–48, 158, 201–2, 209; as dominating Kuzguncuk now, 131, 158–59, 201–4, 208; individual identity as, 14; in Kuzguncuk, 24, 25, 42, 43, 45–46, 57, 74, 81, 100–103, 113–19, 123–26, 128–31, 133–34, 137–39, 147, 148, 155–62, 166, 168, 169, 191, 195, 198–205, 208, 213, 214, 236n56, 243n4; migration of, from all over the world to Turkey, 48, 49; mixed-marriages involving, 46, 55, 138, 155–59; population statistics about, 43, 46, 50, 51, 57, 231n81; relations of, with minorities in Kuzgun-

cuk, 28, 71, 74, 100–101, 109, 113–15, 124–25, 158–60, 186–88, 191, 194–98, 213; rural-urban divisions among, 201; silence of Kuzguncuk's, about minorities' departures, 100–101; Sunni, 9, 50; Turkish national identity linked to, 2, 8–10, 13–14, 28, 47–50, 53, 80, 113, 170, 209–14, 219n1. *See also* Islamists; migration; mosques; national identity; nationalism; religious identity; Turks

name(s): Jews changing their, 172; origins of Kuzguncuk's, 40, 99, 236n53
national identity: and assimilation, 51, 156, 164, 167, 169, 172, 195, 205, 211, 215; and class, 28, 30–31; collective identity and politics of, 14–16, 106–34, 154; as constructed, 11–14, 26, 206; contemporary minorities as excluded from, 8, 87, 128, 131, 204–5; and cultural memory, 23; vs. family identity for minorities, 19; gender as linked to Turkish, 28, 136–39; multiple individual identities linked to, 28, 125; postcolonial, 8; specific ethnic-religious identity linked to Turkish, 1, 2, 8–11, 13–14, 28, 47–52, 80, 162, 170, 209–14, 219n1, 220n13, 220n24, 231n78; Turkey's construction of, 8–11, 13, 47–50, 162, 209–10, 214, 220n13, 231n78; Turkish notions of, as contested, 1–2, 6–15, 17, 24–26, 28, 30–34, 46–58, 87, 107, 109–10, 117, 125, 136–38, 140, 155–60, 170–72, 187–88, 191, 201–6, 208–10, 219n1; and urbanization, 8, 13, 32, 34, 117. *See also* citizenship; community(-ies); nationalism
nationalism (Turkey): vs. cosmopolitanism, 30–34, 46–58, 118–19, 122, 168, 203–4, 206–17; effects of, on urban landscapes and daily life, 9, 17–18, 29,

34, 51, 113, 204–6; and human rights violations against minorities, 7, 10, 36, 109–10, 118–27, 134, 136, 164, 168, 175, 176, 185–95, 205; nostalgia about mahalles as obscuring, 26, 82–83, 87, 104–5, 109–10, 210–11; state's role in constructing, 11–14, 47–53, 133, 175, 187–88, 204–6, 208–12; state's use of, to violate minorities' rights, 109, 110, 119–22, 136, 185, 229n58, 232n106. *See also* Turkification
Navaro-Yashin, Yael, 221n44
Nazis (Germans), 188, 190, 191–92
Ne'emanei Zion, 192
neighborhoods. *See* mahalles; *specific Istanbul neighborhoods*
neighboring (komşuluk): in Algeria, 214; and "belonging" in the mahalle, 27, 39, 67, 112–16, 134, 136–38, 140, 141, 144–62, 187, 213; disappearance of, in Kuzguncuk, 67, 111, 148–49, 152, 154, 207; as intrusive practice, 77, 138, 144–46, 150, 154; limits of, 127; as a mahalle practice among women, 5, 27, 39, 67–69, 79, 100, 110, 112–16, 131, 135–62, 196, 215; proximity in, 137, 142, 155, 158–60; urbanization's effects on, 139, 140–41, 150–51. *See also* knowing (tanımak)
Neve Şalom Synagogue (Galata), 171, 190
Neyzi, Leyla, 19, 169
Nişantaşı (Istanbul neighborhood), 66, 247n98
non-Muslims. *See* Armenians; Christians; Greeks; Jews
nostalgia: for Atatürk, 208–9, 212; for cosmopolitanism, 9, 20–22, 36, 57–58, 62, 67, 168, 207–11; for days before urbanization, 15, 65, 66, 92–95, 113, 201; defined, 15–16, 107; for Kuzguncuk, 59–84, 95–100, 106–34, 163–64, 168; for mahalles, 15,

nostalgia (*continued*)
21–22, 24–26, 59–84, 93, 95, 104–34,
141, 163–64, 205–17; for minorities
in Istanbul, 20–22, 24, 25, 36, 57–84,
102, 106, 112–27, 131–34, 158, 210–12;
nationalist effects of, 34; as obscuring
history, 9, 15, 33, 36, 81–84, 87, 104–5,
118–19, 133–34, 168, 208, 210–11, 213,
216; as rendering mixed marriages
invisible, 160; structural, 15–16. *See
also* collective memory
Nostalgia for the Modern (Özyürek), 208,
209

Odessa (Ukraine), 32
"Odise" (Gökdel), 131–32
Ökte, Faik, 53
Oran, Baskin, 54–55, 232nn106–7,
233n117
Örs, Ilay, 239n6
Ortaköy (Istanbul neighborhood), 23,
177, 179, 180, 182, 185, 193–94, 204
Osmanbey, 183
"other," minorities as, 30, 131–34,
155–206, 210
Ottoman Empire: decline of, 8, 47–48;
1492 invitation to Jews from, 170;
historiography of, 213; Islamists'
cultural memory of, 10, 220n24;
Istanbul as former capital of, 9, 18,
32, 33, 36, 164; mahalles as urban
form of, 2, 10, 36–39, 46–47; minorities in, 7–9, 22, 36–39, 47, 49–50, 131,
160, 179, 213, 214, 244n20; sürgün
policies of, 42, 177–78. *See also* Istanbul; mahalles; millet system
Özyürek, Esra, 208, 209

Palestine, 12–13, 117, 171, 186, 192,
239n14
Paris Peace conference, 47
Penal Code 301 (Turkey), 7
Pera (Istanbul neighborhood), 44

Perihan Abla (television series), 60–62,
67–70, 74, 78, 80–81
Philliou, Christine, 213
Pioneer (Chaluz Zionist organization),
192–93
place (locality): author's focus on, 13–14;
creation of, 104; defined, 86; as
evidence of minority identity, 95–103;
identity linked to, 1, 3, 29–30, 37, 67,
86–87, 93–105, 168, 214–17; lack of,
for contemporary minorities in Kuzguncuk, 46, 78, 82, 104–5, 131–32, 211,
225n97; of memory, 18–19, 205–6;
narratives of, 112–19; national identity
constituted in relation to, 26, 205–11;
nostalgia's transformation of, 16,
207–11. *See also* landscapes; mahalles;
memory; national identity; place of
origin; *specific places*
place of origin: and gender identity, 137;
Istanbul neighborhoods based on
migrants', 177, 178; and Kuzguncuk
identity, 4, 26, 136, 139, 149; migration based on, 38; and Turkish identity, 169. *See also* national identity
plague, 179
Pollock, Sheldon, 34
professionals (and artists): in Kuzguncuk, 27, 70–72, 74, 76–83, 86, 88,
138, 149–53, 199. *See also* Kuzguncuk
Neighborhood Association
property: "abandoned," in mahalles, 20,
55–58, 98, 233n122, 238n23; current
difficulty of determining ownership
of, 55–56, 89, 96–97, 189; destruction of minority, during 1955 riots,
10, 54, 99, 109, 119–21, 123–26, 130,
185, 194–95, 204; as formerly owned
by minorities, 4, 5, 9–10, 20, 24–25,
29, 53–57, 77, 82, 87, 95–101, 103,
117, 123, 152, 194, 199, 208, 209, 211,
213, 233n117; state's appropriation of
departed minorities', 53–56, 87, 88,

96–99, 128, 208, 232n114, 233n117,
238n23; value of minorities', after
1955 riots, 124, 128, 203; values of,
after gentrification, 77, 79, 81, 99,
235nn47, 50. *See also* gentrification;
Jewish cemetery
propriety: defined, 26; in Istanbul
Jews' discourse of Turkish tolerance, 163–64, 169–72, 184, 186, 187;
mahalle's social space as governed
by, 26, 39, 136; mixed marriages as
violating, 156; as price of "belonging"
in the mahalle, 134, 136, 144–46, 148,
160, 211–12; as protecting collective
memory, 147; and speaking hon-
estly about the 1955 riots, 109, 125;
women's neighboring as sustaining,
in mahalle, 27. *See also* collective
memory; silence

religious identity: in Bosnia, 160–62;
Kuzguncuk identity and, 4, 28; as
linked to Turkish national identity, 1,
2, 8–10, 13–14, 28, 47–50, 53, 80, 113,
170, 209–14, 219n1; not as significant
as rural-urban identities, 201; as not
separating mahalle neighbors, 15, 25,
29, 30, 32, 35, 44, 72, 74, 102, 107–8,
112, 113–18, 122, 125–27, 164, 187, 196,
208; Ottoman millet system based
on, 37–39; of *Perihan Abla* characters,
69; Turkish Jews' nostalgia for their,
195–98; and violence, 8, 109–10; and
Wealth Tax, 53–54. *See also* belonging; Christians; ethnic identity; Jews;
millet system; minorities; Muslims;
secularism; tolerance; violence
representational space (defined), 234n11
restoration. *See* gentrification
riots (of September 1955): departure of
minorities after, 19, 21, 36, 54–57, 71,
102, 109, 123, 134, 157–59, 190, 194,
204, 232n107; destruction of minor-

ity properties in, 10, 54, 99, 109,
119–21, 123–26, 130, 185, 194, 204; in
Kuzguncuk, 36, 71, 74, 107, 109, 110,
118–27, 134, 194–95; as marking end
of Kuzguncuk's cosmopolitanism,
118–19; "outsiders" as responsible for,
71, 110, 118–19, 124–26, 195; as result
of nationalist policy, 36, 109–10,
118–19, 185; silence about, 19, 25–26,
109–10, 203–4; state as leading, 109,
110, 119–22, 136, 185, 229n58, 232n106
Romania, 13, 192
Rozen, Minna, 178
Rum. *See* Greeks

Şahin, Haluk, 7
Salacak (Istanbul neighborhood), 96
Salamandra, Christa, 145
Salkım Hanımın Taneleri (film), 20
Şalom (newspaper), 205
Salonica (Greece): anti-Semitism in, 180;
as Atatürk's birthplace, 54, 119, 120;
cosmopolitanism in, 248n12; Saporta
family from, 176, 177, 179, 181
Samatya (Istanbul neighborhood), 60,
67, 75, 235n42
Samsun (Turkey), 180
Saporta, Manuel, 176, 179–81, 188
Sarajevo, 32
Scutari. *See* Üsküdar
Secor, Anna, 221n44
secrets. *See* propriety; silence
secularism: minorities associated with,
248n3; among Muslim Turkish
interviewees, 26–27; and Turkish
Republic, 7–8, 13, 31, 48, 50, 202,
208–9, 241n11
Serverian, Ohannes Amira, 42
Shaw, Stanford, 180, 230n59, 231n81,
246n63
Sifneos, Evridiki, 32
silence: about criticism of the state, 213;
effects of, 26; about impact of

Turks (*continued*)
148, 155, 158–59, 162, 166, 169, 191, 195, 198–205, 208, 213, 214, 236n56, 243n4; rural, as partly responsible for destroying cosmopolitanism, 7, 10, 15, 81, 118–19, 123–26, 128–29, 131–32, 147–48, 158–59, 162, 166, 198–204, 208, 214, 243n4; state creation of identity of, 8–11, 13, 47–50, 162, 209–10, 214, 220n13, 231n78. *See also* migration; Muslims

United States, 118, 121, 124, 216, 242n20
Ünver, Mehmet, 81, 147–48
Uras, Güngör, 92
urbanization (in Istanbul): and bias against rural migrants, 128–29, 201–2; cosmopolitanism and, 7, 32, 201–2, 204–5, 213; forces conditioning, 6; impact of, on neighboring practices, 139–41, 150–51; and Jews, 51, 176, 201, 204–5; and Kuzguncuk, 44, 46, 201–5; landscapes associated with, 57; and national identity, 8, 13, 32, 34, 117; nostalgia for days before, 15, 65, 66, 92–95, 113, 201; as redrawing ethnic-religious boundaries along national lines, 117, 204–5, 213; unplanned, 92. *See also* cosmopolitanism; gentrification; mahalles
Uryanizade family, 43, 61
Uryanizade Street (Kuzguncuk), 5, 60–61, *63*, 70–71, 78–80, 82
Üsküdar (Scutari; Istanbul neighborhood): ethnic and religious makeup of, 42, 179, 228n38, 229n47; Greeks' property in, 96, 121; Kuzguncuk's administrative connection to, 45
Uzun, Nil, 75–76
Uzuner, Buket, 19–20

violence: historical landscapes as obscur-

ing past, 83–84, 210–11; against minorities in Turkey, 6–7, 25, 31, 42, 48, 51, 54–55, 98, 109–10, 112, 119–27, 136, 164, 165, 171, 175, 185–86, 205, 208, 210–11, 216, 229n47, 229n58, 230n66, 231n81, 232n106; symbolic, against Jews, 166. *See also* minorities: human rights violations against, in Turkey; riots (of September 1955); silence
Virane Synagogue (Beth Nisim; Kuzguncuk), 41, 165, 181
Vryonis, Speros, 121

Wealth Tax (1942–1943): effects of, on minorities, 10, 19, 20, 28, 53–54, 57, 98, 159, 169, 171, 188–94, 208; as result of nationalist policy, 36, 53, 190, 192, 229n58
women: bodies of, as preservers of ethnic-religious identity, 156–58; covered, among conservative Muslims, 129, 147–48, 158, 201–2, 209; as limited to home, 39, 140, 144, 145, 196; minority, in riots of 1955, 126; neighboring bonds among, 115–16, 135–62; neighboring by, as a mahalle practice among, 5, 27, 39, 67–69, 79, 100, 110, 112–16, 131, 135–62, 196, 215; single, 151, 153–54; views of contemporary, on modernization, 13, 31, 38–39, 47, 50, 147; as wage-earners, 44, 76, 138, 140, 149–52
work camps. *See* Aşkale (Turkey)
World War II, 20, 54, 175, 188–94

Yiddish language, 38
Yücel, Can, 78, 92
Yücel, Uğur, 74–75, 94
Yugoslavia, 32, 161. *See also* Bosnia

Zionism, 12, 32–33, 171, 186, 189, 191–93. *See also* Israel

CPSIA information can be obtained
at www.ICGtesting.com
Printed in the USA
LVHW021819231121
704246LV00002B/273

9 780820 335742